Connecting in Philadelphia

1000 Great Places to Enjoy Yourself and Meet People Who Share Your Interests

Ruth B. Harvey, Ph.D.
with Janet Gala

Published by
Connectworks Publications
P.M.B. 137
8500 Henry Avenue
Philadelphia, PA 19128

Connecting in Philadelphia:
1000 Great Places to Enjoy Yourself and Meet People Who Share Your Interests

Please note that the information herein was obtained from sources available to the public, as well as phone interviews with group contact persons. It is subject to change and interpretation. Although the author and publisher have re-searched and rechecked all sources for maximum accuracy of information contained in this book, they assume no responsibility for any loss, injury, or inconvenience sustained by any person using this book. Any slights of people or organizations is unintentional. *It is strongly recommended that organizations be contacted before making arrangements to attend events.*

Layout & Graphic Design: Janet Gala, Gala Design
Cover Design & Illustration: Cherie Carter, Carter Design Studios
Maps: Bob Hires, HiRES Graphics
Editors: Carol Ballentine, Kathy Sheehan, Jim Martin

Published by Connectworks Publications (connectworks@earthlink.net)
   P.M.B. 137
   8500 Henry Avenue
   Philadelphia, PA 19128

Printed by: Sheridan Books
     Chelsea, Michigan

Library of Congress Catalog Card Number: 2001118868
ISBN 0-9643708-3-2

Contents

Contents

A team of Philadelphia scullers on the Schuylkill River

Walking, talking, and skating on Kelly Drive

Map: Downtown

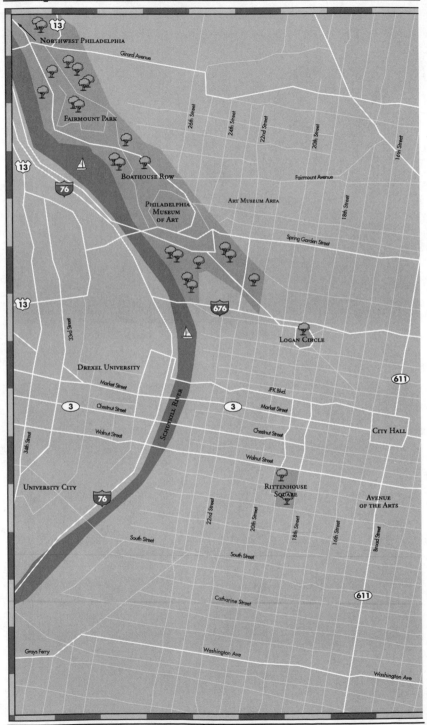

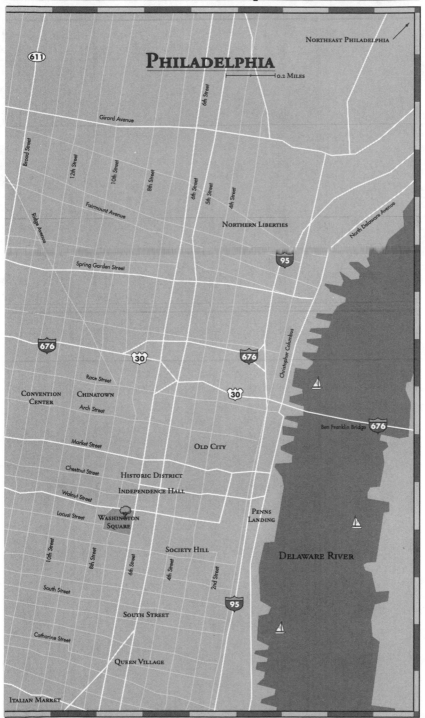

Map: Regional

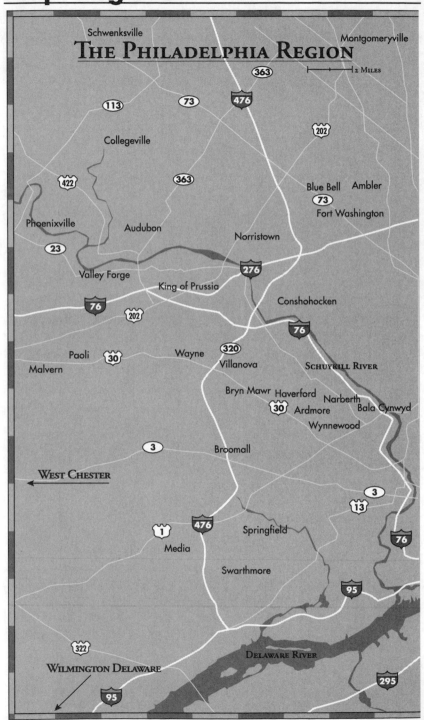

The Philadelphia Region

Map: Regional

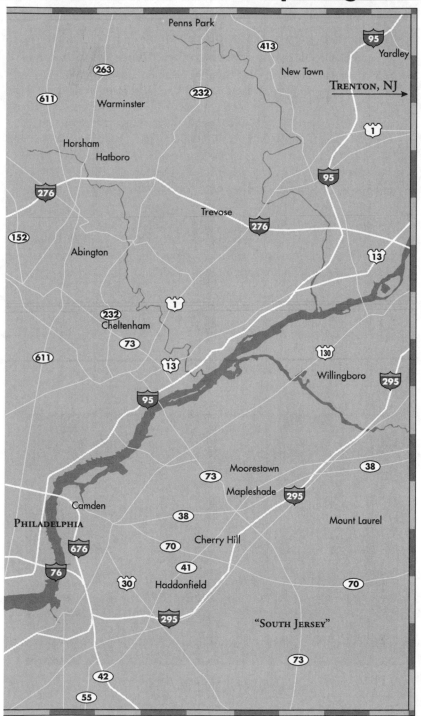

Acknowledgements

People who worked (hard) on this book—
This book could never have been done without you.

Janet Gala (Research Assistant, Graphic Artist & Layout) for design artistry,
    amazing people skills, and outstanding judgement all along the way
Carol Ballentine (Editor) whose eagle eyes and excellent rewrites made sense
    out of nonsense without changing the meaning (*thank* you, sis)
Kathy Sheehan (Editor), for keen observations and great editorial comments
Cherie Carter (Cover), *Carter Design*, for creative design & artistic whimsy
Bob Hires (Maps) of *HiRES Graphics,* for geographic artistry and details
Jim Martin, Joan Enoch, and Leslie Snyder (Trusted Readers)

People who gave support

Jim, again, for great patience, loving support, and best common sense
The Queen Street Group for nurturance and ongoing connecting ideas
Family and dear friends for continued support

Thank you, all of you.

Janet and Ruth

Preface

This is a book about Philadelphia—the historical birthplace of the nation and home of the Philly cheesesteak, Fairmount Park, the Sixers, the Philadelphia Orchestra, and 1.3 million Philadelphians, many of whom are actively engaged in hundreds of exciting local organizations and clubs. This guide was written to acquaint you with these groups and inspire you to join them.

It's exciting to report that over 12,000 people used the first edition of **Connecting in Philadelphia** to find outdoor pleasures, cultural activities, and community service opportunities. New friendships were begun and there were even a few trips up the aisle. The second edition has been expanded to include twice the number of groups and many more types of activities, with descriptive comments that are considerably more substantive and detailed. Web sites and email addresses have also been added.

An exciting new feature in this edition is the over 150 photos of Philadelphia activity groups, so you can see what they look like when they're doing what they do. These are mostly amateur, candid shots taken by participant photographers, so you get a member's perspective on what's happening. And there are two maps of Philadelphia to help you find your way around.

We've also added many more places for young people (in their 20s and 30s) to socialize and be active. We could do this because now there *are* more activities for them in the area, including more dancing, community service/social clubs, outdoor events, etc. Isn't that an encouraging trend! You'll also find full-page write-ups of selected groups and events ("A Closer Look"), as well as numerous "Resources" (books, national web sites, etc.) to assist you in your search for just the right place. The first chapter "Building a Social Network" chapter, my pitch to you about getting out there to find more friends and fun, has been expanded, and includes exercises that can help you examine your own social networking preferences. Hopefully, this will encourage you to develop your own personal action plan.

I could never have completed this book by myself. The Goddess was with me when I walked into the Mermaid and saw a cheerful, pretty, young woman with a book about PageMaker under her arm. Janet Gala was there with her husband Tom, an urban poet and singer/songwriter. Turned out she was a computer graphic designer and an expert in PageMaker, the layout program I'd been using for my **Connecting** books. She signed on to the project; if she hadn't, you wouldn't be reading this right now.

Together we have sweated blood and tears (and laughter) as we worked on **Connecting in Philadelphia II** over the last three years. We talked to

Preface

over 1,000 groups—at least twice, usually more—to get the information you'll find in these pages. The groups responded generously with time and tremendous enthusiasm; their encouragement kept us going when we thought we'd never finish. Despite these efforts (including checking all group stats within the last four months), *there will be changes* by the time you get the book. A directory can give you ideas about what's happening out there, but it suffers from time-accuracy, so *be sure to call* before you go. As hard as managing these many details has been, the rewards have been great fun ("Listen to what this group does—can you believe it?!), especially because we could be excited and share decisions together (a group of two). We worked through my broken leg, a puppy, illness, and surgery. We persevered with the help of huge amounts of sushi and Popsicles and enormous help from friends and family (who are VERY glad we're done).

A note about the volunteer groups contained in many of these activity listings: The staff of many of these groups is truly volunteer. They are people with lives and jobs and responsibilities just like the rest of us. Yet they put in *hours* of time and much energy (often without mention) to keep their groups organized and running. It is a huge amount of work and is frequently done by a small core group of regulars year after year. It is extremely important that we show our appreciation for their efforts and not expect things to run as they would with full-time, paid staff. Janet and I are very grateful for the time and interest we received from these individuals, donated freely from their hearts, for the sake of getting the word out about the activities they love so well.

Ruth working on Connecting in Philadelphia
with help (?) from below

How to use this book

About This Book

1. This guide contains an *overview* of participatory activities in a number of interest categories. It does not include every group and activity in Philadelphia; in fact, there are many, many more. It is intended to provide you with a range of kick-off material to tickle your curiosity and get you started in your search for your own best places.

2. Places close down. They change structure and focus. Contact people change. Please *call* before you set out. We worked very hard to have information current at the time of publication, but things change rapidly (even while this book is at press). Don't go without checking date, cost, place first.

3. The specific events (classes, lectures, films, etc.) listed are meant to give you a *general* idea about the kinds of things offered by the group. Many will change and similar ones will take their place. Call for up-to-date info.

4. Note that there are frequently two phone numbers and two addresses in one listing. In that case, the first address-phone number is that of the organization, and the second is that of the place where the activity is held. You should *call* the organization to find out more about the group and details of the events, but *go* to the location address (after you call).

The activity groups were described using the standard format below.

Activity Type

Organization Name
Organization Address
Organization Phone   *Organization Email*   *Organization Web site*
Activity Location (if different from Organization address): Address & Phone

Descriptive comments about the group

☼ Date   ☕ Time
☎ Contact Person
💰 Cost

Building a Social Network

Dynamic Diversions on a bike ride in Lancaster County

Linda (page 15) keeping a tight hold on the Women's Dragonboat team

Building a Social Network

What is this book about?

Hi out there! If you'd like to find hundreds of terrific activities around Philadelphia and meet people who enjoy the same things you do, then delve into these pages. No matter who you are or what your current relationship status is, this guide will help you connect with a broad social network of active friends.

What this book will lead you to is an amazing number and diversity of both casual and well-organized local groups where people join together to enjoy a broad spectrum of activities. Just a few examples include:

- Groups that hike the Delaware Canal or go backpacking and canoeing in the Pine Barrens

- Downtown groups where people gather in bookstores and galleries to discuss art, politics in Philly, the writings of their favorite novelist or the architecture in their neighborhood

- Group classes where aspiring artists learn to paint, make a computer poster or discover what's so great about those Picasso blue folks

- All-age groups where even first-timers can learn Cajun dancing to live accordion music or sweep across the floor in an old-style country waltz

- Cosmopolitan groups where people discuss French-American affairs (sometimes in French) and sample the first Beaujolais Nouveau or discuss Swedish films or have cocktails and conversation with international dignitaries

- Theater groups where actors, stage-set builders, and costume-makers give a dramatic production flesh and blood

- Groups of people, generous of spirit, who get together to give back to their communities by providing many services, including restoring historic mansions, cuddling newborns, and teaching people to read

In all these activities, people participate because they *choose* to, and they interact with interest, awareness, and enthusiasm because they care about what they are doing. My friend Linda discovered the Philadelphia Women's Dragon Boat Team some months ago. It's not that she didn't have enough to do. It's that this activity and her new boating friends have lit up her schedule. She paddles on the Schuylkill every Wednesday night, as well as on the weekends, with an enthusiasm that's contagious. (She's not alone; they all

Building a Social Network

have it!) They have come together to enjoy each other, learn from each other, and work and play as a team—and their lives have changed as a result.

And here is the real kicker: These activity groups are going on *all the time* right under our noses, and they are filled with people like you and me (not just those who already know *how to do it*). Many are people who share our interests, our passions, and our values. If you're ready to try a new activity, learn a new skill, go new places, and do more socializing, you have a whole world of enthusiastic and energetic Philadelphians out there waiting to meet you.

Who is this book for?

Everybody! We *all* want a life that includes plenty of play and good conversation where we can use our creativity and our ideas, do neat fun things with our bodies, and engage our hearts and spirit. Going to work everyday, doing the bills, and getting the laundry done is not all there is!

Participating in favorite sports and pastimes and discovering groups of people to enjoy them with is a delightful *necessity* for all of us. I firmly believe that there is a group in this book that really suits you. This will be a place that you won't be able to wait to go to and where you'll lose track of all those things you worry about.

Some readers have told me that this guide is especially good for:

- People who are *new to the area*, who want to find their favorite recreation and make friends there

- People who are in *transition in their relationships,* who want to repair and recharge by becoming part of a new social group

- People who are in *transition in their lifestyles* (back from college, semi-retirement, etc.) who have new-found discretionary time and energy

- People who are *single* and looking for life partners

But I think exploring new activities is as important to me, a married, long-time Philadelphia resident, as it is for anyone else, because I love doing new things, meeting new people, and stretching myself.

How about you?

Building a Social Network

Why are you lucky to be in Philadelphia?

You really *are* lucky to be here, if looking for activities where you can be involved with people is what you want. After 15 years of gathering information about interest groups, I'm convinced that Philadelphia is a *great* activity town!

First of all, the unusual *natural beauty* both within the city and in every nearby direction makes the outdoors an appealing place to spend your time. The climate is wonderful, including a variety of seasonal changes (with related activities) and many days when the sun is out, the sky is blue, and the temperature comfortable. It's hard to stay inside on most days! So it makes sense that many games, sports, and outdoors groups take advantage of how close we are to the Jersey shore ("downashore") for beach walks and play, the Chesapeake Bay for sailing and fishing, and the Poconos for ski slopes and hiking trails. Plus, the lovely, expansive Fairmount Park right within the city limits is loaded with walking, hiking, running, and riding trails.

Second, Philadelphia is an *interesting and diverse* city. You'll meet people from different ethnic, racial, sexual preference, and age groups in many of our organizations. (I loved the strong ethnic qualities of Philadelphia's neighborhoods after being raised in the Maryland suburbs where homogenized architecture and culture was the norm.) You'll find people of all types and in all phases of their lives, including young families, college/university students, working people in the trades, an older established crowd, and young, hard-working professionals. Philadelphia culture has the historical, formal qualities displayed in our interactive museums and institutions, as well as a variety of avant garde themes demonstrated in local arts events (such as glass blowing in Old City). The city's Quaker beginnings are still evident in the large number of committed community service organizations involved in the arts and people-for-people work. All these traditions invite each of us to experience our unique creative leanings.

Philadelphia is big enough to have *first-rate cultural activities* that many interest groups include in their repertoire of events. These include a fine visual arts community and an outstanding orchestra, as well as excellent dance, film, and theater productions. For example, SOLOS is a singles group (affiliated with the Philadelphia Orchestra) whose members enjoy socializing at fine restaurants followed by the best in classical music. There are theater groups that sponsor lively theme parties related to their current play. At least 10 major colleges in the area offer every kind of adult evening

Building a Social Network

class you can think of—all taught by excellent teachers and attended by classmates with high-quality minds (like yours). And personal growth experiences are aplenty all around the area. My favorite is a combo of qiGong and t'ai chi taught in a small studio in Roxborough. Opportunities in the mind-heart-spirit arena abound in Philadelphia.

The really nice thing is that although our town is big enough to have first-rate cultural and sporting events, it's also small enough that the average person can figure out how to get around and become part of things. And in addition to the activities in town, there are also things to do in many lively and lovely suburbs less than 45 minutes from Center City.

Philadelphia is a *friendly* town because it has thousands of truly welcoming groups of people following recreational and thoughtful pursuits—from the unusual (climbing the mast on the tall ship Gazela) to the distinguished ordinary (joining a Great Books discussion group). All give you entreé into Philadelphia's social networks. The people in these groups smile at you, introduce you to others in their group, and help you move in to enjoy the action. Check out the Cajun dancers from Allons Danser, for instance. Go, watch, take a lesson, and dance. Notice the way they encourage you to learn to do those special steps and feel a part of their sizeable group that loves to dance (even if you don't do it exactly right). You'll find this is true in almost any group you pick. In this way, Philadelphia really does "love you back!"

Building a Social Network

What's so special about the connections you find in an interest group?

Think about it. When you're happy, isn't it usually because you feel like you "belong" somewhere that you really want to be? And aren't the best times in your life when your relationships are going well and you have good friends with whom to do things you like to do?

If you said yes, you're like most of us. We are wired to be social beings so we can survive the rigors of life on this planet. We band together for support, division of labor, and love. Studies show that when people are isolated from other human beings, they show signs of suffering and mental disturbance. When we don't take care of our needs for social interaction, we often experience many types of unhappy symptoms, including anxiety, depression, insecurity, low self-esteem, and more. It's important to arrange to have pleasurable contacts with people with whom you feel compatible. People who *know* they need people are the luckiest people in the world!

When we think about our social connections, we usually think about family—husbands and wives, parents and children, sisters, brothers, and lots of cousins. If you have a Norman Rockwell family with all those people getting along, that's great. You have all the community you need, gathering for holiday parties, family softball games, and such. But family relationships are not always so perfect. In fact, they can be downright problematic at times. So it's important to have rich sources of social support and affirmation from friends as well as from your family network.

Being part of an interest community is different from being with a partner or family members that you love. First of all, it's largely your *choice* to come and go in the groups you join, depending on how satisfying they are. That's important because we change, and as we change, our relationship needs change. I was very politically active in my 20s and loved being around politically minded friends. Then I had children and wanted to talk to other parents about kid issues. Now my kids are grown and I'm involved in community politics again. (Community activists out there can call me.) It's also fun to find the networks of those who enjoy the games we're playing. (Lady golfers can call, too.)

The way your activity-network friends see you and how they interact with you is very different from the way you interact with your family. You'll get more immediate and openminded feedback with less emotional loading from your community of friends about your new skills, your latest ideas, and the activities you're rabid about. I loved the affirmation I got about what an

Building a Social Network

adventurer I was from fellow sailors hanging out with me high on Gazela's mast. My mother would have worried that I would fall. My husband might have wondered who I was up there with. That kind of thing.

Opportunities for socializing come up often when you join an interest group with a rich schedule of events. And if the organization is large enough, it offers a variety of people with whom you can be friends. When you're in the mood to socialize, you have many phone numbers to call for company.

I frequently hear people say, "But I'm not a group person. I don't like groups." If you're one who says this, consider that there are many *types* of groups. A group is simply two or more people who have come together (maybe only three!) for a reason that appeals to everyone or involves an activity that the members all want to do. Groups can be regular and established, or quite spontaneous. They can meet often, or every now and then, and they can have rules and procedures, or be completely informal. Most likely the key to your comfort level in a group is finding one that feels like the right size and right structure for your lifestyle, that satisfies your interests, and where you feel compatible with at least some of the members. It should feel like *your* group.

Being in an interest community helps you fight feelings of isolation, alienation, and depression. These feelings are *not* resolved by finding a mate or "fixing" a spouse. Taking care of your social needs is a personal challenge and requires you to place yourself in a rich context of compatible friends in addition to your family relationships.

Building a Social Network

5 Good Reasons To Join One Or More Activity Groups

Physical Health

Hey—we *know* that it's all-around good for you to be doing things you enjoy. Having fun lowers your stress level, and the released endorphins give you a sense of well-being; this results in a stronger heart and lowered cholesterol. Any activity that makes you think keeps your brain stimulated, so your mind and memory will work better, longer. Studies have shown that people who play mental games perform far better on tests of mental acuity. (Think how great it will be to know where your car keys are!) If the activity you choose requires body action, you will stay in shape and be stronger, healthier, and trimmer. A ton of studies show the huge advantages to your health of having a full and rewarding social life. It's true—you know it!

When you're doing your recreation in a group, you'll be more likely to make time for those physical activities (play!) you should be doing. Since the group has a schedule of activities (e.g., the running group meets on Wednesday evenings and Saturday mornings, etc.), you're more likely to show up because they (the people you like) are looking forward to seeing you (and vice versa). If you're a little depressed (or lazy) and are having trouble getting yourself moving, an organized activity group could be your motivator. When you get there, you'll be glad you went, and when you come home again, dollars to donuts you'll feel really good and proud of yourself—but put that reward brownie down! Also, if you're out there being active in a group, you'll laugh more than if you were working or at home by yourself. (At least I hope you're not laughing too much in your house by yourself.) We all need to laugh more.

Personal Development

When you are doing the things you love, you become more accomplished (at climbing a mast, writing plays—who knows what?), which enhances your self-esteem. As you move forward with your interests, your curiosity and sense of adventure cause you to press against the edges of the familiar and reach for things completely new (*What's out there?*). You become more interested in life, more interesting as a person, and people will be more attracted to you, which lifts your self-esteem even more. Feeling the transformation (from self-involvement to engagement in outside activities) is exciting. *Very* exciting.

Building a Social Network

A group can help you explore an activity you love. You *could* go taking black and white photos all by yourself, but see what you get when you do it within a club: Regular get-togethers where you watch demos by experts who already know those cool new focusing techniques, trips to pretty places you'd never have thought of where members collaborate on how to frame tricky shots, and the company of cronies who like nothing better than hanging out with their shutterbug friends on a Sunday afternoon. You'll get affirmation for your good shots from your photo friends, laughter at the photo-in-jokes, and genuine enjoyment from each other. And some day, *you'll* be the mentor who helps bring newcomers up to (shutter) speed. That's the group cycle—working for both beginners and old timers.

Social Skills

It's pretty obvious to say that the people you like are often doing the things that you like to do. But there's more to it than that. It's likely that people in your favorite interest group are the same people with whom you share significant values. They can introduce you to all kinds of neat stuff you want to know and lead you into an ever larger network of people in the same community. Your social group could grow like mad, with everyone sharing a common bond. Just *finding* those people—I call them "your people"—is a real coup. You want to keep them in your life and you hope they'll accept you as part of their group.

Speaking of being accepted, finding acceptance is easier in an interest group because you honestly *do* have things in common to talk about. There is less of a struggle to think of something to say. Not only that, if you care about the subject, you'll find yourself thinking about *that* instead of worrying about how you look or act. If you're shy, this is the ticket—forgetting about yourself while you're getting used to new people.

And for those who are shy, there's an added bonus. While you are getting comfortable talking with others about the activity you enjoy— having easy-going chats about it—you are developing and refining your social skills. These are the very skills that are useful in other places, such as at work or in scary social situations where you feel at loose ends. You will actually become more socially fluent and feel more at ease meeting people in general because you've had a place to "practice" just chatting.

When you're not sure what to say to someone you've just met ("*Now* what do I say?"), here's a pointer that you probably already know: If you have developed an interest or two (and have become used to talking about it in your group), talk about *that*. If it is interesting to you, you'll have more confidence and be more natural and enthusiastic. I had a teacher who was normally very quiet and ladylike but noticeably awkward in social situations. At one college tea we stumbled on the fact that she was a licensed airplane pilot. As she related story after story about her airborne adventures with her pilot buds, her face lit up and she became animated and extremely talkative. She relaxed and enjoyed her delighted (and surprised!) audience.

After you've talked about *your* favorite activity, you can listen to *theirs*.

Relationship Building

> *Let friendship creep gently to a height; if it rushes to it, it*
> *may soon run itself out of breath.*
> —Thomas Fuller, 17th century divinity scholar

Beyond simply socializing, if you want to build relationships that are durable and long-lasting (whether close friends or love partners), you have a good chance of finding them in the interest groups you join. First of all, you know you both share a genuine interest in the same subject because you've joined that particular group. (Have you ever dragged someone you like to a group activity that you just love? Their lukewarm response can be such a bummer!) And members of the group often share *other* similar interests. For example, if hiking is your thing, you may also care about environmental preservation, love animals and plants, and work at keeping your body healthy and strong, etc. Having true common interests can be a major foundation for relationships of quality that have more going for them than just romantic or spark-in-the pan qualities. (Not that chemistry isn't important! It's just that there's more, right?)

Second, if you are a part of the group for a while, you have a chance to get to know each other slowly and thoroughly. You can get to know each other's personal qualities so you won't be blinded by the good ones, or devastated by the bad ones. You have time to gain a realistic and balanced understanding of each other. It always seemed to me that it would be a good idea to spend a week in a canoe with someone before agreeing to get into a close relationship with him/her. You'd certainly find out whether that person can solve problems ("Slow up for those rapids!"); will follow your direction (if *you* are in the back); can communicate clearly (if *he/she* is in the back); and has a sense of humor (when you tip the canoe and you're both swimming in the drink). You are more able to determine whether this is really a person with whom you have a good mutual fit.

Building a Social Network

Third, since you'll be in the company of many mutual companions, you aren't in the glare of just one-on-one spotlighted talk. You can watch each other interacting with others when you're not part of what's happening and see how he/she talks to people: warm and interested or distant and unimpressed, hogging the conversation or listening and responding, paying attention to others or ignoring them, etc. You'll see all kinds of interpersonal behavior that will matter to you in your relationship over time.

Often when you meet someone at a fancy social function or on a date, you might try to create an image you'll think the other person will like (this is called "imaging"). But this image is very hard to maintain on an everyday basis—and besides, it isn't really you! If you are seriously looking for someone to be in your life for a long time, you need that person to see you as you really are. (It may sound scary, but you do.) This is where being in an ongoing group can help you.

People in your group will get to know the genuine article when they work with you on a challenging project or while mastering an adventure skill. The really good news about this is that you are your most *attractive* when you are engaged in something you really love. Your face lights up and you are rapt with attention as the experience flows through you. People are very attracted to those who are involved and excited about what they are doing. Being gorgeous isn't necessary. Being high on life is.

For those of you already in committed relationships, it is just as important to find your own activity networks. It can strengthen your connection to your partner if, instead of always relying on that person to make you happy, you introduce new activities and new friends for you both to enjoy. It adds vitality to the way you relate to each other. When your partner sees you with your interest-group peers (appreciating you, knowing you in a different way than he/she does), he/she often gains a new respect for your talents. It's a reminder to you both that you each have your own path to follow, even while you share a life together.

Building a Social Network

Fun

THIS IS THE BIG ONE. Spending more time doing things you love in groups makes life more **fun**. When I asked my *Connecting in Philadelphia* workshop participants to talk about when they last had fun, they looked at me as if I was using an unfamiliar word. You remember fun. It's what you did when you were a kid and could do whatever you wanted. It's what people are doing when they are finding "their inner child." It's the thing you do that doesn't have a reason other than that you like doing it. It frequently has no product or consequences and it helps you not to take life (and yourself) so seriously. It's probably something that you'll want to say, "I did that" when you are on your last legs.

The participants in my workshops believed that having a broad social activities network is part of feeling happy, an idea supported by research reported in a book called *Flow* (Csikszentmihalyi, M., 1991). It concludes that people are happiest when they are immersed in doing something they love and are so involved that they are oblivious to time and their surroundings. Ever happen to you? In other words, your activities can have a powerful influence on your feelings, attitudes, and general disposition.

Think about how good you feel when you have things you really enjoy waiting for you on the weekend or whenever. Don't you find that when you have these activities to look forward to, you're less likely to resent the things you *have* to do? I think that when your life is in balance between your responsibilities and the things you enjoy, you have more fun all the time.

It's also nice to have something you can claim as your particular pleasure, something that helps you identify the fun-loving part of yourself. I'm not a great sailor, but I love the things I do know about sailing. I love to be out there pulling down the jib, or steering a course, or trimming my sails so I can ease past that boat next to me. It feels like *my nifty thing* to do.

SO, what are *your nifty things* to do?

Building a Social Network

A Look At Your Current Social/Activity Network

The first step toward expanding your network is to consider the activity groups you have in place now. If they didn't mean something to you, you wouldn't have continued with them. Be sure not to neglect them as you search for new ones. If, however, they no longer work for you but you don't know how to discontinue them, try reducing the amount of time you spend with them, and if it feels better, slowly taper off.

As you stand back and take a look at how you spend your "leisure" time, consider these questions:

- Do all your activities include the same people, or none of the same people? (That is, what's the overlap of people in your different social circles?)
- Are all your activities of one type, so there is no diversity in your recreation?
- Have you included activities that allow an influx of new people? Or are your social groups closed groups, and, further, are they small closed groups?

An important issue is to acknowledge that you do not have infinite time, money, and energy; you have to pick and choose the activities and people-network that you want to emphasize. We all have different styles about how thin we like to spread our time-money-energy. For example, I like to do lots of different fun activities, trying to fit as many as I can into my schedule. This means I get to enjoy many things but never get especially good at any of them. My husband, on the other hand, likes to do fewer things in depth with more proficiency. (He's a *good* golfer; I'm an OK golfer, recorder player, t'ai chier, singer, folk dancer, endless-discusser, etc. This does require some fancy negotiation between us.) Both ways are fine—it's a matter of preference. You need to decide your style and be realistic about your planning.

Play with the Sociogram (Exercise #1) on page 38. Consider the above questions for ideas about how and in what directions you want to expand your activities.

Building a Social Network

What Do You Love To Do?

Sometimes it's hard to know where to start when you're looking for new things to try. You may not be sure what you like or where to find it.

I suggest that you begin by brainstorming. Encourage your mind to flow freely over all the things you've ever done that have been fun and/or given you deep-down satisfaction. Also, think about the things you've imagined doing but haven't put the needed "oomph" into making them happen. Do these include coasting down a stream in a canoe on a gentle summer afternoon with easy breezes, bird songs, and shade shadows? Attending and discussing the films of your favorite filmmaker with a cinema group? Carefully raising a pot on a wheel in a studio filled with earnest, serious potters? Being part of an exciting, dramatic production in a community theater? Or counting the hawks on Hawk Mountain in the fall with your favorite environmental organization? And wait, how about getting the hang of that waltz step, really getting it, after a bunch of hours trying?

Let yourself mull over all kinds of things that sound wonderful to do without censoring your ideas (e.g., Why you can't do them, why someone else would think it was silly, etc.). If you're having trouble coming up with activity ideas, here's a list of mine. Choose as many as appeal to you. (Keep notes on this in Workshop Exercise #2, page 39.)

Acting	Computers	Running
Archery	Cooking	Sailing
Architecture	Discussion Groups	Science Fiction
Astrology	Environmental Studies	Sculpture
Backpacking	Filmmaking	Singing
Ballroom Dancing	Fly Fishing	Skiing
Basketball	Galleries	Social Groups
Bicycling	Gardening	Swimming
Billiards	Golf	Swing Dancing
Bird Watching	Hiking/Walking	Tennis
Blues	Inline Skating	Theater
Bookstore Browsing	Kite Flying	Vintage Cars
Camping	Martial Arts	Volunteering
Canoeing	Motorcycling	Weaving
Card Games	Painting/Drawing	Wine Tasting
Cat/Dog Lovers	Personal Growth	Windsurfing
Ceramics	Photography	Woodworking
Chess/Go	Play/Poetry Readings	Yoga/Meditation
Coin Collecting	Political Activities	

Building a Social Network

Organize Your Activity List To Fit Your Life

Now think about the activities you've chosen in terms of the way they will fit into your lifestyle. For example, you might categorize activities according to cost, since that is important to most people. You might divide the activities you've brainstormed into three cost categories, such as: 1. Things that are cheap or free; 2. Things that will take a moderate amount of your recreation budget; and 3. Things that will require you to live hand-to-mouth while you save for that wonderful activity (buying a sailboat, a trek to Nepal—people do these things!). You might decide to start saving money for that major trek in Nepal, but in the meantime you could prepare yourself (and have fun) by doing lots of weekly hiking with local clubs that charge only a minimal fee.

Another way to categorize your list of interests is by types:

- **Intellectual** (examples: word and indoor games, idea discussions, hobbies like computer techniques or collecting)

- **Physical** (examples: games and sports, hiking, dancing, fitness)

- **Cultural** (examples: all kinds of arts, such as painting classes, musical participation, theater activities)

- **Spiritual** (examples: Yoga, meditation, journal writing, and wellness activities)

I believe the above categories reflect different parts of your self, all of which need expression. If your activities aren't balanced, you're excluding whole aspects of your personality that need to be exercised and enjoyed. (An example might be if you are a fanatic runner whose running consumes all your discretionary time.) If your activities are too limited or old-hat, you may find that you become bored with yourself, the things you're doing, your friends, and your life in general. If you're feeling this way, take stock of how you are spending your time and what bold initiatives you are willing to take to add a new dimension to your life. For instance, the runner could try a non-physical endeavor, something that uses her head or enlists her artistic creativity, to round out her life.

You can also categorize activities by how much time they take (once a week, five-hour golf games, etc.), and whether the time involved is regular (monthly salon discussion group) or sporadic (a theater production or performing group). It needs to fit in with your schedule, your other activities, and your energy level.

Building a Social Network

Your psychological safety/excitement continuum is a dimension to consider when choosing an activity. You'll probably want to include activities *all across this scale*. On one side are things that are familiar, easier, relaxing, and safe. On the other are things that require you to expand your boundaries (skills, knowledge, new locations, etc.) and are therefore somewhat risky. If you only go places that feel completely safe your recreational life can feel flat. Activities that are more adventurous, such as an in-line skate class or speaking your mind in a discussion group, are important to keep your life stimulating.

You will also want to think about which activity groups will expose you to the people you want to meet. If you are looking for people who are brainy, you should look for intellectual activities. If you are looking for a mate, certain activities might be more likely to help you meet people of the appropriate gender, age, and style. If you like competing, look for games and players. If you are looking for cronies to hang with on a Friday night, choose people who are available for that kind of evening, etc.

A final note. As you think about your pleasurable activities, don't let yourself get stymied by thinking that if you come up with something you have to run out and do it. It may not be something that works for you right now. Write it down so you can consider it for some other time in your life. But don't be too quick to dismiss something that appeals to you, either. Learning sailing might seem impossible ("I can't afford a boat and besides I don't know how"), but new and novice members are always welcome to attend outings with the Philadelphia Sailing Club for reasonable fees. How about: "I'd love to dance, but I'm overweight and would never get a partner." It's true that gorgeous men and women are usually asked to dance first (I won't lie to you), but if you love it, and you're willing to get out there and try, you'll *find* partners in the groups listed in this book. And you'll burn multo calories dancing! (Look at the workshop exercise #3 on page 39.)

Let's summarize where we are in the process of finding your best places.

1. Decide to find new activity groups. Commit time and energy to it.

2. Brainstorm as many lovely things as you can without censoring them. Let your mind loose, imagine, and explore all your options.

3. Then it's time to get a little more real. Put the activities you love into categories of what fits with your lifestyle.

4. Select and get serious about at least two, maybe more, activities. You're now ready to start your research about where to find them.

Building a Social Network

Finding Your Selected Activities

You could, of course, use this book to begin your search for your desired activity. Or you could search the web for your activity from every angle. Look in an assortment of papers: the dailies (*Inquirer, Daily News*, especially the *Weekend* sections), the weeklies (*City Paper, Philadelphia Weekly*), the suburban papers (*Main Line Times, Mt. Airy Express*, etc.), and papers for special populations (e.g., *Milestones* for seniors, *PGN* for gay and lesbian activities) and special interests (*Art Matters*). Pick up fliers and handouts from bulletin boards and public places (libraries, schools, etc.). Call universities, community groups, the Department of Recreation, public libraries, and all groups related to your interests. Talk, talk, talk to your friends and *their* friends to find people who seem to know a lot about interesting events/ groups in the area. If you find someone who is a member of an organization you are interested in, see if you can go with him/her to the next get-together. People usually love to take you along to become acquainted with their favorite places.

Tap into your enthusiasm (It will keep you moving.) as you explore the community for who-knows-what about what's happening. Nifty activities will pop up everywhere around you. (That has certainly happened to me since I started researching this book. I can't keep up with the new and interesting activities that I hear about every day. I just found out about the recumbent bike community. Now I have to make space for it!) You'll likely find more than you bargained for—great news because the more groups you know about, the more options you have to choose from as you look for an activity with the best fit for you and your current lifestyle. Keep notes so you have the phone numbers for interesting activities when you need them.

When you phone or email to request a newsletter and/or to ask your questions, keep in mind that many groups are staffed by volunteers who feel very attached to their groups and take offense at questions that imply that their group isn't wonderful. So with due respect and without taking too much time, make the inquiries necessary to determine if this sounds like a good group for you. Questions might include specific directions about how to get there, where to park, and where the entrance is (especially if it's a night activity). You might want to ask about the participants, including the range of ages, and whether they are mostly men or women. Find out if there is a dress code, and the level of skill needed to be involved. You can even be direct: Given this or that about me, would I be a welcome member? Be sure to get the name of the person with whom you are speaking, so when you go you have a contact person to help smooth your way. (Exercise #4, page 40.)

Building a Social Network

Before You Go

After you have chosen an activity, have called and determined that it sounds like fun, you are ready to venture forth. All right!

You may notice some ambivalence (*strong* feelings in both directions!) as the time to go gets closer. You may start to hear yourself giving reasons why you aren't able to go: you're too tired, it's too expensive, or there is a book (on your shelf for six years) that you've been dying to read. When you hear these excuses running through your head, you have to make a clear decision about the side of yourself you want to support: The one that wants to be comfortable, warm, and safe or the one that wants to break out of the routine and add a new and exciting dimension to your life.

If you decide on the latter, you'll need to actively support your wish to go. The ambivalence doesn't just go away. First of all, there are practical things to take care of, such as making sure you know exactly where the event is located and how to get there (Get a good map!), you have a babysitter ahead of time, you've made plans with a friend if you need someone to go with, and you have the clothes you feel good in out of the cleaners and ready to wear. Does this advice sound mundane? Believe me, these kinds of things can sabotage your efforts to go at the last minute. Don't let them!

The other advance work is psychological. It has to do with facing your anxieties about going somewhere for the first time. Most of us have worrisome thoughts about being uncomfortable with new people in an unknown situation. It is entirely normal to worry about this, but try not to let it stop you from exploring. Try to feel it as excited tension instead of crippling anxiety. Remember that you may find the group friendly, that your discomfort will be minimal, and you could have quite a nice time. And remember that the second time will always be easier!

Also, you may have myths (unsupported beliefs) about the kinds of people you will find. These myths may be negative ("Everybody who goes out dancing alone is either secretly married or desperately single.") or positive ("The love of my life is waiting for me at this event.") These attitudes may sound pretty silly on paper, but negative attitudes often sound this way and operate underground; they'll keep you in your living room alone for years. Try to ferret out these myths and bring them to consciousness in the bright light of day. Talk to yourself (and maybe someone else) about them and defuse them. *Make a decision* not to buy into them. Tell yourself clearly that you are going out to expand your pleasurable activities and have experiences you'd never thought you'd find. Give yourself the

Building a Social Network

freedom to discover new worlds and the people that populate them. I never found that guy in the Harris Tweed jacket with the pipe and a thoughtful expression I thought I wanted. Instead I found someone (in a group) whose style I could never have imagined, whose style is so unique that I am constantly surprised and entertained! (I bet the next great person you find in a group is someone whose charms you never could have anticipated, either. Why don't you go and see?)

Another thing: I always told myself beforehand that I could bail if I was having a really bad time, or if I'd just had enough. Without that, it would be hard to go in the first place. But when you do that, remember that you also want to give the new place, the new people, and yourself a fair chance at that activity. It might be that your discomfort is just a reaction to the unfamiliar ways of the new group. Remember: *A bit of stress is not a good enough reason to leave.* The first time anywhere is always going to feel strange, as you are constantly trying to figure out what is going on, as well as adapt to a whole new crowd. You will not immediately feel that easy-going comfort you have with people you've known and with whom you've developed a history. What is important to consider is whether this place seems to have the *potential* to be your kind of place. You may need the information gathered by several visits to know that this is/is not a place for you, since many factors will influence this decision. So it will be important to be on the alert for the excuses you often use to cop-out prematurely, and plan a self-talk response to them so you can stay until you know what you need to know. Examples of self-talk that I use include:

1. Feeling uncomfortable is OK. Take some deep breaths and relax.
2. Look around and see if anyone here looks approachable. Stand near them and see if you have an opening.
3. It's OK to just sit and listen, or watch what is going on. Just sit here and get a sense of what this place has to offer.
4. Maybe in a while you can ask someone about the activity, either what it means or how to do it. But watch first.
5. No one is thinking about you. They are not thinking bad things about you. They are thinking about themselves.
6. You have every right to be here checking this out. You are fine.
7. It's OK to be new. It's OK to make beginner mistakes. Everyone here was in your shoes once.

(Turn to Workshop Exercise #5 on page 40.)

Building a Social Network

Hot Tips For Socializing When You Get There

When you first arrive:

You look in the door and scan the action. It may look like everyone there is an in-group member and an expert doing whatever the group does. <u>Or</u> it may look boring—the people don't look like your style, and you don't think it's worth your time.

Keep in mind:

Your first impressions are always superficial (looking at the surface, right?) and not the most accurate. These quick observations can give you clues for deciding your first moves, such as how long to wait before joining in or who looks friendly enough to talk to. You usually don't know the whole story about the organization and all its members in the first five minutes. Remember, you are only reacting to the tip of the iceberg, and there is much more to discover as you spend time with this group.

Tips:

Try to be open to people who don't immediately look like "your style." You would be surprised at the qualities people have underneath their looks. True, chemistry and looks are important, but sometimes the sexiest qualities are wisdom, gentleness, and a terrific sense of humor. One woman I spoke to said she never found men her height (5'7") attractive—until she met Michel, who had a sense of humor to die for and who understood her so well he could finish her sentences. She fell hard and stopped looking up.

The most successful approach in socializing is to adopt an attitude of being friendly. Sound corny? Well, watch people in social situations. Who would you want to talk to? Probably someone who projects interest, energy, and a general good humor. So, what does "friendly" look like? Open smiling face, eyes that look at you, not around you, and a body posture that looks toward you instead of looking as if it's moving somewhere else. Try using those friendly ways in the groups you've chosen to explore.

Building a Social Network

Next:

As you watch what is happening, you hang back because the activity is new to you and it looks really hard. You don't want to make a fool of yourself, and you don't want people to be annoyed and held back by your stumbling and bumbling.

Keep in mind:

It's good of you to be sensitive to the needs of the established group and its skilled participants. It's always wise to watch first instead of quickly jumping in without regard for the norms (usual procedures) in the group. That way you get a feel for what is going on and can decide whether it is a good place for you to be active as a newcomer. But in many interest clubs you need to try the activity to see if you like it. You'll never find out if you like the waltz if you don't try it, nor T'ai chi, nor canoeing. If you're not sure when and how to get involved, ask somebody if there is a way for you to fit in without being disruptive. Often they will help you do this in an appropriate way.

Tips:

It's sometimes hard to be totally new, a rank beginner, and try something you've never done before. (I'd much rather be the expert.) But when it's time, you'll have to swallow your pride and just jump in! After all, you are there to have as much fun as you can. Act as if this is the thing you really want to do, become immersed and into *Flow*. Don't hang back observing yourself ("Look how stupid I look!" or "I'll never be able to do this!"). Get into the game. You don't have to commit your life to it—just one evening. Sometimes you (or I) enjoy these things *despite* they're being hard—or even *because* it's a challenge. And you might have a good time!

Building a Social Network

Now you think:

I don't know anyone here. How can I start meeting people—just go up and start a conversation? I wouldn't know what to say.

Keep in mind:

The best way to connect with people is to be part of an activity. When you initiate talk with someone about what is going on, it feels legitimate to both of you. You have a common focus and the conversation feels natural.

Research shows that you are most attractive and interesting when you are engaged and interested in what's going on, and focused on something outside of yourself. You are more approachable and people feel more comfortable with you—which is what they want to feel.

Tips:

Pay attention to cues when you want to approach someone. What did they say or do in the group that interested you? Comment on it or ask about it. You can also look for identifying information, such as jewelry or logos on T-shirts that tell you what this person cares about, and remark on it. Or *you* could wear "information" about yourself, giving others a hook to begin a conversation with you.

There are many other ways to try to take your place in the group (as a newcomer). Offer to join someone in a project, or ask for help in learning something that the group is doing. When I used to go swing dancing, I always asked an expert to dance one dance with me so I could get the feel of how the dance *should* be done. (I was never turned down, even though my partner may have regretted it once the dance started!) If you want to be involved, most people will extend themselves to help you in a gracious manner. They want you to enjoy what they enjoy.

Building a Social Network

What happens if you aren't always the chosen one?

After my one dance, the experienced swing dancers usually looked for another skilled dancer to dance with. People on the Gazela would teach me knots for a while and then find an old hand to go up the mast with them. They did not give me continuous attention for hours, even though I might have wanted them to. It was not about me. It was about my skill level. (Although sometimes it might have been about me!)

Keep in mind:

We all need to learn to deal with rejection. You are going to get slighted, rejected, and disappointed sometimes by some people. It might make you feel annoyed or fearful that you do not belong. Most of the time it's just part of the game. Everybody gets rejected, and the more you are in contact with people, the more it happens. You need to work on how not to take it personally. Learn about rejection by talking to friends, reading about it, and taking workshops where it is addressed. We all need armor and strategies to stop fears about rejection from keeping us home.

Remember that many people feel anxious and awkward. There is a common human concern called the "on stage" phenomenon in which you are sure that everybody is looking at you with a very critical eye. Often the criticism you think they have is the one you have about yourself. Although people may be looking at you, most likely their main concern is how they are being evaluated by the crowd. Knowing that others are uneasy about the impression they make on you should make it easier for you to relax.

Can we talk for a minute about shyness? Sometimes we label our "on stage" feelings as shyness, as in, "I'm too shy to try that." Most people *are* "shy" in unfamiliar situations when they don't know anyone. The feeling is based on not knowing what in the world to do or say, and to whom. One of the reasons for this book is to encourage people who are moderately reserved to go places that liberate their natural friendliness. Many times shyness is more related to the situation than the person. Test this out by being aware of your fluttering anxiety when you go places of different risk value to you. Do you notice your shyness level change? (By the way, if you are extremely shy in most situations, you may want to check out a program to help alleviate those feelings. The universities or the Center for Anxiety and Agoraphobia can help with this.)

Building a Social Network

You might rather just stay home:

You might say to yourself, "I just hate going strange places I know nothing about and risking having a really awful time with lots of stress—all in the name of recreation. My life is hard enough. I have some friends and a good book. I think I'd rather stay home."

Keep in mind:

I really do know what you mean. I have avoided going many places when I've thought about how miserable I might be leaping off into the unknown. It's so easy to stay safe! And I will not press if that's really what you want to do. Trouble is, you'll never know what you missed. It might have been worth it.

• • • •

A Final Note

I thought my father was nuts when he told me he thought if people were lonely they should join a local walking club. I was single at the time—it was thirty years ago—and thought that was the dumbest thing I'd ever heard. I didn't want to go hiking. What I wanted was to meet a handsome man and get married. But I thought I'd try his advice, and was he ever right! Over the course of 16 years of singleness, I was lucky to have a wealth of terrific experiences exploring the city (and surrounding environs) to find the things I loved to do as well as the community that enjoyed them. Now, as a married person, I'm *still* doing them.

The process of finding new interests, new places to have fun, and new people to be active with is exciting. Like any challenge, it takes thought, energy, and nerve. But you'll learn a lot about yourself. Exploring your favorite activity groups furthers your own self-development, regardless of whether you have an intimate partner, children or close friends. The skills you will learn while exploring this great city will always be with you, no matter what happens to you or where you are. This is a golden opportunity!

Building a Social Network

Workshop Pages

Exercise #1: Make a Sociogram of Your Network

1. Make a circle for each group of friends you have.

Dancing   **Work**

Folk   Cajun

Step   YOU!!   **Stamp Club**

2. Label the name of the group and the activity they do together.

3. If the people you know are in more than one group you hang out with, make the circles intertwining with those people on the boundary, to show membership in both groups.

4. If you have a favorite group or cluster of groups, color them red.

5. Draw a line between your smiling self and the circles or circle/cluster and write down the number of times a week/month/year you interact with this group.

_____

_____

_____

_____

Examine what you see.

Do you have friends to do lots of different types of activities with, or are you involved with mostly one type of recreation? Do your friends interlap (my word) or do most of them not know each other? Do you see them as often as you want? Are there circles you'd like to eliminate or add to your sociogram? What are they? Think about what you see and ask yourself your own questions. Let it be a guide to change.

Building a Social Network

Exercise #2: List Activities That Interest You: Past, Present, &
Future

Think about the activities that turn you on. Make notes about the ones
that you'd like to try. Brainstorm *as many options as you can think of* without
evaluating them (That's next.). Look in the papers, on bulletin boards, talk
to people, and use the activity list (page 27) or entries in this book. Take
some time with this, and write them down on paper. (Remember, no
censoring yet!)

Current pleasures?   Past pleasures?   Future pleasures?

Exercise #3: Organize Your Activities

Now choose several favorite activities. Think about how the ones you've
chosen fit into categories of importance to you. Do you want to develop
your strength? Do you want to know more about the city? Do you need to
keep your activities low cost? Do you want to do community service? Do
you need to work around stringent time requirements because of work? Do
you need to stay away from clients in your socializing? Are you looking for a
group of cronies to go out with on Friday nights, or are you looking for a
life long partner? Do you need to find other couples that both you and your
spouse get along with?

Identifying what matters to you can help you choose which activities
you want to look for and invest time in.

Category 1 (Example: Uses my creative abilities. Hi-Med-Low)
_____   _____   _____
_____   _____   _____
_____   _____   _____

Category 2 (Example: Gets me out on the water. Hi-Med-Low)
_____   _____   _____
_____   _____   _____
_____   _____   _____

Category 3 (Example: Helps me meet more men/women. Hi-Med-Low)
_____   _____   _____
_____   _____   _____
_____   _____   _____

Building a Social Network

Exercise #4: Research: Data Collection Notes

Connecting in Philadelphia

_____

Papers

_____

Web sites

_____

Friends

_____

Other

_____

Exercise #5: Are You Ready To Go? Checklist

Practical things

_____
_____
_____

Myths I hold about people	Changed views about this place

Building a Social Network

Notes For People Visiting From Out-of-Town

Our groups and organizations are *delighted* when you (people from other places) want to take part in activities with regular members. *Please* take the initiative and call any group about activities you'd like to do while you are here. Most would love to have you.

Some ideas for your enjoyment: You could join a dance group—whether you're an expert or if you're a complete beginner. Consider folk dancing on Tuesday evenings in the summer. They dance on the Art Museum steps overlooking the Benjamin Franklin Parkway under the moon and the lights of the city. (See page 144) They teach the steps while you dance, and beginners are expected. You could go on a birdwalk on Saturday mornings, an easy bike ride on Sunday mornings or weekday evenings (rentals available), or join an in-line skate club on its tour around the city streets on Tuesdays (you do need to know how to skate for that one). You might want to hitch up with a weekly judo class, a pottery class, or a Wednesday Evening at the Art Museum for a lively multi-cultural experience. Hopefully you can find others throughout the book and will call to inquire about them.

Please do this! You will have a chance to enjoy meeting new people and try out a new (or familiar) activity at the same time. It could give you a chance to go to areas of the city that are off the beaten track and into the very nice and interesting neighborhoods for which Philadelphia is famous. Like the Italian Market in South Philadelphia. You've never seen anything like it, I'll bet, and the people are friendly and have a culture all their own. Engage with "the natives," in groups all over the city and have a whale of an experience! When you get home, you'll have some wonderful stories to tell about your travels.

Philadelphians *will* love you back, especially when they get to know you—and vice versa!

Volunteer crew furls sails on the tall ship Gazela Philadelphia

Art

Art Appreciation • Artists Networking • Classes
Gallery Programs • Multifaceted Art Events
Organizations • Photography • Tours

Art

Art students in class at the Fleisher Art Memorial

When you talk to artists, don't you get the feeling that they "see" things differently? It's as if they see shadows and light, the variations of color, the balance of objects in a landscape, and the ways things move into the distance better than most of us. Whether accomplished or just dabblers, artists seem to have a heightened sense of the visual world. I had some experience with this when I tried a little sketching on my last vacation (*tried* is the operative word). I found that I had to pay attention to qualities about a landscape that I had never noticed before. The view was so different; it was as if I was seeing a tree, a rooftop, for the first time. Doing art can really wake up your senses.

Besides revealing new perspectives, art projects can give you tremendous satisfaction. A good friend of mine in her 70s decided that she wanted to discover the artist in her. She read *The Artist's Way* and started with a drawing class. It began to absorb her and she was harder to make lunch dates with. She moved into oil painting and became thoroughly immersed in her work. (She also has a real job.) Recently she went to Italy for a three-week painting class and came back glowing that it was the experience of her life. Her paintings are full of vitality and very interesting, but what they say about my friend is what is most wonderful about them. She has moved into an expanded relationship with herself and the world around her. And she has developed a community of art friends who share that enthusiasm. (I'm ready to rush down to **Fleisher Art Center** just thinking about it.)

Let's pretend you are thinking about becoming an artist yourself. Where would you start? Well, first, you might want to talk to your supportive friends and share your doubts about whether you can do artistic things. You'll probably want to discuss your (fantasy) worries about how dumb you'll feel when people look at your sketch, standing boldly exposed on some easel in an art class, and wonder what on earth you are doing in that class. You'll go over all the reasons why you can't get involved in art things: No time, no money for the class, no babysitter, the class is too far away, and you wouldn't be any good anyway, etc. Your good friends will reassure you—and tell you to get on with it! You might want to read *The Artist's Way* yourself, which explains how we are *all* artists (just as we are all singers, dancers, and bird watchers, etc.). The deal here is to claim full entitlement to your right to do art in whatever way you choose, and enjoy the heck out of it. Let yourself find pleasure playing around with soft drawing pencils, water colors, or those nifty pastel chalky crayons you see in the expensive art stores. They are for the artist in *you*.

The next part is easy—finding a class that is right for you. You may want to try an adult extension class in a high school or neighborhood art center (**University Arts League, Abington Art Center**, etc.) near your home. One nice thing about these programs is that they offer many kinds of art classes to choose from, everything from papermaking, weaving, and bead work to the usual classes in painting, drawing, and clay. Another nice thing about art centers is that they are a fine gateway for rank beginners (like me) to make art. I don't have to feel out of my league as I struggle to master the most basic techniques and come up with the most "unusual" (that's the word they use for my work) products. Teachers expect people like us and are encouraging and, better yet, kind. Also, these programs are usually very reasonable, so if art does not become an income-producing situation, you can do your thing without feeling like you're losing your shirt.

If you're seeking a specific art activity, you may need to travel a bit for a specialized art center. For example, **Moore College of Art**, the **Art Institute,** and the **University of the Arts** all offer programs in computer graphics, computer illustration and computer animation for those who want to do web graphics and design. **HistoricRittenhouseTown** offers specialized courses in all aspects of papermaking, and the **Clay Studio** provides very professional courses in all facets of clay and pottery work. **Beadswork** will teach you to make beautiful jewelry, and you can learn knitting-art at the **Tangled Web** in Chestnut Hill (listed in Hobbies and Clubs). One of my favorite kinds of fun art is at the pottery shops, **Color Me Mine** and **Kiln Time**, where they provide the clay vase/pitcher/statue, etc., and you apply the glaze. When you give it to your mother for her birthday, you can say (brightly), "I made it for you!" (That is about my speed and it's still art!)

Photography for many levels is offered around the area, primarily by art centers and photography clubs (**Upper Merion Photography Club, JCC Camera Club**, etc.). These groups feature speakers, trips, and social activities as well as seminars in the art of picture taking. If you're an inexperienced photo shooter, never fear. Photography clubs welcome beginners and generously share their techniques and experience to help those just starting out enjoy their new hobby.

Time for a brief commercial, reminding you about the theme of this book: You can meet some very neat people, artists at all levels, to talk about and do art with. If they are on your level and progressing along beside you, if they like to share supportive feedback, then they will likely become part of your art network. You can discuss the blush on the peach you are painting or compare ideas about the teacher's lecture. You might travel to an outdoor site together and set up your easels to paint the river, or attend a conference about handbuilding pottery. You might join a knitting or quilting circle that meets weekly ("It saved my life," one member told me.). Or you might just take in the smells and sounds, the atmosphere of the studio, as you work next to each other without saying a word. Art-making is a grand place to find a community of people who want to see the world in a new light.

To open our eyes to the world the way an artist does, we can study and appreciate art done by others. Philadelphia has more classes than you can imagine where you can learn about famous classic art. The **Philadelphia Museum of Art**, the **Pennsylvania Academy of the Fine Arts** and contemporary art galleries for established and new artists, like the **Nexus Gallery** and the **Painted Bride,** all have single-night lecture/discussions as well as ongoing classes on all kinds of topics. The **Art-At-Lunch** program at the Academy offers presentations about well-known artists and paintings that you can catch on your lunch hour for just $3. And the **Museum of Art** has art events almost every day of the week, as well as the special and ongoing exhibits that you can see anytime. The **Young Friends of the Art Museum** has many single as well as married members who attend special museum openings, tours and lectures, visit artists' studios, view private collections, and meet for relaxed conversations at cocktail receptions. It's a great way to get to know others who share your enthusiasm in a less formal, more social, context. Attending regular lectures at exhibits is also a way to get to know other people who are discovering the world of art just as you are.

You know if you've always wanted to develop the artist in you. You need to think clearly about what has held you back and decide if you will let it continue to do so. If you wish to go forward, you'll have the company of many new and experienced art enthusiasts for encouragement and appreciation.

Art

Photo by Beth Bahl

Painting pottery at Color Me Mine in Chestnut Hill

Members of the Upper Merion Camera Club preparing a photo shoot

Art

Art Appreciation

Institute of Contemporary Art, University of Pennsylvania

118 South 36th Street, Philadelphia, PA 19104
(215) 898-7108   icaup@pobox.upenn.edu   www.upenn.edu/ica

Gain an appreciation for contemporary art through lectures, tours, performances, videos, workshops, and other events. You'll enjoy evenings of symposia
(for example, Wall Power Symposium: Artists, community representatives, and
arts professionals discuss issues related to urban, outdoor wall art), artist
dialogues, films, and receptions with discussions of all kinds. Don't miss the
tours, many led by Alex Baker, Assistant Curator. Call for the Calendar or check
the web site for up-to-date details.

☀ Wednesdays-Sundays   ☉ 10am-5pm
💰 $3 Adults; free to members ($35/yr)   (7pm on Thursdays)

Old City Arts Association: *First Friday*

139 North 2nd Street, Philadelphia, PA 19106
(215) 625-9200   www.oldcity.org
Activity Location: Old City section of Phila., around 2nd/3rd & Arch Sts.

"First Friday is a unique cultural event in Philadelphia and one of the city's most
popular evening escapes. Held the first Friday of each month, rain or shine, this
arts community's 'open house' brings together city dwellers and suburbanites,
contemporary arts and antique collectors, aficionados of classical and contemporary design, and theater and performance buffs. The welcoming informality of
First Friday, with member organizations and galleries of the Old City Arts
Association hosting receptions and exhibition openings, attracts crowds of casual
browsers as well as buyers. All galleries are open to the public."(from OCAA
web page) This is a wonderful tradition in Philadelphia, high energy, a great
street party dedicated to the arts. I go alot, hang out at Big Jar Books on 2nd
Street, look at the art—from the weird to the sublime—and talk to everyone. It's
a lot of fun.

☀ 1st Fri./mo   ☉ 5-9pm

Art

Philadelphia Museum of Art

Benjamin Franklin Parkway at 26th Street, P.O. Box 7646, Phila. PA 19101
(215) 763-8100 or (215) 684-7500 www.philamuseum.org

This premier museum sits proudly on the Schuylkill River where Kelly Drive meets the Parkway and is the heart of many of Philadelphia's finest cultural and recreational activities. With folk dancing and festivals on it's steps, skating, biking, and running on it's pathways, and one of the finest art collections in the world inside, this is a great way to start exploring this city. There are regular and special exhibitions, public and members-only tours, gallery talks, tours of the outdoor sculptures along the Schuylkill, art films, lectures/classes, and Wednesday theme nights with many activities. Check the fine web site or call to join.

☼ Tuesdays-Sundays (Wednesdays until 8:45pm) ⏰ 10am-5pm

💲 Adults $10, Students $7, Seniors $7, Pay what you wish on Sundays

The Creative Collective: *The Craft and Fine Arts Fair*

1216 Pine Street, Philadelphia, PA 19107
(215) 790-0782   creatc@libertynet.org   www.libertynet.org/creatc
Activity Location: Headhouse Shambles, Society Hill, 2nd & Pine Sts., Phila., PA

Every weekend from Memorial Day to the end of September, 25-35 craftspeople and artists exhibit their handcrafted art: Handmade jewelry, glass, clothing, photography, and more under the historic open-air structure called Headhouse Shambles. It's easy to strike up a conversation with artists and other appreciators and you can bring your children to the free arts and crafts workshops on Sundays from 1-3pm. It's free for appreciators; about $95 to exhibit if selected by jury.

☼ Memorial Day to end of September

⏰ Saturday noon-11pm; Sunday noon-6pm

Artists Networking

Artists for Recovery

3721 Midvale Avenue, Philadelphia, PA 19129
(215) 951-0330 x106   www.artistsforrecovery.freeservers.com
Activity Location: Different areas around the city

This is a group of artists recovering from emotional hurts or addiction who meet about twice a week, primarily for open mic performances featuring the many performance artist members. They also hold jam sessions, art exhibits, arts and crafts workshops, rhythm instrument workshops, support groups, and theater improv classes. To support their artists, there are meetings for performers about promoting their work, and meetings for visual artists and writers/poets. They provide performers for art events, and speakers on alternative health care.

ArtistsView

Collegeville, PA
(610) 454-1321   owensjo@aol.com

The goal of this small group (about 12 people) is to find ways/places to show their art. They work together to find galleries to give them shows, and representatives (like interior designers) for their members' works. Once a month they meet for lunch to discuss what is coming up and what needs to be done, as well as to enjoy each others' company

🪙 No entry fee

Creative Artists' Network

The Barclay Hotel, 237 South 18th Street, Su 3A, Philadelphia, PA 19103
(215) 546-7775   canart@libertynet.org   www.libertynet.org/~canart

Since 1984, this nonprofit organization has offered a rich professional development program for talented, emerging visual artists who are selected to be included. For the public, CAN hosts openings every six weeks, plus an excellent lecture/discussion series called "Direct Dialogue." No reservations are needed to attend the lectures. Call or check the web site for current schedule.

🪙 Free

Creative Artists' Resource Project (CARP)

(215) 739-2583   pandiva@earthlink.net

These artists share their trash—since what is not useful to one person may be just what someone else is looking for. Officially, CARP is building a community of people, many of them artists, interested in sharing resources of information and found materials for making art. They work together to encourage each others' projects, using not-new materials in their work. They are affiliated with the Dumpster Divers who go on regular forays for reusables. Look at this web site for other aspects of this group (www.idealist.org/penn.htm).

☎ CDavid Hall-Cottrill

Germantown Pottery Guild, Germantown Women's Y

5820 Germantown Avenue, Philadelphia, PA 19144
(215) 438-6266

If you take a class with the guild you can use its professional studio anytime for the duration of the class. Membership is limited but you can become an associate member and learn how to mix glazes and use the large gas-fired kiln or three electric kilns. The guild also has exhibits for the public to enjoy the members' art work.

☎ Ellen Litwin

Art

National League of American Pen Women, Chester County Branch

(610) 942-4394

Activity Location: Members' homes and Chester County Art Association in West Chester, PA

NLAPW is for women writers, artists, and composers. This Chester County chapter of the national group (meeting since 1897!) has been meeting since 1958, about five times a year, with a speaker, followed by discussion and socializing. In addition to hosting art exhibits and workshops for writers, they share information, learn about each others' work, and provide support and friendship. About 30 members (not all from Chester County) welcome newcomers.

Pennsylvania Guild of Craftsmen

10 Stable Mill Trail, Richboro, PA 18954

(215) 579-5997   pacraft@comcat.com   www.pennsylvaniacrafts.com

Activity Location: Many workshops at the Tyler Craft Center, Richboro, PA (near I-95's Newtown-Yardley exit)

The Guild offers workshops on glass blowing, willow basketry, glass bead making, tin and coppersmithing, and more. This is a nonprofit group that offers its classes for the public to support local artists, and you do not have to be a guild member to participate. It is also a network of chapters (such as the Montgomery County branch and the Chester County Craft Guild) that has developed over the years, providing member craftspeople with local groups that permit more direct marketing, networking, and personal involvement. The twenty chapters are different in flavor and programs, each reflecting the interests of its members. Call or check the web site for the schedule of classes or list of member chapters.

🪙   Membership $25

Philadelphia Guild of Hand Weavers

3705 Main Street, Philadelphia, PA 19128   (Manayunk)

(215) 487-9690   www.libertynet.org/~phweaver

This active organization, about 200 strong, does fiber arts, including spinning, felting, weaving, dyeing, and tatting. They provide outreach demonstrations showing how cloth is made, along with workshops, a monthly newsletter, meetings, and an excellent library for guild members.

🪙   Reasonable workshop fees & $25/yr membership (optional)

Philadelphia/Tri-State Artists Equity Association (P3AE)

P.O. Box 563, Devault, PA 19432
http://region.philly.com/community/artistsequity
Activity Location: Various in the tri-state region

Artists Equity works for improved working conditions for artists and for the protection of artists' rights. By working collectively they can more effectively address the concerns of the profession. Meetings support these goals and also give artists a chance to get to know fellow artists working in a wide variety of media at monthly meetings. Often the 200-member group has speakers on topics, such as "Why do jurors pick what they pick," and other advocacy issues that affect them. In addition, P3AE puts together two group shows a year that are hung in local venues including Ursinus College, Montgomery County Community College, and American College. A newsletter also lists exhibition opportunities. Programs have included: "A Symposium: What Artists Need: 2000 Changes," moderated by Glenn Curry, editor of *Art Matters*. You could join Friends of Artists Equity (215-53-0500), a non-profit that supports artists exhibitions and lectures with activities such as auctions, tours, and other events.

☼ Varies

💰 $30/year, does not include membership in National Artists Equity

Classes

Abington Art Center

515 Meetinghouse Road, Jenkintown, PA 19046
(215) 887-4882

Meet other blooming artists and take an exciting potpourri of studio classes offered here, including Mosaic Ceramics, Bookbinding, Tile Making, Feng Shui, and Multiple Figure Painting. Expand your horizons by experiencing all kinds of art from photography to jewelry making, or meet other art lovers at AAC's fine exhibits, trips and events.

💰 Varies, cheaper with studio membership

Art Institute of Philadelphia

1622 Chestnut Street, Philadelphia, PA 19103
(800) 275-2474   www.aiph.artinstitutes.edu

The Art Institute offers state of the industry classes for serious art students in the daytime and evening. Classes include computer animation, graphic design and multimedia and video production. Check the web site or call to learn more about these excellent courses that will help you upgrade your professional skills.

Art

Beadworks

225 South Street, Philadelphia, PA 19147
(215) 413-2323   www.beadworks.com

You really can make your own jewelry and find others who are talented as well.
If you're brand new, try the Basic Bead Stringing class or the Earring and
Linking class. Specialty workshops are scheduled from time to time, such as
Bead Weaving, and Macramé and Hemp. You can also just walk in empty
handed, gather and arrange beads from their selection, then sit at the back table
with other "jewelers" as you produce your new pieces! If you really enjoy bead
work check out the South Jersey Bead Society as well.

   About $25/2 hour class

Cheltenham Center for the Arts

439 Ashbourne Road, Cheltenham, PA 19012
(215) 379-4660   www.libertynet.org/cheltenham/cca

This adult education center offers many wonderful classes in the visual arts,
including painting and drawing, ceramics, printmaking, jewelry, stained glass,
and more. It also offers theater classes, exhibitions, performances, and guided
tours, such as a visit to Museum of Modern Art in New York.

   Reasonable, cheaper with membership

Clay Studio

139 North 2nd Street, Philadelphia, PA 19106
(215) 925-3453   info@theclaystudio.org   www.theclaystudio.org

The Clay Studio School offers classes and workshops for all levels of proficiency,
from beginner courses to intense workshops geared towards practicing professionals. Classes include Porcelain Workshop, General pottery, Hand-building,
Tiles and Mosaics. There are regular lecture series as well as a Clay Conference
with demonstrations, slide lectures, panel discussions and workshops. This is the
premier clay place.

Community Arts Center in Wallingford

414 Plush Mill Road, Wallingford, PA 19086
(610) 566-1713   info@communityartscenter.org www.communityartscenter.org

A homey place where you can study and practice painting, ceramics, pottery,
jewelry, photography, and many other arts and crafts. They invite us all to "take
a course, visit an exhibit, join us on a trip or come to a lecture, attend a party,
bring a friend, and celebrate with us as we explore the arts and the child in us
all!" Sounds very friendly, doesn't it?

Fleisher Art Memorial

709-721 Catharine Street, Philadelphia, PA 19147
(215) 922-3456   www.fleisher.org

Luckily for us fledgling artists: We have the country's oldest and largest tuition-free visual arts organization for adults and children right here in our town. Workshops have included: Basic Painting, Landscape Painting in Fairmount Park, Sculpture, Chinese Painting and Calligraphy, Photography, Paintmaking, and tons of ceramics classes. There is so much here—you'll be enthralled. Students wanting any of the 22 open enrollment classes can register at any point in the term. Check the gallery to see the quality of work—this is a wonderful place.

💰 Most of the programs are free with materials fees; a membership contribution of $25 for each school term is suggested

Greater Norristown Art League

800 West Germantown Pike (at Sunset Avenue), East Norriton Township, Norristown, PA 19403
(610) 539-3393   www.tgsnational.com/gnaldad.htm

This 58-year-old nonprofit art league holds 10-week classes in clay, sculpture, life class studio, oil painting, and watercolor painting. The cost is low and the quality high. There are also monthly meetings with lectures and discussions, and four shows/exhibits a year mounted at their neat looking studio, once a one-room school house. This 430-member group is very supportive and social. They host bus trips to New York City art museums and Broadway shows, and sponsor a holiday dinner, an arts and crafts bazaar, and even overseas trips to France and Greece. You can take part in all or some part of this!

☼ Day and evening classes; monthly meetings 2nd Tues./mo at 7:45 pm

💰 Membership: About $20/yr adult, $15 senior citizen,
   About $80 for a 10-week (2 hr/wk) class, $65 for members. Trip costs vary.

Hot Soup Glass Studio and Gallery

26 Strawberry Street, Philadelphia, PA 19106
(215) 922-2332   www.hotsoupstudio.com

Opened in November of 1996, Hot Soup is Philadelphia's only public access glass studio and gallery. Check out Hot Soup exhibits on First Friday and view the hands-on demonstrations. Or take a class in glassblowing, or glass paperweights. If you already have experience with glass, rent a bench or sign up for private lessons. If you just like to watch, it's fascinating to see. Stop in on First Friday.

Art

Kiln' Time

4167 Main Street, Philadelphia, PA 19127
(215) 483-6200

Come to this art studio and create your own one-of-a-kind piece of pottery-art. Bisque-fired ceramics are available to paint with help from the staff to direct your learning. The staff fires the piece for you in their kiln and you pick it up a few days later. It's a great place to go to relax, be creative, and get away from your usual activities. You can bring a bit of food and a bottle of wine and really chill out! Open every evening except Sundays, and you should call first and make a reservation. Only $8/hour for painting time. Closed on Mondays.

Color Me Mine

8524 Germantown Avenue, Philadelphia, PA 19118
(215) 242-5555

A ceramic painting studio where you can create your own one-of-a-kind piece of pottery and have it fired by this expert staff. You can come here alone to relax and make art, or you can bring your friends (or make new ones!) and schmooze while you "supervise" each others' projects. These pottery places are lots of fun and you come out with a treasure of your own making! Also in Wayne (610-687-9777). Reservations are a good idea, so you know a place is saved for you.

Main Line Art Center

Old Buck Road and Lancaster Avenue, Haverford, PA 19041
(610) 525-0272   mlacjh@aol.com   www.mainlineart.org

"Art for everyone" is a MLAC motto. You'll find many adult daytime and evening programs, including painting and drawing, printmaking, sculpture, ceramics, jewelry, photography, decorative and fabric arts, flower design, mixed media, and more. Classes are planned specifically for beginners as well as more advanced students. This all-around art organization also sponsors trips—in the area, outside the area, and abroad as well as lunchtime and evening lectures. Wow. A lot happening here!

Manayunk Art Center

419 Green Lane (rear), Philadelphia, PA 19128
(215) 482-3363   www.manayunkartcenter.org

A variety of visual art classes are offered in this neighborhood space, such as drawing, painting, watercolor, and figure drawings. The Friday Night Figure Drawing Group has been meeting for more than ten years. It provides an opportunity to draw live models in the company of a regular group (about $6-$8). Some group members have supper together at the Adobe Cafe after class.

Moore College of Art and Design

20th Street and the Parkway, Philadelphia, PA 19103
(215) 568-4515   info@moore.edu   www.moore.edu

Moore offers outstanding programs in desktop publishing/computer graphics and decorative arts for interiors for the serious public interested in furthering career skills. Look carefully at their class information. Moore also has many fine gallery programs. The Goldie Paley Gallery hosts fine exhibit receptions, lectures, discussions, films, and other activities for the public. Examples of programs at the Paley are: Congo Chronicle: Patrice Lumumba in Urban Art; Urban Art: Philadelphia Style; and Cutting Wit: Philadelphia's Politics of Humor (featuring Tony Auth and Signe Wilkinson, Philadelphia's own editorial cartoonists).

Norristown Arts Building

619 West Washington Street, Norristown, PA 19401
(610) 272-8484   www.drawingworkshops.com

This program is geared toward helping the artist to be connected to his own voice. There are two ways to do this: Take a full residency program (rent space for a few weeks or months, get feedback from other artists, use the library), or take a workshop for three or five days, using a live model, all set in a rich environment for painting. People come from all over the country to study with expert teachers here. This is a vibrant community resource connected to the Pagus Gallery for all to enjoy. Call for complete information.

- ☼ Mondays-Fridays, weekends by appointment   ☎ 9am-3pm
- ☎ Tim Hawkesworth
- ♿ Gallery free to public; Classes are $245 for 3-day workshop, $510 for 5-day workshop.

HistoricRittenhouseTown

206 Lincoln Drive (on Wissahickon Ave., betwn Lincoln Dr & Walnut La),
Philadelphia, PA 19144
(215) 438-5711   HistRitTwn@aol.com   www.rittenhousetown.org

The center of papermaking in America for several decades, and the site of America's first papermill, HistoricRittenhouseTown continues to celebrate the tradition of hand papermaking. You can experience first-hand the magic of making paper in this unique and beautiful setting. An extensive list of summer workshops available through the summer includes "Paper Basics" where you learn to make your own paper stationery or collage by manipulating wet pulp, embedding objects, and building layers of color with personal artifacts like ribbons, lace, and old photos. Other workshops include bookbinding, decorative paper techniques, hidden treasure boxes, pop-up paper structures, Japanese papermaking, and many more. Attend a tour and consider volunteering.

Art

Temple University: *Tyler School of Art Noncredit Courses*
7725 Penrose Avenue, Elkins Park, PA 19027
(215) 782-2828   www.temple.edu/tyler

Try a class in the "Great Masters of Renaissance Art," one example of the interesting art classes at Tyler where you'll find an interesting learning community backed up by one of our area's finest large universities. Or check out Temple's Fort Washington location for classes in professional development (such as "Getting Organized"—so you have time to take that art course, maybe?), and including computer courses—so you can design a terrific brochure for the volunteer group you've joined. There's another branch in Ambler too. Call to get the course guides for updated class schedules.

University of The Arts: *Center for Continuing Studies*
320 South Broad Street, Philadelphia, PA 19102
(215) 717-6095   www.uarts.edu

You can enroll in a certification program in web or print design, or take one of many separate classes in computer graphics (Using a Digital Camera), crafts (Fabric Printing), creative writing (Writing for Film), fine arts, and web design. These are basic classes that will give you a firm understanding of the subject. Call for the brochure.

Wayne Art Center
413 Maplewood Avenue, Wayne, PA 19087
(610) 688-3553   www.wayneart.com

You can find classes in painting, sculpture, wood graining, jewelry making, pottery/wheel throwing, drawing, tile making, and many others here. Check out their gallery and receptions for new exhibits as well. Call for information.

Whitemarsh Community Art Center
P.O. Box 76, Lafayette Hill, PA 19444
(610) 825-0917
Activity Location: 100 Cedar Grove Rd., Conshohocken, PA

There are excellent classes for adults in wheel-thrown pottery, silver-soldered jewelry, watercolor painting, sculpture, and photography in this full-fledged art center. Also try the culinary arts classes and learn how to make sushi, perfect pie crusts, and delicious Thai dishes. Workshops in special topics are conducted here, too. Call to find out about them.

Gallery Programs

Barnes Foundation
300 North Latch's Lane, Merion, PA 19066
(610) 667-0290   www.barnesfoundation.org

The Barnes Foundation was established in 1922 by Dr. Albert C. Barnes, to "promote the advancement of education and the appreciation of the fine arts." This is an art jewel of Philadelphia with a fabulous collection, including the French Impressionists. Barnes offers Art Appreciation classes (a two-year program) and a Horticulture program (a three-year program) as well as many events for the public. You don't want to miss seeing this exceptional collection. Reservations are required and it is suggested you make them 60 days in advance.

☼ Gallery: Fridays, Saturdays & Sundays   🕘 9:30am-5pm
💰 $5 but call for reservation first

Goldie Paley Gallery at Moore College of Art
20th Street & The Parkway, Philadelphia, PA 19103
(215) 568-4515 (Moore) & (215) 965-4026 (Gallery)

The Paley Gallery has fabulous regular exhibitions, with lectures, symposia, workshops, and performances to go along with them. "Friends of the Gallery" help finance these programs and are invited to many special gatherings. These programs are original and very interesting. (See entry under Moore College.)

Nexus Gallery
137 North Second Street, Philadelphia, PA 19106
(215) 629-1103   nexus@libertynet.org

Nexus sponsors lectures, discussions, and workshops, such as the way art relates to contemporary issues. Call for their current listing. Also enjoy their fine exhibits and receptions.
💰 Free

Pennsylvania Academy of the Fine Arts
118 North Broad Street, Philadelphia, PA 19102
(215) 972-2071   www.pafa.org

The Academy is America's first art museum and school of fine arts, collecting and exhibiting works of American artists. Besides their student programs, PAFA offers weekend courses, lectures, and discussions on crafts and art, art history lectures, films, gallery talks, lectures, and Art-at-Lunch. Call for events.
💰 Free or low cost

Art

The Print Center

1614 Latimer Street, Philadelphia, PA
(215) 735-6090   www.printcenter.org

The Print Club encourages the making and appreciation of fine art prints, photographs and artists' books through exhibitions, programs, education, and support for artists, especially those just emerging. You can visit their fine gallery, attend receptions and tours, and go to public lectures and demonstrations. Find fine prints for sale in the Print Club Gallery Store.

Multifaceted Art Events

Allens Lane Art Center

Allens Lane & McCallum Street, Philadelphia, PA 19119
(215) 248-0546   www.allenslane.org

"Draw, act, paint, write, stretch, bend, juggle, sing, perform, imagine, create, dance and tumble" is the defining phrase on the cover of the ALAC brochure. And you truly can do all these things. Above all, it is a family-oriented center although some art classes are just for adults, like Intermediate Sculpture. There are also appealing classes like Vision Thru Art and A Gathering of Painters. This unique center is definitely worth a good look-see, especially if you live in Northwest Philadelphia.

Painted Bride Art Center

230 Vine Street, Philadelphia, PA 19106
(215) 925-9914   www.paintedbride.org

Come to exhibitions of off-the-beaten-track visual art that speaks about contemporary times. An example is *Alien Nation* which features drawings, paintings, sculpture, and mixed media work by artists from Graterford Prison and Kevin O'Neill. Another exhibit, *Discrete Logic* by Margaret Wagner, confronts the relationship between notions of family with the evolution of technology. The Bride hosts a multitude of programs in the arts (dance, jazz, poetry) that "affirm the intrinsic values of all cultures, (and) the inspirational and healing powers of the arts..." (from the web site) Volunteer for a free ticket, and join to help them keep up this outstanding work.

🌢   Very reasonable, cheaper still for members

Perkins Center for the Arts

395 Kings Highway, Moorestown, NJ 08057
(856) 235-6488   create@perkinscenter.org   www.perkinscenter.org

The Perkins Center provides a wide range of creative opportunities for people of all ages and every level of artistic development. They have visual and performing arts classes and workshops at both the basic level and for those more advanced: Life Drawing, Advanced Watercolor, Figure Sculpture, and lots more. They also have 6-week mini courses in Quilting, Portraits in Clay, Pastels, etc. Perkins has music, theater, yoga and dance classes that sound very exciting, as well as special events like Sunday afternoon chamber concerts and a monthly musical event on Friday night at the Moorestown DeCafe Coffee House. Call for information.

💲 $30/adult individual membership, plus course fees

Philadelphia Art Alliance

251 South 18th Street, Philadelphia, PA 19103
(215) 545-4302   www.philartalliance.org

You can enjoy a concert, dance performance, poetry reading or lecture, and tour five galleries filled with work by outstanding artists at the Art Alliance. Juried exhibitions are held at this vital center, where artists and art lovers come to exchange ideas and share experiences, maybe over dinner at the Alliance's Opus 251 restaurant. Consider joining and become a regular at lectures/discussions, events and exhibits; you'll get the membership discount. Drop in to the Gallery to enjoy this place. It's right in the heart of Center City, off Rittenhouse Square.

Philadelphia Folklore Project

1304 Wharton Street, Philadelphia, PA 19147
(215) 468-7871   www.folkloreproject.org

Check out the brown bag lunches, receptions, and parties with artists held by this wonderful non-profit group that pays attention to the experiences and traditions of "ordinary" people like us in the face of powerful institutions. They document, support and present local folk arts in relation to culture and social change with exhibitions, concerts, workshops, and assistance to artists. They also feature discussions on specific issues, such as "Folk Arts in the Classroom," as part of ongoing field research around issues of concern. An organization with very exciting activities all around the Delaware Valley.

Art

Sedgwick Cultural Center

7137 Germantown Avenue, Philadelphia, PA 19119
(215) 248-9229   info@sedgwickcenter.org   www.sedgwickcenter.org

The Sedgwick, dedicated to building community through the arts, provides a common meeting ground for artists and audiences of many ethnic backgrounds, religious traditions, age groups and socio-economic levels from Philadelphia's historic Northwest. ALMA, the Artist's League of Mt. Airy, is a membership organization at the Sedgwich Center that plans a full year of exhibitions in their gallery. When you attend the art openings (free and open to the public) you'll find nice people and good conversation; there are also fine gallery talks and workshops. If you want to be involved, you can help by volunteering for many events. By the way, the concerts here are fabulous with national and international talent performing on a regular basis (see Music chapter). Call for info.

University City Arts League

4226 Spruce Street, Philadelphia, PA 19104
(215) 382-7811   www.ucartsleague.org

Look: You can take Tiles and Mosaics, Introduction to Creative Jewelry, Cartooning, Belly Dancing, or Chinese Language by expert teachers right in a Philadelphia neighborhood. These classes, located in a West Philadelphia "brownstone," reflect all aspects of the cultural life of a community—dance, music, crafts, theater, photography, language, writing, and fitness. They are also home to lectures, concerts and community meetings. I took Flamenco Dancing and it was wonderful!

Organizations

The Plastic Club

247 South Camac Street, Philadelphia, PA 19107
(215) 545-9324   www.libertynet.org/plasticc

Plastic refers to any work of art unfinished, in a plastic state. This club, founded in 1897 for women artists, currently offers three excellent weekly workshops to non-members (of all genders!) for a small charge. A lunch is served at noon on Wednesdays. There are exhibitions throughout the year, with opening receptions once a month on Sundays.

☼ Mondays & Wednesdays   🕑 10am-2pm
   Thursday evenings   6:30-9:30pm

Philadelphia Sketch Club

235 South Camac Street, Philadelphia, PA 19107
(215) 545-9298   info@sketchclub.org   www.sketchclub.org

This small club for serious sketchers has been offering fine low-cost public workshops for years on some evenings and Saturday mornings, sometimes with live models. You need to submit work for review to join this group, but you don't have to be a great artist to "pass." Also you don't have to be a member to take workshops. This is a volunteer artists organization with a mission to promote the creation and appreciation of art through its art workshops, exhibitions, museum, and archives.

☀ 4 days/week

💰 $7/4 hour session

Philadelphia Watercolor Society

P.O. Box 58, Fairview Village, PA 19409
(215) 569-3955   www.pwcsociety.org

Founded in 1900 to promote and exhibit watercolor paintings, today this group includes all works on paper except oil painting. PWS has a large annual exhibit plus regional shows for signature members (who have been accepted to two juried annual shows). Join them for paint-outs at Winterthur Estate in Delaware or attend meetings and sign up for a committee. This is a prestigious group that has over 700 members internationally.

☎ James McFarlane

💰 $35

Urban Painting Partners

(215) 977-8408

Activity Location: Lloyd Hall, 1 Kelly Drive, Phila., PA

Join others for outdoor painting, drawing, photography, and more. The motto of the group is "We are painting Philadelphia." In the warm months (after April 29th) they meet throughout the city to paint it's many views. When the weather doesn't cooperate, the group moves indoors at Lloyd Hall. Open to all and free, but bring your own supplies and be sure to call before you go.

☀ Sundays   ⏰ 10am-2pm

Art

Photography

Churchville Photography Club

(215) 357-1647

Activity Location: Churchville Nature Center, 501 Churchville Lane, Churchville PA
(215) 357-4005

Meetings include speakers and programs, sharing photos and techniques, criticism and contests.

☼ 3rd Mons./mo   ⏰ 7:30pm

💰 Annual membership about $25

JCC Camera Club

(215) 343-3971   http://members.aol.com/jcccc1/

Activity Location: Jewish Community Center, Klein Branch, Red Lion and Jamison Rds., Phila., PA 19116

One of the largest camera clubs in Philadelphia and one of the friendliest. The club web site says: "Programs are typically 'How-To,' Travelogues, or Photo Essays. They are open to guests. We share our techniques and 'secrets' and have a good time socializing with people who share our photographic interests. If you think you would enjoy an evening at our club, you're more than welcome to join us!" Program topics include: How to Photograph Nature; Digital Cameras; and Glass Close Up. There are trips to places like the NY Photo Show and the Cowtown Rodeo, as well as occasional workshops, and monthly competitions.

☼ 2nd & 3rd Tues./mo from September to June

💰 $25-30/individual membership

Main Line Photographic Center, Inc.

1221 Lancaster Avenue, Rosemont, PA 19010
(610) 527-1221

Touted as the only black and white rental darkroom in the metropolitan area, this center offers 10 printing stations, a 9-foot stainless steel sink, and all the chemistry you need. Just bring your own paper, negatives and supplies. The hourly rental fee is low and working photographers are there to answer your questions. Or take a class. Recent offerings include Camera and Darkroom, Master Printing: Advanced Darkroom Techniques, and Natural Light and Location Shooting.

☼ 10am-6pm, Mon., Weds., Fri. & Sat., 10am-10pm, Tues., & Thurs.

💰 Classes $200-$300 for 6-week class, $50 discount for members.
    Rental fees vary depending on equipment used.

Upper Merion Camera Club

(610) 265-0939   www.phillynews.com/umcc
Activity Location: Upper Merion Baptist Church, Valley Forge
and General Steuben Rds., King of Prussia, PA 19406

UMCC welcomes beginners and helps them get started using proper photographic techniques. Meetings include speakers with travel shows, show and tell
with instructional workshops, and, on the last meeting of the month, a slide and
print competition for members. Two long-range field trips are planned each
year, with local excursions for photo shoots on a regular basis. At the year's end,
there is an awards picnic. About 25 people come for the meetings, but the
membership is much larger, with all ages and abilities included. Just $20/year.

☼ Meets 2nd, 3rd & 4th Weds./mo from Sept. to May at 7:30pm
    Weekly workshops from June to August

Tours

Excursions from the Square

P.O. Box 2189 , Philadelphia, PA 19103
(215) 732- 8487, 1-800-831-3351   www.squaretrips.com

If you are interested in tours to places of art interest, you will like these well-
planned, exciting experiences. Begin with a day trip to someplace like NYC, (tea
at St Regis, special museum visits, etc.), or Washington DC ("Art Nouveau"), or
the Baltimore Craft Show. Then try a longer tour to such lovely places as the
mystical streets of Savannah (with side trips to Beaufort and Charleston), or a
three-day weekend in Pittsburgh, to visit the Carnegie Museum, known for it's
French Impressionist paintings, and the city's famous mansions and architectural
highlights, and Paris, where you will see the city's grand monuments, splendid
museums, parks and avenues. Many friends meet on these friendly excursions.

Foundation for Architecture

1737 Chestnut Street, Philadelphia, PA 19103
(215) 569-3187   www.foundationforarchitecture.org
Activity Location: Philadelphia neighborhoods

These excellent small group walking tours will take you through neighborhoods
from Victorian Germantown to Queen Village to 18th century Frankford. Over
40 high-quality tours are offered for only $8, such as Great Philly Homes by
Great Philly Architects. The foundation also has a 4-week architecture lecture
series illustrating the history and development of Philadelphia architecture from
the city's founding to the present. Walks are one hour to 1 hour, 45 minutes.

☼ April to Nov., Sat., Sun. & weekday evenings   ⏰ 11am, 2pm & 6pm

Art

Friends of Independence National Historical Park: *Philadelphia Open House Mural Tours*

(215) 928-1188

The fine products of the Mural Arts Program of the Philadelphia Department of Recreation (www.muralarts.org) are seen in this tour, which also includes lunch at a city tavern with a presentation on the history/accomplishments of MAP, and a discussion with a muralist about the painting process.

 $50 includes lunch

Philadelphia Museum of Art: *Schuylkill Stroll*

West entrance of the Philadelphia Museum of Art
26th Street and the Benjamin Franklin Parkway, Philadelphia, PA

(215) 684-7926   www.philamuseum.org

In the summer, discover picturesque Boathouse Row on the Schuylkill Stroll, led by expert Park House guides, twice a week. When you look carefully at the sculptures and boathouses, you'll be amazed at how interesting and lovely they are! After the tour, go back to sit among them and read your book, watch the scullers, or chat with fellow tour-members.

☼ Wednesdays (6-7:30pm) & Sundays (1-2:30pm) during the summer

Nonmembers $5, Members $3, Children $1

 **Here are some extra resources to check:**

Publications

- *Art Matters*

  290 Commerce Drive, Fort Washington, PA
  (215) 542-0200   artmatters@montgomerynews.com
  An important resource describing all the art happenings in the
  area, including the exhibits in all the galleries. It also includes
  articles of interest to artists.

- *Cultural Resource Directory*

  Put out annually by the Philadelphia Art Alliance

Web Site

- *www.bookarts.com/98badw.html*

  Has listings for paper artists/paper dealers/mills;
  calligraphers; printmakers; artist bookmakers;
  fine printers & publishers; bookbinders/conservators;
  booksellers/dealers/galleries; libraries/museums;
  organizations; periodicals; related services; equipment
  & supplies; schools/workshops.

Art is an answer to reality.
— Tadeusz Kantor

Cafés & Coffeehouses

Coffeehouses & Cafes

Restaurants/Bars with Activities

Tea and Pastry Houses

Cafés & Coffeehouses

Photo by Janet Gala

Friends making music at the Mermaid Inn

Cafés & Coffeehouses

Thank God for coffeehouses and cafés.

It might be that you've just been in the house too long and you want to get out. You haven't got any particular plans. It may not even be a nice day (evening). But cabin fever has set in and you need to go out and be where people are milling around. So you trundle over to your local coffee spot and have a sit with a sweet nibble and a tasty warm drink. You may find a live guitarist, a football game, or darts in the background. Or maybe your favorite café is a peaceful place where you can read the paper or your book and look up on occasion to see everybody else doing the same. Whatever your MO, you can show up when you want, leave when you're ready, and do whatever gives you satisfaction while you're there. It's chill time.

Coffeehouses and cafés are also great places to meet new people whenever you want. If it's your neighborhood spot, then you know the "regulars" and maybe count yourself among them. That's a nice position to be in—you have a coffeehouse/café *community*, where you probably run into someone you know everytime you go and have some kind of conversation waiting for you. I like to take my laptop and work in my local **Starbucks**, stopping from time to time to have a short chat with someone. And if you're looking to expand your network of friends, it's good to do it where you already have some people around that you know. You're protected by your group and can comfortably reach out to a new person. Even if you don't know anyone there, it's still a pretty safe place to start a casual chat.

You've probably guessed that the coffeehouse/cafés described in this chapter will feature activities that patrons can do together. Some activities give you a pretty active role, like playing games such as Quizo (a bar game with competitive teams answering trivia questions), chess, or having a Tarot card reading (**Latte Lounge**). Still other events let you be a bit more laid back but still encourage audience interaction, like art openings (**Dirty Franks**), poetry readings (**Coffee Talk**), comedy improv (**Comedy Sportz**), and open mics for local talent (**Fergies**). During the show, people are encouraged to talk to each other and respond to the performers.

Connecting activities of all kinds have invaded the beaneries and café clubs these days, probably because many of us are looking for more ways to interact with the arts and each other. For example, my favorite

Cafés & Coffeehouses

spot, the **Mermaid Inn** in Chestnut Hill, has an "Open Circle" every first and third Thursday where local folk display their musical talents to an enthusiastic, happy audience. Another example, the "Gathering Girls" at the **Sidetrack Cafe,** is an event where local artists and art-dabblers (men and women) meet to do crafts. Check out the **Bar Noir**, where you can sip wine and watch independent and classic films. What a cool spot to hang around and relax with people you know and people you are just meeting. Also **Coffee Talk** in Norristown appeals to me, where they have presentations on local history with discussions afterwards. Don't you love these kinds of places—informal, comfortable places with fun things to do, making it easy to find people who are interesting and sometimes quite talented who may live just up the street from you?

Since there is an increasing number of hangout coffeehouses/cafés in the area, you can choose just the right one for your mood. You need to go around and test the atmosphere of different places and see where you feel comfortable. Sometimes the places reflect the neighborhood in which they are situated. If you love your neighborhood and a café is close to your house, it may be a winner. Go a few times and see. Check out the activity schedule and go when your favorite thing is going on—you could find a whole different crowd. If you go more than once, people who recognize you will be more likely to say hi because you look familiar.

And, consistent with the point of this book, when there are social activities planned in the café you enjoy, it makes it a heck of a lot easier to identify the people you think you'd like to talk to and get to know better. Just having a common theme to relate to gives you a head start. Having something to do or react to keeps you from feeling like a doofus sitting by yourself staring at your coffee or wine spritzer.

By the way, of all the activities in this book, coffeehouses and cafés are among the most volatile—that is, they are most subject to come and go. Unless you don't mind going somewhere and having it not be there, be *sure* to call before you go or check the web site for hours and current activities.

Cafés & Coffeehouses

Coffeehouses

Brew Ha Ha!

163 Lancaster Avenue, Wayne, PA 19087
(610) 995-2757

At Brew you're encouraged to lounge on the sofas and relax with The *New York Times* or another good read from the huge selection of magazines and newspapers—just as if you were in your very own living room. There are people to chat with as you read and enjoy lunch or a delectable sweet. On some Fridays there is live music, and an open mic night is being planned. Call to check, or better yet, stop by and hang out. Open everyday. You can also find Brew Ha Ha! in Maple Glen (215-619-9950) and Blue Bell (610-239-2411) if you live nearer to those locations.

Coffee Connection

6441 Frankford Avenue, Philadelphia, PA 19135
(215) 331-5903

Carol, the manager, says she makes the best cappuchino in Mayfair. You can drop in and decide for yourself, but while you're there you'll find plenty of neat things to do. Hang out on the sofa and relax with TV, read the paper or a magazine, or surf the web on the café computer. It's one of the few cyber cafés in town. If you're there on Thursday, you can participate in the open mic or just listen. On Saturdays, it's a live music venue. Open weekdays until 11:30pm and weekends until 12:30am, the Connection always gives you a place to go.

Coffee Talk

507 West Marshall Street, Norristown, PA
(610) 275-0199   JMAEigen@aol.com   www.coffeetalkonline.com

Try this sweet spot if only to talk to owners Aleksandra and Joel Eigen, who are founts of information about the wonders of Norristown. Lots of regulars will be there enjoying the coffee/tea and many activities: open stage (requires pre-audition) on Fridays; Saturday concerts; art openings for local artists; local poets' readings; local actors reading new plays; and lectures about everything—How to Put a Sidewalk Together, the Origins of the Civil War, and the History of Norristown. You can't miss here, but check the web site for times before you go.

Cafés & Coffeehouses

Coffee drinkers socialize at Gryphon Café

© 2000 Photo by Jeanie Chadwick - Mamarazzi Photography

Gryphon Café

105 West Lancaster Avenue, Wayne, PA 19087
(610) 688-1988   www.gryphoncafe.com

This is an all-round cultural stop featuring light food and a wide selection of coffee and tea to enjoy while you listen to your favorite music—Celtic, jazz, Scot, bluegrass, folk, and an open mic on Mondays. Gryphon is continually exploring new ways to involve its patrons with discussions on contemporary events, chess, an art gallery, and occasional poetry readings. An interesting and diverse group of people (age and otherwise) are regulars here. Also in Center City.

☼ Everyday

Keswick Coffee

285 Keswick Avenue, Glenside, PA 19038
(215) 884-2001

Not just coffee, tea, pastries and bagels, but water ice is sold here in spring and summer. Activities include games for you to play with your friends, regular poetry readings, and a book exchange. Come and chat at the regular art openings that launch the new works on the walls, and ask about the regular jazz and acoustic music on Friday and Saturday nights.

Last Drop

1300 Pine Street, Philadelphia, PA 19107
(215) 893-9262

Frequented by many University of the Arts students, as well as people who are on their way to work or taking a lunch break, this corner coffeehouse has great coffee and a laid-back atmosphere. There is live music occasionally on weekend nights and some weekdays. It's a nice relaxed place to hang out, read, and have a little something.

Latte Lounge

816 N. 4th Street (near Poplar and Brown), Philadelphia, PA 19123
(215) 629-9808

How many places can you drink fine coffee and explore your astrological chart? Each Thursday at the Lounge is "Love Land" night when you can talk to astrologer Mumin Bey and enjoy poetry—yours or someone elses—at the open mic. On First Fridays there are receptions for the artists whose works you've been watching that month on the Lounge's walls. And on Wednesdays, you can hang out and talk to house music sounds. All told, a good place to hang your hat for a while.

Lighthouse Café

(610) 520-9500   info@proclamation.org   www.proclamation.org
Activity Location: Proclamation Presbyterian Church, 27 Bryn Mawr Ave.,
Bryn Mawr, PA

The crowd here is 20s, 30s and 40s, about 50 strong. They hang out, listen to music, socialize, and play chess or other games in a comfortable atmosphere. (You can bring your own games and find players.) The music is Christian singer/ songwriter style, often by local artists. Don't be surprised if you find a singalong breaking out.

☼ 2nd Fris./ Sept.-June from 7:30-10:30pm

Mom & Pop's Coffeehouse

(215) 547-1124 or (215) 946-6800 (church)   www.fortissimo.org
Activity Location: United Christian Church, 8525 New Falls Rd., Levittown PA

Coffee, tea, and baked goods are served with fine folk music in this convivial and homey spot in a church sanctuary. Volunteers are welcome to help out with about 50-100 patrons, including regulars and delighted newcomers. Call to be on the mailing list for concerts and go to have a great time. Just $7.

☼ 1st and 3rd Fris./mo (Sept.-May)   ⏰ 8pm

Point of Destination Café

Upsal Train Station, 6460 Greene Street, Philadelphia, PA 19119
(215) 849-7771

Enjoy an eclectic mix of music almost every day of the week at this spot in the Upsal Train Station. This state of the art facility is wired with live simulcast and offers seminars, music, and events for patrons to enjoy. They serve coffee and sweets, and restaurant food as well.

☼ Mondays to Saturdays

Cafés & Coffeehouses

Sidetracks Café

14 S. Lansdowne Avenue, Lansdowne (near Baltimore & Lansdowne), PA 19050
(610) 623-2205   www.sidetracks.com

Singers/songwriters and poets entertain at the open mic every Friday, and every second Tuesdays is just for poetry readings. My favorite is Wednesday evenings, when Gathering Girls (a group that includes many local artists) meets to do crafts. Basketweaving, jewelry (beads and metal) making, and drawing are among the activities enjoyed by both gals and guys. You can come on your own to watch and learn, or network with the local craft community. (May be closing)

Starbucks Coffee

8515 Germantown Avenue, Philadelphia, PA 19118 (Chestnut Hill)
(215) 242-3860   www.starbucks.com

Even though they don't have planned activities, it's hard to exclude the major coffeehouse chains altogether. Besides, this is my favorite coffeeshop. They have a space in the back for people who want to sit and write for a bit or work on the book they are having trouble focusing on when they stay home (like some people I know). The coffee is excellent, the staff is very friendly, and it's a nice place to spend time reading and chatting. Find them all over the city, but this one is my hang out.

The Point

880 West Lancaster Avenue, Bryn Mawr, PA 19010
(610) 527-0988   www.atthepoint.com

This community café, which was one of Philadelphia's first performing coffeehouses, features music most nights of the week. Tuesdays boast a large open mic (sign up online or come at 7pm for a 7:30pm event), Wednesdays have an open music circle, and Thursdays through Saturdays showcase national, regional, and local performers. A variety of terrific events, such as art openings, go on here too.

Cafés & Coffeehouses

Restaurants/Bars with Activities

Bar Noir

112 S. 18th Street, Philadelphia, PA 19103
(215) 569-9333   www.barnoir.com

All kinds of wonderful things go on here in this salon/café style spot. Live entertainment—including jazz, cabaret, rock and roll, experimental, and classical music—happens on many nights, and lots of dancing even when the place is filled. They have theater with plays written about this bar, classic films that run continuously, and an independent filmmaker series. Poetry with jazz happens every other Thursday. Try to get there early. This place is hot.

Bob & Barbara's

1509 South Street, Philadelphia, PA
(215) 545-4511

Hard to tell what kind of adventures you'll have at B&B's, but you *will* have them and they'll be different every time. It's hard to keep to yourself here, but who wants to? Two Wednesdays/month there's *Juke, Jerk and Jive*—a night of barbeque, soul music, and happy customers. There's also local rock music on Tuesdays and Wednesdays, and a fabulous drag show at midnight on Thursdays. Great funky juke joint!

Brasil's Restaurant & Bar

112 Chestnut Street, Philadelphia, PA
(215) 413-1700   www.brasils.com

Lots of dancing to hot music at this exciting club. On Wednesdays, Fridays and Saturdays, Latin is the mode, with a free lesson from 9-10pm on Wednesdays. Saturdays you'll find Tango lessons from 8-10pm for only $10, and on Tuesdays, live bands playing music with an international theme: Greek, Turkish and Arabian music with belly dancers from 9pm-2am. Check the schedule for current music and dance lessons. There's more, but you'll have to discover it yourself. This place is hopping! And say hi to owner Waseem Kalla—he's great!

Dickens Inn

2nd Street between Pine & Lombard Streets, Philadelphia, PA 19147
(215) 928-9307   www.dickensinn.com

You don't have to be a Brit to love Dickens Inn, Philly's quintessential English pub. There are plenty of convivial activities, like Scotch malt or port wine tastings, cigar friendly evenings, lively tournament darts to watch or darts to play, and rugby/soccer games to watch from satellite. Call about special events like the Robbie Burns Dinner complete with bagpipes, haggis and ale.

Cafés & Coffeehouses

Downey's

Front and South Streets, Philadelphia, PA 19147
(215) 625-9500

Downey's combines the traditional friendly neighborhood bar with a stylish Irish restaurant. When the person you're chatting with at the 2nd floor bar breaks into song, don't be surprised. They're part of Nicky Dematteo's fine group of piano bar singer-patrons who do classics and show tunes for an admiring group of loyal followers. If you love the music, you can be one of them!

☼ Everyday; Nicky Dimateo plays on Wednesdays & Saturdays

Fergie's Pub

1214 Sansom Street, Philadelphia, PA 19107
(215) 928-8118   www.fergies.com

Test your IQ upstairs for a friendly, funsome, social night of Quizo on Tuesday and Thursday nights, the information game teaser where table is pitted against table. Enthusiasts of all ages make up this rowdy but brainy crowd and you don't have to bring your own friends to take part—just pull up a chair. Stop back for supper and the eclectic open mic on Mondays, or the different bands that play on the weekends. By the way, there *is* a Fergie—say hi to him!

McCrossen's Tavern

529 N. 20th Street, Philadelphia, PA 19130
(215) 854-0923

Stop in at McCrossen's most nights for a bite and a friendly game of darts with the friends you bring or the ones you meet there. Or test your brain in a game of Quizo on Sunday evenings. They are planning a round robin Quizo League with other pubs in the area. This could be the start of something big!

Mermaid Inn

7673 Germantown Avenue, Philadelphia, PA 19118
(215) 247-9797   www.themermaidinn.net

Comfortable and welcoming, this bar has been the place to go to hear folk music for years. On the first and third Mondays the Bothy Club has a featured performer and open mic; Wednesdays has Irish Session; and the first and third Thursdays have Open Circle, a wonderful singalong, jam session, and spoken word combination. Also, there's Bluegrass jam on the third Tuesday, Blues jam on the second Tuesday, Old Time jam on the fourth Tuesday, Big Band on the fifth Tuesday, and bands on the weekends. Wait until you hear these pickers!

Tom Gala, Songwriter & Bothy Club Emcee

Cafés & Coffeehouses

New Wave
784 S. Third Street, Philadelphia, PA
(215) 922-8484

Lots of good interactive stuff happening here (besides good eating and drinking). On Tuesdays there is an Old English dart league; preregistration (but not super skill) is required. TV sports on Sundays draws a good crowd, arriving about noon. The pool table in the back and games like backgammon available behind the bar make New Wave a great place to hang out.

Rembrandt's
741 N. 23rd Street, Philadelphia, PA 19130
(215) 763-2228   www.rembrandts.com

Come in for dinner on Mondays or Tuesdays and sign up for a free Tarot card reading at your table. Or come to the bar on Tuesdays about 9:30pm for the lively Quizo game with at least eight or nine teams in spirited competition. Live music for Sunday brunch and free stock quotes from the fancy machine at the bar round out a great week of socializing at this neat place in Fairmount.

Sugar Mom's
225 Church Street, Philadelphia, PA
(215) 925-8219   www.oldcity.org/memrestaurant/sugarmoms/sugarmoms.htm

Mom's makes beer more interesting than it already is with occasional seasonal learn-about-beer parties where brewers and other experts talk about the various characteristics of beer and beer-making processes. You can compare your notes and favorites with other enthusiasts. Informal and lots of fun. Call to find out when the next event will be held, or keep checking in the *Philadelphia Weekly* or *City Paper*.

Urban Word Café
449 South Broad Street, Trenton, NJ 08611
(609) 989-7777   www.urbanword.com

This Trenton spot is lively every night with something new. On Mondays you'll find Latin music with salsa lesson beforehand. On Tuesdays there's an open mic for those with original material (singer/songwriters, comedians, and poets). Wednesdays look for live music, a jazz jam, with a house band and opportunities for musicians to sit in. On Thursdays there is a poetry slam, a spoken word poetry event. Fridays and Saturdays feature music—live jazz on Fridays and a lounge scene on Saturdays—for dancing and conversation. There is an eclectic bistro-style menu to please the palate.

Cafés & Coffeehouses

Toto's: *Community Dining Table*

1407 Locust Street, Philadelphia, PA
(215) 546-2000

Owner Schiavone Dilullo hits the nail on the head: "What could be more sociable than eating together?" He has installed a table that seats 22 in his fine upscale restaurant, for people who enjoy dinner conversation with newly met companions. Food may be the initial focus, but conversation may lead anywhere with your dinner mates. Also find community dining at Meiji-En, White Dog Cafe, and Buddakan.

Triangle Tavern

10th & Reed Streets, Philadelphia, PA
(215) 467-8683

Get with it South Philly style at the Triangle, where the Tony Dell Trio has performed for the past 40 years on Saturday nights. You have to see them: Hawaiian shirts, rockin' and rollin,' belting out '50s hits by the Everley Brothers, Jerry Lee Lewis, and the King. In this boisterous tavern/ restaurant you can get the best mussels in town and talk to everyone at tables so close you can laugh at their jokes. You have to love it!

Tony Dell Trio on a Saturday night

White Dog Cafe

3420 Sansom Street, Philadelphia, PA 19104
(215) 386-9224   info@whitedog.com   www.whitedog.com

Have a great time finding fellow storytellers at the Salon on Monday evenings; talking to interested people about world affairs at breakfast or in dinner discussion groups (Table Talk); dancing in the street at one of many super fun theme parties; or doing an afternoon of community service with other White Doggers. Oh—and the food and wine are terrific here. You absolutely don't want to miss this place. Read the newsletter to get a flavor of the place and for a schedule of activities.

Woody's

202 South 13th Street, Philadelphia, PA
(215) 545-1893   www.woodybar.com

This well-known gay bar where straight folks are welcome has terrific dancing every night. Try the two-step on Tuesday, Friday and Sunday, move to progressive music on Thursday, or get into regular dancing on the weekends. Besides, there is karaoke on Mondays and Triviata on Tuesdays. Hang out and enjoy music videos or great TV events (sports, Academy Awards) when they come on.

Tea and Pastry Houses

Best of British

8513 Germantown Avenue, Philadelphia, PA 19118
(215) 242-8848

Take a break from window shopping and duck into Chestnut Hill's authentic British tea room, bakery, and import shop. The traditional afternoon tea is offered all day, featuring tea sandwiches, scones and jam, pastries, and beverages. Or take home a sausage pie and fruit tart sold from the beautiful display case on the first floor. A sweet respite in the afternoon (or morning!).

☼ Tuesday-Saturday (9:30am-5:30pm); Sunday (11:30am-4:30pm)

Four Seasons Hotel: *The Swann Lounge*

1 Logan Square, 18th Street at Benjamin Franklin Parkway,
Philadelphia, PA 19103
(215) 963-1500

Pastries, scones, tea sandwiches, and Devonshire cream accompany the delicious teas served at this very classy downtown hotel. Celebrate a special occasion or come anytime just as a treat. Several times a year the lounge has events like book signings. Tea is served on Mondays to Saturdays from 3-4:30pm.

RoseLena's Coffee Bar

1623 East Passyunk Avenue, Philadelphia PA 19148
(215) 755-9697   roselena1@aol.com

This place is like being in your grandmother's parlor. You'll see photographs of RoseLena's wedding on the walls, along with many other family wedding photos from the same art noveau period. Open a menu of tantalizing desserts, including a few delicious diet sweets (I never feel deprived here!), sip a pot of real rich coffee, and take it all in. Just being in this place is a treat. Take a special person to RosaLena's. (By the way, RoseLena's is a restaurant, too.)

A closer look at...

Folk Factory

(215) 848-6246   www.folkfactory.org

Activity Location: Unitarian Universalist Church of the Restoration
6900 Stenton Avenue at Gorgas Lane, Philadelphia, PA, 19150

This Mt. Airy coffeehouse with music has been a staple for relaxed weekend enjoyment for many years. Like coffeehouses of old, it's held in a church with refreshments at intermission. Music with themes related to social change is important to these audiences. You'll hear performances of original songs by songwriters and exciting new works from local and regional East Coast folk acts. Fast Eddie and Professor Louie had my complete attention with a combination of scathing social commentary and very funny songs about everything from "cockaroaches" to people's behavior. Other musicians have included: Tom Juravich and Drew Calvin and Sonia Rutstein and Ferron. Also, storytellers such as Annie Hart and Tom Gala show up to perform. The informal atmosphere allows you to approach the performers at the break and chat with members of the audience while you enjoy a brownie and tea. Call for a schedule of monthly national folk acts or check out the open mic on the fourth Thursday of the month. The music in this real old-style coffeehouse is just plain wonderful.

☼ 2nd Fridays (8pm);
   4th Thursdays (7:30pm)

💰 $8-$25 concerts;
   $2-$8 Open Circle with lite snacks

Cafés & Coffeehouses

 **Here are some extra resources to check:**

Web Sites
- *www.phillytown.com—online source for bars and nightspots*
- *www.philly2nite.com—online source for arts and entertainment*
- *www.phillynews.com—reviews of local nightlife*
- *America Online: Digital Cities—listings of Philadelphia nightlife*

Local Center City newspapers
    provide listings of restaurants, bars, and cafés
- *City Paper (Thursdays)*
- *Philadelphia Weekly (Wednesdays)*
- *Philadelphia Inquirer: Weekend Section (Friday)*
- *Philadelphia Daily News: Weekend Section (Friday)*

Book about coffeehouses in Philadelphia
- *Caffe Philadelphia: A Guidebook to Philadelphia Coffee Culture by Jennifer Linden, Caffe Philadelphia Press, 2000*

Coffeehouse Standards around the city
- *Starbucks*
- *Xando*
- *La Columbe*
- *Bucks County Coffee*
- *Coffee bars in Borders and Barnes & Noble Book Stores*

Cafés & Coffeehouses

© 2000 Photo by Jeanie Chadwick - Mamarazzi Photography

People hanging out at Gryphon Café in Wayne, PA

 A couple of restaurants that are fun:

Coyote Crossing, (610) 825-3000, 800 Spring Mill Ave., Conshohocken, PA
Authentic Mexican Southwestern cuisine with outdoor dining on a heated patio. Popular with many single patrons.

Franco & Luigi's Pastaria, (215) 755-8900, 13th & Tasker St., Phila., PA,
A very sweet restaurant with waiters who sing opera and Italian songs, and a host who gets the whole place singing. Good Italian food.

Liberties Restaurant & Bar, (215) 238-0660, 705 N. Second St., Phila., PA
Great neighborhood bar, but not just local folks go there. TV sports and occasional live music. Lively crowd and neat looking.

Sonoma (215-483-9400) & Arroyo Grille (215-487-1400), Phila., PA
Both in cool Manayunk. Friendly, energetic restaurant/bars with good food and nice atmosphere. Popular places for happy hour meetings. Arroyo located with terrific water views and lots of parking.

Cheap or Free

Cheap or Free

©2000 Photo by Jeanie Chadwick - Mamarazzi Photography

Street performers delight at the Philadelphia Fringe Festival

I t's easy to have a good time if you have lots of money. That's because every large city offers up some very nice entertainment with hefty ticket prices. But I think the hallmark of a *great* city is that it has a large number of recreational and cultural activities available for little or no cost. These events invite everyone, regardless of her pocketbook, to share in the pleasures and richness of the metropolitan environment.

Greater Philadelphia has an abundance of terrific things to do where you can be active and find kindred spirits without losing your shirt. You can see that most of the things listed in this entire guide are reasonably priced to downright cheap, but this chapter highlights activities that are truly great deals. I love to discover things to do that are exciting and free! If you do too, this is your chapter.

For starters, you can't beat Wednesdays for art in Philadelphia for next to nothing. Start with the expert presentations at **Art-at-Lunch at the Pennsylvania Academy of Fine Art**. Not only is the price right ($3), but you can hear the lecture while you eat your lunch during the workday—very convenient for busy working people. And in the evening, make your way to the **Philadelphia Museum of Art** for the **Wednesday Night** programs where you join others to hear outstanding lectures and music, see films, and take tours for just a few bucks.

How about attending an outdoor professional opera performance by the **Delaware Valley Opera Company** for a mere $15. The music is outstanding, the surroundings are lovely, and your opera companions are unpretentious and available for casual conversations. It isn't terribly crowded, either. By the way, you can obtain very inexpensive tickets for the **Philadelphia Orchestra** on the day of the performance, as well.

Many Philadelphia institutions are free and provide unique local "entertainment." There aren't many more stimulating experiences than a morning at the **Italian Market**. Beautifully arranged produce is everywhere, and sellers sing out their enticements for you to buy their wares. (I once bought a small basket of artichokes for $1 there!) You have to be fascinated by stores that sell cheeses larger than you are, spices galore from every conceivable part of the world, fish and fowl that look alive, and weird hardware items that you can't help but finger under the

Cheap or Free

shopkeeper's watchful eyes. Stop and catch your breath over the best coffees in the city, and pick up a pie from Isgro's or Termini's before you leave. It doesn't cost you a thing to go, but you probably won't get away without buying some very cool and delicious stuff for cheap.

The **Fringe Festival** has to be one of the best all-around art and performance events happening in the city. In the same neighborhood as **First Fridays** (free—a gallery-hopping party), Fringe hosts events that are the closest thing to the New York avant garde art scene I've ever seen. (Of course, I think it's better than NY.) For about sixteen days, Fringe hosts numerous concurrently running events in about a five-square-block area. Viewers can purchase tickets to one or more of the hundreds of events, or can take part in outdoor installations happening at the moment. I saw an act where three actors sat yukking it up in a brightly colored car, and an "audience" person was invited to be the fourth person in the car. From that moment on, the act proceeded in a zany fashion to the delight of all of us on the sidewalk. It's hard to know what is scripted and what is spontaneous—and that's the fun of it! One ticketed event was Eric Schoeffer's dance group whose members emerged from gauze cocoons hung from a warehouse ceiling over the heads of the astonished and delighted audience. Just hanging around the art, music and performances at the Fringe, outside and inside, is great fun, and gives you a lot to talk about with others who love art on the edge.

In warm weather, you'll find people out and about many outdoor activities, including the college and high school regattas on the Schuylkill River, which you can watch from the **Kelly** or **West River Drives**. In the summer, West River Drive is closed to automobiles but open to any vehicle that you can ride or glide on, as well as your own two legs. You'll be surrounded by happy, recreational enthusiasts zooming past you on all sides, taking advantage of the wide-open road for their sports. Or maybe you'd rather be enjoying the sun in town. No matter who you are, you can sit with a hot dog in **Rittenhouse Square** on a beautiful day, watching the dogs and the kids and the painters and the runners, while you enjoy the flowers. It's a hoot of urbanites in their "backyards" doing what people do at leisure. You'll want to be there.

Some cheap or free events take place twice a year, like the summer **Schuylkill Stroll** led by the Park Guards from the Philadelphia Art Museum who will give you the facts about Boathouse Row and the sculptures along the river. Another wonderful annual event is the

Philadelphia Folk Festival, held on the weekend before Labor Day, where you can immerse yourself in folk and bluegrass music for four wonderful days. If you want to go for free and meet lots of nice music enthusiasts, call to volunteer to help with parking, service booths, etc. They'll even feed you for your help, although the wonderful music is reward enough.

When you hang out in these places, you'll find yourself with people who are there to enjoy the dancing, the boat race, the inline skating, or the historic mansions—just like you are. You'll have reasons to chat and connect around your common interests, and really enjoy yourselves together. Get into the day, and into the experiences you are sharing. Enjoy the flow with people around you!

Photo by Mark Garvin

An artist evaluates his work at Fleisher Art Memorial

A closer look at...

Photo by Nate Clark

Free Library of Philadelphia
1901 Vine Street, Philadelphia, PA 19103
(215) 567-4341   www.library.phila.gov/writers

The Philadelphia Lectures

Meet people with ideas at these evenings (formerly called "Rebuilding the Future") where major authors like John Updike, Toni Morrison, Margaret Atwood, and Kurt Vonnegut discuss their recent books. Meet the author, get your book signed, and enjoy talking to the participants about the topic and other books. This is a very social event with refreshments afterwards.

☀ Almost weekly on Thursdays, Sept-May   ⏰ 8pm

💰 $12 in the auditorium (Get your tickets early thru Upstages)
   $6 for video simulcast in the East Gallery

Cool Books, Hot Topics

Choose your fun summer reading based on these popular book discussions held in June and July with exciting authors like Peter Mayle, E. Lynn Harris, Zadie Smith, Dave Eggers, and David Hajdu. Structured very much like the Philadelphia Lectures, except these talk/discussions are free!

☀ Usually every week on summer weeknights   ⏰ 7pm

💰 Free (and it's air conditioned!)

Appalachian Mountain Club of Delaware Valley

P.O. Box 1393, North Wales, PA 19454
(215) 979-1174   www.amcdv.org
Activity Location: Valley Forge Park, Wissahickon
Creek, Delaware Water Gap, Peace Valley Nature
Center, and many other areas.

AMC will definitely keep you busy and healthy!
Every week there are plenty of hikes as well as
backpacking, rock climbing, canoeing, and
bicycling trips. There are workshops, overnight
trips, and an active singles group that goes whale
watching and to Broadway shows and enjoys the
many outdoor activities for which AMC is famous.
Members spend time at the Delaware Water Gap
center with weekend workshops like fly fishing,
llama lore, and Irish song and dance.

DV-AMC on the trail

☼ Activities everyday

🐷 $40 per year; hikes are free, additional cost (low) on some events

Bucks County Audubon Society

6324 Upper York Road, New Hope, PA 18938
(215) 297-5880   mail@bcas.org   www.bcas.org

Go on bird counts throughout the region with this group, or enjoy bird
watching within BCAS's 120 acres of trails, woods, and streams. The Honey
Hollow Environmental Education Center runs several hundred workshops (e.g.,
Natural Landscaping) a year, as well as seasonal festivals. Check the Nature
Centers in the Nature chapter to find other free outdoor activities near you.

🐷 Memberships available for individuals and families

Cafe Roma

6179 Ridge Avenue, Philadelphia, PA 19128
(215) 482-3222

If you want to feel like you're in Italy without taking a plane, if you want to taste
some *fine* cappuchino for a tiny amount of money and sample *real* Italian sweet
cakes, head up to Roxborough and have a sit in Angelo's Cafe Roma. Listen to
the Italian spoken at the next table by the regular patrons and look for Angelo—
he's the cute one with a twinkle in his eye. I love hanging out in this place. And
the baked goods are to die for.

🐷 Cappuchino for $1.50 (He ought to go to *at least* $2.00)

Cheap or Free

Curtis Institute of Music: *Classical Music Recitals*

1726 Locust Street, Philadelphia, PA 19103
(215) 893-5261 (hot line)   www.curtis.edu

Activity Location: Student recitals are at Curtis (215) 893-5252; Curtis Symphony
Orchestra plays at the Academy of Music at Broad & Locust Sts., Phila., PA

Enjoy a night out listening to exceptional solo recitals and chamber music. Each
year more than 100 student recitals are offered to the public. You can also attend
symphony orchestra concerts at the Academy of Music or a fully staged opera
production at the Prince, both given three times a year. If you sit in the amphi-
theater, it's free (with a ticket), and the family circle is only $4.

☀ Mondays, Wednesdays and Fridays   ⏰ 8pm
💰 Free or $4

Danzeisen & Quigley Plaza:
Ski, Snowboard & In-Line Skate Swap Shop

1720 East Route 70 (near Rte. 295, NJ Turnpike), Cherry Hill, NJ 08003
(856) 424-5969   www.dandq.com

Skiers, snowboarders and in-line skaters get together when D&Q sponsors an
equipment swap several times a year. Skaters of all levels can learn a lot at
D&Q's clinics on Wednesday nights and Saturday mornings—only $15 for
equipment rental and several hours of expertly taught group lessons. It's lots of
fun, not intimidating, and you'll come out skating! (If you see someone
stumbling, it'll probably be me...) D&Q is a great place for bringing people
loving outdoor activities together. Check it out!

Delaware Valley Opera Company

(215) 745-4171   www.libertynet.org/dvoc
Activity Location: Hermitage Mansion, 700 E. Hermit Ln., Phila., PA
(off Henry Ave. in Roxborough)

For just $15 you can hear a fully staged opera performed by a fine local
repertoiry company. You're invited to a lovely informal evening of fine music
and soft summer breezes outside a lovely old mansion in Fairmount Park where
you bring your own lawn chair and flashlight and meet the community of opera
lovers. On some evenings, a buffet dinner is offered; on others, you are encouraged to bring your own picnic on the grass. If you really want to get to know
people here, feel free to volunteer to help serve the dinner, design sets and make
costumes, and work on the gardens to fit the current performance. By the way,
there are indoor and outdoor performances. For those of us opera/nature buffs,
these evenings are as good as it gets.

☀ Many Thursdays and Saturdays in the summer   ⏰ 6:30-8pm

Ethnic Festivals at Penn's Landing

(800) 668-5724 Philadelphia Visitors Center
(215) 922-2FUN   www.pennslandingcorp.com
Activity Location: Columbus Blvd. at Spring Garden St., Phila., PA

Go to Penn's Landing on the Delaware River almost any summer weekend and you're likely to run into an exciting festival with a nationality or musical theme. Examples include the *Jam on the River* featuring well-known blues and jazz artists where you'll find lots of people having fun. Other festivals include: *Portuguese Heritage Days, Mellon Jazz Festival, Irish Festival, WPEN Big Band Series, Hispanica Fiesta,* and more. Call Penn's Landing to find out what's happening this weekend.

Fairmount Park Commission: *International Folk Dancing*

(215) 945-1316
Activity Location: Steps of Philadelphia Art Museum, 26th St. & Benjamin Franklin Parkway, Phila. PA

You won't believe how lovely it is to listen to lively folk music on the Art Museum steps as you learn the steps to dances of many cultures. Arrive about 7pm for instruction and a chance to let more experienced dancers refine your technique every Tuesday from June to September. (From October to May, they dance at 8-10pm in Lloyd Hall down the hill on Kelly Drive.) It costs about $3 to dance with this friendly community of dancers. Wear comfortable clothes and leave your stage fright at home. (Look at www.phillydance.com for all area folk dancing.) Go on Mondays and see the really good jugglers doing their thing in the same spot.

☼ Tuesdays   ⏰ 8-10pm
💰 About $3

Fairmount Park Rowing Program

Schuylkill River Development Council, 2314 South Street, Philadelphia, PA 19146
(215) 985-9393   lt@srdc.net   www.srdc.net
Activity Location: Schuylkill River near the Strawberry Mansion Bridge

This organization offers a rowing program to the community during the summer. If you'd like to see if rowing is for you, try the hour-and-a-half introductory class on Saturdays for about $35. To continue, you can take three weeks of instruction for co-ed beginners and intermediates taught by rowers from boat house row. Schedules for classes are varied enough to accommodate most work schedules. Also, look at www.boathouserow.org for info about classes at the Bachelor Boathouse and the Girls Rowing Program.

Cheap or Free

Fall Line Ski Club

P.O. Box 1535, Cherry Hill, NJ 08034
(856) 931-4462 (hot line) www.fallline.org
Activity Location: Mt. Laurel, NJ

Fall Line offers ski trips to all kinds of places—from Vermont to Italy, just about every weekend in the winter. Summer activities include sailing on the Chesapeake, canoeing and camping, rafting, golf, and tennis. The club has social events like Friday happy hours and dances all year. General meetings are held the first and third Tuesday of each month in Mt. Laurel from 8:30 until 11pm. That's where you can sign up for trips, hear announcements, get up-to-date information, and have a great time socializing.

☼ 1st & 3rd Tues./mo   ☎ 8:30-11pm

First Friday of the Old City Arts Association

139 N. 2nd Street, Philadelphia, PA 19106
(215) 625-9200 www.oldcity.org
Activity Location: Old City section of Phila., around 2nd/3rd & Arch St. Galleries

On the first Friday of the month, fifty or more galleries stay open late to greet a crowd of art lovers making their way along the Old City art strip. An exciting Philadelphia tradition, this evening is for socializing while experiencing fine art, much by local artists. (More on this in the Art Chapter.)

Fleisher Art Memorial

709-721 Catharine Street, Philadelphia, PA 19147
(215) 922-3456 www.fleisher.org

Excellent art classes very reasonably priced (or free) are given in South Philly on weekdays and evenings for adults. You can draw, paint, sculpt, do glass casting, monoprints, pot on the wheel, and build ceramic tiles to your heart's content, all the while connecting with the art community.

Foundation For Architecture

1737 Chestnut Street, Philadelphia, PA 19103
(215) 569-3187 www.foundationforarchitecture.org
Activity Location: Philadelphia neighborhoods

These excellent small-group walking tours will take you through neighborhoods from Victorian Germantown to Queen Village to 18th century Frankford. Over 40 high-quality tours are offered for only $8 each, such as Great Philly Homes by Great Philly Architects. Plus they have a four-week architecture lecture series.

☼ April to Nov., Sat., Sun., & weekday eves.   ☎ 11am, 2pm & 6 pm

Photo by Kathy Sheehan

Gazela sailors furling the sails high above the Delaware River

Gazela Philadelphia

801 South Columbus Boulivard, Philadelphia, PA 19147
(215) 218-0110   gazela@usa.net   www.gazela.org
Activity Location: Penns Landing area

For the cost of dues and insurance (around $85/year) and an inexpensive pair of kakai pants to go with your Gazela shirt, you can be crew on the oldest, largest, (sweetest) wooden, square-sailed ship still sailing in the world. She's an old Portuguese cod fishing boat that is retired from fishing off the coast of Maritime Canada and Greenland in 1969 and now lives near Penn's Landing in our fair city. The volunteer crew does maintenance (painting, tarring, rigging, etc.) in the winter and sails in the summer to places like Nova Scotia, Boston, NYC, Baltimore, and Norfolk. You'll feel like you're part of an old sea adventure as you help to hoist sail, stand watch or steer the ship, but you'll sleep very well at night after evenings of socializing and singing sea shanties. I did this—it was super. (Each volunteer is asked to contribute a minimum of 50 hours towards maintenance or ship support before applying for a sail berth.)

Gershman YMHA

401 South Broad Street, Philadelphia, PA 19147
(215) 545-4400

There are many excellent programs at this downtown Y with an emphasis on Jewish culture. There's regular Israeli folk dancing, volleyball, and a Jewish Film Festival with discussions afterwards. Plus members go on trips to New England or the Canadian Rockies, and have a very active social group called The Adult Network. You don't have to be Jewish to join.

☼ Everyday

💰 Reasonable

Cheap or Free

Historic Philadelphia, Inc.

123 Chestnut Street, Su 401, Philadelphia, PA 19106
(215) 629-5801   http://historic.philly.com
Activity Location: Sign up for tours at Visitors Center at 3rd and Chestnut, Phila.
(800) 76-History   (Try it; it works!)

So—even if you live here, how much do you really know about our history? From May to September, you can experience history brought to life in the 270 street performances given in and around Independence Hall each week. Stop by the Visitors Center to get the Historic Philadelphia Gazette which lists the performance schedule. This is a fun and educational activity. If you have out of town guest, or are new to the city, or want to see history reenacted through first-person monologues.

☀ Everyday from May to September   ⏰ 10:30am-5:30pm

💰 Free

Insectarium at Steve's Bug Off

8046 Frankford Avenue, Philadelphia, PA 19136
(215) 338-3000   insectarium@aol.com   www.insectarium.com

The Insectarium is one of the largest all-insect museums in the United States, with more than 40,000 specimens both living and dead. Museum educators will show you a variety of arthropods, including exotic cockroaches and scorpions. Also available is an insect petting corner. Geared very much toward education and school groups, this is a fun place to visit on a rainy afternoon. Check out lectures (such as Insects & Architecture), tours, and special events, or sign up to be a volunteer. Can you imagine a place with 40,000 bugs! Only $5.

☀ Mondays - Saturdays   ⏰ 10am-4pm

Italian Market

South 9th Street, Between Catherine & Wharton Streets, from Pat's Steaks to
Sarcones Bakery, Philadelphia, PA (South Philadelphia)
(215) 922-5557 (Fante's, in the Italian Market Merchants Association)
www.italianmarket.com   or   www.fantes.com

You can't *not* interact in this South Philly phenomenon of hanging pigs, fresh blue crabs, and vegetables/fruits galore. (I got a basket of artichokes for a dollar once.) The merchants call out to you to check out the freshness of their wares and the walkways are crowded with a diverse clientele, there for the business and the atmosphere. It's a real experience *and* you'll find some great buys in food, spices, coffee, pasta, olives, and cheeses bigger than you are. Enjoy!

☀ Everyday but Mondays and Sunday afternoons

💰 Free except for your purchases

Cheap or Free

Manayunk Art & Crafts Festival

www.manayunk.com (Manayunk Development Corporation)
Activity Location: Main St. between Shurs Lane & Green Lane, Phila., PA

On the last weekend in June, Main Street in Manayunk is alive with outdoor kiosks of fabulous crafts by some of the finest artisans in the country. (They say it isn't easy to get a booth here.) I found a totally wonderful and unusual rocking chair from the mountains by a wood craftsman, but you'll see amazing paintings, photography, jewelry, clothing, pottery, and more at this wonderful event. Also food, demonstrations, and lots of your neighbors. There are many other festivals in this trendy neighborhood, such as the Indian Summer Festival in September, which features the nifty boutiques and restaurants here, and the First Union Bike Race. These are great events for mingling!

Mellon PSFS Jazz Festival

(610) 667-3559 (hot line)   www.mellon.com   or   www.festivalproductions.net

A 10-day celebration of jazz music from be-bop to hip hop to Dixieland to the avant-garde takes place in concerts in parks, theaters, museums, and markets all over the city, including a free Saturday night concert at Penns Landing. Jazz greats like McCoy Tyner and Greg Osby are examples of the talented performers on the festival bill with well-known Philadelphia favorites. There are over 40 different events at this exciting musical celebration. Concert locations are listed in the *City Paper,* so watch for it in June.

☼ Mid-June

💰 Mostly free, but some concerts around $14

Morris Arboretum of the University of Pennsylvania

100 Northwestern Avenue, Philadelphia, PA 19118
(215) 247-5777   www.upenn.edu/morris

This amazing Victorian public garden from the turn of the century has wonderful garden structures and free tours with price of admission ($6). Morris offers a variety of interesting and useful classes and workshops, such as Building a Bluebird House, Making Flower Boxes, Gardening with Shade Perennials, Using Native Plants, Photographing and Painting Nature, Making Soap from Plants, and Chinese Herbs to Ease Aging. Your garden will never be the same!

☼ Open everyday all year   ⏰ Varies

⏰ Classes from $10 to $100

Cheap or Free

Mt. Airy Learning Tree

6601 Greene St., Philadelphia, PA 19119
(215) 843-6333   www.mtairylearningtree.org
Activity Location: Various Locations Around Mt. Airy

A community-based adult education program where experts and neighbors teach unusually high-quality classes, including T'ai Chi, Ballroom Dancing, Dog Obedience, Japanese Flower Arranging, Traveling as an Air Courier, Stand-up Comedy Writing, Bellydancing, Cooking, and Horseback Riding. You will keep coming back season after season to these interesting and social classes.

💰 *Very* reasonable

Pennsylvania Academy of Fine Arts: *Art-At-Lunch*

118 North Broad Street, Philadelphia, PA 19102
(215) 972-2071   www.pafa.org

Every Wednesday around noon, art professors and guest speakers offer lectures and discussions on topics such as the Legacy of Frank Furness, The New Abstraction, and Conserving Maxfield Parrish's Paintings. You can bring your lunch while you learn about these exquisite works. By the way, the museum also has a Thursday visiting artist series, musical performances, exhibit tours, and low-cost art history courses.

☼ Wednesdays   ⏰ 12:15pm
💰 $3

Pastorius Park Concert Series

(215) 248-8810   www.chestnuthilllocal.com
Activity Location: West on Willow Grove Ave., parking at end of Lincoln Dr., Phila.

Treat yourself to dinner at a fine Chestnut Hill restaurant (not free) on a Wednesday summer evening and stroll down to the Victorian walking garden in Pastorius Park for a concert under the stars. A variety of different musical groups, all excellent, perform each week, including the Philadelphia Boys Choir, the City Rhythm Big Band, the Quaker City String Band, and the Sousa Band from the Philadelphia Orchestra. Check the web page, the *Chestnut Hill Local*, or the *Philadelphia Inquirer "Weekend"* section for the schedule. This is one example of outdoor concerts given in neighborhoods in the area, such as Gorgas Park (Roxborough) and Clark Park (West Philadelphia). Check with your local neighborhood organization.

☼ Wednesday evenings in June, July, and the first two weeks in August
💰 Free or donation gratefully accepted

Philadelphia Fringe Festival

211 Vine Street, Philadelphia, PA 19106
(215) 413-9006   www.pafringe.com
Activity Location: Many venues in Old City in early September every year

There's a lot of 'entertainment on the edge' to experience at this festival every September. Venues include a parking lot, a loading dock, an old factory, a restaurant supply showroom, historic churches, galleries, and even theaters "filled with some of the most exciting experiments in the performing arts today as more than 180 artists and ensembles invade Old City for a 16-day (in 2001) outbreak of the avant garde. Find theater and performance art, dance, music, poetry, puppetry, and the impossible to pigeonhole." (from Fringe brochure) $10 is the average ticket price. In 2001, the event has become a sixteen-day festival of theater, film, art, spoken word, and music events. There are daytime art classes, lunchtime theater, and many, many evening performances. International, national, and local artists will fill the neighborhood with their works.

Philadelphia Museum of Art:
Wednesday Nights at The Philadelphia Museum of Art

26th Street & Benjamin Franklin Parkway, Philadelphia, PA 19130
(215) 684-7506   www.philamuseum.org

Each Wednesday, PMA puts on a fabulous evening of film, music, performances, gallery tours, storytelling, and food (including wine tastings) all tuned to a related theme. To give you an idea, here's *one* night in August with the theme *Philly Folk Review*: *Film*: "Days of Heaven" starring Richard Gere and Brooke Adams; *Music*: Distinctive swing with Jive Five Minus Two; also folk songwriter/guitarist Patty Larkin; *Gallery Talk*: Philly Folks—Portraits of Prominent Philadelphians with Martha Halpern (assistant curator for the Fairmount Park Houses); *Chef's Special*: Chef's fried chicken with country potato salad. All in one night! It's like that every Wednesday with lots of socializing before, during, and after.

☼ Wednesdays   ⏰ 5-8:45pm

💰 $10 & Free for Museum Members

Cheap or Free

Philadelphia Museum of Art: *Schuylkill Stroll & other tours*

26th & Benjamin Franklin Parkway, Philadelphia, PA
(215) 684-7926   http://pma.libertynet.org
Activity Location: Meet at West Entrance of the Art Museum for bike tour

Here's that museum again! The Schuylkill Stroll, a walking tour of Boathouse Row, the Water Works, and statues along Philadelphia's most famous esplanade, the Walkway by the Water are led by expert guides. Check out the many other tours inside the museum as well. If you go on Sunday, you pay whatever you wish all day! This is the bargain of the town.

☼   Wednesdays (6-7:30pm) & Sundays (1-2:30pm) during the summer
💰   Nonmembers $5, Members $3, Children $1

Philadelphia Orchestra: *PNC Concert Series*

123 South Broad Street, Su. 1930, Philadelphia, PA 19109
(215) 546-7900 (administrative offices)   mannphila@aol.com
Activity Location: Mann Center for the Performing Arts, 52nd St. and Parkside Ave., Phila., PA   (215) 878-7707 (box office) or (215) 893-1999

Probably one of the most terrific summer musical things happening in the city—great music under the stars—and it's only $5 (PhilaCharge) if you're ok on a blanket in the grass. Friendly, easy chatting with people around you and you may see some of your friends. Also, check into the reduced summer tickets at the Academy. For about $20 you can attend jazz, Broadway theater, and PECO Pops as well. Check into the Access Concerts for only $15, too.

Reading Terminal Market: *Saturday Morning Breakfast Club*

Pennsylvania General Store, 12th and Arch Streets, Philadelphia, PA 19107
(215) 592-0455
Activity Location: Meets at Demonstration Kitchen area near Arch Street entrance

Grab some coffee and pastry and head over to the Reading Terminal's kitchen for a lively discussion on the science, history, and culture of cuisine. All for free. Reservations are not needed to talk food with this group. Learn about Jewish Specialities, Creative Breads, Making Truffles, or Winter Soups. Started by Pennsylvania General Store's Michael Holahan, the talks are presented in collaboration with the Philadelphia chapter of the American Institute of Wine and Food. This is a really fun way to start your Saturday (9am), plus you can shop for the ingredients at the market. Free concerts by some of the best Philadelphia jazz artists, and cooking classes are happening at the terminal too!

Roller-skating, In-line skating, Biking, Jogging, & Walking on West River Drive

West River Drive, Phila., PA

On summer weekends we have the greatest roller rink in town when West River Drive is closed to cars and open to roller skaters, bikers, joggers, and walkers. There's all kinds of recreational activity around you—happy campers all. Where else would you want to be?

☼ April-October on Saturdays and Sundays　　🕑 7am-5pm

Secret Cinema

www.voicenet.com/~jschwart

Activity Locations: various, including Borders (1727 Walnut), Moore College of Art (20th & Race Sts.), and The Print Center (1614 Latimer St.), Phila., PA

If you want to have a truly fun evening, try any of the films dug up by Jay Schwartz. These offbeat, obscure (Jay says "neglected") cult films ("16 MM on a giant screen, no video—not *ever*") of the '50s, '60s, and '70s are totally amazing, especially when viewed with a large, enthusiastic crowd. Occasionally there are special thematic programs (such as "The Sugar-Charged Saturday Morning Supershow"—nostalgic early '70s children's TV shows like the Banana Splits). Notable speakers sometimes too. The web site tells you a lot about the films coming up (if you need to know what you are letting yourself in for), as well as other activities such as the group trip (cuts costs) to the Syracuse Cinefest, a festival of vintage films. You can get on an email list for current films.

☼ Jay Schwartz

💰 $5

Thomas Eakins Head of the Schuylkill Regatta

www.hosr.org (for Eakins Regatta)　　www.boathouserow.org (for all regattas)

Activity Location: Go to Kelly Drive on the Schuylkill River

The Eakins Regatta takes place on the last weekend of October. It's an all-day event with a 3-mile race and 4,000 competitors rowing from 1,000-1,100 boats. The Eakins Regatta is hosted by the University Barge Club #7, Boathouse Row. Many other regattas are featured on the Schuylkill. In Spring (March-June) you'll find college regattas every Saturday and high school matches every Sunday. When local club matches are held in June and July, it's exciting. Kelly Drive is blocked off and filled with fans cheering for their teams, with bikes, Frisbees, dogs and runners all around to watch the sculls. You won't be bored! If you want to be a sculler, check the Games chapter.

☼ Spring/Summer weekends

💰 Free

Cheap or Free

Trocadero Theater: *Balcony*

1003 Arch Street, Philadelphia, PA 19107
(215) 922-LIVE

Check out the free movies shown on the Balcony at the Troc on Monday nights.
Usually an eclectic mix of films selected for an eclectic, over 21, crowd. Fun.

☼ Mondays   ⏰ 8pm

💰 Free

Wagner Free Institute of Science

1700 West Montgomery Avenue, Philadelphia, PA 19121
(215) 763-6529

*Activity Locations: Various institutions such as libraries, Academy of Natural
Science, and Pennsylvania Horticultural Society*

Free 12-week classes on the natural sciences for the public, including
anthropology, biology/medical, geology/paleontology, population biology,
plant physiology for gardeners, and more. What a deal!

☼ Mondays to Thursdays & Saturdays

💰 Free

Weavers Way Food Co-Op

559 Carpenter Lane, Philadelphia, PA 19119
(215) 843-2350   www.weaversway.org

Meet interesting people and fellow food enthusiasts at this cooperative market
where member-volunteers do the work that make the market function (such as
stocking shelves, packing food, and even making middle-of-the-night trips to
the food distribution center in South Philly). I love packing with Dale and other
co-operators while having terrific conversations. But work isn't all that's going
on. They have dinner/meetings, book conversation groups, games, and other
functions drawing this community together. Besides, you'll love food shopping
(for healthy foods) where you see all your friends. That's the point.

💰 $30/year to belong and shop and 6 hours work/year for each adult member
of the household

*You will do foolish things, but do them
with enthusiasm.*

~ Colette

Community
Service

Animals • Arts • Civic • Environment
Meals & Shelter • Medical
Neighborhood Organizations • People for People
Political Activities • Teaching/Tutoring
Walks/Runs for Charity

Community Service

Friends of the Wissahickon are fighting the vines—and winning!

Participants in the Walk Against Hunger meet on the
Philadelphia Art Museum steps

Community Service

What is it about giving our resources and time that lifts our spirits? You always hear people say that *they* got more from "helping out" than the people who received the help. Maybe it's just because being fully engaged with others takes your mind off yourself. When we are voluntarily lending what we have to uplift those who could use a hand right now, it occurs to us at some level that we all have times of strength and times of need; that the human condition is about the ebb and flow of trouble and triumph, and we all take our turns along that wavy line. It *feels* right to reach out and share your current resources when you're in a position of strength. It also gives perspective to have real contact with the world that extends beyond your personal needs and have a working connection with some living, breathing part of your community.

Beyond the opportunity to expand yourself is the real bonus of finding other people involved in community service who believe in those values, people who make time in their busy lives (like yours) to care about others and don't just talk about it. They don't just look good—they *are* good. When you find people who are busy putting their hands where their mouths are, so to speak, you can see what they really care about and the values they hold. They can see yours too.

It's amazing to discover the variety of activities around Philadelphia where you can give your time and energy and meet others doing the same. For instance, you can attend theater performances or do outdoor activities like rowing on the Schuylkill for no cost when you enjoy the company of a disabled person who could not go without assistance. By lending your strong arm to someone with a strong spirit, you can do something wonderful while you make a friend. It doesn't get much better than that.

You could get involved and meet those who support the fine cultural and civic institutions in the city. Meet them backstage in the theater, ushering at the **Philadelphia Film Festival** (and see all those amazing movies), or helping to raise money for the outstanding **Philadelphia Orchestra**. You could become a docent and lead tours for the **Foundation for Architecture**, be a community representative in support of the **Free Library**, help out at the **Atwater Kent** (re: history) or **Balch** (re: culture) museums, or be part of **Philadelphia Renaissance**, a group of

Community Service

young people who want to participate in service that moves our city forward. One thing that is different in the second edition of this book is the large number of listings for young people (Young Friends of...) who want to take part in volunteer work for the major Philadelphia institutions, like **Landmarks**, the opera, the orchestra, the library, and more. There is a fine web site that lists many of these groups (http:// FUNN.org), so you can discover all the types of community service in which you can participate.

There have always been exciting ways to support efforts to keep our environment clean and safe, including activities with large organizations such as **Riverkeeper**, the **Sierra Club**, **Earthwatch**, and the **Appalachian Mountain Club** (listed in the Nature chapter). They sponsor serious earth-care-taking activities as well as many outdoor recreational events enjoyed by a whole slew of people. When you help establish clean trails, plant native plants to prevent erosion, monitor the flora and fauna in an endangered area, and the like, you know you are doing something really important. It's very satisfying. Speaking of fauna, there are ways to do service by helping animals, at the **SPCA**, the **Philadelphia Zoo**, and other places where we protect our four-legged and feathered friends.

If you want to work with people, you can pretty well choose what you love and do it with someone who will appreciate it. Teach gardening skills to a community that wants to learn, tutor (and mentor) a child or an adult, take meals to someone who never gets visitors, read stories to someone who is blind, teach urban teens how to ride and care for horses, or help a homeless family rebuild a house ravaged by flood waters. These opportunities are endless. Check the web sites of the large resource organizations (such as **United Way**) that will link you to the type of volunteer work you wish to do.

If you want to have a really good time while you participate in service, check into the events sponsored by your neighborhood community organization. They raise money for neighborhood play areas, form pairs for **Town Watch**, have street parties, dinners and many other delightful activities so you can meet your neighbors. Also, look into the tours and discussions sponsored by the **White Dog Cafe**, as they seek to encourage people-to-people understanding and mutual support. You'll learn about people you'd never have met otherwise, do good things for each other, and have a whale of a good time.

Community Service

I've heard people say that they are afraid to volunteer their time because they have so little of it and they are worried that they will get pressed into more service than they can manage. I think the opposite is true: One of the best things about volunteering is the control you do have over what and how you give your time. Most organizations understand the heavy demands you labor under and appreciate what time you can give. However, it's important to be as clear as possible about your situation so they can develop clear expectations. You should be free to commit a lot of time or very little without guilt, which, of course, means you can wade in slowly, or jump in head first and really do a job.

Another concern some have is that they ought to have special skills to be able to help—which is true sometimes and not true other times. If you call and explain what you have to offer, the group can determine if there is a way you can be useful; then you can decide if you wish to participate.

And, as always, a third concern you may have is that you will not know anybody there. Believe me, when there is an important job to do—a wall to spackle and paint, a child to be loved into reading—people get to know each other through the job and feel like buddies in no time.

Friends of the Wissahickon

Community Service

A closer look at...

Philadelphia Cares

100 S. Broad Street, Su 620, Philadelphia, PA 19110

(215) 564-4544   www.philacares.com

You want to make a difference.
You want to feel connected and give back to your community.
At Philadelphia Cares, you make a real difference, one project at a time.

Philadelphia Cares mobilizes people to address the critical social, educational, and environmental needs of the Greater Philadelphia region through volunteer action. What kinds of action?

- Reading to children at local hospitals and community centers
- Sorting food for donation to community agencies
- Maintaining trails and landscaping parks
- Building or renovating housing for families in need
- Planting or helping out with community gardens
- Helping at fairs and picnics at local hospices or social service agencies
- Playing bingo with senior citizens

One well-known annual PC event sends volunteers into more than 100 public schools to refurbish classrooms and playgrounds. Another is Neighbors in Action which restores playgrounds and reinvigorates neighborhoods (see photos). There are social activities too—such as the PC Turkey Ball where you can dance, mingle, and give thanks with other volunteers.

Animals

Academy of Natural Sciences

1900 Benjamin Franklin Parkway, Philadelphia, PA 19103
(215) 299-1029   kuter@say.acnatsci.org   www.acnatsci.org

People from all over the country come to see the exhibits at the Academy, one of Philadelphia's finest museums. You can be a part of the experience for these visiting learners by becoming a volunteer. As a volunteer, you could be trained to care for live animals, ranging from small alligators to butterflies to armadillos. (The Academy houses over 100 undomesticated animals.) You could also work with the staff on "The Dig," where visitors dig up fossils and uncover a buried dinosaur skeleton. Or you could organize exhibits of specimens or lead tours of adults and school children. Volunteers say they love being involved and learning here.

☎ Lois Kuter

💲 $30/yr individual membership, entrance fee about $9, seniors $8.25

Marine Mammal Standing Center

3625 Brigantine Boulevard, Brigantine, NJ 08203
(609) 266-0538   www.mmsc.org

Volunteers are trained to assist professionals in their work rescuing and rehabilitating seals and other mammals. They also lead tours at this educational museum, and help with special events such as the Ocean Swim Race. Since training is provided, a regular ongoing commitment is necessary.

New Jersey State Aquarium

1 Riverside Drive, Camden, NJ 08103
(856) 365-3300, x305   www.njaquarium.org

"Discover the world under the sea where aquatic adventure greets you at every turn." (from the Aquarium's brochure) There are exciting volunteer opportunities for diving, educating, doing biology lab work, and assisting in the office. You can get involved in everything from exhibit interpretations to seal feedings to tank cleanings to occasional canoe trips. You'll learn while being part of this marvelous presentation of the natural environment.

☎ Volunteer Services

Community Service

Pennsylvania Society for the Prevention of Cruelty to Animals

350 E. Erie Avenue, Philadelphia, PA 19134
(215) 426-6300   www.pspca.org

Help the PSPCA rescue animals and find them good homes in your available time and you'll get back more than you give. Opportunities include socializing with animals and assessing their behavior, going out with educators to help teach kids how to handle animals properly, and greeting prospective parents and assisting them with all aspects of the adoption process. *Special* heroes get involved with the nitty gritty of animal care: feeding, bathing, and grooming—which actually can be satisfying to you both (volunteer and animal).

Philadelphia Zoo

34th Street & Girard Avenue, Philadelphia, PA 19104
(215) 243-5200   www.philadelphiazoo.org

Many volunteers at America's oldest zoo serve as guides, photographers, ZooShop personnel, gardeners, and clerical staff. Although volunteers do not work with the regular animal collection, they do work with the domestic animals in the children's petting zoo. They also handle small animals used in educational programs, such as toads, turtles, snakes, opossums, ferrets, a prehensile tail porcupine, and exotic birds. The Docent Council provides a training program for those who lead tours at the zoo and conduct programs in schools. Call the Volunteer Office.

Schuylkill Center for Environmental Education (SCEE)

8480 Hagy's Mill Road, Philadelphia, PA 19128
(215) 482-7300   www.schuylkillcenter.org

For many years the SCEE has taught us about the natural environment within our city's limits. Volunteers are important here to give classes to children, greet newcomers at the reception desk, man the gift/book shop and the library, and participate in outdoor land management, such as removing vines from trees. The SCEE Wildlife Rehabilitation Clinic trains people to work with rescued animals, including feeding, cage care, and even taking home critters who need constant care. The Clinic also needs people to help in the office, do fund-raising activities, and give talks about the care of wild animals to community groups. If you like the outdoors, you'll love this place. Check out the center and/or take a nature hike (guided tour or alone with a prepared map) in their 4000 acres of forest, all within the city limits.

Volunteering at SCEE - forest restoration

Community Service

Work to Ride Program

Chamounix Stables, 98 Chamounix Drive, Philadelphia, PA 19131
(215) 877-4419   worktoride@worldnet.att.net   www.worktoride.net
Activity Location: Chamounix Stables is in Fairmount Park

Chamounix's raison d'etre is to be home base to the Work to Ride Program that gives youth at risk a chance to be involved with horses and riding. This is a great way to be involved with inner city kids, as you do horse and barn care together, ride, and enjoy interaction with the horses. There are also many opportunities to join the group for horse shows, parades, and other equestrian events. (WTR sponsors the only minority interscholastic polo team in the country.) If you just want to ride, you can take group adult riding lessons in balanced seat riding and a bit of jumping. Call Lezlie Hiner for information.

Arts

Artreach, Inc.

3721 Midvale Avenue, Philadelphia, PA 19129
(215) 951-0316   artreach@libertynet.org   www.art-reach.org

Free tickets are provided for volunteers who assist disadvantaged and disabled member groups to attend performing arts events. It's a win-win situation. You have the pleasure of assisting those who might not otherwise be able to go and enjoying the performance yourself.

☎   Joyce Burd

Curtis Institute of Music

1726 Locust Street, Philadelphia, PA 19103
(215) 893-5279   www.curtis.edu

When you volunteer for this terrific local school of music as a Friend of Curtis, you can take tickets, usher, and do clerical work. Or you could adopt an out-of-town student, be a post-recital reception host, and conduct tours of the Curtis buildings. Don't forget to attend their superb concerts (free on Fridays!) as well.

Foundation for Architecture

1737 Chestnut Street, Philadelphia, PA 19103
(215) 569-3187   www.foundationforarchitecture.org

Be a tour guide and learn about Philadelphia's magnificent architecture and neighborhoods. The Foundation gives excellent training for guides who lead 42 different walking tours around the city. If you take the training, you'll need to make an four-month commitment. Most people stay around for years and continue to learn things about the city the rest of us never know!

Community Service

Philadelphia Festival of World Cinema

(215) 895-6542   ihouse@libertynet.org   www.libertynet.org/ihouse

More than 400 volunteers sign up to help with this outstanding annual international film festival. They arrange parties, escort guests, usher, and do office work and telephoning. Be part of this exciting event, meet other film aficionados, and take in some great flicks!

Philadelphia Folk Song Society: *Philadelphia Folk Festival*

7113 Emlen, Philadelphia, PA 19119
(215) 247-1300 or (800) 556-Folk   www.pfs.org or www.folkfest.com
Activity Location: Old Poole Farm, Schwenksville, PA

Volunteers love being part of the greatest folk music festival around. Three wonderful days of music, dancing and crafts, and if you volunteer you'll get free admission and camping—and be fed as well. Volunteers work on everything from planning the Fest to promotional art graphics to taking care of the grounds and supervising parking. See you there!

☼ Weekend before Labor Day

Philadelphia Opera Guild

Academy House, 1420 Locust Street, Su 415, Philadelphia, PA 19102
(215) 735-3637   www.PhillyOperaGuild.com

This nonprofit volunteer organization is dedicated to providing financial support and volunteer services to the Opera Company of Philadelphia. Volunteers host a variety of educational and social programs for opera lovers in the area, and manage hospitality events for visiting artists. Guild activities include special fund-raising events, a boutique, a lecture series (Pre-performance Opera Digest) related to the current opera, pre-opera dinners, parties, and more.

Philadelphia Orchestra Volunteers

260 South Broad Street, Philadelphia, PA 19102
(215) 893-1956   www.philorch.org

Volunteer for the Orchestra and help plan and create (and enjoy!) the parties for Opening Night at the beginning of the season, as well as the Academy Ball in January. Or you could join one of 12 regional volunteer committees that friend-raise and fund-raise for the Orchestra. That means you are out and about, giving information that develops interest in the Orchestra's programs. It's fun, and it spreads the word about these fine concerts. Also ask about the Young Friends for the Philadelphia Orchestra for those 40 and under. Young Friends' activities include audience development, fund raising, parties like the Halloween Ball, and happy hour events before a concert.

Community Service

Point Breeze Performing Arts Center
1717-21 Point Breeze Avenue, Philadelphia, PA 19145
(215) 755-1014   www.pbpac.org

If you love helping children and adolescents develop ability in performing arts, you should look into PBPAC, whose mission is "to use the performing arts as a social action strategy that cultivates talent, revitalizes communities" and "to celebrate the cultural heritage of African Americans." The volunteers, a multi-cultural group, help with clerical work and exciting art projects. They may also become Board members of this South Philadelphia organization that addresses community development issues as well. To start, you could attend the fine programs showcasing neighborhood young talent. Call for information.

University of PA: *Museum of Archeology and Anthropology*
33rd & Spruce Streets, Philadelphia, PA 19104
(215) 898-9307   www.upenn.edu/museum

Volunteer mobile guides take artifacts from the museum into the public schools and lead discussions. They also conduct tours in the museum. Other volunteers help organize artifacts in the museum's vast collection. Since there is training involved, volunteers must commit to no less than one morning a week of time. There is a volunteer coordinator to help you sign up.

Village of Arts and Humanities
2544 Germantown Avenue, Philadelphia, PA 19133
(215) 225-7830   www.villagearts.org

The Village seeks to build community through innovative arts, education, construction, and social programs. In all of its activities, it seeks to do justice to the humanity of people who live in inner city situations, especially North Philadelphia. Volunteers assist in art classes for children, gardening, community outreach activities, and work in the office, and tutor local teens and children.

Walnut Street Theatre
9th & Walnut Streets, Philadelphia, PA 19107
(215) 574-3550 x558

Be an usher for the theater and see shows for free or receive discounts on some theater tickets. You'll meet others who also love the theater when you help out, working in subscriptions and development, data input, or mailing notices of upcoming plays.

Community Service

WWFM, The Classical Network

P.O. Box B, Trenton, NJ 08690
(800) 622-WWFM   www.wwfm.org

Activity Location: Mercer County Community College, 1200 Old Trenton Rd.,
Trenton, NJ

Many who enjoy the classical music on this public radio station come together
to help out during the biannual fund drives that take place in the spring and
fall. Volunteers of all ages help to take telephone pledges from listeners at the
station's studios on the West Windsor Campus of MCCC. They chat while they
help with mailings and a variety of office tasks.

Young Friends of the Art Museum

P.O. Box 7646, Philadelphia, PA 19101
(215) 684-7750   www.philamuseum.org

This is a friendly group of young professionals whose mission is to raise funds
for special museum projects through a variety of educational and social activities. Young Friends are given membership to the museum and are invited to
three fund-raising events—the Young Friends Black-Tie Ball (to which the
public is invited), a Rodin Garden Party, and a holiday party. During the year
there are many events, such as First Friday happy hours, gallery tours at local
galleries, and day trips to other museums. For greater involvement, some
members join subcommittees to plan special events.

💰 $100/year

Young Friends of the Opera

Academy House, 1420 Locust Street, Su 210, Philadelphia, PA 19102
(215) 893-3600   www.operaphilly.com

For opera enthusiasts under the age of 35, a wide variety of benefits, such as
discounted subscriptions and a wide variety of social activities. These activities
include happy hours with opera performers, pre-opera dinners at fine restaurants, educational programs in which members meet the artists in intimate
settings. Join over 300 members who enjoy "Opera Friendship" activities.
(Other support for the opera company comes from three donor groups within
the Club Bravi Circle who donate $1200/year to the opera company. They
include Operaesq, lawyers, Operadocs, medical professionals, and Divas, women
philanthropists. Each group participates in their own fun events, relating various
operas to the details of their professions. Call the above number for more
information.)

Civic

Atwater Kent Museum

15 S. 7th Street, Philadelphia, PA
(215) 922-3031   www.philadelphiahistory.org

Atwater Kent is the official history museum of Philadelphia with exhibits, displays and lectures, and workshops and tours. If you volunteer, you might lead general tour or school groups, or label and organize artifacts. Activities here relate to the development of Philadelphia as an industrial city, so you'll be learning about our common heritage and sharing this information. Volunteers can also help by working in the museum store, or at the reception desk. Call the Education Department for more information.

Pennsylvania Convention Center (PCCA)

(215) 418-4700

Volunteers are welcome to be involved in activities that support tourism in the city. They participate in special events (like *Freedom America*) by taking tickets, working the information booth, and coordinating activities. They also work in the Visitor's Center and give airport greetings to conventioneers as they first hit Philadelphia soil. Contribute your personal touch to our City of Brotherly Love.

Friends of the Free Library of Philadelphia

www.library.phila.gov/friends

Friends support neighborhood libraries by raising money for branch programs, designing and sponsoring programs, encouraging volunteers to get involved, advocating for the library before elected officials, supporting literacy programs, and serving as liaisons between the library branch and the community in which it lives. Call your local branch librarian to get connected.

Friends of Landmarks

321 S. 4th Street, Philadelphia, PA 19106
(215) 925-2251   landmarks4@aol.com

The mission of this group is to raise money to support four fine historical house museums (Physick, Powel, Grumblethorpe, and Waynesborough). They do this by sponsoring and attending a variety of enjoyable cultural events. An arm of the Philadelphia Society for the Preservation of Landmarks, Friends is for people 21-45, who enjoy many outings, parties, trips, and other exciting events together. Additional benefits to being a "Friend" include free tours of historical places, advanced notice about lectures (such as "Childhood in the 18th Century" and "Spotting Fakes and Forgeries in Antiques"), Oktoberfest, Holiday Cheer, Wine Tastings, at the museum-houses, and a newsletter.

Community Service

Independence National Historical Park: *Volunteer Guides*

313 Walnut Street, Philadelphia, PA 19106
(215) 597-9669   www.nps.gov/inde

Take part in welcoming visitors to Philadelphia! Guides work at many sites included in Independence Park, such as the Edgar Allen Poe Site, the Gloria Dei (Old Swedes') Church, or the Deshler-Morris House, leading tours, providing information for visitors, and assisting in the bookstores. Volunteers also help collect and preserve historical resource materials such as photos, cultivate park gardens, and work in administrative positions. (Call 215-597-1586 for information about guiding groups to the Liberty Bell and other sites throughout Independence Park.)

League of Women Voters

1218 Chestnut Street, Suite 400, Philadelphia, PA 19107
(215) 829-9495   http://pa.lwv.org/pa/philadelphia

This nonpartisan group promotes active and informed citizen participation in government. If you work with them, you'll do research and and be active in current political issues such as campaign finance reform. You can be an observer in city agencies, work the election day hotline, help first-time voters, assist in community forums, and work on the Voter's Guide or the Legislative Reference Directory. There's lots of interesting work to do on a time-available basis.

🪙 $60/year dues, gets you three newsletters

National Park Service

200 Chestnut Street, Philadelphia, PA 19106
(215) 597-7890   tom_davies@nps.gov   www.nps.gov/volunteer

Help maintain the landmarks of our national heritage. Parks from Valley Forge National Historical Park to the Delaware Water Gap National Recreation Area abound with unpaid positions in administration, library work, archaeology, interpretation, and maintenance. Call Tom Davies for information.

Norristown Business and Professional Women

(610) 277-9500 Montco Chamber of Commerce

One of many active working women's groups that acts as an advocate for working women and provides peer support as well as skill-building programs. Interesting meetings ("Time Management" and "Women in the Arts") and terrific speakers give experienced and new entrepreneurs business support. They support community relations by working with different organizations in the community. Important for all working women and fun too! Dues are about $75 per year.

☼ 3rd Thurs./mo. from September to June   ⏰ 6-8:30pm

Community Service

Philadelphia Museum of Art: *Park House Guides*
Box 7646, Philadelphia, PA 19101
(215) 684-7926   www.philamuseum.org

The Park House Guides (volunteers) offer a variety of year-round tours highlighting the history, architecture, culture, and decorative arts in the Fairmount Park Houses, such as Mt. Pleasant, Cedar Grove, Laurel Hill, Strawberry Mansion, and Lemon Hill. This is a rich, scholarly experience for the volunteer participant, including a year of weekly training sessions at the Philadelphia Museum of Art, with writing assignments followed by a work requirement. A new training class starts every three years; the next one is in Fall 2003.

Philadelphia Renaissance
(215) 925-4555   bret_perkins@hotmail.com   www.jjmb.com/philaren

A premier group for young professionals (25-40) who are interested in exploring Philadelphia, working on interesting short-term community projects in the city, and socializing with others who value community service. Lots of singles attend the regular happy hours, which are easy-going, low maintenance, and highly social affairs. Volunteer opportunities have included school cleanups with Philadelphia Cares, a Thanksgiving volunteer event put on by the Little Brothers of the Frail Elderly, the Art Museum's Holiday Candlelight Tour of the Fairmount mansions, and activities with the volunteers from the White Dog Cafe. Find your niche with other young, committed, civic-minded people.
☎   Bret Perkins

Young Professionals Network
of the Greater Philadelphia Chamber of Commerce
200 South Broad Street, Philadelphia, PA 19102
(215) 790-3744   www.ypn.gpcc.com

YPN is a personal and professional development program designed to allow young business people to interact socially, exchange ideas, share common interests, and meet regional business leaders and public officials. They offer regular networking events, such as golf outings, monthly networking evenings, sporting events, a black tie awards banquet, and the like. They are involved in community service events, like the Walk for Hunger and Philadelphia Cares Day. Check out networking opportunities with YPN in the suburbs, too.

Community Service

Environment

American Littoral Society

(609) 294-3111   www.littoralsociety.org

This national organization (like the River Keeper Network in Lambertville: 609-397-4410) promotes the conservation and study of coastal areas. Their outings, lasting one day to two weeks, may be to observe the hawks on the Delaware or to monitor water quality and land use. They also sponsor recreational/social activities like beach walks, fishing, and canoe trips.

☎   Angela Anderson; Elizabeth in Sandy Hook (732) 291-0055

Chesapeake Bay Foundation

Old Waterworks, 614 N. Front Street, Harrisburg, PA 17101
(717) 234-5550   www.savethebay.cbf.org
Activity Location: Various around the Chesapeake Bay

The Chesapeake Bay is one of the finest estuaries in the world and it needs your help. Activities of this group that protects the Bay include field trips (canoeing), a stream restoration program, and discussion groups, with a newsletter for members. By the way, if you haven't been to the Chesapeake lately, try visiting Rock Hall, Maryland. It's a jewel of a town and only two hours from Philly.

Earthwatch

3 Clock Tower Place, Su 100, Box 75, Maynard, MA 01754
(800) 776-0188   info@earthwatch.org   www.earthwatch.org
Activity Location: Various branches all over the country

Earthwatch's mission is to assist the conservation of natural resources and our cultural heritage with the help of scientists, educators, and volunteers doing field research all over the world. Another mission is education and research. You could very likely be involved in field work, recording pods of whales in the Bahamas or describing housing conditions in Turkey. Whatever excursion you choose, it will likely be a life-changing experience that will connect you to others who really care about our planet.

Friends of Philadelphia Parks

(215) 879-8159   friends@philaparks.org   www.philaparks.org

FoPP promotes the care and development of parks throughout Philadelphia. They also help with community outreach and education around park issues. If you value our lovely green parks and want to volunteer, FoPP can help you find a group where you can be involved. Call for the newsletter for some terrific ideas about main-tining and protecting our park areas.

Community Service

Friends of Pennypack Park

Verree Road at Pennypack Creek, Philadelphia, PA
(215) 934-PARK

The Friends of Pennypack Park take part in many work projects around the park, including clean-up activities and planting. There are meetings about current environmental issues with speakers and programs. The Friends of Pennypack Environmental Center (215-685-0470) help by raising funds, doing carpentry, and helping with festivals. Friends of the Fox Chase Farm take walks, lead tours, and do gardening. You can reach the farm through the Center. These are just a few of the projects undertaken by volunteers around Pennypack.

Philadelphia Sustainable Lifestyle Campaign

135 South 19th Street, Su 300, Philadelphia, PA 19103
(215) 751-9398   ecoteams@mindspring.com   www.globalactionplan.org

A local field office of the national organization Global Action Plan, the Campaign provides people with grass roots training in ecologically sound lifestyles in a support group approach to environmentalism. Groups of 6-10 neighbors meet bi-weekly over a period of four months and work to reduce the amount of garbage they produce, the water and energy they use, how much they purchase. They try to be more efficient about around-town travel. It's a great chance for neighbors to get to know each other while learning how to be good to Mother Earth.

Preserve Your Park

(215) 685-0039

Now you can help protect and improve Philadelphia's greatest natural resources. Part of the Fairmount Park Commission, this program aids restoration and encourages stewardship of natural areas in the park. This means you can care for the outdoors and do trail work, restore stream banks, remove invasive plants, and install native plants. Training and support will be provided.

Sierra Club

P. O. Box 34659, Philadelphia, PA 19101
(215) 592-4073 (hot line)   www.sierraclub.org/chapters/pa/southeastern

A well-established (since 1892) national group, the Sierra Club leads local outings, nature explorations, and hands-on projects that protect and restore the quality of the natural and human environment. Their motto is to "explore, enjoy and protect the wild places of the earth." Fun activities include lots of hiking, biking, and boating, and educational programs about ecological issues (like a weekend natural history expedition to watch bald eagles). The Club has a chapter for singles, and an Inner City Outings Group takes inner city kids for overnights in the wilderness. Sierra Club is a strong advocate for a cleaner Earth.

Community Service

Meals/Shelter

Aid For Friends

12271 Townsend Road, Philadelphia, PA 19154
(215) 464-2224   www.aidforfriends.org

The "Friends" part of this group matters. They take home-cooked meals to isolated home-bound people of any age at no charge. But maybe more importantly, these volunteers go once a week for a real visit to people who often don't have many visitors. Volunteers are needed either to visit, to drive the visitors, or to cook the meals. Aid For Friends operates in five local counties, where there are freezer sites (300 of them!) that store the meals.

Bethesda Project

1630 South Street, Philadelphia, PA 19146
(215) 985-1600 jmorissette@bethesdaproject.org   www.bethesdaproject.org

Volunteers with this group are asked to "be as family with those who have no family." Helpers serve homeless people who frequently have physical and/or mental disabilities. Every effort is made to provide placement into a permanent home in one of seven residential communities, including My Brother's House. Volunteers visit and get to know residents. They also help out by serving meals and doing general repairs on the community homes.

Christmas in April of Philadelphia (RTCIAP)

P.O. Box 42752, Philadelphia, PA 19101
(215) 568-5044   www.rebuildingphilly.org

This organization of volunteers makes essential home repairs for low-income homeowners, many of whom are elderly or disabled. At the present time (2001), more than 2,000 volunteers worked on homes in North and West Philadelphia. Volunteers, who include many UPenn students, can be involved in selecting the houses they wish to work on. Besides the fun of working on the houses, there is an Open House and a party at the completion of repairs.

Community Outreach Partnership

c/o Trinity Memorial Church, 2212 Spruce Street, Philadelphia, PA 19103
(215) 732-2515   trinity@libertynet.org

This interfaith, nonsectarian organization provides compassionate volunteer work, meals and shelter to the less fortunate among us. Wintershelter is a warm, safe place to stay with food and social services. Communicare matches volunteers to help elderly persons. Training (with commitment) is provided in this program. This is a great place to volunteer, especially for Center City folks.

Habitat For Humanity of North Central Philadelphia

1829 N. 19th Street, Philadelphia, PA 19121
(215) 765-6000, ext. 23   habitatncp@aol.com   www.habitatinnercity.org

The mission of this fine organization is that since a stable community begins with homeownership, those who have this opportunity can take more control over their own lives and neighborhood. You can help make this possible, whether or not you have construction experience. People from all walks of life get involved doing painting, landscaping, insulation, office tasks, or planning fund raising events. There are activities that require great skill as well as those you can learn in 20 minutes—everybody can help. Great co-workers, too!

☎   Volunteer Coordinator

People's Emergency Center

3902 Spring Garden Street, Philadelphia, PA 19104
(215) 382-7523, x221   www.pec-cares.org

An important program that assists women and children in emergency situations, the center provides basic shelter and food for close to 100 families. In addition, volunteers help tutor kids, teach literacy skills to adults, and help give workshops about job training, parenting skills, and money management. The center also provides job placement and permanent housing.

☎   volunteer coordinator

Philabundance: *Share the Harvest*

3616 S. Galloway Street, Philadelphia, PA 19148
(215) 339-0900   www.philabundance.org

Philabundance fights hunger by reclaiming surplus food from the food industry and distributing it to community organizations serving people in need. Volunteers are highly valued to: organize food and penny drives, collect food at special events and trade shows, pack and sort food, grow food for "Share the Harvest," and take part in group gift wrapping at bookstores at holiday time.

Community Service

Philadelphia Committee to End Homelessness

802 North Broad Street, P.O. Box 15010, Philadelphia, PA 19130
(215) 232-2300   pceh@juno.com   www.libertynet.org/~pch

You can join members of PCH doing community outreach by providing information, hope, and friendship to people living on the streets of Center City Philadelphia. Relationships built on trust are established; when people are ready to use community resources, you will be able to assist them in gaining access to this help. About 10 people walk in groups for PCH each night after being trained. The commitment is about two hours each week. Volunteers meet at the beginning and end of each walk, and provide support to one other.

Project H.O.M.E.

1515 Fairmount Avenue, Philadelphia, PA 19130
(215) 382-1622, x211

A major organization that provides assistance to people who are homeless, H.O.M.E. provides many opportunities for volunteers, including helping out at their thrift store, cafe, and bookstore (Cornerstone). Volunteers also serve meals at H.O.M.E. residences, take part in adult learning/literacy projects, provide after-school programs for children, and do advocacy work on issues related to homelessness. There is a full plate of important projects for volunteers.

Medical

ActionAIDS

1216 Arch Street, 6th flr., Philadelphia, PA 19107
(215) 981-3303   www.actionaids.org/volunteer.htm

ActionAIDS is Pennsylvania's largest AIDS service organization, currently serving over 2,500 individuals and 110 families living with or affected by HIV/AIDS. In addition, they educate over 25,000 youth and adults in diverse communities. ActionAIDS is committed to responding to all communities in need, and developing and maintaining positive relationships within these communities—making friends for life. The volunteers are the lifeblood of this organization, providing one-on-one emotional support and companionship, as well as occasional assistance with the tasks of daily living, such as food preparation and prescription pick-ups. Both an adult and pediatric clientele are served. Because of the wide range of volunteer opportunities, you are encouraged to tell the staff if you have a skill, a talent, or the ability to provide a special service so that there can be a match between the organization's needs and your abilities.

Community Service

Family Home Hospice of the Visiting Nurse Association of Greater Philadelphia/New Jersey

1 Winding Drive, Monroe Office Center, Philadelphia, PA 19131
(215) 581-2046   1 (888) 467-9330

You can become part of a hospice team in a variety of ways: doing clerical work in the office, joining the speakers bureau, doing community outreach, and going on home visits (in your neighborhood) to offer companionship and help with small tasks. Twenty hours of training are provided and a commitments of two-four hours/week of time is requested. You'll be rewarded with the companionship of the really special people who are part of the hospice movement.

☎ Elayne Aion, Volunteer Coordinator

MANNA

12 South 23rd Street, Philadelphia, PA 19103
(215) 496-2662   www.mannapa.org

MANNA was organized in 1990 as a volunteer group whose members prepare and deliver daily meals to persons living with HIV/AIDS, provide support to clients and their families, and promote understanding of the role of nutrition in fighting AIDS. The food consists of an HIV-specific diet needed to fight the disease. Volunteers come from every walk of life, from all neighborhoods, and from all age groups (including students). They would welcome your help!

Methodist Hospital

2301 South Broad Street, Philadelphia, PA 19148
(215) 952-9229   www.jeffersonhospital.org/methodist

Many hospitals, like the ones in your neighborhood, are delighted to have volunteers. For example, Methodist needs people to act as liaisons between the operating room, intensive care, and the patient's family; to let the chaplain's clerk know to notify the patient's church so they will be included on the prayer list; to feed patients; and to take the juice/snack cart around in the evenings.

Philadelphia Community Health Alternative

1201 Chestnut Street, Philadelphia, PA 19107
(215) 563-0652   sarch@pcha1.org   www.pcha1.org

Volunteers have an important supportive role in this group, especially for fund-raising activities such as the World AIDS Day Awards Dinner, a black tie benefit where participants nosh top-quality hors d'oeuvres, watch a fashion show, and schmooze every December 1st. Volunteers also support the annual bike ride by riding (8-100 miles) or by passing out water and picking up exhausted riders, etc. Any way you cut it, you'll have fun networking while you support an excellent organization.

Community Service

Neighborhood Organizations

Center City Residents Association

1616 Walnut Street, Philadelphia, PA 19103
(215) 546-6719

If you're a center city resident, here's a way to get together with your neighbors and work on issues that you have in common in your community. These include zoning issues, education, and street cleaning. The association has held educational forums and sponsored events like a center city house tour, meet-your-neighbor covered dish dinners (sometimes with a square dance!), and a celebrity auction. If you want to be very involved, there are subcommittees to join.

NICE

22 Iona Avenue, Narberth, PA 19072
(610) 668-8413 (Ted Ahearn)

This group, which began 34 years ago, continues under the steam of Ted Ahearn with the goal of building community by creating beautiful (and friendly) spaces in Narberth for residents and visitors to enjoy. NICE volunteers are involved in holiday decorating in the business area, planting projects, bulbs in the fall, annuals in the spring, as well as painting benches and other public structures.

North Light Community Center

175 Green Lane, Philadelphia, PA 19127 (Manayunk)
(215) 483-4800   www.northlightcommunitycenter.org

This very active community center offers tons of volunteer opportunities, such as tutoring, aiding the after-school program, taking part in North Light's theater activities, coaching athletic teams, fund-raising, manning community events, and being active in community issues. Neighborhood centers are a great way to be truly involved in *your* community and make friends with your neighbors.

Computer Lab   Playground Dedication
North Light Community Center

Old City Civic Association

Betsy Ross House Building, 239 Arch Street, Philadelphia, PA 19106
(215) 440-7000   oldcitycivic@hotmail.com   www.oldcity.org

This is one of Philadelphia's most active community organizations. In addition
to serving as a liaison to federal, state, and municipal agencies, OCCA works
diligently to preserve the unique character of the neighborhood. Whether it is
serving as a forum for ideas or sponsoring environmental, social, and educational, activities, OCCA is committed to enhancing the quality of life for all
members of the Old City community. The association also has lively social
events, including about six neighborhood parties a year.

Rittenhouse Police Partnership & Town Watch

NE corner of 20th & Sansom Streets, Philadelphia, PA 19103
(215) 496-9050

Join your neighbors on this patrol and reduce the crime in your neighborhood.
Evening partnership volunteers are needed to operate the base radio and patrol
with a partner. You may volunteer once a week, month, or more frequently. If
this is not your neighborhood, look for a town watch where you live.

People For People

American Red Cross

23rd & Chestnut Street, Philadelphia, PA 19103
(215) 299-4000   www.redcross-philly.org

Everyone knows that the Red Cross is the first outfit to help victims of natural
disasters. Volunteers are crucial to both their disaster relief efforts, and local
activities, including conducting school and community training (in CPR, for
example), planning for fund-raising events, public speaking about a variety of
safety topics, and working on blood collections. Or you might be interested in
the activities of Friends of the Red Cross (usually people between 20 and 40).

Associated Services for the Blind

919 Walnut Street, Philadelphia, PA 19107
(215) 627-0600, x3275   www.asb.org

Computer-literate people are sought to help blind and visually impaired
individuals learn computer skills. Two hours a week are requested. ASB will
work around your schedule, provide training, and once a year hosts a volunteers
recognition luncheon. Volunteers also escort groups of clients around the city,
read mail and books, help out with paper work, and read articles on the radio
for ASB's Radio Information Center.

Community Service

Big Brother/Big Sister

2037 Chestnut Street, Philadelphia, PA 19103
(215) 557-8600   www.Beabig.org

Join BBBS and help provide a positive adult role model and friend for boys and girls growing up in single-parent homes in the Philadelphia area. You'll be spending quality time with your little brother or sister on a regular basis—talking, hanging out, and doing fun recreational activities. Seven branch offices match volunteers to a child near their own neighborhoods. BBBS provides an orientation program and quarterly activities for mentors to enjoy, some with the children and some without.

Boys & Girls Clubs of Metropolitan Philadelphia

1518 Walnut Street, Suite 712, Philadelphia, PA 19102
(215) 735-8818   www.bgcphila.org

This program for inner city children has after-school programs in seven sites in the city where educational and recreational activities are offered. Volunteers receive an orientation to help with homework, recreational play, and crafts. Volunteers are also needed for the summer camp and evening program for teenagers, as well as the day-care program for children as young as six months.

Center in the Park

5818 Germantown Avenue, Philadelphia, PA 19144
(215) 848-7722   ctrpark@libertynet.org

This community-based nonprofit senior center offers many wonderful classes and support services. Volunteers are invited to participate in a variety of ways, such as teaching classes, doing clerical work (in the office, on the newsletter, etc.), joining the advisory groups on health, and decorating the center for special occasions. You can meet your neighbors and be of service at your local community center—yet feel like *you* got the most out of the experience.

Executive Service Corps of the Delaware Valley

119 Coulter Avenue, Suite 200, Ardmore, PA 19003
(610) 649-2284   www.executiveservicecorps.org

The goal of ESCDV is to mobilize the management and technical talents of both active and retired executives and professionals to provide (volunteer) management consulting assistance to nonprofit clients. Strategic planning, human resources, marketing, information systems, and fund-raising are among the activities the volunteers do. ESCDV provides training and holds periodic networking meetings of volunteers to discuss experiences and share insights.

Global Volunteers

375 East Little Canada Road, St. Paul, MN 55117
(800) 487-1074   www.globalvolunteers.org

Join a team for one to three weeks and work on much needed human and economic development projects, like teaching kids in the Mississippi Delta area or building community facilities such as schools or community centers abroad. From all backgrounds and of all ages, the volunteers become "servant-learners," working with and learning from people in 21 countries. An extremely rich experience awaits you here. "You're going *where?*"

💰   US $450, plus transportation; international $995-$2,395

Pegasus Therapeutic Riding Academy

8297 Bustleton Avenue, Philadelphia, PA 19152
(215) 742-1500   www.pegasusridingacademy.com

On five mornings and three nights, Pegasus volunteers assist physically and mentally challenged people to ride horses in their outdoor facility. Volunteers help groom the horses, saddle them (with special saddles or therapy pads), and lead the riders along the trail near Pennypack Park. Rich Tatum says you should see the faces of the riders (and volunteers) as they experience the mastery and thrill of horseback riding.

Philadelphia Futures

230 South Broad Street, Philadelphia, PA 19102
(215) 790-1666   www.philadelphiafutures.org

Mentor city teens and expand their life options. Futures' Sponsor-A-Scholar program prepares motivated but financially needy high school students for college and careers by providing one-on-one mentoring, academic support and enrichment, college prep activities, and financial incentives. Mentors should meet with "their" student at least once a month, with telephone contact in between. Mentors are supported by regular staff contact, and periodic roundtable discussions where they share experiences and insights.

Philadelphia Rowing Program for the Disabled (PRPD)

#4 Boathouse Row, Philadelphia, PA 19130
(215) 765-5118   pacenter@aol.com   www.centeronline.com

PRPD makes rowing accessible to people with physical disabilities. Volunteer "instructors" learn to row and help carry boats and oars. About 150 people take part in this activity in which each boat is jointly commandeered by one able-bodied and one disabled person. Call Isabelle Bonn for more information.

Community Service

St. Christopher's Hospital for Children: *Cuddling Program*
Erie & Front Streets, Philadelphia, PA 19134
(215) 427-5000

You can offset the distress experienced by young children who are in the hospital by feeding, holding, rocking, and bathing them. How about playing, reading (Caring Thru Reading), and drawing with the older tykes? Just your touch and your smile can make the difference. Pennsylvania Hospital and Children's also have Cuddlers Programs. And, don't forget the myriad other volunteer opportunities all hospitals need so badly: support for families and patients, greeting/admissions, and food services. Call about their volunteer opportunities.

William Way Lesbian, Gay, Bisexual & Transgender Community Center: *Gay & Lesbian Peer Counseling*
1315 Spruce Street, Philadelphia, PA 19107
(215) 732-TALK or -2220   wwcenter@yahoo.com   www.waygay.org

Volunteers from a variety of backgrounds receive many hours of intake training on all kinds of issues to prepare them to do peer counseling. This is supervised, nonprofessional, short-term counseling where all sorts of concerns are discussed, free of charge. WW has many *other* types of volunteer opportunities, too, related to their many programs and special events. Volunteer Orientations are conducted on the first Wednesday of the month at 7pm at the Center.

Women in Transition
21 South 12th Street, 6th floor, Philadelphia, PA 19107
(215) 564-5301; x118   www.libertynet.org/~wit

Volunteer counselors staff a 24-hour hotline from home to help save the lives of battered women (heterosexual, lesbian, and bisexual) and those struggling with addictions. WIT provides 45-hours of training that lasts over two months and involves close work with a supervisor. Volunteers meet for inservice groups and also get together to talk at various invitation-only events.

WOMENS WAY
1233 Locust Street, 3rd floor, 19107
(215) 985-3322   www.womensway.org

This very important funding federation raises money for organizations that provide women and families with vital services in counseling, health care, education, legal assistance, and much more. Volunteers participate in all aspects of fund-raising, as well as make educational and outreach presentations at work sites, provide clerical help, and make phone calls. There is a strong Young Women's Initiative with networking (happy hours/then attend a talk, or go to a play, etc.) and a yearly volunteer event serving a local service organization.

Community Service

Political Activities

American Friends Service Committee

1501 Cherry Street, Philadelphia, PA 19102
(215) 241-7024   quakerinfo@afsc.org   www.afsc.org/qic.htm

The volunteer opportunities related to AFSC are too numerous to adequately summarize here. Please go to the above web page, which describes "workcamps, internships, camps, other potentially transformational experiences, and some perennial jobs—Quaker and non-Quaker; short, medium, and long-term; both domestic and international." These are opportunities for activities such as building construction in the wake of natural disasters, conflict resolution in various communities, or providing services on Native American reservations. The work locations are all over the world. AFSC offers amazing opportunities for rebuilding with people.

Brandywine Peace Community

P.O. Box 81, Swarthmore, PA 19081
(610) 544-1818   brandywine@Juno.com   www.geocities.com/brandywinepeace
Activity Location: University Lutheran Church, 3637 Chestnut St., Phila., PA

BPC is a faith-based peace activist group committed to war resistance. They engage in nonviolent action to promote the economic conversion of weapons-producing corporations. They meet for a monthly potluck (everybody brings a dish) supper program in University City for speakers, discussion and eats.

☼ 2nd Sun/mo   ⏰ 4:30pm

Democratic City Committee

1421 Walnut Street, Philadelphia, PA 19102
(215) 241-7800   www.democrats.org (national web site)

Be behind the scenes of the electoral process and find the community of those who make our two-party system work. Volunteers can work to support the candidates or be involved in party organization and politics. If you want to work for a particular candidate, call her/his headquarters and volunteer. The campaign will be delighted to have your help. (If you don't know the candidate's phone number, call the above number for information.)

Also, check out *Democrats with Attitude*—it's a group that injects a sense of humor and fun into politics!

Community Service

Log Cabin Republican Club of Philadelphia

(215) 465-5677 (hot line)   www.lcrphiladelphia.org
Activity Location: Warwick Hotel, 17th & Locust Streets, Phila., PA 19103

This nationwide, primarily gay and lesbian Republican club, meets monthly (3rd Wed./mo at 6pm) to insure that the party takes moderate stances on various platform issues. Each month, an appropriate speaker presents useful information to interested members of the community. Speakers to the club have included such noteworthy individuals as Senator Arlen Specter and State Republican Chairman Alan Novak.

White Dog Cafe

3420 Sansom Street, Philadelphia, PA 19104
(215) 386-9224   www.whitedog.com

The White Dog encourages civic participation for progressive social change by sponsoring regular activities, tours, and discussions about contemporary social issues. These have included tours of public murals, a fall walk around Tinicum Marsh, discussions about children around the world, and papermaking in Tibet. Also, there are events with groups such as the Village of Arts & Humanities Tree Farm and Habitat for Humanity. Keep in touch with the White Dog to connect you to a community that thinks and contributes.

Women's International League for Peace and Freedom

1213 Race Street, Philadelphia, PA 19107
(215) 563-7110   wilpf@wilpf.org   www.wilpf.org

Working since 1915, WILPF'ers are currently focused on three major issues: challenging corporate power, disarmament, and truth and reconciliation about racial justice. Volunteers are involved at many levels of time and energy. At the local area branches, activities include educating other members and writing letters to and phoning representatives. On a national level, volunteers are involved with all aspects of legislative action and national issue campaigns.

Love is a verb.
~ Clare Boothe Luce

Teaching/Tutoring

Center for Literacy

636 South 48th Street, Philadelphia, PA 19143
(215) 474-1CFL   www.centerforliteracy.org

Become a volunteer tutor three hours a week for the center. This group will train you to tutor adults 16 and older in reading, writing, and possibly math, either one-on-one or in a small group, and then help connect you to a tutoring situation. You need to make a commitment for a minimum of six months, meeting with your student twice a week in a CFL tutoring site.

Philadelphia Reads

1401 JFK Boulevard, Suite 1000, Philadelphia, PA 19102
(215) 686-4450   www.phila.gov/philareads

A city program that helps people connect with volunteer sites (such as after school programs or summer camps) where children from Kindergarten to 3rd grade get help learning to read. Training for volunteers is held approximately once a month, with a commitment requirement of at least one hour a week (although most volunteers do more.) Reads helps Volunteers find a volunteer opportunity near to their home so it is easy to get to. Reads also sponsors Power Partners, a business connection to kids who need reading help.

Police Athletic League Homework Club

2524 E. Clearfield Street, Philadelphia, PA 19134
(215) 291-9000 x103

Activity Location: 23+ neighborhood centers

You can be involved helping children learn to read after school at a local PAL center near you. The rewards are huge.

Community Service

Walks/Runs for Charitable Organizations

Walk Against Hunger participants fill the streets

Coalition Against Hunger: *Walk Against Hunger*

(215) 430-0555   www.hungercoalition.org   www.hungerwalk.org

The Coalition is the vehicle through which groups that fight hunger can work together. They sponsor the Walk Against Hunger on a Saturday in April from the Art Museum steps. Volunteers can help organize and sign up walking teams from their neighborhoods, families, or places of work. You'll have more fun walking together for a good cause. Check the web site (or call) for other volunteer opportunities with participating agencies of the coalition as well.

☼   A Saturday in April

Broad Street Run

Philadelphia Dept. of Recreation, Broad & Sommerville Sts., Phila., PA
(215) 685-0150

Popular 10-mile charity run sponsored by the City for the American Cancer Society. On the first Sunday in May. $18 entry fee.

Multiple Sclerosis Society: *Walk*

#1 Reed Street, Philadelphia, PA 19147
(215) 271-1500   www.pae.nmss.org

Like many charitable organizations, the MS Society sponsors a fund-raising walk in the spring. Participants request donations for the number of miles they walk (or run). You can check the web site for the exact date or find it in the *Philadelphia Inquirer* or *Daily News*. These walks are fun and include much socializing, before, during and after.

Here are some extra resources to check out

Books & Guides

- *Volunteer Vacations: Short-term Adventures That Will Benefit You and Others*
  by Bill McMillon (Chicago Review Press, $13.95).
  This paperback lists volunteer vacations at archaeological sites, parks and work camps.

- *Invisible Philadelphia: Community Through Volunteer Organizations*
  by Jean Barth Toll and Mildred Gillam
  (Atwater Kent Museum)
  The authors have compiled an excellent 1,364-page guide to the depth and breadth of the region's volunteer organizations, both past and present.

- *The Call of Service: A Witness to Idealism*
  by Robert Coles (Houghton Mifflin)
  A moving book by psychiatrist Coles (*Children of Crisis*) that examines the satisfactions and costs of service to others. He distinguishes between different types of service, including community work, charity, religious activities, goverment action groups, political activity, and service to the country. It includes interviews and personal experiences. It's terrific.

Global Volunteers

Community Service

- *Volunteer! A Comprehensive Guide to Voluntary Service Opportunities in the U.S. and Abroad.*
  5th Edition. 1995. This is produced bi-annually and costs $12.95, plus $1.50 for bookrate postage. Publications Department, Council on International Educational Exchange, 205 East 42nd Street, New York, NY 10017. Phone: (212) 661-1414, ext. 1159.

- *Access the Arts, Etc.*
  80-Page guide to museums, theaters and other cultural institutions in the Philadelphia area that are accessible to people with disabilities, published by Artreach. $5 copy. Call Artreach (215) 951-0316

- *Directory of Volunteer Opportunities in Philadelphia* put out by United Way (215-665-2474) lists and describes volunteer opportunities in the area. It is extremely comprehensive and clear. www.uwsepa.org is the United Way website and www.vp.org is for a UW volunteer opportunity.

- *The Green Guide* is an environmental directory for the Philadelphia area put out by the Clean Air Council at (215) 567-4004. Check the web site, www.cleanair.org, for current activities.

Web Sites

- *www.Americaspromise.org* (888-559-6884) gives you many ways to help kids in your community.
- *www.campfire.org* (800-669-6884) provides opportunities in community service, youth leadership and camping programs.
- *www.mentoring.org* Resources for adults who want to mentor young people in their local area
- *www.orbyss.com* for green activities

- ***www.volunteermatch.com*** VolunteerMatch is a premier online service that utilizes the power of the Internet to help individuals nationwide find volunteer opportunities posted by local nonprofit and public sector organizations. You list your zip code as well as your interests and this huge data base opens up all kinds of opportunities for you. (I liked Frog Watch USA where you monitor wet lands and learn frog and toad calls.) Don't miss this web site for an extensive list of volunteer organizations

- ***www.Ymca.net*** (888-333-9622) needs youths for its Teen Leadership program and African-American adults as mentors for its Black Achievers program.

- ***www.libertynet.org*** lists many community service activities in the Greater Philadelphia region.

- ***http://FUNN.org*** is the web site for Friends United in Need Network, a local non-profit organization whose mission is to use the Internet to increase participation and get the word out about great events and happenings in the Greater Philadelphia region.

Organizations

- ***United Way Volunteer Center of Southeastern Pennsylvania*** If you're not sure what kind of volunteering you want to do, this umbrella organization provides training in volunteer work and refers you to agencies that need the kind of service you are interested in providing. Call (215) 665-2474 in Philadelphia and (610) 558-5639 in the suburbs.

- ***Foundation for Community*** (888-784-9001, www/fce-community.org) is a national group based on principles by Scott Peck (The Road Less Traveled).

- ***Rotary Clubs of Philadelphia*** are service organizations located in neighborhoods of the area.

- ***One-To-One Philadelphia,*** 215-665-2467, provides mentoring referral services to individuals and technical assistance to organizations with mentoring programs.

Community Service

*The vocation of every man and woman
is to serve other people.
~Leo Tolstoy*

Dancing

Ballroom • Cajun • Clogging

Contra, English & Scottish Country

Country & Western • Folk • Irish

Jazz & Tap • Latin • Movement-Ethnic

Polka • Square • Swing

Dancing

Cajun dancing with Allons Dancer at the TK Club

Dancing

O K, dancers and would-be dancers. It's time to get serious. Since the first edition of this book in 1994, this chapter has grown from 49 places to 94 places. That's twice as many places to dance! Why? Because Philadelphians and their friends are going dancing in record numbers. And don't forget, our listings just include the places that have lessons and dance parties. There are probably three times as many places where you can go to just dance without structured lessons if you'd rather.

Another reason there are so many more places to dance is that we like more *kinds* of dances. We're not content with the same old box step and simple folk dances. No. We're doing the Hustle, the Argentine Tango, Balkan or Scottish Country dances, Cajun with bands straight out of Louisiana, period dances, and all manner of Swing dancing—from Retro to basic Jitterbug. If you are like my husband who only wants to learn the Texas two-step, you can find a place to teach you and a place to dance.

Let's get one thing out of the way. Dancing should *not* only be done by those who already know how, or by the graceful, the knowers-of-the-steps, the people who get chosen by partners. "No, I don't dance" is an all too common refrain at many joyous dancing affairs. That probably means, "I don't dance well," or well enough to be seen dancing. To those who feel that way, I suggest that you ask yourself: Do you really want to miss this wonderful activity just because the sideline watchers (who you usually don't even know) don't like how you do it? The people you *do* know, and who matter to you, care only that you are joining them to have fun! Moving to music is your birthright.

Now, do you think that Fred Astaire and Ginger Rogers (who did it backwards and in high heels) just fell off the truck and started dancing? They didn't. They took lessons and practiced and danced a lot before they could do what we see them do on the screen. (That's how they got so thin.) Well, my friends, my *dancing* friends, we have to do that too. That's why this chapter lists places where you can take lessons—to get you on the road to Fred and Ginger. It may be awkward at first, but persevere; you'll be gliding across the floor like a pro in no time!

Could we review what is so wonderful about dancing? Let's start with Ballroom dance. If you're dancing with a well-known partner, it's a chance to take a break from the little stuff you deal with, like picking up

Dancing

the dry cleaning or driving someone to the orthodontist. Instead, you'll be feeling the music together, trying to master that sexy Tango turn. My Ballroom dance teacher at **Temple** used to say that the woman was the flower and the man's job was to help her bloom. (Sigh) Dancing can be a shot in the arm for your relationship.

And here's the best part. If you do *not* have a partner to learn to dance with—not to worry. Most dance places in this chapter *expect* that. Teachers wouldn't let you dance exclusively with the partner you brought with you anyway. You really *can* go alone. You will dance with every person in the room, giving you experience with partners of all levels and sizes in a variety of musical styles and rhythms. That's the best way to learn, and it certainly gives everyone the opportunity to learn those wonderful steps together.

So where are our teachers? With 30 Ballroom spots listed here, you should have no problem finding a place that suits your style, or is near to your house. Some places (**DiscoAmerica, Mostly Waltz**) specialize in certain kinds of dances, but most places offer many types of Ballroom lessons. The teachers will help you decide where you should start. One very important Good Thing now offered by most Ballroom places: Lessons are almost always followed by a dance party, where you can practice (*practice, practice*) what you've just learned with partners you've just learned it with. For people like me, that really helps. I need to dance with people who know the same steps I know, at least while I'm learning. When I get good, I can deal with people who are introducing variations left and right. And besides, these dance parties are *fun*, and they give you the opportunity to spend more time with your favorite dancers. And, who knows, you might just go out and dance somewhere else with that partner!

Latin dance is taught at most Ballroom studios, but there are also many clubs that feature Latin dancing with lessons and live bands—and they are really hot! **Brasil's**, for instance, has wonderful bands that inspire even the most hesitant of people to get out on the dance floor. Some dancers look like experts and others look like they just learned—but when you look at their faces, you can see that they are *all* having the time of their lives. A premier teacher of Tango, Jean Fung, teaches at **Tokio Ballroom, Philly Total Fitness**, and in New York City. She has mounted a web site (www.dancing.com/phillytango) where you can find out about

Tango happenings in the area. (You know, when you can dance the tango, you feel like you've really arrived—it is so awesome.) Latin dance has become a staple on Thursday and Sunday nights at the cool **Five Spot**, which, if you haven't been there, feels like a nifty supper club from the '40s. My friend Talia, who is a Latin dancing fool, told me about a Trenton place (**Urban Word Café**) which she says has fabulous music and great Latin dance. Since she is a regular dancer, she has found a Latin dance community that travels around to dance wherever Latin music is happening. Even if you're not ready to do the Merengue yourself, these places offer terrific music and dancing-people watching.

Partner dancing is picking up in all forms, including Swing—whose popularity has skyrocketed in the last decade. If you can figure out the differences between East Coast and West Coast Swing, the Lindy Hop, and the myriad other variations, you're doing better than I am. One expert explained it this way: East Coast Swing incorporates the dances like Lindy Hop (very popular right now), Jitterbug, and Bop. Do it to Swing music of the '40s and rock and roll of the '50s, dancing in a circular motion. Find it on Wednesdays at the Tokio Ballroom. West Coast Swing is a more stylized version of Swing, danced in a slot, often to rhythm and bluesy type music. It's more interpretive, more slinky and sexy, instead of perky like East Coast. Find it on Sundays at the Tokio. She adds that there are many places to do Swing, but one of the best is the **Philadelphia Swing Dance Society**, which has a great web site (www.swingdance.org) that describes its dances, and gives the necessary details of upcoming events. Just about every PSDS dance has a large dancer-friendly dance floor, free refreshments, and a dancing lesson before the dance party, with dance tips and demonstrations during intermission. But check for yourself, and go whirling about to the lessons of Jane Liebman, who really appreciates working with new dancers.

My husband, who is not a big dancer, promised me he would take dance lessons to do that Texas two-step. I found lessons (ha!) at the **Mt. Airy Learning Tree**, **Woody's**, and **Club 92.5**. Club 92.5, in King of Prussia, is probably one of the largest places for Country and Western dancing of all kinds, and gets a sizeable energetic crowd. You can learn Line Dancing and get out on the floor without waiting for someone to ask you. And it *is* fun! Woody's is a gay bar with lots of activities, including a Country and Western dance night that is more fun than you can imagine. (If you're straight, you're also invited. People have too much

Dancing

class at Woody's to make you feel uncomfortable.) Outside of the Line Dancing, most Country is partner dancing, with a fast pace and lots of easy-style movement. If you want a fun place to start dancing, check out these spots. Notice there are also a number of neighborhood halls offering Line and Country dancing; these are just a few of the ones I found. Watch the paper for more organization-sponsored country dance places (like the **Polish Association**, etc.).

We never went to the Texas two-step lessons because we found Cajun dance first. The biggest Cajun dance I've found in the area is in Conshohocken at the **TK Club**, where **Allons Danser** gives lessons and a big Friday night Cajun dance about every other Friday. With a nice group of regulars and newcomers showing up all the time, these simple partner dances start with a lesson anyone can follow (I know whereof I speak). The live bands have usually driven 19 hours from Louisiana to play—washboards, accordions, and all. You really can't stand still while they're playing, so get out there and dance, any old style!

There are many dances that are done in groups, like Line folk dances, Square dances, Contra dances, Israeli and Irish dances. You can find a place for one of these dances any night of the week, even if you go on the spur of the moment. And you don't need to find someone to go with you. They all offer lessons for the novices, as well as opportunities for fast-beat, high-stepping for those more advanced. You'll feel welcome in all the group-style dance places, but check out the **Beaver Folk Dancing** group in Fort Washington on Wednesday nights for a wonderful basic folk dancing experience. There are also groups that specialize in certain kinds of group dances, like Irish Set dancing, Royal Scottish folk dancing, International folk dancing and Israeli folk dancing, to name a few. Notice that Israeli folk dancing takes place almost every night of the week. Trouble is, there are so many places to go, I don't know how to steer you because they are all fun. You will see many of the same people who round robin around the groups, so they can be dancing several nights a week. To help you choose, there is an unusually good web site for all these dances: www.phillydance.org listing about 15 places to dance for every day of the week all around the tri-state area.

One thing to mention about the folk and country dancers. They very often create a community that socializes in other ways, like potluck suppers and going to the movies together. A prime example of this was told to me by a member of the **Thursday Night Contra Dance**. She said that some members of the group make quilts for other members who have babies. Now that's community. These are people who really like each other.

I don't want to be pushy about dancing, but quite frankly, it is one of the nicest networking activities you can do. The music is lovely in and of itself. The movement of a bunch of people swaying and stepping together, their faces attentive and full of enjoyment, will entice you to join them. Dancers are unusually tolerant people, eager to help those who want to learn. Don't let shyness or worry about performance stop you. Life is too short to miss dancing. (And will you let me know about your dancing experiences? I really want to hear.)

Getting into the swing of things at Disco America

A closer look at...

Photo by Janet Gala

Art Museum Folk Dancing

(215) 945-1316   Find on www.phillydance.com
Activity Locations:
(June-Sept.) Steps of the Philadelphia Art Museum, 26th St. & Benjamin
Franklin Pkwy., Phila., PA   on Tuesdays from 8-10:30pm
(Oct.-May) Lloyd Hall, 1 Boathouse Row, Kelly Drive, Phila., PA
on Tuesdays from 7:30-9:50pm

The folk dancing above the steps of the Art Museum (sponsored by the Fairmount Park Commission) has to be one of the most wonderful summer activities in Philadelphia. It's dusk, the moon is coming out, and the sweet sweet strains of folk music are in the air. Even if you just watch, it's a terrific evening but don't do that—join in! Come at 8pm to catch the well-taught lessons (mostly by Jerry Schiffer, with arm raised in the photo) at the start of each dance. You can dance by yourself behind the line of dancers until you have the steps almost down, and then reach out a hand and the line will take you in. You can feel the music guide your movement. Line dancing members are very welcoming, and you don't need a partner for most dances (except the Salty Dog Rag, mucho fun). Sometimes there's even live folk music for your listening and dancing pleasure, bands like the International Folk Sounds. Delightful.

If you enjoy this group, check out the International Folk Dancing at the Westfield Friends School in Cinnaminson, NJ on the 1st and 3rd Saturdays of the month (from 8-11pm) from September to May. It's also led by Jerry Schiffer, and you'll find lots of the same nice people there.

Ballroom

Crystal Ballroom

728 Philadelphia Pike, Wilmington, DE 19809
(302) 764-3262   dnccrystal@aol.com
www.dcdancenet.com/crystalballroom

You can get private and group lessons in American and International Ballroom almost every day here, learning from teachers who are themselves competitive dancers. On Fridays, there is a lesson at 7pm and then dancing from 8-ll:30pm. Everyone is welcome to this social, which includes dancers of all ages, with a large number in the 35-55 age group.

☀ Fridays   ⏰ 7-11:30pm

☎ Pete Taylor

💰 $10/party, includes lite food

Cut-a-Rug DJ & Dance Enterprises

P.O. Box 1307, Roslyn, PA 19001
(215) 784-9906   www.cut-a-rug.com
Activity Location: Several, including Tokio Ballroom, 122 Lombard St., Phila., PA

Paul's motto is that we can all learn to be good dancers if we take the time to do it. (He's right—I took several wonderful sessions and dance quite respectively now!) Cut-a-Rug gives lessons in American style Ballroom, Swing, and Country-Western (Line Dances!) at Tokio on Friday nights, with a dance party after-wards. The lessons, for beginners and advanced beginners, are at 8pm with dancing until 10pm. People of all ages are welcome to attend.

☎ Paul Wilburn

💰 $10

Dance Nights

(610) 644-0828
Activity Location: Congregation Ohev Shalom, 2 North Chester Rd. (off Route 320), North Wallingford, PA 19086

Here's a hot tip for avid dancers: You can really learn a dance by taking the lesson for the same dance every Tuesday (8-9pm) for a whole month. General dancing follows on the same night from 9-11pm ($4-$6). On the 3rd Saturday of the month, there is a public dance where for $10 you can enjoy theme party dancing with a little buffet. Couples and singles are invited for these fun evenings and afternoons. Call for their newsletter with an events calendar.

☎ Barbara Magozzi or Irma Stichter

Dancing

Dancers Extraordinaire

135 South Main Street, Doylestown, PA 18901
(215) 340-7780

Expert dancers teach all types of Ballroom, Latin, and Swing in group and private lessons. Also, Ballet, Tap, Jazz, Modern, Hip Hop, and Kick boxing. On some Saturday evenings at 7pm you can take a lesson and stay for the dance party from 8-11pm for only $7/lesson or $10/both, including snacks. One Saturday a month is a theme party, like "Vegas Night," with games, light food, and a professional dance show. Mixed ages; singles and couples. A great time!

☼ Saturdays   🕐 7-11pm

☎ Janelle Presti

💰 $7-10

Disco America

(215) 482-9992   donnaboyledisco@aol.com   www.discoamerica.com
Activity Location: Radisson Valley Forge Hotel & Convention Center,
King of Prussia, PA

Get out and have fun learning the Hustle from Donna, who has been teaching Saturday Night Fever dancing with a passion for over 20 years. Disco America offers other kinds of Ballroom dance, including Swing and West Coast Swing, that you can do in the city's hot spots or at somebody's wedding. Many singles. The web site tells you what happens when. Go ahead and "do the Hustle!"

☼ 3rd Sun./mo at the Radisson

☎ Donna Boyle

Fiesta Dance Club

(610) 485-7274
Activity Location: St. John Chrysostom Church, 617 S. Providence, Wallingford, PA.

This dance club is really a warm community, hosting social dances since 1951 with lessons in American Ballroom, Latin, the Hustle, and Line Dancing for both singles and couples. It's not unusual for 150 people to show up, and President Frank Falcone says, "People who come can't believe what a good time they have! It's a great place to make friends." Check out Frank's great newsletter. Lots of the same people attend the Medalist Dance Club (same phone for info), which meets on some Mondays for instruction and dancing.

☼ Wed. 8-11pm; 2nd Sat./mo. from 8:30-11:30pm

☎ Frank Falcone

💰 $3-$4 includes group dance lesson on Wednesdays

Fortuna's Universal DanceSport Center

Route 130 South, Collingswood, NJ 08103
(856) 869-0010 universa@bellatlantic.net www.timetodance2.com/universal

You can learn both competitive and social Ballroom dancing here every day of
the week in group lessons, as well as Salsa merengue, Hustle, and Argentine
Tango. Dancers are all ages, with an average age of 30, and you may come with
or without a partner. Find out about the terrific dance parties and "practice
sessions" featuring one type of dance (such as Ballroom, Latin, or Hustle) where
beginners and advanced dancers mix. The jam-packed newsletter gives details of
many other activities. These dances will bring out your artistic side as they
strengthen your body! There are trips to NYC, other people's dance parties, and
formation dances (group of people doing one dance routine), and the finest
international competition in the area in the beginning of April every year—all
sponsored by this dance center.

Gershman YMHA

401 South Broad Street, Philadelphia, PA 19147
(215) 545-4400

Don Rosenblatt, a master teacher, has been teaching couples and singles to
dance at this YMHA "forever" and loving every class. These are small group
classes (from 10 to 20 people) so you have individualized instruction, and all
ages attend. It's not necessary to bring a partner to the classes, which include the
Waltz, Swing, Foxtrot, Rumba, and Tango. Some participants are beginners,
while others are honing steps they've learned before. Come alone or bring a
friend!

☼ Wednesdays   ⏰ 6-9pm

Mostly Waltz

(215) 643-4397 or (215) 483-0726 www.mostly waltz.com
Activity Location: Varies, often in Chestnut Hill

All types of live music and dancing—Waltz, Country, Viennese, Pop, English,
anything that goes 1,2,3—are featured on these Sundays. Other couple dances,
however such as Polkas, Schottisches, Swing, Tangos, and Zweifachers are mixed
in for variety. Two lessons Basic (beginners) and "Flourishes" (advanced) take
place simultaneously from 3-3:30pm, so don't worry if your Waltz step is a bit
rusty. Dress is from casual to dressy, and you needn't bring a partner to these
dances presented by the Waltz Project. Tip for women: At Mostly Waltz, it is
perfectly acceptable and usual for women to ask men to dance. To help break
the ice, there is a Waltz mixer near the beginning of every Mostly Waltz event.
Call for locations. Times are 2:30pm for instruction and 3-6pm for dancing.

☼ 4th Sun./mo   ⏰ 2:30-6pm

Dancing

Paso Doble Ballroom

4501 New Falls Road, Levittown, PA 19056
(215) 547-2311   http://dolphin.upenn.edu/~ballroom/places/pdballroom.html

The Paso Doble Ballroom probably has the largest dance floor in the Greater
Philadelphia region. It generally has live bands mixed with some taped music.
Mostly an older, married crowd; singles are welcome, but you might find it
easier to go with a partner, except on Friday nights, which are *Singles Nights*.

☼ Fridays: 8pm-1am; Saturdays: 9pm-12:30am

🍷 $5-8

Quickstep, Inc.

49 E. Lancaster Avenue, Ardmore, PA 19003
(610) 649-6655   www.quickstepinc.com

Everyone is invited to Quickstep on Friday nights for lessons (beginning at
8:15pm) and/or a dance party (at 9pm) where you can do Latin, Smooth,
Disco, Salsa, and Swing dances. About half are single in this mixed-age group,
which also enjoys occasional dinner dances during the year. Small group lessons
are offered for both beginners and advanced dancers during the week.

☼ Fridays   🕐 8:15-10:30pm

✉ Trudy Sellers

🍷 $7 for Friday dance party & lesson

Stardust Ballroom

Route 73 & Haddonfield Road, Pennsauken, NJ 08110
(856) 663-6376   www.stardustdance.com

A *very* popular ballroom that hosts different dancing groups for Ballroom
dancing for a mixed, happy crowd. On the first and second Saturdays of the
month there is Merengue dancing to a fine Salsa beat. On certain Sunday
afternoons, couples from the Imperial Club work on steps for competition. On
Thursday and Sunday evenings (8pm with a lesson first), the Single Parents
Society cuts a lively rug—great for people newly in transition. What is really
neat about the lessons is that on Wednesdays, Fridays, and Saturdays of each
month they specialize in one type of dance. By the end of the month, you can
be terrific! Call for their full and current schedule, because it changes.

Sundays in Bala Cynwyd

(610) 896-5221

Activity Location: 332 Trevor Lane, Bala Cynwyd, PA 19004

Tish Sweeney will tell you that the point of Ballroom dancing is to have fun— and that's just what happens at these Sunday dance parties (including lessons) when people dress up and spend the evening dancing elegant dances (Ballroom, Latin, and Swing) in elegant surroundings. Although the Swing dancing draws a younger crowd, most who attend are in the 40 to 60 age range, with all ages welcome. You can take private and group lessons during the week from Tish and Michael so you can really strut your stuff on Sunday. Doesn't that sound like so much fun!

☼ Sundays   ☎ 4-7pm

☏ Tish & Michael Sweeney

💰 $10

Tokio Ballroom

122-124 Lombard Street, 2nd floor, Philadelphia, PA 19147
(215) 922-2515   www.lechampignon-tokio.com

Start with a beginner dance lesson from expert instructors at the Tokio, and then enjoy a great dance party afterward. The current schedule is: Mondays and Tuesdays: Lindy Hop; Wednesdays: Argentine Tango; Thursdays: West Coast Swing; Fridays: Hustle, Swing, and Ballroom on different weeks; Saturdays: likewise with Argentine Tango and Salsa; and Sundays: West Coast Swing with the Swing Dance Society of Delaware Valley. But schedules change, so check the web site or call before you go!

💰 $10 includes lesson, refreshment with cash bar

Top Hat Dance Studio

3114 Willits Road (off 95 at Academy Road exit), Philadelphia, PA 19134
(215) 676-3100   jaanderson@quixnet.net   www.tophatdancestudio.com

Brush up on all your steps at Top Hat, where they offer lessons in Smooth Ballroom, Latin (including Samba and Salsa), West Coast Swing, and Hustle. Both social and competitive dancing happens here, as well as Wedding dancing for people coming with and without partners. Everyone is welcome to check out the dance parties on Saturday evenings or Sunday afternoons.

☏ Allen

💰 $10 group lesson

Dancing

Trocadero Ballroom

2030 Sansom Street, Philadelphia, PA 19103
(215) 665-8411

If you'd like to become a really good dancer, check out this dance studio. It offers private lessons in Ballroom, Latin, and Swing and specializes in competitive dancing. On Sundays, the studio sponsors a fun social afternoon for experienced dancers with one advanced lesson, dancing, and a hot dinner buffet. These dancers know what they're doing and love doing it! Also check out the Sunday Tango Tea Dance on the 2nd Sunday (with a lesson included). Call for schedule.

☀ Sundays   ⏰ 5-8pm

☎ Ken Calowy

💰 $10 includes buffet and beverages

University City Arts League

4226 Spruce Street, Philadelphia, PA 19104
(215) 382-7811   Ray/Mitchell: kray1@erols.com

You won't believe the spins and turns you'll find yourself performing when you take these great classes by Kelly Ray and Leslie Mitchell in Ballroom, Latin, Argentine Tango, and Swing. And when you just want to dance, you can join your new dancing buds at Friday (Argentine Tango) and Saturday (1st & 3rd for Ballroom, Latin, and Swing) dance parties to practice your steps! Come with a partner or meet new dancers. For private lessons, contact Ray/Mitchell at (215) 574-9555.

☀ Fridays & Saturdays   ⏰ 8:30pm-12am

💰 $5

University of Pennsylvania Ballroom Dance Society

(215) 898-5000, ask for Student Affairs
ballroom@dolphin.upenn.edu   http://dolphin.upenn.edu/~ballroom

During the school year, PBDS offers dance lessons every Sunday afternoon for $40/semester for non-students. There is no partner necessary, no experience necessary, and your first Sunday is free so you can check it out and decide if you want to come back. The school also has workshops and dances throughout the year, like the big winter and summer balls. Sounds like a great deal and lots of fun.

UPBEAT

623 South Taney Street, Philadelphia, PA 19146
(215) 546-7068   upbeat@ix.netcom.com   www.upbeatdancefitness.com

Get up and dance with this predominantly young group in their late 20s and early 30s! You can try their lessons at a lively open house to help you decide whether to start Ballroom dance classes, including the Waltz, Foxtrot, Tango, Swing, Mambo/Salsa, Hustle, Cha-cha, Jitterbug, and more. Dance off to local hot dancing clubs together or join them for Swing dancing Thursdays (with a free lesson at 6:30pm) to big band music at Penn's Landing in the summer (WPEN). All ages are welcome!

☎ Denel Keister

💰 $45/advance ($55/door) for 4 one-hour weekly sessions

Wanna Dance

(215) 855-2711   vbeiswenge@aol.com

Activity Location: Pennsylvania Academy of Performing Arts,
125 S. Main St. in North Wales, PA (Shearer Square)

Wanna Dance teaches Ballroom and Latin dancing on Friday and Sunday evenings. (Be sure to check the most recent schedule for these dances.) A free beginner hour lesson is included, followed by an evening dance party. An expert dancer herself, Vivian loves teaching beginners to do the Rumba, Cha-cha, Tango, Sambo, Hustle, Mambo, Swing, Foxtrot, and more. No partners are needed to attend a terrific evening of dance.

☼ Fridays & Sundays   🕐 8-11:30pm

☎ Vivian Beiswenger

Cajun

Allons Danser

(215) 576-0839   kpearle@email.msn.com

Activity Location: TK Club, East Hector & Apple Sts., Conshohocken, PA
(610) 828-9352

Allons Danser is the heart of Cajun dancing around the Delaware Valley. Get on the mailing list to hear about area Cajun dances, mostly at the TK Club, with dancing and instruction to the finest live Cajun music (accordions and wash-boards included!) outside of Louisiana. Everyone is willing to help you, and you'll have a great time learning these dances. A tip: Get there by 7:30pm for the lesson—it really will turn you into a dancer!

☼ About two Fridays a month   🕐 7:30pm-12am

💰 $10/members; $12 all others.

Dancing

Clogging

Fiddlekicks Appalachian Clogging

(215) 643-6497   www.ipcc.com/heritage/fiddleki.htm

Activity Location: Allens Lane Art Center, Allens Lane & McCallum St.,
Phila., PA 19119

Enthusiastic dancers have been Appalachian Clogging in Philadelphia since
1996. Everyone is welcome, whether experienced or inexperienced, who is
willing to learn steps, work on routines, and whoop-it-up to old time and
bluegrass music. Other styles of Clogging, such as French Canadian and Cape
Breton, are also explored. Cloggers are also welcome to dance when musicians
hold an Old Time jam session at the Mermaid Inn (7673 Germantown Avenue,
Phila., PA) on the fourth Tuesday of the month.

☼ Saturdays

Contra, English & Scottish Country

Arden Folk Guild

Arden Club, 2126 The Highway, Arden, DE
(302) 478-7257   http://home.sprynet.com/~rbrat

Live music and well-known callers lead afternoons of Contra dance fun for
dancers of all levels. Instruction for beginners starts at 1:30pm, followed by
dancing from 2-5pm. Arden also has a full schedule of Cajun (3rd Sundays,
4-8pm) and Square and Folk dances (Wednesdays) throughout the season, often
with live music. They have holiday dances, too. Check the web site for info.

☼ 1st Sun./mo   ⏰ 1:30-5pm

💰 $6/$7

English Country Dancing

(215) 836-0426   http://www.culture-at-work.com/gcd.html

Activity Location: Summit Presbyterian Church, Greene & Westview Sts., Phila., PA.
(West Mt. Airy)

For a lovely kind of dancing, try English Country Dancing with the
Germantown Country Dancers on these Saturdays.

☼ 1st Sat./mo from Nov. to May (except Dec.)   ⏰ 8-11pm

Dancing

Germantown Country Dancers

(215) 836-0426   http://www.culture-at-work.com/gcd.html
Activity Location: Merion Friends Meeting Hse, 615 Montgomery Ave., Merion, PA

Experts preform dances of 18th century England and America and invite you to join in afterwards. Wear soft-soled shoes and, if you wish, bring snacks to share for tea. Live bands and callers provide the music that makes you feel like you've gone back in time. GCD is a Philadelphia area group affiliate of The Country Dance and Song Society, which sponsors national dance events.

☼ Wednesdays

🕐 8-10:15pm

🐝 $5

7:30pm instruction

Lambertville Country Dancers

http://www.stockton-law.com/lcd_dance/lcdmain.html

LCD is also a member of CDSS (Country Dance & Song Society) and holds New England style Contra Dances with live bands. It's lots of fun, with lively steps and callers, and no partners needed. Dances are held on a special events basis at the Yardley Community Center. Check the web site above for specifics, or call (609) 882-7733.

LCD also sponsors English Country dancing at the United Methodist Church of Titusville in Titusville, NJ. English Dancing is held on the 1st Friday/month at 8pm with live bands. Please carry in clear soft-soled shoes to wear. You'll be dancing the same dances they danced in Jane Austin's *Pride and Prejudice*. (www.princetonol.com/groups/pcd/lcd/) (609) 393-3762

Pineland Country Dancers

(856) 779-9084
Activity Location: Westfield Friends School, Rte. 130 & Riverton Rd., Cinnaminson, NJ

Try English and Scottish Country dancing and some Contra dancing with this enthusiastic and welcoming group. There's instruction and a chance to practice the steps before the evening dance so you'll know what you're doing. Also ask about the Country Dance group on the 3rd Tuesday/month in Haddonfield, NJ, for more dancing.

☼ Every Monday from September-June

🕐 8-10pm

Dancing

Princeton Country Dancers

(609) 683-7956   http://www.princetonol.com/groups/pcd

Activity Location: Suzanne Patterson Center,
Nassau St. & Rte. 206, Princeton, NJ 08540

Each week, traditional dances of the United States and England (Contra and English Country dances) are taught with live music by different bands. A beginner's workshop is held at 7:40pm and you do not need to bring a partner. Occasionally there are Saturday night dances as well as some terrific special events, including weekend long dance events. Check the web site for up-to-date information on these wonderful activities.

☼ Wednesdays   ☎ 7:40-10:30pm

Scottish Country Dancing

(215) 487-9056

Activity Location: Germantown Unitarian Society, 6511 Lincoln Drive, Phila., PA

Instruction and dancing for dancers at all levels. This is beautiful dancing—go just to watch and listen. For experienced dancers, Scottish Country dancing takes place at the Performing Arts Center Dance Studio at Swarthmore College every Thursday at 6pm.

☼ 2nd & 4th Fri./mo   ☎ 8-10:30pm

Tapestry Historic Dance Ensemble

327 Kenmore Road, Havertown, PA 19083
(610) 446-6356

This semi-professional group performs dances from the 17th, 18th, and 19th centuries. The Ensemble holds classes for new and experienced dancers to learn historic period dancing on Thursday evenings in Ardmore, PA.

Thursday Night Contra Dance

(215) 885-9370   www.voicenet.com/~squeeze/phildance.html
Activity Location: Glenside Memorial Hall, Waverly Rd. & Keswick Ave.,
Glenside, PA

Beginners are most welcome to dance to live music by Maia Bang, Wild Asparagus, Sarah Heibert, Bob Stein, Bob Pasquarello, Please and Thank You String Band, and others. Come for instruction about the dance figures, with a walk-through between 7:30-8pm, and be sure to wear your soft-soled shoes. Or try the Contra and Squares Dance at this location on the third Saturday/month from 8-11pm, also with live music and callers.

☼ Every Thurs./mo & the 3rd Sat./mo   ☎ 7:30-11pm

Country & Western

Club 92.5

Find on: www.marlindj.com

Activity Location: Radisson Valley Forge Hotel, 1-76 and the PA Turnpike, Valley Forge, PA (610) 337-2000

Leave it to our own country radio station WXTU to give us local country music live with Country Dancing, Line Dancing, including lessons and all! So y'all come on out and hoop and holler with people having a great time. Wednesday is beginner's night, and on Thursdays there are lessons for couples in Two-step and Swing. Fridays and Saturdays are everybody-dance nights. A very mixed crowd comes out for these lively evening dances. About $6.

☼ Weds. 6pm-2am; Fris. 5pm; Sats. 7pm (lessons 7-8pm, Fris. & Sats.)

Dancercize

Ralston Wellness House, 3615 Chestnut Street, Philadelphia, PA
(215) 386-2984

Morning Line dances are taught here on the weekends, mostly for the over- 55 crowd, but all are very welcome. Dances are especially designed for a good-for-the-heart workout, but provide much fun and good community as well. Ralston also offers t'ai chi, qiqong, Feldenkrais, and other programs for people interested in the mind-body connection, all for very reasonable fees.

☎ Ralston or Evelyn Jacobs, (610) 352-5284

North Penn Elks Club

Trewigtown Road, Colmar, PA
(215) 997-7688   www.marlindj.com

Lots of C/W dancing here: Tuesdays (7:30-8:30pm until 11pm), Fridays (7:30-8:30pm until 11:30pm), and Sunday (6-10pm). Always a lesson first and a free mini-buffet for energy!

Polish Association Home Ballroom

9150 Academy Road, Philadelphia, PA
(215) 997-7688   www.marlindj.com

Dance at the Country Night until 10:30pm on a wood floor.

☼ Mondays   ⏰ 7:30pm lesson

Dancing

Prospector's

3050 Route 38 & Ark Road, Mt. Laurel, NJ 08054
(856) 235-1121   www.prospectorsrestaurant.com

Come for Country & Western dancing on Wednesday through Saturday nights at 8pm. Line dancing is taught on Wednesdays, couple dancing on Thursdays, and a live band plays on Fridays and Saturdays so you can dance up a storm and show what you've learned! It's a great time. $5 at the door.

Woody's

202 South 13th Street, Philadelphia, PA
(215) 545-1893

In the afternoons, this wood-paneled gay club with five bars plays show tunes and Swing music. At night, it turns into a dance club with Disco, good food, and cappuchino, too. On Tuesdays, Fridays, and Sundays, you can learn to dance Country & Western to your heart's content. This friendly place is lots of fun for gay dancers, and also for straight dancers who have their values in order.

☀ Tuesdays & Fridays at 8pm; Sundays at 5pm

Folk - International

Arden Folk Guild

2126 The Highway, Arden, DE
(302) 762-2818 or (302) 764-2682   http://home.sprynet.com/~rbrat

Kick up your heels at International folk dancing here every week. On the 2nd Wednesday/month they bring in a caller to include square dances too. Instruction is part of the deal.

☀ Wednesdays   ⏰ 7:30-9:30pm

Beaver Folk Dancing

(215) 233-9399 until 9pm
wadlinge@voicenet.com   www.voicenet.com/~wadlinge/folkdance
Activity Location: Or Hadash, 190 Camp Hill Rd., Fort Washington, PA

Instruction happens from 8:15-8:45pm officially, but actually it goes on for the entire evening as there follows a mix of both easy and challenging dances. Advanced dancers show the rest of us how it's supposed to look, and learning by dancing behind them is standard practice. Circle, line and couple dances from all nationalities taught by two terrific teachers. I loved it. $5

☀ Wednesdays   ⏰ 8:15-10:30pm
✆ Bill Wadlinger

Beaver Folk Dancing Photo Peggy Tietz

Glenside Folk Dancing

(215) 885-7650   *Find on www.phillydance.com*

Activity Location: Behind the church at Mt. Carmel & Limekiln Pike, Glenside, PA

Instruction and dancing every week.

☼ Tuesdays   ⏰ 9:30-11am

Kimberton Dance Society

Kimberton & Prizer Roads, Kimberton, PA
(610) 935-1092

Dancing and instruction at these weekly Friday night evenings from 8-10:30pm.

Princeton Folk Dance Group

(609) 924-6930

Activity Location: Riverside School, Riverside Dr., Princeton, NJ

This group is known to be great fun! Instruction at 7:30pm and dancing from 8:30-10pm on Tuesdays. Beginners are welcome to learn and attend class here. A more advanced group dances on Fridays, usually at the YWCA, Paul Robeson Place & Rte. 206 in Princeton, NJ, from 8-11:15pm. (For current info, call 908-369-8906, or http://ourworld.compuserve.com/homepages/hunt_smith)

South Jersey Folk Dancers

(856) 829-5059

Activity Location: Westfield Friends School, Rte.130 & Riverton Rd., Cinnaminson, NJ

There's terrific folk dancing here as well as country dance on Mondays.

☼ 1st, 3rd Sats./mo from September to July   ⏰ 8-11pm

Dancing

Folk-Israeli

This is not just folk dancing the way you remember it from years ago, but also dancing to modern music, and includes circle, partner, and line dancing.

Sunday

Klein Branch, Jewish Community Center
Red Lion Road & Jamison Street, Philadelphia, PA
(215) 698-7300

⏰ 7-11:30pm with instruction for all levels from 7-8:30pm

💰 $6   ☎ Host Rob Markowitz

Germantown Jewish Centre
Lincoln Drive & Ellet Street, Philadelphia, PA
(215) 247-9614

⏰ 10:30am-12:30pm

💰 $6

Tuesday

Beth Shalom
8230 Old York Road, Elkins Park, PA
(215) 379-0641   spolsky49@cs.com

⏰ 7:30-10pm—dancing for beginner through intermediate levels

💰 $5   ☎ Host Sharon Polsky

Congregation Beth El
2901 W. Chapel Avenue, Cherry Hill, NJ
(215) 893-0727   schill@dca.net

⏰ 7-10:30pm, 7-8pm instruction

☎ Host Don Schillinger, of RAK-DAN Israeli Dancing

Thursday

Temple Beth Hillel/Beth El
1001 Remington Rd., Wynnewood, PA (summers at the Art Museum-Rocky statue)
(215) 893-0727   schill@dca.net

One of the largest dance groups in the area. Early in the evening is for families and beginners; after 9pm, the dancing is for adults.

⏰ 7:30-9pm instruction, 9-11pm dancing

☎ Host Don Schillinger, of RAK-DAN Israeli Dancing

Folk-Italian

Ballerini e Voci D'Italia

(215) 487-3229   ptorna@erols.com

Activity Location: St. Nicholas of Tolentine School, 9th & Pierce Streets, Phila., PA

Group or partner dancing Italian dances like the Tarantella. No partner needed.

☀ Saturdays   ⏰ 10:30am-noon

Folk-Swedish

Gammaldans

American Swedish Historical Museum, 1900 Pattison Avenue, Philadelphia, PA
(215) 389-1776

Several different kinds of Swedish folk dancing are taught here every week, including the Hambo, the Schottis, Snoa, Vals, and Polka. All levels of dancers are included in the lessons and general dancing. Remember the basic Schottis? One, two, three hop, four, five, six hop, hop-hop-hop-hop. And again. My mom taught me and we'd do it for anyone who would watch. Easy and fun. Call first.

☀ Fridays in some months   ⏰ 7-9pm

Dancing

Irish

This includes *set* dancing—a flat, traditional quadrille, with four couples in a set—and *step or Ceili* dancing, done by individuals in a line, like *RiverDance*.

Irish Step Dance

(215) 885-2304

Activity Location: Glenside Knights of Columbus Hall, 235 Limekiln Pike, Glenside

These Step or Ceili classes are conducted by Rosemarie Timoney who says her purpose is to get people out to enjoy dancing and have lots of fun. She teaches beginners on Wednesdays (7pm), intermediates on Mondays (7pm), and advanced on Tuesdays (8pm). She's one really good teacher—been at it for 30 years—and is a delight to learn from.

Irish Set Dancing

(610) 446-9338

Activity Location: MacSwiney Club, Greenwood & Walnut St., Jenkintown, PA

A relatively small group of three or four sets.

☼ Thursdays (not in Jan., Feb., July, Aug.) ⏰ 8-10pm

Irish Set Dancing

(856) 428-4546   gbuckley@netaxs.com   www.shanagolden.com

Activity Location: Cadbury Center, Rt. 38 (beside Cherry Hill Mall), Cherry Hill, NJ

Classes held downstairs in the ballroom.

☼ Mondays ⏰ 8-10pm

Irish Set Dancing

(856) 428-4546   gbuckley@netaxs.com   www.shanagolden.com

Activity Location: Knights Of Columbus Hall, Broad & Elm, Palmyra, NJ

☼ Wednesdays ⏰ 7:30-9:30pm

Irish Set Dancing

(856) 428-4546   gbuckley@netaxs.com   www.shanagolden.com

Activity Location: VFW Hall Post 6253, 34 Chestnut Street, Berlin, NJ

Fiona Buckley says on the web site: "These dances are more then just people coming together to dance They're community events. People come to dance, to learn, to share food, to listen to wonderful music, and to have fun. Everyone is made to feel welcome." She teaches wonderful Set Dances in New Jersey.

☼ About 6 Sundays/year ⏰ 1pm (workshop)-6:30pm

Hoolie (Irish Dancing)

(609) 429-0312   www.shanagolden.com

Activity Location: Knights of Columbus Hall, Broad & Elm, Palmyra, NJ

The South Jersey Irish Society sponsors Hoolies (an evening of Ceili dancing).

☼ 1st Fri./mo   ☎ 8pm

Philadelphia Ceili Group: *Irish Music and Dance Festival*

6815 Emlen Street, Philadelphia, PA 19119
(215) 849-8899   www.netselect.net/pcg/default.htm
Activity Location: Memorial Hall, Fairmount Park West, Phila., PA

An annual festival in September with the finest musicians, dancing, crafts, and everything Irish. Dancing includes Step dancing, beginning and advanced, Set dances and Waltzes. These are internationally famous musicians playing inside and outside the Hall. PCG also sponsors mini Irish music festivals in fall and spring, and regular Friday night activities at the Emlen Street center.

Jazz & Tap

Afro-Caribbean Dance

Hawthorne Cultural Center, 1200 Carpenter Street, Philadelphia, PA 19147
(215) 685-1848

Shawnta Smith-Taylor, international touring performer, and traditional drummer Kenneth "Skip" Burton teach this exciting dance every Monday from 6:30-8pm. Bring a loose Caribbean skirt and move to this exciting music! On Weds., from 7:30-9pm, learn traditional West African dances with live drummers.

Gwendolyn Bye Dance Center

3611 Lancaster Avenue, Philadelphia, PA 19104
(215) 222-7633   www.gbyedance.com

Ongoing classes for beginners to professionals in Modern, Ballet, and Jazz dance. Special workshops, too.

☼ Weekdays 4-8pm, and Saturdays

Tap Jam

(215) 233-0708

Activity Location: Allens Lane Art Center, Allens Lane & McCallum St., Phila., PA

You can shuffle off to Buffalo in the Thursday Tap Jam in West Mt. Airy. Led by Audrey Bookspan, this delightful evening activity costs only $5. Bring a snack to share and meet fellow tappers in a comfortable setting.

Dancing

University of the Arts, School of Dance: *Dance Extension*

211 South Broad Street, Philadelphia, PA 19102
(215) 717-6110   www.uarts.edu

Do you ever wish you could dance like (or with) Gene Kelly? Must confess I have trouble keeping still when I watch him—maybe it's time to take a tap lesson (At my age? Yes!) at the University of the Arts. There are excellent evening classes in exotic jazz dances, like Samba, Jazz, and Brazilian as well as African Dance, Ballet, and Movement styles. Also check out the summer and daytime classes and the four-week intensive workshops for serious dancers (if you're one of them).

Latin

Brasil's Restaurant & Bar

112 Chestnut St., Philadelphia, PA
(215) 413-1700   brasils@brasil.com   www.brasils.com

Lots of dancing to hot music at this exciting club. You could take a lesson in Argentine Tango/Milonga and then show your stuff to live music. Wednesdays (10pm-2am) are *Latin nights* with Latin Swing (Salsa, Merengue) and a free lesson at 8:30pm. Fridays are also Latin nights with Salsa Merengue and club music. The music and dancing on Saturday *International Nights* vary with the band. You could find Latin, Brazilian, or Caribbean music and dancing, and perhaps a Tango lesson ($10) from 8-10pm—but always call to check on the lessons and the music schedule for that evening.

☼ Wednesdays, Fridays & Saturdays for Latin dance

💰 Free on Wed.; Fri. & Sat. varies—$5 to $10.

Club Cancun

4th between Chestnut & Market Streets (Bourse Building), Philadelphia, PA
(215) 625-4835   www.salsaflava.com/cancun.htm

You don't have to get on a plane to the south to find hot Merengue and Salsa. DJ Monchi plays great dance music with a band on Saturdays. Large dance floor and friendly crowd greet real dancers.

🕙 10pm-2am

💰 $10

Dancing

Eighth Floor

800 North Delaware Avenue, Philadelphia, PA 19123
(215) 922-1000   www.eighthfloor.com

This Latin evening is very highly rated by patrons—as you will see when you check the web site. The Eighth Floor is well known for many types of dancing nights, but Friday is Latin night, when lessons are offered from 8-9pm followed by a hot night of dancing to live music. (On Saturdays, find 95.7FM Jamming Gold '70s Disco, and on Sundays 97.5FM presents late '70s, '80s and '90s dance music.) Many changes all the time, so check the web site.

☼ Fridays   ⏰ 8pm

Five Spot

34 Bank Street, Philadelphia, PA 19106
(215) 574-0070   www.thefivespot.com

Latin happens here with fervor on Thursday nights, with a lesson at 8pm and live music. Other nights you'll find Rockabilly—old fashioned rock 'n roll mixed with Swing and Western. Five Spot is famous for its Swing lessons as well, followed by dancing on Tuesdays, Wednesdays, and Sundays. If you prefer contemporary dance music (House, HipHop, etc.) you'll find that too, especially on Fridays and Saturdays. Two floors support all kinds of dancing at this popular, cool, supper club and lounge.

☼ Tuesdays-Sundays

💰 $5 cover charge

Philly Tango Grapevine

P.O. Box 466, Ambler, PA 19002
(267) 625-6678 or (917) 252-6074   phillytango@yahoo.com
www.dancing.com/phillytango
Activity Location: Tokio Ballroom, 122-124 Lombard St., 2nd floor, Phila., PA
(215) 922-2515

If you really want to learn Tango, show up at the Tokio Ballroom on Wednesdays at 7pm where Jean Fung specializes in teaching newcomers. On Thursdays she teaches at the Pennsylvania Performing Arts Academy, and on Tuesdays she's at Fortuna's Universal Dancesport. Or try the Tango practice session on Sundays at Philly Total Fitness and Dance (7140 Germantown Avenue) from 8:30-11:30pm. No partners needed. Call or check the web page to find the class that will best help you learn this fluid, graceful Latin dance. Jean's classes are terrific!

☼ Wednesdays   ⏰ 7pm

Dancing

Movement-Ethnic

Dances of Universal Peace

(610)544-2778 http://hometown.aol.com/dancingpeace786/myhomepage/faith.html
Activity Location: Media Friends Meeting, 125 W. 3rd St., Media, PA

These dances combine simple folk dance movements with the singing of sacred phrases from many of the world's spiritual traditions. Jeanne says sacred song and dance can heal the inner spirit. All dances are taught and no partners are needed. Wear casual dress. Held in many locations; call for newsletter.

☼ 2nd Sat./mo   ☎ 8pm

☏ Jeanne Ayesha Lauenborg

Group Motion

Community Education Center, 3500 Lancaster Avenue, Philadelphia, PA 19103
(215) 387-9895

Express yourself doing free style dancing led by well-known dancer Manfred Fischbeck. Everyone here is your partner. Housed in a building with other dance companies (Kumquat), you'll find classes in Modern dance, HipHop, Capoeira, and Pilates (exercise) too. Call for a schedule listing many exciting activities.

☼ Fridays   ☎ 8-10pm

Moving Arts Studio of Mt. Airy (MaMa)

Carpenter Lane and Greene Street (West Mt. Airy), Philadelphia, PA 19119
(215) 842-1040   muze@erols.com

Highly trained dancers teach African Dance (with live drums), Tap and Jazz, HipHop Funk, Tai Chi (push hands), Swing and Latin, aerobic classes, Pilates, '60s-'70s style Line Dancing, Yoga rhythmics and Yoga at this friendly neighborhood dance studio. This is an exciting studio only 12 minutes from Center City.

☼ All days

💰 Very reasonable

Mt. Airy Learning Tree: *Belly Dancing by Naja*

6101 Greene Street, Philadelphia, PA 19119
(215) 843-6333   www.mtairylearningtree.org

You can swirl to the dance of the seven veils in Naja's belly dancing class, which ends in a big party with Middle Eastern food and dancing. Other outstanding dance classes at MALT include Ballroom, Argentinian Tango, Cajun, and Swing, as well as harder-to-find dances like Hip Hop. There's a new schedule of classes out every four months. Dance while you meet your neighbors!

Dancing

Painted Bride Art Center: *Movement Research Workshops*
230 Vine Street, Philadelphia, PA 19106
(215) 925-9914 www.paintedbride.org

These workshops are but one example of the exciting dance and movement experiences at the Bride that invites even the non-professionals among us to dance with them. Call to find out about the next one offered. Also, ask about the master dance classes.

Philadelphia Folklore Project
Urban Education Center, 4801 Market Street, Philadelphia, PA
(215) 468-7871

Philly Dance Africa workshops and dance parties combine live music, singers, and dancers, and you can move in to dance with and around them. It's amazing!

Susan Hess Studio
2030 Sansom Street, Philadelphia, PA
(215) 665-9060

This premier dance studio sponsors Dance Lab workshops by well-known and experienced teachers. Classes in Modern Dance and Contact Improvisation are examples of the offerings here. Reasonably priced and very fine teaching.

Polka

Frank & Ziggy Polka Party
Stardust Ballroom, Route 73 & Haddonfield Road, Pennsauken, NJ 08110
(856) 663-6376 www.stardustdance.com

Everyone is invited to this lively, happy dancing place where about 300 people of all ages polka together!

☼ Sundays   ☎ 2:30-6:30pm

Eddie Blazonczyk & the Versatones
Activity Location: TK Club, E. Hector & Apple Sts., Conshohocken, PA
(610) 828-9352

This band out of Chicago plays for Polka dances in the area, such as the TK Club, the Gilbertsville Fire Company, and halls in Clifton Heights. The best way to know when the dances are held is to subscribe to the Polish newspaper, the *Post Eagle*, from Clifton, NJ, for just $10. The TK Club is home to Cajun and other dances as well.

☼ Some Sundays   ☎ 3pm

Dancing

Square-Club Dancing

Buckaroo Square & Round Dance Club

(215) 343-3483   *mrmrs02@cs.com*

http://communities.phillyburbs.com/home/buckaroos

Activity Location: Lessons at the Titus Elementary School, 2733 Lower Barness Rd., Warrington, PA. Dances are at St. Paul's Methodist Church on Palimino Drive.

The O'Botts gave me the scoop here: You need to take about six months of lessons to be able to dance with most Square dance *clubs*. That's how long it takes to learn and respond quickly to about 60 calls. Then you're probably ready for the club dancing. Good news is that the lessons are tremendous fun with many clubs to dance with in the area and a terrific yearly convention of about 20,000 dancers. This club is 43 years old and going strong. Wow.

☀ 2nd & 4th Fris./mo club dances   ⏰ 7:30-10:30pm

    Every Wednesdays for lessons   7:30-9:30pm

💰 $3

Club Sashay

(610) 328-4533   *http://members.aol.com/clubsashay*

Activity Location: C.C. Hancock Memorial Church, Sproul (Rte.320) & Wesley Rd., Springfield, Delaware County, PA (off Blue Rte., Exit 3)

"Forget your woes and start dancin'!" says the web site of the oldest Square dance and Round dance club in the Delaware Valley which offers dances on the Plus Level twice a month. Notice that the large groups offer dances on different nights. That gives Square and Round dancers the chance to dance several times a week, and many of them do!

☀ 2nd & 4th Sats./mo, Sept. to May   ⏰ 8-10:30pm

💰 $10/couple/non-members

Dixie Derbys Square Dance Club

(215) 675-8848   dixies@dixiederbys.com   www.dixiederbys.com
Activity Location: During the school year: Upper Moreland Middle School,
Orangeman's Rd., Upper Moreland, PA; in summer, Bryn Athyn

The web site says this is the largest Square dance club in the Delaware Valley
with a full Square and Round dance program with lots of classes for beginners
and advanced dancers and dances on the weekends. Round dance is a ballroom
dance where everyone is doing the same steps at the same time. It takes about 30
weeks to be proficient dancer. Dixie Derbys offer "class level" dances for learned
beginners (those who have attended at least 15 weeks of classes) around the area.
There's no drinking/smoking at the dances themselves, but it's OK for the lively
socializing afterwards! This club performs in various public parades. Square
dance lessons on Tuesdays; Round dance lessons on Mondays thru Thursdays.

☼ 1st & 3rd Fris./mo   ☎ 8-10:30pm dance
💰 $4

Independence Squares

(215) 408-9058   www.maplecherry.org/indsq.html
Activity Location: William Way Center,

The Independence Squares was founded in 1988 as a mixed group of gay and
lesbian dancers (with a smattering of straight folk) from Pennsylvania, New
Jersey, and Delaware. The club teaches classes in the Mainstream, Plus, Advanced, and Challenge 1 programs of modern Western Square Dancing. Classes
are open to all and membership is contingent on completing the Basic program
and paying dues. The Squares offers GCA dances on Friday, Saturday, or Sunday
nights once a month. The fee is whatever you feel like paying, and the atmosphere is casual and fun. Dance levels are adjusted to the folks who are there.
Check the web site for the schedule of these dances.

King Squares Square Dancing Club

(610) 356-9368

Activity Location: Wayne Senior Center, Across from PennDot Railroad Station,
Wayne, PA

All ages dance in this very active and large Western Square Dance club that
dances to callers every week. To join the dance, you'll need to be an intermediate
level dancer (Mainstream and Plus). There may be beginner classes in Fall, 2001
to, so you can be a regular club dancer!

☼ Wednesdays   ☎ 7:30-10pm
💰 $5 for visitors, $40/each quarter of the year if you join

Dancing

Square-Open Dancing

Russellville Square Dance

www.voicenet.com/~frysing/dance/index.html

Activity Location: Russellville Grange Hall on Rte. 896, just north of Rte. 10, about halfway between Cochranville and Oxford, PA, (717) 529-6256

Formerly the Cochranville Dance, this is a "dance" not a "club" so beginners can go and learn the calls as they dance. No Contras, all Squares, a live band, and a great hall with wood floors and great acoustics. Come with or without a partner.

☼ 2nd Sat./mo, Sept.-May   ⏰ 8-11pm

Arden Square Dance

(610) 277-0844   http://home.sprynet.com/~rbrat

Activity Location: Arden Guild Hall, 2126 The Highway, Arden, DE

You can sashay here at this Square dance on the very first night. They give instructions and then a dance and you learn while you twirl. International dancing on these evenings also. Check the web site for up-to-date info for other evenings when dances are held.

☼ Wednesdays   ⏰ 7:30-930pm

Tuesday Night Square Dance Guild

St. Mary's Parish Hall on Penn's Campus, 3916 Locust Walk, Phila., PA
(215) 477-8434

This is a local Square dance that has been very popular for years. Come as you are and learn the calls as you dance—no experience (or partner) needed. Many singles and couples too. I've only heard wonderful reports from these dances.

☼ 2nd Tues./mo   ⏰ 7:30-10:00pm

💰 $5

Upper Merion Senior Service Center

(610) 265-4715

Come to this Square dance, learn some calls, and raise your level of dance. All abilities are invited to come and have a lot of fun. George Polk, Jr. is the caller.

☼ Monday afternoons   ⏰ 1-2:30pm

Dancing

Swing

Beat Street

77 Buck Road, Huntingdon Valley, PA
(215) 962-4957 (Bill's cell phone)   paswingguy@earthlink.net

You can trip the light fantastic at a monthly social dance on the first Friday of the month with these dancers, who get a lesson first at 7:30pm. Or you can take group classes or private lessons in Ballroom, Swing, Hustle, and Country dancing during the week. (Bill is the organizer.)

☀ last Fri./mo   ⏰ 7:30-9pm (lesson); 9-? (dancing)

Club 92.5

The Sheraton Building, First Avenue and Gulph Road, King of Prussia, PA
(215) 679-9480 (Larry Tarr)   www.wxtu.com/club925.htm

You can learn four dances, from start to finish, every Wednesday night and then brush up on your style Thursday nights with intermediate and advanced lessons. At Club 92.5, you never need a partner. Class is at 7:30pm, with dancing all evening after the class. Instruction is by Larry Tarr and is hosted by DJ Sound and Lighting.

☀ Wednesdays & Thursdays   ⏰ 7:30pm

Eighth Floor

800 North Delaware Avenue, Philadelphia, PA 19123
(215) 922-1000   www.eighthfloor.com

Cut a rug on Sundays when DJ Perry A. spins for Q102, and many, many patrons do the Hustle on a large dance floor with terrific views. Or come for Swing dancing on Fridays with classes by Greg Avakian.

☀ Sundays

Five Spot Cocktail Lounge & Supper Club

5 South Bank Street, Philadelphia, PA
(215) 574-0070   www.thefivespot.com

Bring some romance and civility back to your nightlife at the Five Spot, where you can dance Swing on Sundays, Tuesdays and Wednesdays. Lessons are given first on all three days. The City Rhythm Orchestra plays on Sundays for a great night of dancing. (By the way, come for Latin dancing on Thursdays.)

☀ Sundays (7pm lesson), Tuesdays, Wednesdays (8pm lessons)
💰 $5/cover charge

Dancing

North Penn Elks Club

Trewigtown Road, Colmar, PA
(215) 997-7688   www.marlindj.com

People are raving about the great dance floor in this terrific new dance place. Lots of West Coast Swing along with Two-step, Waltz, and Hustle. A mixed generational group, mostly single, dances to DJ music until 11:30pm.

☀ Wednesdays   ⏰ 7:30-8:30pm Instruction

Philadelphia Lindy Project

(215) 476-8287 (Greg Avakian)
swingboypa@aol.com   www.phillydance.com
Activity Location: Tokio Ballroom, 122-124 Lombard St., Phila., PA
(215) 922-7181

The Lindy Project is a Thursday night Swing Dance hosted by Greg Avakian and Laurie Zimmerman, with a specialty lesson from 7-8pm and dancing to a DJ from 8-11pm. It's only $8 for the dance plus lesson, and $5 for the dance alone. On Mondays from 7-8:30pm, Greg teaches a beginner lesson in Lindy Hop. On Tuesdays he teaches the same dance, same time, followed by an intermediate lesson in Lindy Hop from 8:30-10pm. So come on by and learn your stuff and then show us what you can do on Thursday nights!

Philadelphia Swing Dance Society

(215) 576-6864   (9am-9pm)   www.swingdance.org
Activity Locations: Commodore Barry Club in West Mt. Airy, Phila., TK club in Conshohocken in the winter, and Germantown Cricket Club, Phila. and Glenside Memorial Hall in the Summer

Try one of the best dance activities in the area, with a Jitterbug lesson at 7pm, a Lindy lesson at 7:45pm, and dancing from 8:45pm to midnight. Get carried away as you move to the hopping sounds of some of the best bands around. This organization was a pioneer in introducing Swing Dancing to Philadelphia, with Jane Liebman and Jim Zaccaria as founding teachers. From time to time there are whole weekends of Swing dancing. Check the outstanding web site for dates and locations of many dance events (not just Swing), or call for fliers. People of all ages and skill levels are welcome, with and without partners. Trust me, these dances are so much fun.

☀ 2nd & 4th Sats./mo   ⏰ 7:30pm-midnight
💰 $10 ($3 off with baked goods); $3 for students

Peppermint Dance Club

Church on the Mall, Plymouth Meeting Mall, Germantown Pike,
Plymouth Meeting, PA
(610) 872-2547

Steve Culver and Betty Krout turn this nontraditional church into a lively
dancing hall with an extensive sound system and a friendly crowd. They teach
all kinds of dances, including Swing, Salsa, Two-step, Waltz, Tango, and Cha-
cha. Beginners and intermediates are all welcome, with lessons specifically
geared to this level. A dance follows, with everyone joining in.

☼ Saturdays, except first Sat./mo   ⏰ 7:15pm-midnight
💰 $6

Temple University, Center City

1515 Market Street, Philadelphia, PA 19102
(215) 204-TUCC tucc@blue.temple.edu   www.temple.edu/tucc

Temple offers a variety of dance classes, including Ballroom, Swing, and
Bellydancing! The teachers are among the best, and the students are all ages,
eager to learn. It's central location makes the classes accessible by public
transportation, and the fees are reasonable. Again and again, Temple comes
through for us with classes you'll really enjoy. Check the web site for current
listings, or call for a catalog to be mailed to your door.

Tokio Ballroom

122-124 Lombard Street, Philadelphia, PA
(215) 922-7181

Intermediate West Coast Swing Dance lessons begin at 7:30pm, with a dance
party from 8:30-11pm. $10 admission includes the lesson, the party, and a hot
buffet. The Tokio has become a center for excellent dancing in Philly.

☼ Sundays   ⏰ 7:30-11pm

Festival Pier

Columbus Boulevard at Spring Garden Street, Philadelphia, PA
(215) 922-2386

A different big-band plays every Thursday evening from 7-9pm on the Delaware
River waterfront during the summer. You can take a swing dance lesson first (at
6:30pm) so you can show off when the dancing starts!

💰 It's all free

Dancing

 **Here are some extra resources to check**

Ballroom
- *Resource Ballroom Dance Association*
  www.cssi.org/usabda
- *Where to Dance Hotline*
  (800) 447-9047
- *United States Amateur Ballroom Dancers Association*
  (215) 855-2711
  Check out Greater Phila. Ballroom Dance Month

Country
- *Country Dance & Song Society*
  P.O. Box 338, Haydenville, MA 01039
  If you want to get a little more serious and go to dancing camp, this group has dances, concerts, song gatherings, festivals, camps, and a newsletter. Write to them for a full schedule of events.

- *Country and Western dance web site*
  www.marlindj.com. Great site! It has lots of pictures for each place, schedules, directions, links, and even dance steps.

Folk
- *Folk Dance Council of Delaware Valley*
  C/O Janet Amato, 7011 Sprague Street, Phila., PA 19119
  Will send listing that tells you where you can folk dance every night! This folk dancing hotline (215-828-8918) provides up-to-date information about upcoming folk dancing in the area.

 **Here are some extra resources to check**

Latin

- *Philly Tango Grapevine*
  P.O. Box 466 , Ambler, PA 19002
  (267) 625-6678, www.dancing.com/phillytango
  Call for information about Argentinian Tango in
  the Philadelphia area.

- *Latin web site: www.bailamos.org or www.salsaflava.com*

Philadelphia Dance & Music Network
(215) 828-8918 (#166)

Square

- *Federation of Delaware Valley Square*
  and Round Dancers, PenDel Branch
  (800) 892-8828

Swing

Web sites for swing bands
- *Total Swing: www.totalswing.com*
- *Hep Cat: www.hepcat.com*
- *Pennsylvania65000: www.pennsylvania65000.com*
- *Royal Crown Revue: www.rcr.com*

- *www.phileswingdance.com An outstanding site for the*
  swing dances in the Greater Philadelphia Region

Dancing

Here are some extra resources to check out

Web Site

- *phillydance.com is a great web site site for all kinds of dancing in the area*

Event

- *Heritage Dance Association*
  Phila., PA 19101-2415
  (215) 849-5384   www.ipcc.com/heritage

  This dance organization sponsors dances many weekends, many of which are in Mt. Airy, are cheap and are well run with instruction. They also sponsor a wonderful (outstanding) dance festival in fall and spring.

Jump into the middle of things, get your hands dirty, fall flat on your face, and then reach for the stars.
- Joan L. Curcio

Discussion Groups

Art, Music & Films • Cultural Issues
Food & Wine • Literature & Reading Groups
Political & Social • Professional Development

Discussion Groups

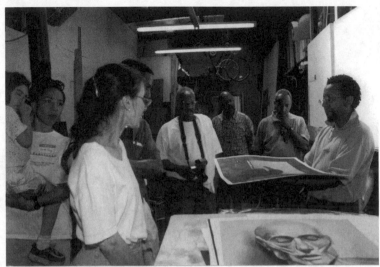

Photo by Karen Mauch

Members of the Art Sanctuary make a studio visit with James Duprée

Foundation for Architecture volunteer tour guide, Ginny Warthen,
giving the new regional tour: "*West Chester*" in July 2000. Tour attendees
are gathered in front of the West Chester Historical Society building

People *like* to talk to each other. It's the way we become acquainted and keep connected with the people we like. We chew the fat, gossip, explore our personal lives, share new information, argue about ideas, compare notes, develop trust, and challenge and synthesize what others think with what we believe. Personally, I *love* to talk. It satisfies my deepest needs to tell people what I think and get their response to my ideas, to my feelings—to *me*. But I also love to know what someone else is thinking and feeling because I'm curious about *them*, and because I have a craving to know things new. My own ideas interest me (maybe too much), but at some point they become stale and I'm dying for a new look and some new facts so I can expand my thinking. If I didn't, I would always be caught in my own narrow personal biases, and I would certainly bore myself to death!

I don't think I'm much different from you. I think most of us look for places where we can find a few friends or a small group with whom to discuss our lives, feelings and ideas on a regular basis.

Discussion groups take these conversations to the next level. These are small groups of about 8 to 25 people who get together for all kinds of discussions that are more than just talk. They have a focus, or topic, that is known ahead of time (unless it shifts during discussion). There are norms or guidelines for the group to follow. These usually include having regular meeting days with starting and ending times, perhaps a requirement to have seen a movie or read a book beforehand, and the assumption that everyone will keep an open mind or at least make a sincere and courteous effort to listen to and understand each others' perspectives. Moderators are often present to support these guidelines to allow for a more deliberate and fair exchange of ideas instead of a verbal free-for-all.

Groups may be set up very differently. Some have a definite agenda while others are more free flowing. Some feature experts on a subject, catalytic speakers, while others simply have open participation by members of the group. In some groups, especially small ones, you need to be a front-and-center, active participant most of the time, while in others you can sit back, say less, listen more, and mull things over. Choosing the style of group that fits *your* style is important if you want to keep up your interest. It is also important to observe and respect the norms of the group when you first go so when you do start to participate you'll be in the swing of things (your "When in Rome..." attitude).

Discussion Groups

Some groups meet for only one session with no anticipation of future sessions. But a number of the groups listed here have regular meetings and are more interesting when at least a certain number of participants return and provide continuity from session to session. It may be an advantage for you to make a limited commitment to a particular group, at least for several sessions. When you go more than once, you'll get to know other "regulars," get an idea about how they approach different issues, and learn how they'll parry this possibility or that new fact. You'll be able to agree and disagree with other members and still have respect and enjoyment for them as people. (Do you know how many people write others off after one disagreement?) You'll form bonds that have depth and increasing mutual understanding. This really becomes *your* discussion group. It's a great feeling to have these kinds of networks, especially when they are outside of any other part of your life and where you belong because you really enjoy it.

If being part of a conversation "salon" interests you, you are *very* lucky to be in Philadelphia where there are so many discussion groups of high caliber covering a tremendous range of subject matter. The ardor for meaningful conversation knows no bounds here. Look at just some of the listings here: In fine arts and music, you can attend conversations about music at the **Curtis Institute of Music** or **Philomel**. You can attend workshops and parties with artists at the **Folklore Project**, or you can take in fine tours and conversations with artists at the **Institute of Contemporary Art**.

For all things Philly, you can go on informal but informative neigh-borhood tours with the **Foundation of Architecture**, attend *Philadelphia Magazine's* salons about local Philadelphians and current topics at **Barnes & Noble**, or learn about the city's history in interactive forums at the **Atwater Kent**. For international connections, look into the wonderful happenings at the **French Chamber of Commerce** or **Alliance Francaise**, as well as nationality groups such as the **German, American-Italy,** or **Lithuanian Societies** that have regular social and informative get-togethers.

If you're a Philadelphia foodie, you might be interested in the **Saturday Morning Breakfast Club** at the **Reading Terminal** (a great place for all kinds of informal conversations, by the way), or any one of a number of friendly wine and beer groups (great homework). For literary discussions, there are specialty groups that focus on one author, such as **Sir Arthur Conan Doyle** (Sherlock Holmes), **P.G. Wodehouse, Jane Austen,** or **Carl Jung.** Others zero in on a topic like sci-fi (**Science Fiction Society**), the future of the world (**World Futurists**), or world affairs (**World Affairs Council,** or the **International Visitors Council**).

There are tons of book discussions meeting regularly at the local **Borders** and **Barnes & Noble** bookstores. Try any one that appeals to you and discuss mysteries, romance, spirituality, or all kinds of novels with others who love to read as much as you do. The book stores in your neighborhood are often responsive to the reading interests of their clientele, so if you have an idea for a book discussion group that you think would attract others, talk to the community events coordinator. And if you don't find a group that wants to discuss your favorite topic, how about starting one of your own? Take a look in the *Inquirer's Sunday Book Review* section. Every week there is a small local book club whose reviews of one book are printed. Each group was started by someone like you.

Those interested in professional networking will want to check out the major organizations that sponsor interactive meetings to help you expand your business or become more marketable. These include the **Greater Philadelphia Chamber of Commerce** and the **Center City Proprietors Organization.** Being a member gives you access to all kinds of events with useful presentations where you can find others who are consumed with the same issues you are. Besides, they have great net-working parties.

There are many opportunities to engage in scholarly forums. Once a year the **Penn Humanities Forum** presents many events around a theme (such as *Style*) and the **Art Alliance** offers superb periodic *Conversations with Legends* with the likes of writer Edward Albee and Metropolitan Opera baritone Robert Merrill. Some require advance reading (**Great Books Discussions**) and others stimulate you to run out and read afterwards. Sometimes we lose track of the fact that this is a city with outstanding universities that offer a wide range of courses at all levels. You don't have to write papers and take tests. If you audit, you just go to class, join the discussions, and learn. Make sure you have the really exciting course schedules on hand to remind you to sign up. The descriptions alone will turn you on!

Discussion Groups

And finally, if you really care about the larger issues in life and society, you can find others who want to talk about how to make the world a better place at nearby **Pendle Hill** and **Fellowship Farm** or in West Philly at the **White Dog Cafe**. These organizations have a sincere interest in offering opportunities to talk about (and maybe act on) socially responsible agendas. Their discussions help people learn, re-group, and reassess their priorities.

Whom will you meet in discussion groups? You will certainly meet people who are interested in things, want to learn, want to bat ideas around to further their own thinking, and want to have their ideas on the table for reaction. You'll meet people who do not want to spend their lives watching TV and who prefer being in an active rather than a passive mode. After all, they got there, didn't they? And they probably enjoy interaction with people, which is why they are out there interacting—the way you are!

Whatever group you choose, do try to find one. The rewards of sharing ideas and expanding your thought-horizons are huge. Small groups have always been the locus of change and development in society. As we raise our personal understanding and expand our connections, we make a difference in our communities, and meet a lot of wonderful people in the process.

Foundation for Architecture tour director, Ken Hinde, giving the *"Society Hill Stroll"* tour in May 2000, on the 200 block of Delancey Street in Society Hill

Discussion Groups

Art, Music & Films

Curtis Institute of Music: *Conversations at Curtis*

1726 Locust Street, Philadelphia, PA 19103
(215) 893-5279   www.curtis.edu

Attend any of a variety of lecture series at Curtis and hear lectures about the influence of renowned conductors or singers in musical history. Each series consists of three or four lectures, free to the Friends of Curtis, but only $5 for the public. Receptions are held first (usually about 6pm), followed by the "Conversations" program. And, by the way, check the web site for info on current outstanding performances by Curtis students/alumni. They are the best!

☎   Ask for Friends of Curtis, and reservations are necessary

Foundation for Architecture

1737 Chestnut Street, Philadelphia, PA 19103
(215) 569-3187   www.foundationforarchitecture.org

These excellent small group walking tours will take you through neighborhoods from Germantown to Queen Village to 18th Century Frankford. Over 40 high-quality, inexpensive tours are offered; plus the Foundation has an 8-week architecture lecture series. Latest tour: "Great Philly Homes by Great Philly Architects."

☼ April to Nov., Sat., Sun.,   ⏰ 11am, 2pm & 6pm
   & weekday evenings
💰 About $8

Harlan Jacobson's: *Talk Cinema*

P.O. Box 686, Croton-on-Hudson, NY 10520
(800) 551-9221   Harlan@Talkcinema.com   www.talkcinema.com
Activity Location: Ritz Theater, 2nd & Walnut Sts. Phila. PA, Ritz in Voorhees, NJ

An interactive film series where participants preview independent and foreign films well before they are released. Take part in discussions with distinguished film critics and filmmakers following the screenings. These are all high quality films, including early showings of Oscar winners. Series fills up quickly so register early.

☼ Some Saturdays   ⏰ 9:30am (door);
💰 $99 for 7 films   10am (film)

Discussion Groups

Institute of Contemporary Art

118 South 36th Street, Philadelphia, PA 19104
(215) 898-7108   www.upenn.edu/ica

At ICA you not only can enjoy the fine exhibit of contemporary artists, but you can hear the perspective of an expert ("Curator's Perspective") on the opening day of the exhibit. These are very interactive, with questions from participants encouraged. You can also hear artists' talks (e.g., "After Mapplethorpe") and panel discussions, and join tours by local artists for certain exhibitions. Call ICA for a newsletter of current events.

☎ Assistant Curator

♿ Free with admission to exhibit ($3 general admission)

Pennsylvania Academy of Fine Arts: *Art-At-Lunch*

118 North Broad Street, Philadelphia, PA 19102
(215) 972-2071   www.pafa.org

For $3 you can hear a first-rate presentation, such as one on Maxfield Parrish or Frank Furness or any number of topics on art, music or Philadelphia history. These fine talks, often related to the current exhibit at the museum, are held during lunch time, so bring your sandwich and prepare to meet others who love art. Other events include a Thursday visiting artist lecture series, free Community Days with musical performances, and more. You really need to receive this newsletter!

Photo by David Graham
Art-At-Lunch

☀ Art-At-Lunch on Wednesdays   ⏰ 12:15pm

Philadelphia Folklore Project

1304 Wharton Street, Philadelphia, PA 19147
(215) 468-7871   www.folkloreproject.org

Check out the brown bag lunches, receptions, and parties with artists held by this wonderful non-profit that pays attention to the experiences and traditions of "ordinary" people like us in the face of powerful institutions. It documents, supports and presents local folk arts in relation to culture and social change through exhibitions, concerts, workshops, and assistance to artists and features discussions on specific issues such as "Folk Arts in the Classroom."

Philomel Baroque: *Concerts & Conversations*
(215) 574-0523   info@philomel.org   www.philomel.org

You can stay after *any* of the chamber concerts and talk to the musicians who are committed to talking with you about the music and the instruments. But in January, Philomel presents a three-concert series (C&C) when soloists will share insights on their music, introduce their instruments, and answer questions from the audience. Also, their *Listener's Guide to Baroque Music* will help you understand what you are listening to and answer some of your questions. Besides regular performances, musicians visit and play at senior centers around the area all year, with interaction built into the events. Get on the mailing list to see where they'll be playing next.

Cultural Issues

Alliance Francaise
1420 Walnut Street, Ste. 700, Philadelphia, PA 19102
(215) 735-5283   www.alliancefrancaisephiladelphia.com
Activity Location: Center City Philadelphia and the Main Line

Take part in this international organization and learn about France through any number of French classes and/or a plethora of exciting cultural activities. Expand your French lingo during monthly lunches in Center City, Chestnut Hill, and the Main Line; book clubs; films; happy hours and dinner dance; wine tastings; concerts; excellent lecture discussions, and many other events. And if you really want to kick up your heels French style, celebrate Bastille Day with Alliance in July!

🏦 Yearly membership $45

Instructors and students at a cocktail party at the Alliance Francaise

Discussion Groups

America-Italy Society

1420 Walnut Street, Suite 1206, Philadelphia, PA 19102
(215) 735-3250   americaitalysociety@rcn.com

Regular Italian lunches are the tip of the iceberg offered by the America-Italy Society, where you can practice your conversational Italian. But there are a host of other activities here: Lecture-discussions about Italian painters, about Italian music, and about Italy; films; trips to NYC art museums; concerts with members of the Philadelphia Orchestra; and a large language school with classes on literature and conversation. Ciao!

Atwater Kent Museum

15 South 7th Street, Philadelphia, PA 19106
(215) 922-3031   www.philadelphiahistory.org

The Atwater Kent is about all things Philadelphia. Take a look at the active series of programs at this museum of Philadelphia history and you'll want to know more about this amazing city. Just a few events this museum has sponsored: "Riding the Rails," a fall trip on most of the rails in and around the city as a study of Philadelphia's transportation system; a tour of local breweries every October; a summer music series in the AK garden; a street food festival in May specializing in Philly foods; and in February a "Books & Authors" series with discussions. Also you can find special presentations related to current exhibits. Truly a place for Philadelphiaphiles!

💰 $3 entrance; $2 students & seniors

Balch Institute for Ethnic Studies

18 South 7th Street, Philadelphia, PA 19106
(215) 925-8090   www.balchinstitute.org

Learn about the immigrant experiences and cultural traditions that represent your background and those of your neighbors in programs and workshops for people of all ages. Balch programs encourage lively discussions about public programs, such as the work of Asian women filmmakers as they explore family roots and relationships. These are extremely thoughtful and exciting programs with discussion and learning for everyone present. Check the web site for current programs that would interest you.

Discussion Groups

Church of the Advocate: *Art Sanctuary*

1801 West Diamond Street, Philadelphia, PA 19121
(215) 232-4485   www.artsanctuary.org

Photo by Karen Mauch
A studio visit with
James Duprée

Art Sanctuary is an African-American lecture and performance series designed to bring the best of our contemporary creators of arts and letters to speak, read, perform, exhibit, and demonstrate their art in a stunning cathedral in the heart of the black community. Open to all, Sanctuary presents lectures, performances and workshops with opportunities to be involved and meet featured performers such as Terry Gillen and John Edgar Wideman. Occasional trips to places like Harlem's Schomburg Center on Black Culture are part of the exciting schedule. Call for current material on these outstanding events.

Free Library of Philadelphia/Community College of Philadelphia: *Café for the Mind*

1901 Vine Street, Philadelphia, PA 19103
(215) 686-5415   www.library.phila.gov

Activity Location: The Library (above address) or
Community College of Philadelphia, 18th & Spring Garden Sts., Phila. PA

You and I (the public) are invited to join a group of college scholars for coffee and discussion in a series of diverse and interesting contemporary topics, such as, "Love and Death: Readings by Samuel Beckett and Other Dramatists," and "Fractals II: The Construction of Sound and Image." Also, don't forget that all branches of the Free Library hold presentations and discussions on a frequent and regular basis. Stop by and pick up the newsletter for upcoming events. (You'll be amazed at the quality and variety!) Free.

☼ Tuesdays 🕰 6:30-8:00pm

Friends of Landmarks

321 South 4th Street, Philadelphia, PA 19106
(215) 925-2251   landmarks4@aol.com

The mission of this group is to sponsor cultural and fun events that raise money to support four fine historical house museums (Physick, Powel, Grumblethorpe, and Waynesborough). An arm of the Philadelphia Society for the Preservation of Landmarks, Friends is for people 21-45. Their activities include many outings, parties, trips, and other exciting events. Benefits include tours of historical places, notice of lectures (such as "Childhood in the 18th Century" and "Spotting Fakes and Forgeries in Antiques"), Oktoberfest, Holiday Cheer, wine tastings at the museum-houses, and a newsletter.

Discussion Groups

International Visitors Council of Philadelphia

1515 Arch Street, Philadelphia, PA 19103
(215) 683-0999   www.ivc.org

If you'd enjoy one-on-one contact with the world's rising leaders, you should look into this group that offers the opportunity to socialize with international visitors here for State Department high-level exchange programs. As a member, you can be a host for the home-stay program, or invite guests for receptions or dinners in your home. If you'd be more interested in an international salon, attend the receptions at the Warwick on the first Wednesday of the month; international visitors, members, and non-members are welcome. Or try one of the Conversations with International Visitors which take place in an upscale restaurant three or four times a year. Compass is the young members group (20-45) that participates in all functions, including activities of its own.

💰 $50/yr membership for networking and socializing

Philadelphia Art Alliance: *Conversations With Legends*

251 South 18th Street, Philadelphia, PA
(215) 545-4302

Get up close to and talk with legendary figures in the art world at these out-standing events at the Art Alliance. You will hear them interviewed by an expert in their field, followed by questions and perhaps discussion in the audience. People such as Edward Albee, Metropolitan Opera singer Regina Resnick, and movie musicals star Jane Powell are examples of the inspiring legends the Art Alliance has brought for us all to hear. You also won't want to miss the well-attended art programs at the Alliance, often related to the current exhibits.

⏰ 7pm
💰 $15 non-members

Philadelphia Magazine: *Salon Series*

(215) 665-0716   www.barnesandnoble.com
Activity Location: Barnes & Noble, 1805 Walnut St., Phila., PA

For an insider's view of what's happening in Philadelphia and an opportunity to add your 50 cents, join this monthly group sponsored by Barnes & Noble that discusses current articles from *Philadelphia Magazine*. Meet the writers from *PM* and sometimes the subject of their work. For example, they've had the editors of the "Best of Philly" issues, "Best Docs," and those who've written profiles of Philadelphia personalities in the political and entertainment world. You'll certainly learn about the city and have fun meeting your Philadelphia neighbors.

☀ One Weds./mo   ⏰ 7pm

Discussion Groups

Philosophy Discussion Series at Barnes & Noble, Center City: Dialogue on the Square

1805 Walnut Street, Philadelphia, PA
(215) 665-0716   www.barnesandnoble.com

This popular evening series (since 1997) hosted by Temple University Chair Richard Shusterman explores philosophical topics with prominent authors. Discuss writers from Plato to Jacques Derrida, with those who have published books about them. At least 50 people regularly show up for this non-academic look at academic topics.

Food & Wine

IWC (Independent Wine Club)

P.O. Box 1478, Havertown, PA 19083
(610) 649-9936   iwcwine@aol.com
Activity Location: Jack's Firehouse, 2130 Fairmount Ave., Phila., PA

If you want to know which wine goes with what meat, or you just enjoy learning about types and styles of wine, you'll want to try IWC's wine tastings with lectures and discussions. They are offered almost every Thursday evening, with lots of time for sampling and socializing. IWC also offers other events, such as excellent one-night courses on Monday and Tuesday evenings. Call for a newsletter to whet your palate.

☼ Tastings many Wednesdays & Thursdays   ☲ 7-9pm
✆ Neal Ewing
💰 $35-$55 for each event for non-members

Pennsylvania General Store: *The Breakfast Club*

Reading Terminal Market, 12th & Arch Streets, Philadelphia, PA
(215) 592-0455

My friend Alonna Smith recently conducted a "Who Makes the Best Bagel," tasting early one Saturday at the Market and it was a lot of fun—besides giving great info about bagels! It's not just dyed-in-the-wool foodies who will enjoy the variety of programs in this informal group that has discussions about organic foods, Pennsylvania Dutch cooking, and the most important ingredients to have in your kitchen. We 'sometime-cooks' get a lot out of it as well. One of the best things about the Breakfast Club is you can shop for terrific Terminal foods when you're done. (Don't forget to get a pretzel from Lancaster County.) The Reading Terminal Market is a cultural jewel in Philadelphia, open Monday to Saturday.

☼ Saturdays from October-July   ☲ 9:30-10:30am

Discussion Groups

Sugar Mom's

225 Church Street, Philadelphia, PA 19106
(215) 925-8219

Mom's makes beer more interesting than it already is with occasional seasonal learn-about-beer parties where brewers and other experts talk about the various characteristics of beer and beer-making processes. You can compare your notes and favorites with other enthusiasts. Informal and lots of fun. Call to find out when the next event will be held, or keep checking in the *Philadelphia Weekly* or *City Paper*.

Literature & Reading Groups

Barnes & Noble, Rosemont: Mystery Book Club

720-730 Lancaster Avenue, Rosemont, PA
(610) 520-0355   www.barnesandnoble.com

We hear that the members of the book clubs in this store would cause pain and mayhem if any of the clubs were cancelled—that's how devoted they are. And look at all the choices! The Mystery Group discusses award winning British and American authors who sometimes show up to read aloud to the group. But there are also groups for Romance Reading, Fiction Books, a Film Forum Discussion Group, a Speculative Fiction Readers Group, an African-American Readers Group and a Philosophy of Religion Book Club. Now really, what else could you want?

Barnes & Noble, Plymouth Meeting

2300 Chemical Road, Plymouth Meeting, PA 19462
(610) 567-2900   www.barnesandnoble.com

One of the new kids on the block, this is a beautiful new bookstore located nicely for the northwestern suburbs. There are already a number of book clubs scheduled for a variety of interests. My favorite is the Book & Film Group, in which books based on popular movies are featured and discussed (3rd Wed./mo at 7pm). There is a Fantasy Book Group (on the 3rd Sun./mo at 6pm), a Mystery Book Group (last Tues./mo at 6pm), and a Literary-Fiction group (last Sun./mo at 6pm). There is a café where you can scan new books to buy, and music on some evenings. Stop by, pick up a flier, and choose your group.

☀ Mondays to Saturdays   🕐 9am-llpm
    Sundays   11am-llpm

Discussion Groups

Bookfriends Association of Philadelphia

(215) 743-1690

Activity Location: Williamson's Restaurant, GSB, City Line Ave., Phila. PA

If you're curious about why and how books get to be written, look into this comfortable but very interesting book group that has been meeting for over 25 years. Members hold three dinner meetings a year (usually October, February and May) with talk and discussion about and with local recently published authors.

💰 Membership $10 for 3 events, then about $25/30 for dinner

Borders Books, Chestnut Hill: *Book Groups*

8701 Germantown Avenue, Philadelphia, PA 19118
(215) 248-1213   www.borders.com

Chestnut Hill Borders has a number of very creative ongoing book discussion groups: Spiritually Speaking, a discussion of not necessarily Christian literature (such as *Seven Habits of Highly Effective People*) viewed from a Christian perspective, and People of the Book that holds Judaica-oriented book discussions. Other groups include the African-American book group that features black authors, a fiction group that reads hot popular paperbacks, a semi-regular Star Trek Group, and the Creative Writing Group whose members do writing exercises in the group. Talk to the community representative if you want to start a book club about your specific interest. They're free.

Borders Books, Springfield: *Book Groups*

1001 Baltimore Pike, Springfield, PA 19064
(610) 543-8588   www.borders.com

Expect a good turnout for these book groups with interesting themes. Along with the fiction (classics and contemporary), mystery and sci-fi groups, there is a group talking about Gay and Lesbian literature, a creative writing group (Pen in Hand), Books that Changed My Life, and the Spirituality Book Discussion Group (non-denominational, natch). You've got to find something for yourself here!

💰 Free

Discussion Groups

Friday Morning Book Group

Unitarian Society of Germantown, 6511 Lincoln Drive, Philadelphia, PA 19119
(215) 844-1157

Activity Location: Meets in members' homes

This small but very friendly group likes to read and discuss all types of books, usually picked from the public library.

☼ Usually 1st Fri./mo   ⏲ 10am

💰 Free

Great Books Program

(215) 576-8836   (800) 222-5870   ngwash@temple.edu   www.greatbooks.org

Read the finest of literature with people in Great Books groups, using "the shared inquiry method of discussion" led by a trained leader. These fine, sophisticated discussions held all around the city are about the ideas that have sustained men and women since the beginning. (One group meets every other Tuesday from 7-9pm at the central branch of the Free Library.) These discussions are free and engaging.

Jane Austen Society

(610) 642-1719 or national: (573) 474-9682

The Southeastern Pennsylvania region of the Jane Austen Society meets four times a year for a luncheon, with a speaker and much discussion about their favorite author. They also celebrate her birthday in December. People who meet at the regional meetings often form their own local book discussion meetings.

P.G. Wodehouse Society, Philadelphia Chapter

(609) 465-3043

Activity Location: Dickens Inn, 2nd & Pine Sts., Phila., PA (215) 928-9307

You don't have to be a literary expert to join the Wodehouse group at the Dickens Inn every other month for lunch on a Sunday afternoon. Au contraire—you only have to enjoy the books and his particular brand of humor! His fans come to take 'noms de plume,' toast his whimsy, raise money for the newts at the Philadelphia Zoo, read stories aloud and such, all in a delightfully unserious vein. This crowd also has picnics and travels to national Wodehouse conventions together. (The national conference will be in Philadelphia in October 2001.) Don't come to their meetings for a pretentious literary experience (even though he *is* an excellent writer); come to laugh and have fun, Wodehouse style.

☼ One Sunday every other month   ⏲ 1pm

Discussion Groups

Philadelphia Science Fiction Society (PSFS)

1 (877) 656-3914 (hot line)   www.psfs.org

Activity Location: Currently meets at International House, 37th & Chestnut St., Phila., PA

This group meets monthly to discuss and promote science fiction and fantasy in literature, the arts, and popular culture. You'll hear guest speakers such as writers, editors, artists, and publishers, and then discuss what you've heard in a general "Meet and Greet" hour. PSFS sponsors an annual science fiction conference (*Philcon*, www.philcon.org), and also has many special interest subgroups such as the Book Discussion Group and the Special Events Group (which attends science fiction and fantasy movies and other events). And don't forget the Halloween Party—it's terrific! Check out the web site or call for info.

☀ 2nd Fri./mo

🌑 8pm business meeting

💰 $18/yr for individuals; $30/yr for couples

9pm program

Political, Social & Personal Growth

Brandywine Peace Community: *Monthly Potluck Dinner*

P.O. Box 81, Swarthmore, PA 19081

(610) 544-1818   www.geocities.com/brandywinepeace/index.htm

Activity Location: University Lutheran Church, 3637 Chestnut St., Phila., PA

Military disarmament, peace and justice are the focus of this 22-year-old organization. Each month the community hosts a potluck dinner, followed by a close up discussion with a speaker or film to inform the audience. Recent topics have included "The Effects of the Sanctions Against Iraq" and "Money and Electioneering: Whose Politics Is It Anyway?" Members also conduct non-violent demonstrations for peace.

☀ 2nd Sun./mo except May & August

🌑 4:30-5:30pm potluck

✉ Robert Smith

5:30-7pm program

💰 Free

Discussion Groups

Bryn Mawr Presbyterian Church: *Community Forums*
625 Montgomery Avenue, Bryn Mawr, PA 19010
(610) 525-2821   www.bmpc.org

You can find many discussion opportunities at the fine community forums offered at the BMP Church where people explore issues of significance in contemporary society. Known speakers such as Daniel Shorr, Donna Shalala, and Mary Pipher (*Saving Ophelia*) make presentations which are followed by informal discussions. There is also a literature group, a Great Decisions (world events discussions) group, and more offered by the Presbyterian women. The general public is invited to take part in these activities.

Fellowship Farm
2488 Sanatoga Road, Pottstown, PA 19464
(610) 326-3008   www.fellowshipfarm.org

In this beautiful natural setting near Pottstown, you can feel the tension fall away as you take part in the educational and personal growth programs offered here. The essense of the Farm is to promote equality and justice; the diverse community you meet here addresses these issues. Help to create an interdependent sense of community by volunteering for activities around *your* sense of purpose. You can also volunteer for projects to help in the upkeep and development of Fellowship Farm and it's mission. This place is *all* about community and is eager to welcome new participants.

Discussion Groups

Henry George School of Social Science

413 S 10th Street, Philadelphia, PA 19147
(215) 922-4278

This school offers classes in the economic ideas and social philosophy of Henry George. Examples of the interesting classes offered are: "Applied Economics, Protection & International Trade," "The Philadelphia Dilemma," "World Perspectives," and more. Classes are free with a small ($15) materials charge.

☼ Tuesdays, Wednesdays, Thursdays   ⏰ 7-9pm

Men's International Peace Exchange

P.O. Box 36, Swarthmore, PA 19081
(610) 872-8178   mipe00@aol.com   www.PeaceExchange.org

Although MIPE does not have frequent discussion meetings, it hosts a yearly conference in October that provides terrific opportunities for men and women interested in all areas of peace and non-violence to meet each other, exchange ideas and develop plans for action. As members put it, these activities give a port-of-call to "many men and women seeking a place to hang their peacemaking hats." Examples of conference themes: "Changing a Culture: Building a Community of Support."

Mt. Airy Learning Tree: *A Survey of Philadelphia History*

6601 Greene Street, Philadelphia, PA 19119
(215) 843-6333   malttree@aol.com   www.mtairylearningtree.org

Delve deeply into the people, places and events of Philadelphia's colorful past in this in-depth discussion class at MALT. Or you can read and discuss "The Philosophy of Happiness" or take "A Journey Through the African Continent" with other enthusiastic folks. Of course, different classes of this caliber as well as discussion groups about books, jewelry, professional development, and more are offered each semester, so you'll need the latest catalog from MALT to choose where you jump in. I'm not kidding: The classes here are outstanding.

Discussion Groups

Pendle Hill

338 Plush Mill Road, Wallingford, PA 19086
(610) 566-4507   www.pendlehill.org

Pendle Hill is a place that invites seekers, people who choose to explore their spiritual path alone as well as in the company of fellow travelers. There is a wide selection of weekend workshops and retreats with topics ranging from artistic workshops for learning art ("Painting on Cloth"), poetry, and street theater to spiritual programs that cross all spiritual lines, such as a weekend on spiritual autobiography to personal growth programs, including massage and energy work. Founded by the Quakers in 1930, this pastoral retreat center is a haven for serenity, contemplation, and community.

Penn Humanities Forum

University of Pennsylvania, 3619 Locust Walk, Philadelphia, PA 19104
(215) 898-8220   humanities@sas.upenn.edu   http://humanities.sas.upenn.edu

Scholars and the community meet on common ground to explore themes of importance to all of us at this year-long forum with regular speakers, seminars, courses and cultural programs. The theme in 2001 was *Style*. These are exceedingly fine presentations and discussions that stimulate and encourage our thinking in an age of sound bytes. Call for a brochure to see the outstanding speaker/discussants at these events. Also, try the walking tours provided by Penn History graduate students as part of the program.

Philadelphia Association of Critical Thinking

P.O. Box 1131, North Wales, PA 19454
(215) 885-2089   www.phact.org

If you like tough questions and don't always accept the first answer you get and if you like to challenge unsupported information, you may enjoy this group. PhACT encourages responsible scientific investigation of paranormal and fringe-science claims. Their activities include a newsletter and educational meetings and lectures, such as "Keeping Fiction Out of Science," "How Do You Know That's Impossible?," and "Fanaticism in Cyberspace." This is a well-educated and thoughtful group that asks, "What's the evidence?" Check the web site for topics of meetings over the last few years.

Discussion Groups

Philadelphia Ethical Society: *Weekly Sunday Platform*

1906 South Rittenhouse Square, Philadelphia, PA 19103
(215) 735-3456

For years the Ethical Society has provided rich opportunities to explore and discuss issues that relate to our values and ethical principles. The *Weekly Sunday Platform* begins with a speaker presentation followed by coffee and exciting thought-provoking discussions. Call for information about other forums there, such as a monthly salon and a bimonthly video (usually of a famous speaker like Noam Chomsky), with discussion that focuses on contemporary political and social issues.

☼ Sundays   ⏰ 11am

💰 Free

Results (Responsibility for Ending Starvation Using Legistration, Trim-Tabbing and Support)

(215) 247-5916   www.results.action.org
Activity Location: Various members' homes

This is a grassroots citizen's lobby whose goal is to end hunger and poverty. Twice monthly members have discussion and letter writing sessions on topics like primary healthcare for children and economic reform. Microcredit "legistration" is a timely subject for them. Call to find out what that is.

💰 $25/yr suggested donation

C.G. Jung Society of West Jersey

(215) 985-4525   http://region.philly.com/community/wjjung
Activity Location: Moorestown Community House, 16 E. Main St., Moorestown, NJ

The C.G. Jung Society of West Jersey is a public lecture series which is offered in an open and friendly atmosphere. The lectures and discussions are focused on the applications of Carl Jung's thought to understanding our culture and ourselves. Jung utilized mythology, fairy tales, and folk tales as they relate to the struggles we all face in our lives (for example, "Through the Dark Forest: Drawing Inner Wisdom from the Adventures of Little Red Riding Hood"). Also, for serious students of Jung, there are the Philadelphia Jung Seminars eight weekends a year in Center City.

☼ Sunday afternoons, twice a month

💰 Nonmembers $10 at the door; Membership $60 admits you to 12 lectures

Discussion Groups

White Dog Cafe: *Table Talks—Serving Food with Thought*

3420 Sansom Street, Philadelphia, PA 19104
(215) 386-9224   info@whitedog.com   www.whitedog.com

Enjoy a wonderful three-course dinner followed by a speaker and discussion. Make a reservation, and if you are attending alone you will be seated at a table with others. Recent topics include "Cloning and the Genetic Revolution," "Challenge of Cyberspace and Constitutional Rights," and "The Corporate Response to the Global Warming Debate." The White Dog sponsors many types of speakers/discussion dinner events that focus on interesting current topics and human relationship topics, such as *Monday Storytelling Nights*. Get on the mailing list—and try these topnotch evenings!

☀ Mondays

💰 $30 per person, $25 seniors and students

Table Talk on "Environmental Justice" at the White Dog Cafe with Judy Wicks introducing former US Congressman, Peter Kostmayer

Discussion Groups

World Affairs Council of Philadelphia

1314 Chestnut Street, Philadelphia, PA 19107
(215) 731-1100   wac@libertynet.org   www.libertynet.org/~wac
Activity Location: 1314 Chestnut St. and Center City Hotels

The Council is a major organization helping to educate the public about world and domestic policy issues. To do this, it sponsors informative dinners, discussions, lectures, seminars, exhibits, and films. The distinguished speaker series hosts extremely interesting people such as Ted Turner, Madeline Albright, and Queen Noor and a regular book club with author appearances. The tours are both substantive and fun, ranging from having tea at the British Embassy to visiting special art exhibitions. Members enjoy business and social networking. Call for the rich schedule of events and you'll find that this group is especially welcoming to newcomers.

💰 $10-$15 for most speaker events, meals additional

World Future Society

(215) 895-2455 (A.Shostak)   shostaka@drexel.edu   www.wfs.org
Activity Location: currently at the Ethical Culture Society, 1904 Walnut, Phila. PA

The WFS local chapter holds regular meetings to discuss the social and technological developments shaping the future. Lively audience participation follows talks on "Foods of the Future" (Restaurant School presentation), "Corporate Culture in 2010," and "Space Settlements" (with the L-5 Society). Not a heavy academic thing—these debates are exciting. With 35,000 members in 72 countries, this organization has terrific national conferences once a year, with Philadelphia WFS hosting in 2002. Look for *The Futurist* in local bookstores.

☼ 6 meetings between September and May

Professional Development

Center City Proprietors Association

1528 Walnut Street, Su 2020, Philadelphia, PA 19102
(215) 545-7766   www.centercityproprietors.org

Business owners around Center City will find useful professional support and networking opportunities in this vital group. Members meet throughout the year for seminars such as "Web 101" and "Motivating without Money," specifically designed to help the small entrepreneur. They also enjoy casual networking/social opportunities, including the *City Stroll*, business card exchanges, marketing discussions, and a series, *Meet the Presses*, when journalists are invited to share ideas on particular topics such as culinary arts, design and architecture, and health care. These events are not expensive. Call for info.

Discussion Groups

Macintosh Business Users Society (MacBUS)   Photo by Irv Herzog

Free Library of Philadelphia, Central Branch

1901 Vine Street, Skyline Room, Philadelphia, PA 19103
(215) 686-5436   www.library.phila.gov

This series of workshops by the Workplace Career and Job Information Center
of the Free Library helps you identify your employment interests, learn about
the needs of specific employers, and develop the skills you need to find a better
job. Recent topics include "Decision-making and the Job Search Process,"
"Libraryland: a World of Job-hunting Resources," and "Resume Writing, and
Interviewing Skills." An added bonus is the use of the center's vast career
resources during the week. If you are exploring your job situation, take advantage of the considerable expertise you will find here. Free.

:☀: Workshop on Wednesdays   🕑 6:30-8:30pm

Greater Philadelphia Chamber of Commerce:
Business AfterHours/Business BeforeHours

200 South Broad Street, Philadelphia, PA 19102
(215) 545-1234   www.gpcc.com

This is a great place to enjoy an interesting professional community. Besides
taking part in seminars for small businesses, start-up businesses, and home-
based businesses, as well as workshops on every conceivable issue useful for
professional development, these people enjoy themselves! Informal networking
in casual settings takes place several times monthly and often includes social
events such as attending a Sixers Game, golf outing, or the William Penn Gala.
An essential networking venue for entrepreneurs.

🖢 $15 BAH for non-members; membership fees vary

Discussion Groups

Macintosh Business Users Society (MacBUS)
P.O. Box 96, Glenside, PA 19038
(215) 732-8727   www.macbus.org
Activity Location: Currently at the FMC, 4th & Chestnut Sts., Phila., PA

MacBUS is one of the few user groups around to focus on business and professional uses of the Macintosh. Come to hear excellent speakers, such as presenters
from Adobe or Apple who will explain new Mac software. Bring your Mac
problems to the experts within the group who could take apart your computer
and put it back with no missing parts five times over. Any questions you have
will get answered, even if you have to give your shoe size when you introduce
yourself. Lots of problems are solved along with terrific good humor (including
bad jokes, often mine). If you're a Mac user, probably the single best tool you
can give yourself is a membership in MacBUS.

☼ Last Tues./mo   ⏰ 6:30-9:30pm
💰 $40/yr

National Association of Women Business Owners
Park Towne Place, Su 108 North, Philadelphia, PA 19130
(215) 557-9917   www.nawbophila.org

This is an established business woman to business woman networking organization that has monthly meetings with speaker/discussions, professional peer
interaction, and events just for socializing. They learn from each other and have
fun besides. Activities are held in Center City and the surrounding suburbs.

Panorama Club Toastmasters
(215) 546-4409   www.toastmasters.org
Activity Location: Panorama Club, 1500 Locust St., 46th flr, Phila. PA

Overcome your fear of public speaking in your local branch of Toastmasters.
There are 24 chapters in Philadelphia alone so there's got to be one near you!
You'll brush up on presentation skills and techniques, get feedback from others
new to public speaking, and have numerous opportunities to speak with
confidence. It's a plus that the meeting room offers a great view of the city.
(Maybe takes your mind off your upcoming speech?) Planned and extemporane-
ous presentations are made at each meeting. Another Toastmaster group meets
at the Northwest branch at the Philadelphia College of Textiles in Hayward Hall
(usually room 113), on the first and third Wednesdays of the month from
7:30pm to 9pm. Call: (215) 482-8765 for more information.

☼ Every other Wednesday   ⏰ 7:30-9pm
💰 $16 one-time fee, $48 yr dues

A closer look at...

University of Pennsylvania College of General Studies: Non-Credit Programs for Adults

3440 Market Street, Suite 100, Philadelphia, PA 19104

(215) 898-6479   www.sas.upenn.edu/cgs

The university offers non-credit programs for professional development and personal enrichment. These seminars and workshops for adults, which meet on and off campus, are presented throughout the year in the evening, on weekends, and during the day. There is a wide selection of programs in writing, communication, personal development, trips and tours, financial management, history, contemporary issues, music, art, literature, anthropology, and archaeology." (from UPenn catalog) Examples of courses that have been offered are: *Philadelphia and the City Beautiful Movement; The Golden Age of American Cinema: Classic Films from 1900-1950; The Musical World of Cole Porter; Diversity;* and *The Culture of Medicine and Alternative Health Beliefs*. UPenn also sponsors trips and tours, such as a *Trip to the Santa Fe Opera* (at time of writing, 5 days is $2645 and includes everything but lunch!) Note the special fees for seniors. Check out the interesting looking Penn lectures by Penn faculty, which are open to the public for $10.

💰   Non-credit programs about $50/4-hour session

Temple University Center City: Institute for Continuing Studies

1616 Walnut Street, Philadelphia, PA 19103

(215) 204-6946   www.temple.edu/TUCC

"ICS is a non-credit program at TUCC dedicated to the personal enrichment of adult students. For the past 20 years, we've continued to offer a wide variety of practical, provocative, and unusual courses ranging from *Wine Appreciation* to *Belly Dancing*. Our courses are designed for adults and involve stimulating discussion and ample opportunity to meet and socialize with like-minded individuals." (from TUCC catalog) Many courses encourage lively discussion and sharing of ideas, like *Connecting in Philadelphia* (I'm shameless) and *Comedy Improvisation 101*. If you see a course by Harrison Ridley on some aspect of jazz, sign up quick because the course is quickly filled. Mr. Ridley is a gem, and does he ever know his jazz in a personal way. Be sure to check the many TARP courses (Temple Association for Retired Persons), such as *Singing Voices of TARP* (your chance to sing for fun and pleasure), *Learning at Lunch* (all kinds of lunchtime lecture/discussions), or *Shakespeare for Fun* (amazing).

Discussion Groups

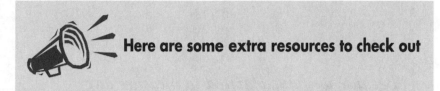

Here are some extra resources to check out

Excellent discussions can be found in adult education classes.

Lifelong Learning (non-credit) courses can be found at:

The Art Institute of Philadelphia	*(800) 275-2474*
University of the Arts	*(215) 717-6095*
Philadelphia University	*(215) 951-2900*
Villanova University	*(610) 519-5555*
Drexel University	*(800) 2 DREXEL*
Harcum The Learning College	*(800) 345-2600*
Menlha Buddhist Center	*(215) 848-4644*
Aware: Women's Self Defense	*(215) 241-5720*
Chestnut Hill College	*(215) 248-7125*
Moore College of Art	*(215) 965-4014*
Immaculata College	*(610) 647-4400*
Rosemont College	*(610) 527-0200*
Cabrini College	*(610) 902-8600*
Holy Family College	*(215) 637-7203*
PA Academy Fine Arts	*(215) 972-7632*
West Chester University	*(610) 436-1009*
Penn State University, Abington	*(215) 881-7351*
Community College of Phila.	*(215) 751-8010*
St. Joseph's University	*(610) 660-2000*

"Because we have learned to measure our manhood by things that can be quantified, we become poor in experiencing the richness of the small daily pleasures that must be savored moment by moment."

~ Sam Keene

Film

Film Discussion Groups • Film Festivals
Film Series • Filmmakers' Activities
Travel and Cultural Films

Film

Scribe filmmakers working in neighborhood outreach *Community Visions* Project.

M ost of us love going to the movies. It's a major American pastime. But my neighborhood theater doesn't feel like a place where I can meet other film lovers to discuss the meaning of the films I've see there. Does yours? So there I am, filled with all kinds of reactions to the film, and no place to hash it over. I *always* want to talk about a movie I've just seen. (What did *this* mean? Why did she do *that*? Etc.) Talking about it takes the movie experience to another level for me. It also provides a jump-off point for discussing why people do what they do with a bunch of thoughtful people. So where can you find places to hang out and discuss movies?

Never fear. Interesting movie discussions are happening in any number of fine film groups all around the area, with "Why did that happen?" conversations built into film-watching evenings. You'll find that it's especially nice to talk with others who have *chosen* that particular movie because they have knowledge about and interest in the subject of the film. You'll probably see them again and again at similar programs, and lo, a community will start to develop. For example, there is a following that attends travel documentaries at the **Geographical Society**. They attend regular presentations in Center City where the filmmaker/ explorer often is the speaker. But they also have brunches, hear speakers and take trips to nearby cities to see similar high-quality films about other parts of the world.

One very good reason to attend organized cinema programs is that the films have been selected by an expert who thinks they have merit in some subject area. Whether it's a classic film, a fine international independent film, a totally outrageous horror flick, or a top rated sci-fi movie—*someone* has decided it is special enough in a certain category to invite you to see it (and not just to make the money from your ticket). Attending a movie night in these groups greatly reduces the chances of seeing a movie so bad that you wish you'd stayed home. (I hate it when that happens.)

If you want to meet the filmmaker, actors, director, or others intimately involved in making the film you're seeing, look for them at festivals and film series because they frequently show up to lead discussions and answer questions when their film is shown. Also, experts on the film topic, or just experts in cinema overall, may be present to raise

Film

points that the audience may not have tuned in to, but which make the film more meaningful. It's really exciting when there are events and workshops that encourage you to jump in and get active in all areas of films and filmmaking. Organizations that offer such events, such as the **International Festival of World Cinema** and **Films at the Prince**, are committed to developing and maintaining a community of those who take their film watching seriously (even if they are campy flicks). Films are, after all, an educational experience, especially if the subject is human nature. And learning by watching movies...well, is there any way of learning that is more fun than that?

So, where will you find all these terrific activities? The Film chapter is organized into *Film Discussion Groups, Film Festivals, Film Series,* and *Filmmaker Activities,* depending on the primary focus of the group.

There's certainly plenty of talking going on! Among the *Film Discussion Groups* is a local branch of the national **Harlan Jacobson's Talk Cinema** at the Ritz in Haddonfield that chooses outstanding films to see and discuss. And take a look at the first-rate offerings from the **Villanova Film Series** for a discussion group led by an expert speaker following the film. Whichever style suits you best, the main function of these groups is to encourage stimulating conversation. A more recent addition to local film activities has been the outstanding **Film at the Prince** (Theater), which hosts film activities of all kinds (for example, *Classics for the Big Screen*).

Film Festivals attract a community who want to see movies with particular themes, and you're likely to find the same people going to many of these films over the life of the festival. Some festivals include discussion groups and Q & A, but even when they're not planned, discussions frequently break out at intermission or around the refreshment table (Don't they all have refreshment tables?) because people attending share an interest in the festival subject. The festivals in this town are excellent. To name just a few: the well-known **International Festival of World Cinema**, which undergoes changes in format from year to year, but always includes films of high quality. In different years, the public has been a part of "cine-cafes," discussions with directors and screen-writers, seminars, and great parties as the films opened and closed. There is a broad spectrum of film themes, from the **Features at Five** (a terrific independent film festival) to the erudite **Margaret Mead Festival**, to the **Braniff Festival** featuring outdoor climbing adventures. And the **International Gay and Lesbian Festival** is days and days of great films with tons of creative activities for all to enjoy.

Film Series are regularly shown films chosen because they speak to a common theme (i.e., feminism, horror, etc.), because they are unusual (**Secret Cinema, Exhumed Films**), or just because they are fine entertainment. The films may be shown in a comfortable venue (outside at **Frankford Style**), in an accessible venue (**Free Library**), and for reasonable cost, if not free. A truly all-evening of outstanding entertainment happens every **Wednesday Night at the (Philadelphia) Art Museum**, in which a film event is accompanied by an eclectic mix of music, performances, tours, demonstrations, and food—all related to one topic. During the Van Gogh exhibit, for example, the theme was "Night Cafe," with a gallery talk on the artistic impressions of Van Gogh and Monet with a related movie *(The Sweet Hereafter* by Egoyan). By the way, there is also a **Members Film Club** at the Art Museum, with a lecture/discussion followed by a movie.

If you really want to be active, try getting involved in filmmaking yourself. You can learn to make your own films in a filmmaking class, such as the fine workshops at Scribe (see *A Closer Look*, page 221). Or you can audition to be an extra in a movie in the making, now that Philadelphia is a hot spot for major Hollywood film productions in which even your neighbor has appeared. My friend Diane DeCastro, who has done such things, says, "You don't have to be gorgeous, but you do have to submit photos and meet certain requirements. If you qualify, you'll have a chance to work with struggling actors, make a few bucks, eat a catered lunch, and maybe get to play the role of human landscape." Keep an eye out for auditions in "Notes for the Arts" in the *Inquirer*.

Philadelphia has really become an outstanding film town. With a variety of outstanding festivals and series, great interactive programs, and many fine international and independent films (especially at the Ritz and Roxy Theaters), we are learning more about the art of cinema and the way it helps us learn about ourselves, our families and neighbors.

Film

Special Note: For the shyest of shy interactors, going to film events is one of the easiest things to try. Going to the movies is easy, and going to a discussion group about a movie is pretty easy too. If you are nervous about joining the discussion, you can just listen. At first, it might be hard to go alone, but try it. Once you get used to it, it's kind of neat because you can go on the spur of the moment, even when you're supposed to be doing the dishes or mowing the lawn. Also, you don't have to find someone who is in the same mood you're in to see what you feel like seeing. It's a luxury to go alone—and once you're there, you might be more inclined to take a risk, chat with the person next to you, and eventually be a "regular" in the discussion group. You'll make a place for yourself in the community of people who love films.

Film Discussion Groups

Chestnut Hill Film Group: *Tuesday Nights at the Movies*

Free Library/Chestnut Hill Branch, 8711 Germantown Avenue, Philadelphia, PA
(215) 248-0947   www.armcinema25.com/chfg

A free weekly repertory screening series that features vintage classics
("Casablanca"), new classics ("Babette's Feast"), local premieres ("Magdalen"),
and off-beat fare, such as evenings spotlighting the work of special directors (like
Edgar Ulmer). Since 1973, CHFG projects film, never video or DV, takes pride
in its Cinemascope screen, and offers a diverse range of genres (noir, comedy,
foreign, musicals, etc.). Offerred in a comfortable, neighborhood setting with
great sound, free refreshments, handouts, speakers and lots of conversation.
Donations are encouraged.

☼ Tuesdays   ⏰ 7:30pm

Film at the Prince

The Prince Music Theater, 1412 Chestnut Street, Philadelphia PA
(215) 569-9700   www.princemusictheater.org

"It's a gathering place for filmmakers, film lovers, actors, writers, students and
families to see exciting new and classic films, socialize, and exchange ideas. We'll
have *Classics for the Big Screen, Silent Film with Live Music,* and *Philadelphia
Filmmakers* with screenings of work by local media artists. This is the *Sharon
Pinkenson Film Project* presenting innovative film programming from historic to
fantastic, silent to musical, classic to kitsch, doc to drama, and local to international." (Exerpted from the **Film at the Prince** brochure.) You can sit in the café
and socialize, or join a variety of events, including discussions about the films
with directors and actors following the cinema. A terrific new venue with
delicious offerings. Be sure to stay in touch with their web site.

💰 Prince FilmPass Special: $25/5 film admissions or $7/per film

Harlan Jacobson's: Talk Cinema

P.O. Box 686, Croton-on-Hudson, NY 10520
(800) 551-9221   Harlan@Talkcinema.com   www.talkcinema.com
Activity Location: Ritz Theater, 2nd & Walnut Sts. Phila. PA, Ritz in Voorhees, NJ

In this interactive film series, where participants preview independent and
foreign films well before they are released, you can take part in discussions with
distinguished film critics and filmmakers following the screenings. These are all
high-quality films, including early showings of Oscar winners. Series fills up
quickly so register early.

☼ Some Saturdays   ⏰ 9:30am (door); 10am (film)
💰 $99 for 7 films

Film

Members Film Café

Philadelphia Museum of Art, 26th Street and the Benjamin Franklin Parkway, Philadelphia, PA

(215) 684-7926   www.philamuseum.org

Meet others and participate in a lecture/discussion following a fine film as you enjoy food and drink from the museum cafeteria in an intimate atmosphere.

Movie Discussion Night at Barnes & Noble Bookstore

Market Fair, 3535 US Route 1, Princeton, NJ 08540

(609) 897-9250   www.barnesandnoble.com

Attend regular movie discussion nights and find out what others think about contemporary and classic films.

☼ 2nd Tues./mo   ⏰ 8pm

Movies & Conversation at The Sedgwick Cultural Center

7137 Germantown Avenue, Philadelphia, PA 19119
(215) 248-9229   www.sedgwickcenter.org

Classic movies and new works are introduced by film experts and film lovers with great interest in the subjects and in filmmaking. Discussions about themes and the artistry of the films follow the screenings.

Temple University: *CinemaTUCC*

1515 Market Street, Philadelphia, PA 19102
(215) 204-TUCC www.temple.edu/tucc

Non cedit offerings include film discussion classes, such as "History Hollywood Style" taught by Steve Friedman ("Mr Movie" Film scholar and WPHT 1210 AM radio host) in which the class examines "the reel aspects of some of the most colorful people in history...and their ongoing cinema legends." (from TUCC catalog) Other classes in films are offered as well.

Villanova University: *Cultural Film and Lecture Series*

(610) 519-4750 (info)   (610) 519-7262 (box office)
Activity Location: Connelly Center Cinema, Villanova, PA

Every weekend during fall and spring, you can find thoughtful art and foreign films based on universal human themes, such as 'rites of passage' or 'the ties that bind.'Attend on Monday nights to hear an introduction by a guest expert and join a discussion that will include *your* expertise, following the film.

☼ Saturdays (7pm), Sundays (3:30pm, 7pm), Mondays (7pm)
💰 $4, Students $3

Film

Film Festivals

Banff Festival of Mountain Films

(Sponsored by the Philadelphia Rock Gym, 610-666-7673)

Activity Location: University of Pennsylvania Museum of Archaeology/Anthropology 33rd & Spruce Streets, Philadelphia, PA 19104

Be brave! Experience the thrill of ice climbing, kayaking whitewater rapids, and the like while safe in your movie seat. The Banff takes place one weekend in February or March and focuses on high adventure outdoor sports.

Features at the Five

(215) 901-3771   www.armcinema25.com

Activity Location: Five Spot, 5 South Bank Street, Phila., PA, (215) 574-0070

An annual film festival that takes place over five consecutive Monday nights in May/June and premieres two local indie/underground feature length movies each week. Producer-Directors are on hand to introduce their films and answer questions. The hip atmosphere gives audiences a chance to view new works from up-and-coming independent filmmakers and provides a great networking opportunity for local industry professionals. $5 cover with cash bar.

Jewish Film Festival

Gershman Y, 401 South Broad Street, Philadelphia, PA 19147
(215) 446-3033

Political thrillers, comedies and documentaries about the Jewish cultural experience are shown on the big screen in the auditorium at the Y. When you attend on Saturdays or Sundays, the screening is preceded by a speaker, usually the filmmaker. A sample of films shown include *Hannah*, *Arguing the World*, and short comedies by young filmmakers.

☼ Saturdays ($9), Sundays ($7), Mondays ($6) from October to April

Philadelphia Festival of World Cinema

International House, 3701 Chestnut Street, Philadelphia, PA 19104
(215) 895-6542   ihouse@libertynet.org   www.libertynet.org/ihouse

This outstanding and noncompetitive festival is not to be missed. Approximately 100 films are screened at downtown theaters and International House. Besides the films, there are discussions with the filmmakers, seminars on topics such as "Making a low-budget film," and an awesome closing party where you can meet the who's who of independent film and dance until 2am.

☼ About eleven days beginning the last Thursday in April

🐞 $7.50, unlimited pass $125, $49 for 7 tickets

Film

Philadelphia International Gay & Lesbian Film Festival

234 Market Street, 5th floor, Philadelphia, PA 19106
(215) 733-0608   www.tlavideo.com/piglff
Activity Location: A variety of Center City venues & International House

With more than five successful years under its belt, this has been a movie festival with lots of opportunities for interaction: Concerts and parties, stars and filmmakers. It's a great place for lesbians and gays and their friends to get together and relax, chat, and have a good time. The feature films and shorts always get rave reviews from viewers and reviewers alike as they present the changing, ever-broadening gay and lesbian images, with an international perspective from 27 countries. They also include segments of the straight world with the real life issues gays and lesbians confront. This festival is a class act and everyone who loves great cinema will enjoy it. Look for it annually in July.

PhilaFilm

2623 Sorrento Drive, Su A, Philadelphia, PA 19131
(215) 879-8209   www.philafilm.org
Activity Location: Various theaters in Center City, Phila., PA

Filmmakers from around the world travel to Philly for this international competition of independent films. The 40-45 finalists from nine categories (feature, short narrative, documentary, animation, music video, student, experimental, Super 8, and TV series) are screened and available for general viewing. The public is invited to attend the awards ceremony, a black-tie gala, or take part in excellent workshops on screenwriting and directing.

☼ 3rd week in July

✆ Larry Smallwood

💰 $5, 50% discount for seniors and students

Margaret Mead Traveling Film and Video Festival

University of Pennsylvania Museum of Archaeology & Anthropology
33rd & Spruce Streets, Philadelphia, PA 19104
(215) 898-4015, Education Department

This annual film festival focuses on anthropological and cultural themes and takes place all in one weekend, usually around the end of February. Examples of recent films have been *Lumumba: Death of a Prophet*, *Cracks in the Mask*, and *Mother of the Tribe*. Films are sometimes accompanied by discussions led by anthropologists as background for the films. A very high-quality festival.

Film Series

Creative Access

230 Vine Street, Philadelphia, PA 19106
(215) 592-0946   craccess@aol.com   www.creativeaccess.org
Activity Location: Various theaters around the Delaware Valley

The region's only advocacy, art-service, and presenting organization dedicated to making the social, cultural and political life accessible to deaf and hard-of-hearing people (and deaf/hearing families) of all ages in the Greater Philadelphia area. Major services include: Theater Access Project (sign-interpreted theater), Movie Access Project (advocating captioned movies), Deaf Performing Artists Initiative, and Sign Language Interpreter Services and Classes.

Community Education Center: *Feminist Film/Video Series*

3500 Lancaster Avenue, Philadelphia, PA 19104
(215) 387-1911   www.libertynet/cec.org

See cutting-edge films by women filmmakers in March as part of the celebration of Women's History Month. Emphasis is on new and innovative work by local and national independent women media artists. Recent themes have included the search for cultural identity and the effects of society's expectation of how women should look, live and behave.

☼ One weekend, usually in March
💰 $8, $6 members, seniors, students

County Theater: *Hollywood Summer Nights & Cinematheque* Series

20 East State Street, Doylestown, PA 18901
(215) 345-6789   www.countytheater.org

If you've missed the classics on the big screen, this cool nonprofit community theater that features art and independent films is a neat place to see them. Should be, since they've been showing movies since 1938! You can catch *The Maltese Falcon* or *Vertigo* in the Hollywood Summer Nights Series. Or attend the screening of a local independent film once a month, followed by a discussion with the filmmaker. Try being a kid again on a Saturday afternoon for a matinee of *The Fly* or *The Princess Bride*, with the breathlessness of your 10-year old movie-watching self! A terrific web site informs you about all upcoming events and their film archives.

💰 $7.50, members $4, seniors & students $5.50

Film

Exhumed Films

www.exhumedfilms.com

Activity Location: Hoyt Theater, Rte. 38 & 70, Point Shopping Center, Pennsauken, NJ (856) 910-2340

If you want to try something off the beaten path, take a peek at this web site to see the old movies showing at Exhumed Films. Where they were exhumed from we don't know, but an evening with them is nothing but fun and worth the ride. Either horror or cult films are shown, sometimes with a discussion with the director, and always with fun lobby activities and door prizes. Now you can get your horror fix once a month on Friday nights.

☼ Fridays/once a month   🕙 10:30pm

💰 $8/double feature

Frankford Style: *Summer Screen*

4620 Griscom Street, Philadelphia, PA 19124
(215) 744-2990 ext. 222   fkdstyle@libertynet.org
Activity Location: The Art Lot at Jack's Cameras Frankford Avenue and Unity Street

Walk around to the lot next door to Jack's Cameras on a Wednesday or Friday summer evening and have a seat for a free movie or performance by a local band. Frankford Style, a nonprofit arts organization, hosts *Summer Screen* for anyone who happens by. In the past, Wednesdays have been the Hollywood movie nights, and Fridays have been stage nights for musicians of all styles of music. But check on Frankford Avenue for a program, or just stop around and see what you can find out. Very casual, comfortable and fun!

☼ July-August evenings

💰 Free/Optional Donation

Film

Medford Township Municipal Center

17 North Main Street, Medford, NJ 08055
(609) 654-2512   www.medfordtownship.com

Bring your blanket or beach chair and spend a warm summer night under the stars viewing a popular Hollywood film. Family entertainment is the emphasis here with most of the films coming from Disney Studios.

☼ Tuesdays at dusk

🜚 Free

Neighborhood Film and Video Project

International House, 3701 Chestnut Street, Philadelphia, PA 19104
(215) 895-6533   ihouse@libertynet.org   www.libertynet.org/ihouse

Each year-round series of new international and independent films, as well as classic films, is usually planned around a theme and often followed by discussions. Recently, Indian cinema, Egyptian cinema, animation, and local filmmakers have been featured. One year seven Mary Pickford films were shown, some with live piano music! Get the Arts Center calendar for a schedule of film screenings, which includes excellent music events as well.

☼ Wednesdays-Sundays

🜚 $6.50, $20 for 4-show pass

Philadelphia City Institute Library

1905 Locust Street, Philadelphia, PA 19103
(215) 685-6621   www.library.phila.gov

See your favorite classic film stars like Marlene Dietrich or Gary Cooper, or directors like Akira Kurosawa at free film series given several times a year at this branch of the Free Library. The films shown are sometimes based on themes like opera or women in film from the 20's and 30's. Great fun. The City Institute also gives lecture/discussions periodically. You can find out from the newsletter from the Free Library, a jam-packed publication about numerous events in the library. You'll be surprised!

☼ Different nights in the spring & fall

🜚 Free

Film

Philadelphia Museum of Art: *Art Around the World*

Benjamin Franklin Parkway at 26th Street, Philadelphia, PA 19101
(215) 763-8100 or   (215) 684-7506   www.philamuseum.org

Each Wednesday night PMA presents a wonderfully eclectic mix of films, music, performances, tours, demonstrations, and food–all related to a particular country or topic. Some Wednesday night topics have included: "Philly Folk Preview" (film: *Days of Heaven*), "A Night to Remember" (film: *A Night to Remember*), "This Sceptered Isle" (film: *Looking for Richard*). On some Saturdays, there is the Members Film Club, when a film showing is often accompanied by a lecture discussion. In addition, a variety of films are shown in conjunction with the current exhibits, such as a Japanese film series during the Celebrate Japan event. It is hard to overestimate the value of these extremely high-quality programs. The Wednesday night series is an informative and very social evening that you will really enjoy. I have been to many of these programs and they have all been outstanding! Come from 5pm - 8:45pm and enjoy the evening.

Secret Cinema

www.voicenet.com/~jschwart

Activity Locations: Various, including Borders (1727 Walnut), Moore College of Art (20th & Race Sts.), and The Print Center (1614 Latimer St.), Philadelphia, PA

If you want to have a truly fun evening, try any of the films dug up by Jay Swartz. These offbeat, obscure (Jay says "neglected") cult films ("16 MM on a giant screen, no video–not *ever*") of the '50s, '60s, and '70s are totally amazing, especially when viewing them with an enthusiastic crowd. Occasionally there are special thematic programs (such as *The Sugar-Charged Saturday Morning Supershow*–nostalgic early '70s children's TV shows like the *Banana Splits*) and sometimes notable speakers. The web site tells you a lot about the films coming up (if you need to know what you are letting yourself in for), as well as about other activities such as the group trip (cuts costs) to the Syracuse Cinefest, a festival of vintage films. You can get on an email list. Only $5.

☼ Jay Schwartz

Film

Sunday Cinema and Perlmutter's Picks

National Museum of American Jewish History, 55 North 5th Street,
Independence Mall East, Philadelphia, PA 19106
(215) 923-3812 nmajh@nmajh.org www.nmajh.org

Twice a year on Sundays the museum presents Perlmutter's Picks, a film
screening and lively discussion led by film critic Archie Perlmutter. Six times a
year the museum offers films that reflect the themes of their exhibits, such as
Next Stop Greenwich Village and *Avalon*. Other programs explore American
Jewish history and identity, including an annual family program, "Being Jewish
at Christmas," held on Christmas Day. You can keep up with the many programs offered from a public programs brochure, but a more efficient method is
to consult the web site or be placed on an electronic mailing list where you will
learn about upcoming events.

💰 Free with $3 admission, $2 seniors & students

University of Delaware: *International Film Series*

Trabant University Center Theater, 17 West Main Street, Newark, DE 19716
(302) 831-4066 www.english.udel.edu/lrussell/calendar.html

Run by students, this outstanding free film series offers international films that
are hard to find, like the Russian film *Prisoner of the Mountains*, all shown with
subtitles. The schedule may change each semester so call ahead. The web site
lists many other events (like open mics) taking place at the university as well.

☼ Sundays   🕐 7:30pm

William Way Community Center: *Movie Night*

William Way Lesbian, Gay, Bisexual & Transgender Community Center,
1315 Spruce Street, Philadelphia, PA 19107
(215) 732-2220 wwcenter@yahoo.com www.waygay.org

Recent releases, classics, and documentaries are shown, like the *Life and Times of
Harvey Milk, Dr. Strangelove, Sunset Boulevard,* and *Delores Claiborne*. All who
are lesbian, gay, bisexual, transgender, and their friends and supporters are
welcome. This center sponsors a variety of many many wonderful activities and
is very responsive to the wishes of its members. $2 suggested donation.

☼ Sundays at 7pm

Film

Filmmakers' Activities

Learning Studio

412 East King Street, Malvern, PA 19355
(610) 578-0600   classes@learningstudio.net   www.learningstudio.net

"Anyone Can Make a Movie" with Lance Weiler has been a popular course at LS. The brochure asks: "How many times have you gone to the movies and left feeling like you could have done a better job of telling the story? Movie making is now becoming accessible to the masses. All you need is access to a desktop computer, a camcorder, and some additional inexpensive hardware and software and you can be your own movie studio. Join Lance as he discusses the ins and outs of digital filmmaking, film festivals and how to distribute your movies."

💰   Members Club$29 Non-members $35
    $3materials fee payable to instructor

Philadelphia Feature Film Project

(215) 308-6522   admin@filmproject.org   www.filmproject.org
Activity Location: Center City, Phila., PA

PFFP describes itself as "...an organization open to all those interested in building an active local 'film community' and fostering a viable commercial feature film market in the greater Philadelphia area." It holds events several times a year and 100-200 industry-savvy people show up. Besides hosting notable filmmaker speakers (e.g., Eugene Martin, *Edge City*), there are presentations on technical topics like "3-D Modeling of Action Films." It's useful information and an excellent networking affair combined with a great party. Check the web site or get on the mailing list for events.

☎   Rick Gamble
💰   Free to $5

Philadelphia Independent Film and Video Association

International House, 3701 Chestnut Street, 6th floor, Philadelphia, PA 19104
(215) 895-6594   (215) 387-5125 International House
pifva@ihphilly.org   www.libertynet.org/pifva

Check out the films at the free monthly Open Screen & Potluck or attend the many workshops, such as "Approaches to Documentary" or "Guerilla Marketing for Film & Video." Members pay less for workshops, get an information-packed newsletter, and can apply for the PIFVA subsidy program, which provides completion funds for independent productions. Check the web site for an excellent listing of important film links.

☼   Year-round

Travel and Cultural Films

Geographical Society of Philadelphia:
Travel Adventure Cinema

Box 67, Haverford, PA 19041
(610) 649-5220   www.geographicalsociety.org
Activity Location: Academy of Natural Sciences Auditorium,
19th Street & Benjamin Franklin Pkwy, Phila., PA

Robert Perry showed slides to the Society when he returned from the North Pole in 1909. Nowadays you can see outstanding travel and nature films of amazing and beautiful places which are introduced and narrated by their internationally acclaimed filmmakers. Subject matter might includes films about Scotland, the Baja Peninsula, and the Canadian West. With renowned speakers and refreshments, these programs for $10 are the best deal in town. The group is active in other ways, enjoying day-long excursions to places like Baltimore's Evergreen House-Museum (contains an indoor theater), luncheons, and dinners. Call for a brochure to see the schedule of these excellent programs."

☼ 8 Wednesdays from October to March   ⏰ 2:00pm & 7:30pm

⅋ Non-members $10, members $8 for films. $65/yr membership

An off-line editing class at Scribe Video Center

Film

 **Here are some extra resources to check out**

Web Sites

- *www.filmmag.com* is the web site for independents.
- *www.ifp.org,* the web site for the Independent Feature Project, lists independent film events in New York, including screenings, volunteering opportunities, and many classes, workshops, and seminars.
- *www.madscreenwriter.com* is a great resource for people in screenwriting.
- *www.ritzfilmbill.com* has information about the films playing at the Ritz theaters. Also has a film archive, movie links, soundtracks, & local film events.
- *www.suntimes.com/ebert/ebert.html* for Roger Ebert's movie reviews.
- *www.us.imdb.com* An amazing database of movie info.

Classes

- *Learning Studio* (www.learningstudio.net; 610-578-0600) in Malvern has had many, many film classes such as: "How to Make It in TV and Film," (with Mike Lemon, premier Philadelphia casting director), "Dinner and a Movie" nites, "Become a Commercial Model & Actor," "Desktop Video Editing," "Screenwriting Basics," and more. Check on the current class line up.

A closer look at...

The Scribe Video Center

1342 Cypress Street, Philadelphia, PA 19107, (215) 735-3785
www.libertynet.org/scribe

This media arts center seeks to explore, develop and advance video as an artistic medium and tool for social change. Professional instructors will teach you every aspect of video production, as well as provide the encouragement you need to put your concerns and stories on tape. You can rent equipment at low cost, with classmates as your production crew. Scribe holds *Producers Forums*, which are screenings and discussions by highly acclaimed award-winning filmmakers. A *Community Visions Program* supports nonprofit organizations in creating videos about their work. Also from Scribe, *Street Movies* present free outdoor screenings of independent films at 12 city community centers in August. You can start learning with others new to video in a beginner's class, such as "Camera & Lighting for Video Production," which gives plenty of hands-on experience with the camera. Experienced students take more advanced classes, such as "Post-production and Visual Design," or join the *Producers Working Group*. There's always something neat going on at Scribe, which encourages participation from people of color or with low incomes, women and elders.

☼ Year-round   ✆ Louis Massiah

💰 About $10 per hour of instruction, Producers Working Group - free, Producers Forums -$10

*For an actress to be a success she must have
the face of Venus, the brains of Minerva,
the grace of Perpsichore, the memory of Macaulay,
the figure of Juno, and the hide of a rhinoceros.
~ Ethel Barrymore*

*I love acting. It is so much more real than life.
~Oscar Wilde*

Games & Sports

Baseball & Disc Games • Biking

Canoeing, Kayaking & Rowing

Climbing & Caving • Golf

Horseback Riding & Polo

Indoor Games • Lacross, Rugby & Soccer

Martial Arts • Miscellany

Recreational Groups • Running • Sailing

Skating: In-line, Roller & Ice • Skiing

Swimming & Scuba • Tennis & Racquetball

Games & Sports

Divers with Aqua Hut hanging out

Dynamic Diversions at the summit

Philadelphia is a great outdoors city. It has natural beauty and four full-fledged seasons with plenty of sunshine, a huge natural park, and the mountains and seashore right around the corner. It welcomes "hikers, bikers, climbers, swimmers, runners, skiers, kite flyers, golfers, sailors, bowlers, motorcyclists, rowers, cross-country skiers, windsurfers, para-gliders, and advocates of every conceivable contraption that one can mount, strap on, glide on, ride, or float through" the natural areas of the Delaware Valley. (Quote by Diane DeCastro, coauthor of **Connecting in San Francisco.**)

Playing games and sports is probably the way most people have fun no matter what age they are. If you're looking for your "inner child," you'll probably find her/him somewhere playing games. After all, isn't that what you did when you were 10 years old on a Saturday afternoon after you'd cleaned your room for your mom and could do whatever you wanted to? One advantage to playing games is that you will stay trim and lower your stress level. Another advantage is that you will not meet any couch potatoes there. The people you *will find* care enough about themselves to get moving while learning and having fun at the same time. Those kinds of people are fun to spend time with, *n'est pas*? They'll think that about you too!

Fortunately there are all kinds of games/sports to play around Philadelphia, so you have lots of choices. You can go out to play all day (golf), or spend just an hour or so (tennis). You can compete hard (Ultimate Frisbee), or not at all (Sunday morning bike rides). You can be outdoors in the water (canoeing and kayaking with the **Philadelphia Canoe Club**) or inside painting historical figures that refight historical battles (with **Center City Miniature Gamers**). There are *tons* of groups around the area who would love to have you join them play and have fun—while you all put the week at work aside.

That is the deal here. How to forget about work (even if you *love* your work!). And how to find friends who want to have fun. When I ask people in my workshops what they do to have fun, they look at me like I'm using a word they've never heard before. *Fun*. That's that stuff you do when *you* chose how you are going to spend your time. It's what you do when you want to just goof off and test your mettle, or be silly and laugh. It has no real negative consequences, like getting told off by your boss when you do a lousy job, and it gives you a chance to let down your

Games & Sports

hair and kick up your heels. Fun is when you get away from your responsibilities so much that you don't even remember them, when you escape your naggers, the phone calls, the housework, and the kids. This is *your* time. You need it, you deserve it, and by gum you're going to take it. ("By gum" is what my mother used to say when she really meant it.)

Listen to the stories of people that do sports. In *Rowing Against the Current: On Learning to Scull at 40*, Barry Strauss, a scholarly Cornell professor, describes his adventure when he took up rowing. Starting out as a rank beginner at 40, he progressed from the initial awkward stage of being completely out of sync, hitting teammates with oars, to becoming a competent athlete. Art Carey (*Philadelphia Inquirer*) describes Strauss, "The appeal of rowing took a quantum leap. It had something to do with solitude, the intimate connection with nature, and the changing seasons. It had something to do with the Zen-like ecstasy when every-thing is moving right and the boat seems to fly, as well as the other gifts of rowing: a sense of discipline, mastery, self-control and proportion."

That's why you do it.

This chapter will give *you* some starting ideas on where to go and who to join if you want some places to play and have fun. You already know some of the major groups taking part in play activities, such as the **Appalachian Mountain Club** that hikes, bikes, canoes, does trail mainte-nance, and has social outings. Or the **Philadelphia Bicycle Club**, whose members you see biking in the area on Sundays. (They have both beginner and advanced rides. Nice folks, and they watch out for you the first few times.) Or the **King of Prussia Ski Club** that goes on all kinds of excursions—way more than skiing—all year.

But there are so many more—including some that really tickled my bones. How about the **Philadelphia Women's Dragon Boat** group, whose members row in sculls that look like dragons, either for fun or for competition (international!). Right here in Philadelphia. The group meets weekly for motivational and fitness activities. These women become true comrades who have fun but are also really serious about rowing. On the other end of the spectrum is the **Narberth Chain Smokers**, a bike riding group that is so relaxed that they may or may not show up at the appointed place for the weekly ride (They usually do.). Their motto is that they have no rules, no stress, while they enjoy riding.

The **Hash Harriers** run about and then socialize afterwards, with the objective to have fun together. The **Tandem Bikers** are devoted to their unusual bikes and trust their partners to steer them on safe paths. They party with other riders who also ride tandem all over the Atlantic coast. (By the way, many motorcycle groups also have large riding and social gatherings.) The **Adaptive Sports** group includes abled and disabled members who share the bond of fun and movement as partners while rowing, biking, and skating.

If you're not afraid of heights, try rock climbing at places like **Go Vertical**, a real hangout for outdoor enthusiasts of all kinds. I love the **Executive Women's Golf League**, which says that women can do business on the links as well as men and work on their short game at the same time. These gals are really fun and the socializing is the best. (Singles can check out the **American Singles Golf** group listed in the Singles chapter to meet other unattached golfers.) Despite the insurance issues with horseback riding, there are lots of horseback riding places in the area with many, but not all, out of the city. And martial arts groups are going strong. Check the **Philadelphia Judo Club** with Art Bourgeau (who runs the Whodunit Bookstore on Walnut Street). He's a great teacher.

Periodic **Gay Bingo** nights are popular events with lots of fun and laughs. The host group (**Action AIDS**) welcomes the entire community (but make a reservation because the evenings fill up) and the profit goes to fight AIDS. Most people who attend go back again and again. Other regularly held indoor games where you can test your mental acuity, cunning, and clever strategies include Chess, Bridge, Scrabble, pool/ billiards, and fantasy gaming. Most of these are low cost or free. How long has it been since you've gone all out to win one of these fun games?

You can also find exciting sports like sky diving and fencing, try your hand at boxing or fishing, or join a classy group whose members go exploring. You'll discover groups in picturesque settings: Learn to juggle in front of the Art Museum at sunset, glide along the rivers and creeks in a canoe or scull on the Schuylkill River, go kite flying along the Jersey shore, or learn to windsurf on Lake Nockamixon.

If you like activities that command a large following, like sailing, skiing, or tennis, you will meet Philadelphians galore who will join you. The **Philadelphia Sailing Club** meets monthly for terrific evenings of sailing travelogues, upcoming events, schmoozing and sailor stories. Ski clubs include **Fall Line Ski Club** which has trips to the Poconos, Canada, and Switzerland, as well as lots of other kinds of activities like biking,

Games & Sports

canoeing, and picnics. **The Philadelphia Social Club** is another multi-activity group for "those looking for activities now that they are out of college"; they offer coed football, softball, and volleyball games for those who love to play. Just peek in these pages for a gigabyte of companions whose interests you share.

Anyone who knows me knows that I fell in love with the **Gazela Philadelphia** after I fell out of love with a guy whose boat I shared. The Gazela is a big sweetie, a real historical museum (circa 1870's), on whom you can work, learn about ships, and become proficient at handling huge square sails. If you want to climb the 95-foot mast to help unfurl the sails, you can. (I got as far as the first yard arm, 35 feet above the deck, higher over the water, and said this is fine, thanks. But others are happy to go all the way up every weekend!) You can steer under the captain's direction and prepare meals in the galley, and you will sleep in a fisherman's bunk below when you put out to sea on your way to Nova Scotia or points south. Everything you do will be just as it was 100 years ago. You'll be with the other volunteer sailing crew, who wear gear for cutting lines and fixing sails, and who are ready to teach you, and talk and sing with you. One evening we took off for New York to join a flotilla of tall ships sailing into NY Harbor. I was at the helm (imagine!), instructed by the pilot, with the coastal lights of New Jersey off our port side. The square sails were illuminated before the dark sky, and there were crew hanging out in the bow singing sea shanties. I felt like I had died and gone to heaven. In my whole life I will never forget that night. (It's fair to say that you work hard on that ship, painting, fixing, tarring, etc. But you do it with companions—like Ed Astair the best dancer on board—and it's "fun" work. Don't ask me why. It just is.) When we put into port, we were ambassadors for the ship and Philadelphia, giving tours of this old cod-fishing vessel, the oldest, largest, square-sailed ship still sailing in the world. Whenever I was on her (every weekend), I never once thought about the job, or paying my bills, or whether my hair was messed up (it was). Nothing mattered except the ship and her crew.

Learning to sail a tall ship may not be your cup of tea. Maybe you'd rather be playing a game of Scrabble (which I hate, regularly dumping the board in my always-winning husband's lap...). But choose *something* that you will enjoy playing, because we all need a respite from the routines and responsibilities in our lives. Whether it's hiking or Monopoly or soccer, get out there with old friends and new friends and have some fun. It's all out there for you.

Baseball & Disc Games

Andorra Softball Association
(215) 483-3201

This group welcomes new members to join teams for a slow pitch, unlimited arc, men's league that plays from 10am-4pm on Sundays in Roxborough and Andorra. The group is a member of the Amateur Softball Association, so your team will be eligible to play in larger tournaments if you win. Since you are signing up for a league, you'll need to call before you go.

City of Brotherly Love Softball League
(800) GO-CBLSL   CBLSL@libertynet.org   www.libertynet.org/cblsl/index.html
Activity Location: Dairy fields in East Fairmount Park, Phila., PA

Organized over 15 years ago, the City of Brotherly Love Softball League is the largest gay sports organization in Philadelphia, with over 350 members. Double headers are played on Sundays with practice days decided by each team. Although serious about their softball, members enjoy socializing together, too. Each week a different sponsor bar is dubbed the "Bar of the Week," and players from all divisions often unwind after the games with other players there. This is a great opportunity to meet new friends and relive the day's most spectacular plays, as well as the best bloopers. Also, members of CBLSL hold fund-raising events, participate in community activities like Pride Fest, and take trips away (really away—like San Diego) to watch league games.

☼ Sundays: mid April to mid July

Philadelphia Area Disc Alliance
(800) 705-2483   info@pada.org   www.pada.org
Activity Location: Edgely Field in Fairmount Park

Ultimate Frisbee is the game these people play. It looks like touch football and soccer combined only played with a frisbee. If you're interested in local league play, this is the place for you. There are five leagues: Three coed leagues (spring, summer, fall) and two all-women leagues (summer, fall) are open to everyone 16 and over. At the beginning of the season, PADA offers clinics to beef up the skills of newcomers as well as advanced players . Besides the leagues, there are many pick-up games that are listed and kept up-to-date on the web site. Actually, it is best to get most of your information about PADA on the web.

Games & Sports

Philadelphia Comets Amateur Baseball Team

brett@libertynet.org   www.libertynet.org/blacksox

"League players may be lawyers, local businessmen, or police officers during the week, but enjoy baseball as a serious hobby each weekend." (from web site) This local member of the national Men's Adult Baseball League gives men age 18 and over the opportunity to play real competitive-level baseball on a regular basis in a professionally run environment. Aside from a few rule changes, the MSBL/MABL conforms to standard baseball rules. Teams wear major league style or replica uniforms, play on the best available fields, and play nine-inning games or two seven-inning games as part of a double header once a week, generally on Sundays. The league conducts championship playoffs and an all-star game, and the teams compete in local and national tournaments. All you Mike Schmidts out there, contact them through the web site!

Roxborough YMCA: *Softball, Volleyball, Basketball, etc.*

7201 Ridge Avenue, Philadelphia, PA 19128
(215) 482-3900   www.ymca.net

Bring your own friends or come by yourself to league play at the Roxborough Y. In the summer you'll find sand volleyball and softball, and in the winter there are full-court basketball teams for men of all ages. Most are team entries, but if you come alone they'll try to find a place for you. These are currently all-men's teams, but they used to be coed. If there was an interest, maybe they would be again... Check your nearest Y for the latest team offerings and many classes.

💰 Very reasonable: about $25-40/person/season

Biking

Bicycle Club of Philadelphia (BCP)

P.O. Box 30235, Philadelphia, PA 19103
(215) 735-2453 (hot line)   info@phillybikeclub.org   www.phillybikeclub.org

You can't miss the BCP riders if you're out and about on Sundays. They regularly schedule four bike rides on that day: A morning (8:45am) breakfast ride for intermediates; an advanced ride at noon; a ride for intermediates at 12:15pm; and a beginner's ride at noon. Call to find out where they meet. But there is much more going on with these folks, such as the *Spring Bike Bazaar & Swap Meet* and ad hoc rides like a 40-mile jaunt to Doylestown. When they describe special rides, they always give you the difficulty level so you know if you have a flying chance of keeping up. Members receive a newsletter (*Quick Release*) that includes many bike rides and events in the region. For local bicycle riders, this is a great group to join.

Bicycle Coalition of Greater Philadelphia

252 South 11th Street, Philadelphia, PA 19107
(215) 940-0801   info@bcdv.org   www.bcdv.org

BCGP is a bicycle network that fights for improved road conditions for cyclists and sponsors many bike events to educate the public about the value of biking as a means of regular transportation. The *Freedom Valley Ride* on the Philadelphia to Valley Forge Bike Trail in May is a major local biking event that you won't want to miss. (By the way, BCGP was heavily involved in the development of that wonderful, heavily traveled bike trail. I'm on it all the time.) Also, in August, the annual *Light of the Moving Bikes* involves hundreds of bikers starting out at 8pm on a Saturday evening to visit local mansions on a moonlight ride. These events are fun, and joining them helps BCGP improve biking conditions. Newsletter. (Go to www.geocities.com/Colosseum/6213/pa.htm for a list of bike clubs in PA.)

💰   Voluntary dues averaging about $35/yr

Bilenky Cycle Works: *Tandem Biking*

5319 North 2nd Street, Philadelphia, PA 19120
(215) 329-4744   artistry@bilenky.com   www.bilenky.com

One of six major mid-Atlantic manufacturers of tandem bikes, this shop is a local contact point for tandem riders. Are you ready for a new and exciting sport? People who ride tandem gather for many organized riding/social events in the region, such as the *Eastern Shore Memorial Day Event*, with activities like a ride to Chestertown and a Skipjack sail to Rock Hall. There are tandem bike organizations in Baltimore ("Crabs") and Washington ("Potomac Peddlers") that frequently get together with Philadelphia riders for regular biking activities, as well as picnics, evenings at the theater, and such! Try Bob and Willa Freeman (703-978-7937) for info about tandem events. (By the way, Bilenky makes all types of custom bikes for enthusiasts and recreational riders.)

💰   The tandem bikes are pricey; the activities are not.

Brandywine Bicycle Club

P.O. Box 3162, West Chester, PA 19381
(610) 458-8153   www.geocities.com/brandywinebikeclub

Every Wednesday and Thursday this bike club sponsors different level rides. The leaders and their phone numbers are listed on the web site so you can decide which is right for you. There is also a monthly meeting with a supper followed by a guest speaker. At one recent meeting, the speaker's topic was *Cycling in the Himalayas*. This active group has lots of special rides too, some with camping.

☼ 3rd Wed./mo   📷 7:30pm

Games & Sports

Brooks Country Cycling & Hiking Tours

140 West 83rd Street, New York, NY 10024
(212) 874-5151   www.brookscountrycycling.com

You may not feel rested when you return from a bike vacation, but the change of pace is definitely refreshing! BCCT arranges tours to have you riding through beautiful scenery on quiet country roads while your luggage goes by van to the next inn. One of my friends reports that the accommodations are lovely and the meals are delicious. Bike routes average 25 to 35 miles a day with varying levels of terrain difficulty. They sponsor national and international tours, including several in Pennsylvania (such as PA Dutch area and Bucks County). You can go for a week or for a day, and meet new riders and new friends. Take a look at their web site.

Delaware Valley Bicycle Club (DVBC)

P.O. Box 156, Woodlyn, PA 19094
(610) 565-4058   ira@dvbc.org   www.dvbc.org
Activity Location: Various around the area, especially west of Philadelphia

DVBC has many interesting rides for all levels of riders to different places around the area, some with stops for food. This modest-sized group (about 180 members) is probably the oldest bike club in the area. They also present lectures, seminars, planned rides, and other activities to educate the public about the safe use of the bicycle. Check the terrific list of cycling links by Chris Harendza on their web site.

Motor Maids of Pennsylvania

(610) 489-2293 amafrloish@aol.com   www.motormaids.org
Activity Location: Collegeville, PA

These are durable motorcycle riders who get together for riding activities, often traveling 400 miles or so to conventions with riding and socializing events. The group attracts many professional women, but all who really love cycling are most welcome. Lois rides a full-dress Harley and is a member of the Ladies of Harley and Women in the Wind as well, so you can call her for information about all these groups. They get together for camaraderie and to share a love for riding.

☎ Lois

Narberth Chain Smokers

(215) 885-9500   www.chainsmokers.com

Activity Location: Rides leave from Mainly Bikes, 229 Haverford Ave., Narberth,
PA (610) 668-2453

You have to love a group whose web site includes the following: "We are a fun
loving informal group of all levels of riders. There are no club dues, newsletters
or rules. We only ask that you ride safely and enjoy yourself! Our rides are show
and go. We typically divide up into at least three groups based on speed. We try
to accommodate everyone. We convene after the ride for food and libations in
one of the taverns in the immediate vicinity." I don't know about you, but I love
the spontaneous fun I hear from the Smokers!

☼ Tuesdays & Thursdays   ⏰ 6pm

Suburban Cyclists Unlimited (SCU)

(215) 675-1536   www.suburbancyclists.org

Activity Location: Horsham Township Municipal Building,
Horsham Rd., Horsham, PA (about a mile N of HH High School)

Although SCU sponsors weekend rides, the staple rides are on Tuesday and
Thursdays at 6:30pm. In groups of between 10-12 riders, there are bike hikes at
different levels of difficulty, reflected in pace and number of miles. This
accommodates both beginner and experienced riders. Also, there's lots of
socializing here: Picnics, an annual banquet, trips, ice skating, bowling, and
happy hours—something for everyone!

☼ 1st Thurs./mo (general meeting)   ⏰ 8pm

Trophy Bikes: *Great British Bike Weekend*

311 Market Street, Philadelphia, PA 19106
(215) 625-7999   mcget@aol.com   www.trophybikes.com

For a great weekend, try the tons of activities at the *British Bike Weekend*
sponsored by Trophy (& Via Bicycle Shop, 215-627-3370). Lovers of these
"noble city steeds" congregate to appreciate each others' Raleighs and Robin
Hoods, swap stories and parts, and ride and hang out together on a bike and
pub crawl. Young and old love this annual event. Trophy also sponsors a picnic
where people bring in their hamburgers and hot dogs on their bikes—it's worth
going just to see that! And they sponsor an annual *Multi-faith Blessing of the
Bikes* in early April to give a special send-off to your biking season. Call these
nifty bikers for more event info.

Games & Sports

Canoeing, Kayaking & Rowing

Buck Ridge Ski & Hiking Club

P.O. Box 213, Springfield, PA 19064
Activity Location: Masonic Hall, Rte. 420, Springfield, PA

Buck Ridge is an outdoor club for people of all ages who wish to find companions for skiing (includes recreational downhill and cross-country skiing for people with novice, intermediate and advanced capabilities), biking, hiking, sailing, canoeing, kayaking, rafting, golfing, in-line skating, and more. Trips range from one-day trips to overnights for a weekend or longer. As an all-around club, you can enjoy a consistent group of members from the tri-state area for many different activities

☀ 2nd Wed./mo   ⏰ 8pm
💰 About $20/individual

Fairmount Park Rowing Program

2314 South Street, Philadelphia, PA 19146
(215) 985-9393   gen@srdc.net   www.srdc.net
Activity Location: Schuylkill River near the Strawberry Mansion Bridge

This organization offers a rowing program to the community during the summer. The four cycles include 13.5 hours of instruction for $140-$180. There are beginner and intermediate co-ed classes taught by the Temple Women's Crew team for all aged adults, most of whom are in their 30's-40's. Schedules for classes are varied enough to accommodate most work schedules. If you'd like to see if serious rowing is for you, try the Introductory Class: 4 Saturdays for $35! I'll see you there!
(Note Summer 2001: These classes may be on hold for this season, but hopefully will resume soon. Call to check.)

Pennsylvania Center for Adapted Sports

#4 Boathouse Row, Philadelphia, PA 19130
(215) 765-5118   pacenter@aol.com   www.centeronline.com

This center makes the outdoor world accessible to people with physical disabilities. Members ski, ride tandem and hand bikes, and go in-line skating, canoeing, kayaking, walking, and running. Volunteers join in the activities, lending their abilities to others so they can do it together. And everybody has fun.

☎ Isabelle Bonn

Philadelphia Canoe Club

Colony Castle, 4900 Ridge Avenue, Philadelphia, PA 19128
(215) 487-9674 (hot line)   info@philacanoe.org   www.philacanoe.org

If you love the water, paddling may become your passion. To find out, spend some time with this group for excellent classes and a wide variety of canoe/kayaking experiences throughout the Delaware Valley. Training includes White Water Kayaking, Sea Kayaking, and White Water, Flat Water, and Moving Water Canoeing. It's best to start at the monthly meeting held in the old stone clubhouse (castle) on the Schuylkill River to get an idea about their trips and social activities, like dinners, dances, and the Thursday supper pot luck. You might also stop in at the club's summer *Open House* event for more information. Look at the web site (http://peteandedbooks.com/cclubs.htm) for links to a canoe club near you, such as the South Jersey group, the Lehigh Valley group, etc. There is a fine informative newsletter for members.

☼ Meets on 3rd Mon./mo except January   ⏰ 7:30-10pm

Philadelphia Women's Dragon Boat Team

(610) 642-8881   lindnercll@aol.com

Experience this ancient Chinese sport under the instruction of Philadelphia's nationally competitive Dragon Boat Team. You are invited to paddle in a 39' teakwood craft with a dragon's head at the bow and a tail at the stern. Each boat seats about 20 people, with a drummer and steers-person. Women between the ages of 26 and 75 are involved, with one competitive team, a breast cancer survivor team, and a recreational group who does it for the love of it. Members get together during the winter for all kinds of training and conditioning (and bonding!) to prepare for a busy and enthusiastic spring and summer of paddling, competitive and otherwise. I have done this and I can promise you that it is a glorious experience to be on the Schuylkill in one of these boats paddling in sync (or trying to!) with 19 other paddlers.

REI (Recreational Equipment Incorporated)

Ridge & Butler Pikes, Plymouth Meeting, PA 19428
(610) 940-0808   www.rei.com/storelocator/conshohocken

REI offers orienteering, canoeing, canoe camping, and kayaking clinics/discussions and occasional outdoor activities (hikes, trail maintenance, etc.) for beginning and experienced outdoors people. These sessions are most often presentations by expert sports-people about their excursions in the wonderful wilderness of this country. Since schedules vary, call for the newsletter (or check the web site) to learn about the upcoming clinics. By the way, REI also sponsors great adventure trips all over the world using these skills.

💰 Free

Games & Sports

Climbing & Caving

Doylestown Rock Gym/The Adventure Center

3853 Old Easton Road, Doylestown, PA 18901

Activity Location: Doylestown Rock Gym, Doylestown, PA   (215) 230-9085

With multiple climbing walls in 7000 square feet of space, including one 30' high, this facility sponsors many indoor climbing activities. There are many classes for beginners and advanced climbers. The parent company, Adventure Network, offers guided outdoor trips. Call (215) 997-9270 to find out about classes or check www. adventure-network.net.

Go Vertical

950 North Penn Street, Philadelphia, PA 19123
(215) 928-1800   www.govertical.com

The only Philadelphia indoor climbing spot, this premier facility has more than 13,000 square feet of multicolored stucco walls with dangling ropes for you to develop your climbing skills. This activity develops your physical abilities as well as your mental agility, such as strategic planning. The staff provides instruction geared to your needs: Beginners learn to be self sufficient on the wall, and intermediates are guided to the next level in top rope, lead climbing, and bouldering. This center has become a community for active people, acting as a springboard for finding friends for climbing and other outdoor activities. Lots of "hanging out" and conversation around here.

💰 $65 for beginners (includes 2 hrs. of instruction & 3 days of climbing); $15 for day pass

Mountain Sports: *Adventure School*

107 Sidney Road (Rte. 617), Annandale, NJ 08801
(908) 735-6244   director@gorockclimbing.com   www.gorockclimbing.com

This school, accredited by the American Mountain Guides Association, gives Level One and Level Two courses, teaching fundamentals and more intermediate skills in rock climbing, bouldering, and ice climbing. They travel to areas in the tri-state area, such as the Delaware Water Gap, the Catskills, and the Adirondacks, to climb. Call for information or check out the web site for a complete description of all courses.

Philadelphia Grotto

(215) 836-1565
speleotab@erols.com   www.caves.org/grotto/philly

This is a nonprofit caving club, chartered by the National Speleological Society, dedicated to cave conservation, exploration, education, research, and just plain fun. I love this statement from the web site: "We are a group of individuals from the Philadelphia area who like to drive 14 hours (sometimes less) round trip to crawl around and get dirty in caves... Why do we do this? Few of us actually know this answer. It's probably a combination of a spirit of exploration, natural beauty, friendship and physical challenge." The way to get involved is to go to a meeting. If you like what you see and hear, sign up for a beginners trip, and take it from there.

☼ 1st Thur./mo   ⏰ 7:30pm

Philadelphia Rock Gym

422 Business Center, Oaks, PA 19456
(610) 666-ROPE   www.philarockgym.com

PRG is a professional climbing school with a 35-foot-high indoor climbing wall, lead wall, and extensive bouldering area. Whether you're a beginner or advanced climber, you'll find classes and experiences to challenge you. Outdoor trips are also offered. They put it this way: "An exciting and adventurous total body workout that combines grace, precision and skill...a complete experience for the body as well as the mind." All aged adults—men and women climbers—are welcome. You can sign up with other climbers on their cork board listing of events and climbing partners.

💰 $30 for Introductory Class, including gear

Vertical Reality

67 Old King's Highway, Maple Shade, NJ 08052
(856) 273-1370   www.climbinside.com

"We at Vertical Reality have designed a facility that challenges both the first time climber as well as the seasoned wall rat. We truly enjoy the sport and look forward to sharing our enthusiasm and knowledge with you." (from the web site) This indoor climbing gym allows for controlled climbing for beginners and avoids bad weather climbing for serious climbers. They provide indoor classes, outdoor trips, and slide shows by experienced climbers.

💰 $30 for beginner's package, including day pass, lesson and all rental gear, as well as a day pass for another day; $12/day pass for all

Games & Sports

Golf

Cobbs Creek Golf Course

72nd & Lansdowne Avenue, Philadelphia, PA 19151
(215) 877-8707

Cobbs Creek was voted the sixth best municipal course by *Golf Week Magazine*. This area golf course offers a Men's Association in which you can sign up, develop a handicap, and enjoy tournament play. They had a Women's League for a number of years, but whether it is held depends on customer interest, so make your wishes known! At Walnut Lane Golf Course (Walnut Lane & Magdalena Street, 215-482-3370) they have offered an After Work League for anyone who wanted to play. Most public golf courses offer open leagues where you can meet people to play golf with, and clinics in the spring to sharpen your skills. Call the course near you and tell them what you'd like!

Executive Women's Golf League

(610) 668-3866 (hot line)   www.ewgaphilly.com

EWGA sponsors league play, outings at fine courses, and several social events to provide an opportunity to network. All who enjoy playing golf are welcome, regardless of ability. The chapter has three leagues (Mondays, Tuesdays and Thursdays) as well as a league for beginners on Wednesdays. There are a variety of fun and challenging events held every third week as well as a banquet at the end of the season. Beginners can use the golf lessons at the beginning of the season. There are other perks to membership, but you'll have to call them and find out for yourself.

Longknockers Driving Range

1500 N. 33rd Street (at Oxford), Philadelphia, PA 19121
(215) 236-6794   billstev@earthlink.net

The best deal in town for golf hitting practice, this well-kept secret driving range is right in Strawberry Mansion. If you could use a lesson (who couldn't!), there is a golf pro for individual lessons and regular weekly clinics in some aspect of the golf swing. Longknockers is home base to an all-age men's golf club that meets every other week and plays at local courses every week. They sponsor younger newer golfers too. Say hi to Bill who always has a useful word as you come in. And if you get too frustrated at golf, they have Baseball Batting Cages where you can relieve your stress!

☼   Every day
☎   Bill Stevens

Horseback Riding & Polo

Ashford Farms

700 River Road (between Barren Hill Road and Hart's Lane), Miquon, PA 19452
(610) 825-9838   ashfordf@bellatlantic.net   www.siteblazer.net/ashfordfarms

A fifty-acre equestrian facility offering trails, dressage, jumping, and an outside hunt course. You'll feel like you're riding in the country at Ashford in nearby Miquon where they offer group (3-5 people) and individual lessons in English riding. In the summer there are evening classes in 'Horse Care' so you get the whole feel for horse ownership. Every level of rider can try riding the trails at Ashford Farms, but you have to make a reservation to do this. These activities are good places to meet fellow riding enthusiasts.

Circle K Stables

4220 Holmesburg Avenue, Philadelphia, PA 19136
(215) 335-9975

Individual Western riding lessons are offered at Circle K, with horse care instruction as part of the lesson. After three lessons, you can rent a horse and ride him into Pennypack Park with a guide. Circle K is tough to find, so call first and get directions.

Little Bit O' Farm

901 Cherry Lane, Penns Park (Bucks County), PA 19843
(215) 598-7744

Little Bit Farm is a full-scale show barn on 18 acres where they give private and group (2-5) lessons. They also have an indoor riding academy with a heat-controlled lounge for watchers. They teach English hunt seat riding and basic dressage and their riders attend a lot of shows. Students also can take advantage of the 60 acres of trails as part of their lessons. Leslie says riding is a real stress buster: her clients say that when they are riding they don't think about anything but being on horseback.   Check it out; it's lovely out there.

☼   Mons. thru Sats.

☎   Leslie Molinari or Vicki Peters

Games & Sports

Monastery Stables

1 Kitchen's Lane, Philadelphia, PA 19119
(215) 848-4088   www.members.aol.com/monasterystable

There are private, semi-private and group lessons for adults here, from beginner through jumping and dressage with emphasis on "balanced seat" riding. Beginners take one private lesson before being placed in group instruction. Persons not owning a horse can ride by joining the Philadelphia Saddle Club. (Call 215-233-0341 for details.)

Northwestern Equestrian Facility: *Fall Horse Show*

9700 Germantown Avenue, Philadelphia, PA
(215) 685-9286   www.fow.org/newsletter/horse_stables.htm

You can watch local equestrians care for and train their horses in this pretty spot across from Chestnut Hill College (or Brunos, a terrific neighborhood eatery). There are several small horse shows here from time to time. If you want to learn to ride and care for your horse, group and individual lessons are offered.

Philadelphia Polo Association

www.cowtownpolo.com/ppc_home.htm
Activity Location: Fairmount Park West, Belmont Ave. & Edgely Road, Phila., PA

If you own your own horse and have experience playing polo, you can take part in these fast-paced polo games in the Park. They play about 12 games a year, which draw interested spectators who love good sport. Whether you want to watch or play, check out the web site which lists events, and attend a game.

Philadelphia Saddle Club

Monastery Stables, Kitchen's Lane, Philadelphia, PA 19119
(215) 233-0341

It's not easy finding places to ride with others in the area, but the Saddle Club is one of the best. Located in our own Fairmount Park, the club owns eight fine horses, and for a monthly fee ($155 currently), members can ride as often as they wish. There are no more than 24 members (3 to one horse), both men and women, who are required to take several lessons upon joining. This is a lively club that participates in local shows and parades, carriage driving, a Halloween horse show in costume, and social events like cookouts following riding activities. Meetings and newsletter part of the deal.

☎   Tom Fitzpatrick
🏇   Initiation fee $350; $155/monthly thereafter (includes tackle)

Riders of the Wissahickon

Courtesy Stables, 901 Cathedral Road, Philadelphia, PA 19128
(215) 482-9303   www.courtesystable.com

Riders is an organization that has a broad spectrum of educational goals, including safe riding, as well as a 4-H program in which members teach animal care with live animals at Courtesy Stables. In addition, the organization works to raise awareness about the care of local natural areas like Wissahickon Park. Adult volunteers are always needed to care for and work with the animals. Home to the Riders club, Courtesy Stables offer riding lessons to the public, including group (4-6) and private classes, in jumping and dressage. Initiative and sincere interest are the bywords for the Riders advocacy group and this interesting, local stable.

Woodedge Equestrian Center

116A Borton Landing Road, Moorestown (Burlington County), NJ 08057
(856) 235-5623   weshorse@aol.com www.woodedge.com

Only 11 miles from the Liberty Bell, people are taking private and group lessons in English and Western riding for recreational and competitive show riding purposes. This is a year-round facility where you can get involved in all aspects of horsemanship as well as horse care. Since they run many horse shows in South Jersey, students can get fully involved in these events—and do!

Photo by Jonna Naylor

Each Spring Mt. Airy Learning Tree sponsors a group ride
from Rittenhousetown to Valley Forge

Games & Sports

Indoor Games

AIDS Fund: *Gay Bingo*

1227 Locust Street, Philadelphia, PA 19107
(215) 731-9255   www.aidsfundphilly.org
Activity Location: Gershman YMHA, Broad & Pine, Philadelphia, PA

People come from as far as Boston to attend this hilarious gay bingo game to raise money for local AIDS organizations. You don't have to be gay to play. It's open to everyone who cares about getting rid of that damn disease; you can even give your winnings back to the AIDS fund. If you get "Bingo" watch out for the BVDs (Bingo Verification Divas) dressed up for the theme of the evening. They'll glide over to you on roller skates to be sure you have a true Bingo! The whole evening is a riot of fun. Better make reservations in advance and plan on coming back again.

☀ One Saturday a month

💰 $15 for balcony; $18 for floor

Bridge Club of Philadelphia

1530 Spruce Street, Philadelphia, PA 19102
(215) 732-1148   www.phillybridge.com

The Bridge Club is likely the only player owned bridge club in the Delaware Valley. On Wednesday evenings, there is a beginner's broup from 7-10pm with supervised play. On the other days, regular games are offered, with special games on Saturday afternoons.

☀ Mondays, Tuesdays, Wednesdays, & Thursdays

💰 $7/game

Chess Club at Barnes & Noble

Activity Location: Barnes & Noble, 102 Park Ave., Willow Grove, PA
(215) 659-1001

People of all ages (predominantly 20s-40s) arrive on two Wednesdays a month to win chess matches. Just bring your board and be prepared to play!

☀ 1st & 3rd Wednesdays   ⏰ 7:30pm

💰 Free

Games & Sports

Center City Miniature Gamers

(215) 729-1561   john.a.desmond.cgs80@alumni.upenn.edu
CCMG used to meet regularly in downtown Philadelphia to paint toy soldiers
and refight historical miniature battles. They may still do so. You can check.
☏ John Desmond

Eastern Pennsylvania Gaming Society

www.epgs.org

*Activity Location: Best Western Fort Washington Inn, 285 Commerce Dr., Fort
Washington, PA 19034 (215) 542-7930*

EPGS is the largest strategy gaming club in the Philadelphia metropolitan area,
and caters to all kinds of gamers and the games they enjoy playing. With an
average monthly attendance of over 50 people per meeting and an overall
membership of 150 plus, there is never the lack of something to do! Whether
you are new to the strategy gaming hobby or a real "grognard," EPGS is the
ideal place to find new opponents, learn new games, and get the opportunity to
blow the dust off some of your old ones. (from the EPGS web site) No matter
when you get there, they say there is always someone to play a game with.
Other Gamer groups include Penn Gamers (pgamers@dolphin.upenn.edu) and
the Philadelphia Area Gaming Enthusiasts, or PAGE (www.philagamers.org;
santillo@mac.com). Check on the web for information on these groups. Or you
might do best to go to EPGS and find out about the other groups there.

☼ 3rd Sat./mo   ⏰ 10am-10pm

Games & Sports

Fergie's Pub Quizo Nights

1214 Sansom Streets, Philadelphia, PA 19107
(215) 928-8118   http://fergies.com

Every Tuesday and Thursday nights you can match gaming wits with friendly strangers in a challenging game of Quizo. Table competes against table, trying to come up with answers to questions about everything from food to Shakespeare to the constellations. Bring your own table of about 8-10 people or try to prove your value to an existing group. About 60 people each time, with regulars who can knock your socks off—but everybody's having fun. Winning tables win a nice credit on their (delicious) food tab. This is a neat center city place with "eclectic ambience inspired by the mad genius of its namesake, yet the place still remains faithful to the Old World style of the pubs of The Emerald Isle." (from Fergie's web site)

☼ Tuesday and Thursdays   ⏰ 9:30pm

Franklin Mercantile Chess Club

1420 Walnut Street, Su. 460, Philadelphia, PA
(215) 546-1883

www.uschess.org/clubs   national web site for chess gives local clubs
Also   www.chessclub.com/clubs   for local clubs

These are real players at the FMCC, a club over 100 years old, so you need to know how to play. Several local chess clubs have regular games as well, and include the Main Line Chess Club in Gladwyne. Call (610) 649-0750 to reach Dan about the Main Line group, or go to his web site: members.home.net/danheisman/chess.htm for lots of information about chess as well as a listing for chess clubs in the state. You don't have to be a real good player to join these clubs, but you have to know how to play and want to learn more.

☼ Monday-Saturday   ⏰ 12:30-10:30pm

Scrabble Club

(610) 269-1723

Activity Location: Fairfield Inn, 5 N. Pottstown Pike (Rtes. 113 & 100), Exton, PA

Members of the Exton Scrabble Club are serious players, following competition rules of NSA. But they include people of all skill levels, including beginners who play within the club to prepare for tournaments. They meet weekly to play and arrange tournament schedules. In between games, these word lovers know how to socialize! Newsletter. Check for other clubs on the web site for Pennsylvania scrabble clubs (www.teleport.com/stevena/scrabble/clubs/pa.html).

☼ Mondays   ⏰ 6pm
💰 about $3/evening

Lacross, Rugby & Soccer

Philadelphia Box Lacross Association

6006 Augusta Street, Philadelphia, PA 19149
www.phillyboxlacrosse.org

"The Philadelphia Box Lacrosse Association is a non-profit incorporated lacrosse organization that is dedicated to the promotion and growth of lacrosse in the Delaware Valley through competitive league activity, tournament organization, as well as instruction to novice players of all ages. The PBLA is in its fourteenth year of existence and consists of players from all levels such as pros, college, intermediate, high school, and players who have never played organized box lacrosse. Even though the league was founded on the principles of good sportsmanship, fairness, and the competitive spirit of lacrosse, we must make it clear that this is a competitive league and Box Lacrosse is a full-contact sport." (from their web site) This sounds like a pretty exciting sport. You can register online once you enter the web site.

Philadelphia Women's Rugby Football Club

P.O. Box 42896, Philadelphia, PA 19101
(215) 309-0422 (hot line)   www.pwrfc.org

Activity Location: Pumpkinfest Tournament: 14th annual competition, Edgley Field (Fairmount Park), Phila., PA

PWRFC is an open and welcoming crew with a nice balance of serious competitiveness along with healthy fun and social events. Anyone, regardless of rugby playing experience, is welcome to join. "PWRFC is the oldest senior women's (rugby) team, and the premier senior women's team in the tri-state area. Our success is due to the efforts and talents of our veteran players, but *more importantly* to the steady stream of new players who join our ranks. And even if you don't want to play rugby, we'd love to have you as a social member! For us, it genuinely is a case of 'the more the merrier.' Come on ... give us a shot! If you have any inclination to play or continue to play this sport—we're the one to join! Seriously!" (This was abstracted from their web site. It has to be the most welcoming web site I've ever seen!) This group also has movie nights, dinners out, a park fitness run, and other fun-sounding social events!

Schuylkill River Exiles Rugby Football Club

(267) 200-0687   info@skillrugby.com   www.skillrugby.com

Activity Location: Practices at 4th & Washington Ave., Phila., PA; Games at FDR Park, South Broad St., Phila., PA

SRERFC says they are the only rugby club playing and training in center city Philadelphia. They welcome new players and provide a high standard of coaching to both beginners and experienced players. There are fall and spring season games as well as Summer 7's, usually in Fairmount Park. This club says if you are looking for rugby in Philadelphia, you have found it! This is a men's team. They socialize at O'Neals on 3rd and South Street after their games. Check the web site before you go looking for them—it's updated regularly with all their events.

Martial Arts

Aikido Koki Kai

43 N. 3rd Street, Philadelphia, PA
(215) 829-1777

Owner Cecilia Riccioti emphasizes that Aikido is the only spiritual/martial art that is one hundred percent defensive. You can protect yourself and your partner at the same time! This school is over 20 years old, holds ongoing classes six days a week, and includes men and women of all ages. All levels of classes are held and include between 4-15 participants. There is an affiliate branch in Germantown.

Aikido Seishinkan Dojo

50 East Germantown Pike, Norristown, PA 19401
(610) 239-9950   www.aikidoseishinkan.org

Classes seven days a week during the day and evening classes five days (no weekends) for students at all skill levels. Generally there are between 10-20 people in each class. Be prepared to go at least twice a week if you want to develop proficiency. You can take one week of unlimited free classes to see if it's for you.

💰 $70/month for unlimited classes, discounted for family members

Disston Recreation Center: *Karate Class*

Hellerman & Hegerman Streets, Philadelphia (Tacony), PA
(215) 685-8734

Classes are held for interested adults at the very reasonable rate of $20/month. You can bring your child with you, too.

☀ Mondays and Wednesdays   ⏰ 7pm

Philadelphia Judo Club

(215) 567-1478   (Art at the Whodunit Book Store)
Activity Location: Central YMCA, 1425 Arch Street, Phila., PA

There is no feeling so wonderful (to me) as throwing someone bigger than yourself down on a mat. In judo you will learn stretches and exercises for throwing and off-balancing "games" (you "play" judo), and the Kada necessary to advance through the belts. All levels are welcome on all days. About 25% of the players are women in classes that average between 10-25 people. You must be a member of the Y to take these judo classes taught by Art, one of the finest teachers you'll ever meet. (I know. He made me throw him once. It was grand!)

☀ Mondays, Thursdays, & Fridays from 7:30-9:30pm, Sundays -10am-12pm

Games & Sports

Miscellany

East Coast Pool League

802 Sansom Street, Su. 3D, Philadelphia, PA 19107
(215) 925-EAST   george@poolleague.com   also www.barsports.com

Eighty-one teams have emerged after only three years, including those in Fishtown, Jersey, Center City, North Philly, and the suburbs. You need to be over 21 to belong, but all abilities are welcome, since your score is handicapped. Women and men enjoy some serious shooting, and also have fun and lots of laughs. $20/year gets you a yearly membership, including a league (logo) shirt and a membership patch. Also, you can win some pretty hefty cash prizes (from match fees) if you make it to the divisional playoffs or national tournament.
💰 $6/player/weekly match

The Explorers Club

(732) 477-8404   steve@diversion2.com   www.explorers.org/philadelphia.html
Activity Location: Various around the city

Have you always yearned to be an explorer but haven't gotten around to the high adventure yet? Come to the Explorers Club and enjoy the company of others like yourself while you listen to people who have hot air ballooned over the North Pole, climbed Everest, or worked on the NASA space project. They meet 8-10 times a year in nice spots like the Pyramid Club, and all are welcome. The society is dedicated to the advancement of field research and scientific exploration, and the ideal that it is vital to preserve the instinct to explore. It serves as a meeting point and unifying force for explorers and scientists worldwide. The national group offers high-end wonderful educational trips. (Participants who qualify may be reptile researchers, divers, and archaeologists.)

Fencing Academy of Philadelphia, Inc.

3519 Lancaster Avenue (Powelton Village), Philadelphia, PA 19104
(215) 382-0293   maestromasters@msn.com   www.fap-fencing.com

They say that fencing is the world's oldest modern sport. At the Fencing
Academy you can see lots of dueling going on but not the violent type. "It's the
kind of thrilling competition that promotes physical, intellectual, and creative
flow," and includes considerable strategy. The director is a former national
champion, and he makes champions out of his students if they are really serious.
Even if they aren't, this game is challenging and fun for all ages, both men and
women.

💰 $230 for 10 weeks (twice a week) with equipment and materials included

Fitness Works Philadelphia Boxing Center & Gym

938 South 8th Street, Philadelphia, PA 19147
(215) 599-3939   www.fitnessworksforyou.com

Formerly "Rocky's Gym," this renovated facility includes free weights, circuit
training, and cardiovascular equipment, as well as a complete boxing center with
a USA Boxing-approved 20-foot boxing ring. The center offers speed bags,
heavy bags, and over 15 boxing classes each week. You can also learn from a
personal trainer.

Hi Spot Lanes

Pechin & Hermit (Roxborough), Philadelphia, PA 19128
(215) 483-2120

This is a small, unpretentious bowling alley in Roxborough where everyone feels
comfortable. They don't offer classes, but do offer League play Monday to
Friday evenings and again on Sundays, where local experts will be sure to give
good advice. You can go in the fall and be part of the leagues that play tournaments all year. Men's leagues and mixed leagues are offered.

Moving Arts of Mt. Airy (MaMa):
Physical Theater & Equilibristics, Arts of the Impossible

(215) 842-1040
Activity Location: Corner of 550 Carpenter La. & Greene St., Phila., PA 19119

Try circus arts for beginners, including tightwire, juggling, unicycle,
stiltwalking, tumbling, plate-spinning, and more—every week, something new.
This is fun and challenging as well. MaMa offers tons of exciting classes in an
intimate, pleasant space with regular students. Call for a class schedule.

💰 $95/10 lessons

Games & Sports

Main Line Fly Tyers

(215) 885-0917

Activity Location: Schuylkill Valley Nature Center, 8480 Hagy's Mill Rd., Phila. PA

The men and women in this group meet to discuss the best fishing spots and the tried and true techniques of fly tie fishing. Experts are invited to discuss their expeditions and fishing wisdom with the group. Beginner and advanced classes are offered so everyone can be included on the group fishing trips.

☼ September to May 3rd Thurs./mo   ⏰ 7pm

O'Neils

3rd & South Streets, Philadelphia, PA 19147
(215) 574-9495   www.onealspub.com

O'Neals has a competition-quality English darts set-up. Darts are available at the bar. You can compete in Philadelphia Area Old English Darts Leagues here and at the Dickens Inn (2nd Street between Pine & Lombard Streets, 215-928-9307).

Para-Flying

(610) 644-3200   www.para-flying.com
Activity Location: New Hanover Airport, Pottstown, PA

Barry Shellington says para-flying is so simple to learn that most people can learn to do it in about an hour. You steer with your feet, right or left, and move the throttle forward to climb or back to descend. Sound simple? Well, it sounds very exciting! If you want to ask about it, Barry will answer your questions.

Philadelphia Hash House Harriers

www.voicenet.com/~huxster/Phhh/OnHHH.html

This web page is very smart alecky. This is a running group, sort of. I think they run weekly, probably go for beer afterward, and have no rules. See what you think. "A drinking club with a running problem. Runs/Apres are on Tuesday nights at 6:30 pm during the summer and Saturday at 3:00 pm for the rest of the year. New boots welcome." About 40-50 men and women show up regularly for weekly hashes which are between a half hour to two hours over hill and dale. There is socializing, after the workout. You have to look at the web site to see where the next run is. Directions (and really fun music) are provided, but there's no phone, so my information is as good as yours.
I'm going to try this one.

Philadelphia Jugglers Club

(215) 808-8859   Dickr7@juno.com
www.hal.com/services/juggle national web page
Activity Location: Year-round in Lloyd Hall, Boathouse Row on Kelly Drive

The more the merrier for this group, which for 20 years has been riding unicycles and tossing balls, clubs, and all kinds of props into the air. Very welcoming to newcomers, they'll teach you how to juggle. About 20-40 people show up to have fun. The group also holds a free 2-day festival in October.

☼ Mondays   ☎ 7:30-9:30pm

River City Billiards

4258 Main Street, Philadelphia (Manayunk), PA
(215) 482-7410

This is a nifty little place in the heart of Manayunk with an upscale feel where you can play some serious billiards. The walls are adorned with art and fun collectibles so you'll feel like you're playing in somebody's living room. There's even a non-smoking area. Dubbed Philly mag's "Best of Philly: Billiards and Place to Have a Party," it's the place to go when you're in the mood for a night of friendly challenge and game playing. The crowd is between 18 and 70 and includes plenty of women at one of the 20 tables or having a game of foosball. (What? Well come and find out!) A great place to hang out, improve your game, and meet people at the next table. The advice is free. So is the chalk.

☼ Every day   ☎ noon-1am

Games & Sports

Skirmish USA

Rte 903 HC-2, BOX 2245, Jim Thorpe, PA 18229
(800) 754-7647 www.skirmish.com
Activity Location: Rte. 903, 10 mi N of intersection Rte. 209 North, Jim Thorpe

Paintball these days is for the mainstream—women players, fathers and sons, and people who remember how much fun it was to play chase games. It's a version of Capture the Flag, involving lots of strategy and comaraderie. The *Inquirer* said, "the thrill of victory and the agony of the splat." Using washable paint balls in your gun, the idea is to spray your opponent with color and eliminate them from play. On one of 42 fields on 700 acres, you'll play in groups of from 10 to 20 people. If you don't come with your own friends, you'll be put on a team with other game-loving players. Games last about 30 minutes; you can then play again on another field. For those still not interested, Skirmish, an adventure organization, also has white water rafting, biking and hiking.

Sky High Hang Gliders sailing through the clouds

Sky High Hang Gliding

P.O. Box 911, Bryn Mawr, PA 19010
(610) 527-1687

Learn to fly! Sky High offers certified instruction in hang gliding with sophisticated, incredibly stable aircraft for "a fun and safe form of weekend recreation when done with proper training and education."

☎ Bill Umstattd

💰 $115 for an introductory tandem flight
with instructor at your side in a special
two-person glider.

South Jersey Kite Flyers

(215) 722-4092
www.geocities.com/Colosseum/Sideline/8309
Activity Location: Gloucester County Library, Mullica Hill, NJ (15 minutes from CC)

Come to a meeting where kite flyers talk about participating in upcoming kite festivals like the Wildwood Kite Festival (May) and the Core Creek Festival in Buck's County (May). Enjoy other players and lite refreshments and then you're off for kite flying for the afternoon. They know the best kites to buy, the best methods for getting them off the ground and out of the trees, and the best places to watch your kite soar while you forget your troubles and run like mad. You have to love it. You can find all the events and activities from the American Kiteflyers Association (1-800-252-2550; www.aka.kite.org).

☼ 3rd Sun./mo 🕐 1pm
☎ Mike Dallmer, President
💰 $10/individual; $15/family

Westbrook Lanes

1 Creek Road, Brooklawn, NJ 08030
(856) 456-2692   www.westbrooklanes.com

Westbrook is a family operation and has the friendly atmosphere you would expect. It is really crowded on most weeknights, which are the big league nights. Most of the leagues are mixed, but there are a few men's and women's leagues as well. If you need a few lessons, you can sign up for them here. You'll find that most bowlers are from 18 to 65 years and going strong, having a great time.

Windsurfing: *Ebbtide*

Route 309 & 463, Montgomeryville, PA
(215) 368-9095   www.dplus.net/ebbtide

You can take a great lesson at Ebbtide Windsurfing, where they claim to get anyone up and sailing. Contrary to what some think, this is not an issue of how strong you are. It's actually technique and balance that count, so a good lesson is important. Beginners will learn how to stand properly and how to turn, and more advanced students will learn a variety of maneuvers. $80 gives you two-plus hours of class and water instruction, rental equipment, and a book worth about $25. You should need only one lesson to start and then lots of practice.

Games & Sports

Recreational Groups

Appalachian Mountain Club, Delaware Valley Chapter

(215) 979-1174   info@amcdv.org   www.amcdv.org

This first-rate, enthusiastic, well-attended outdoor organization sponsors a variety of outdoor activities for all ages and experience levels: day-hiking, biking (regular road biking and mountain biking), canoeing, backpacking, climbing, and snowshoe trips. Beginners who are non-members are welcome on many trips, but it's easier to keep up to date if you are a member since there is an extensive newsletter. Members supply their own equipment. If you are at all interested in being outdoors, this is a terrific group to join.

💰 $40/yr

Black Women in Sport Foundation

P.O. Box 2610, Philadelphia, PA 19130
(215) 763-6609   www.blackwomeninsport.org

"The Black Women In Sport Foundation, founded in 1992, is dedicated to facilitating the involvement of Black women in every aspect of sport in the United States and around the world, through the "hands-on" development and management of grass roots level outreach programs." (from BWSF brochure) Programs include Black Women in Sport workshops, sports clinics, mentor programs, awards Banquets, coaching, etc. This group primarily focuses on creating many opportunities for young African-American women to be involved in sports. As part of this activity, there are many opportunities for adults to be involved in sports themselves.

Dynamic Diversions

P.O. Box 1775, Southeastern, PA 19399
(215) 849-9944   dynamicdiversion@hotmail.com   www.dynamicdiversions.org

Now in its 24th year, Dynamic Diversions has always been one of my favorite groups after many happy skiing and local canoeing trips. The events are well chosen, well organized, and very reasonable. You'll find hiking, biking, sailing (on the Chesapeake & Virgins), local and international skiing trips (Vermont and Switzerland), cross-country skiing, horseback riding, rock climbing, and more. There are occasional Sunday brunches with slide shows of DD in action. Participants are mostly—but not all—single people between ages 20 and 60 with the majority in the 30-40 range. Joe says the goal is for people to experience new adventures with new friends. Fits right in here!

☎ Joe Feisel

Eastern Cooperative Recreation School

(215) 729-6738   www.ecrs.org
Activity Location: Different places in and outside of the city

ECRS typically sponsors about 10 events a year: four weekends, two one-days, two week-long camps. These activities are great fun, but you learn about leadership and cooperative play as well. You can try games, drama and singing in a supportive atmosphere and have a great time playing your heart out. ECRS events are usually attended by between 30 to 50 people of all ages and styles.

💰   Very very reasonable

Outdoor Club of South Jersey, Inc.

P.O. Box 455, Cherry Hill, NJ 08003
(609) 427-7777 (hot line)   www.voicenet.com/~ubert4/ocsj

"The Outdoor Club of SJ is a nonprofit organization dedicated to providing low-cost opportunities for extending the individual's awareness, knowledge, appreciation, and enjoyment of the environment through experiences in outdoor activities." This club offers backpacking and hiking, bicycling, camping, cross-country skiing, and canoeing in a year-round program led by member volunteers. With 2000 members of all ages, many hikes draw 50 or more participants from all over the region. There are also many special activities like campfire evenings and activities weekends. Only $8/individual/year.

Philadelphia Sports Connection

317 Stony Hill Drive, Chalfont, PA 18914
(215) 996-0929   www.phillysportsconnection.com

This is a sports-based special events planning organization that brings friends, co-workers, and individuals together on a casual basis through coed sports leagues and special events. PSC offers terrific sports leagues for everyone, from the recreational player to the competitive athlete. If you miss the enjoyment and friendly competition of your college intramural program, it's time to get in the game! Activities include football, volleyball, basketball, soccer, floor hockey, softball, and include all who are interested in playing. Games take place primarily in the Bryn Mawr, Haverford, Manayunk areas.

South Jersey Ski Club

(609) 386-8841   sjsc@sjskiclub.com   www.sjskiclub.com
Activity Location: Meetings: Cherry Hill Holiday Inn, Rte 70 East, Cherry Hill, NJ

This club has been one of South Jersey's leading adult ski and social clubs for 39 years. With membership of about 500 members from all over the region, they have trips for all levels of skiers and an active year-round social schedule.

☼ 1st & 3rd Wed./mo   ⏰ 8-11pm

Games & Sports

Running

Bryn Mawr Running Club

P.O. Box 743, Bryn Mawr, PA 19010   *www.runbmrc.org*

Activity Location: Bryn Mawr Running Company, 828 W. Lancaster Ave.,
Bryn Mawr, PA (610) 527-5510

This group of about 250 members doesn't just run, they socialize too. Wednesday is the big day for them. They meet at 6 pm at the Bryn Mawr Running Company for a group social run—a fun run of 5-10 miles—followed by supper somewhere. (1/2 mile is a fun run for me...) On Tuesdays, they do a track workout at the Haverford College track. And on Saturday mornings, they run at 8:30 am, with some folks going out after. If you can keep up, you can have fun with them too!

☼ Runs on Wednesdays at 6pm & Saturdays at 8:30am

💰 $20/yr; $15/renewal

Frontrunners/Frontwalkers of Philadelphia

(215) 545-6990 (hot line) info@frontrunnersphila.org www.frontrunnersphila.org

FR/P is a diverse runners club in center city with runners of all abilities, races, creeds, and orientations. They incorporate track and field events such as relays, discus, and javelin. Activities have included participation in the local running events, the Gay Games, a Drag Race, and the Philadelphia Distance Run as part of their "Anniversary Weekend" with activities all weekend. FR/P also has regular running/walking workouts every week which are listed on the web site. The workouts are noncompetitive activities at various speeds for distances up to five miles. Participants meet at local eateries for a light meal and conversation afterwards. For many, FR/P has been an introduction to the gay and lesbian community, but for everyone it is a family of friends.

Fast Tracks runners still standing after a 10 mile race!

Fast Tracks

(610) 640-0331   info@fasttracks.org   www.geocities.com/runfasttracks
Activity Location: Saturdays at Betzwood side of Valley Forge Park (entrance to Bike Path) and Wednesdays at Conestoga High School track, Berwyn, PA

During daylight savings, Fast Track runs on the Conestoga track with different programs each Wednesday. There are four groups, so you can run at the pace best suited to support your athletic development and goals. During the winter there are fun runs in lighted areas. Babysitting is provided on Wednesdays. On Saturdays, rain or shine, they run the bike path and various trails in VF Park. Generally the run is about 6 miles, but you can run any distance and the group will fit you in. After the run, enjoy refreshments and great talk. All ages and all levels (and all weights, they told me!) are invited because the group is committed to supporting developing runners, as well as those at marathon level. If running interests you at all, you can find your niche here. Meetings and social events are also an important aspect of this organization.

☼ Runs on Wednesdays at 6:30pm & Saturdays at 8:30am

Sailing

Cooper River Yacht Club

P.O. Box 188, Collingswood, NJ 08108
(856) 869-9145   www.erols.com/wolf6001/cryc/cryc.htm

You can take lessons even though you don't belong to this private yacht club, which has an active weekend racing schedule (April to November). Beginners and advanced sailors learn sailing on small boats (10'-14') on weekdays and evenings from May to August. Then, when you fall hopelessly in love with sailing, you can buy your own small sailboat and join the club and race with them every Sunday. What a way to spend a weekend!

💰 8 lessons, 2 hours each, $120

Games & Sports

Women's Dragon Boat Team (page 235)

Gazela Philadelphia

801 South Columbus Boulevard, Philadelphia, PA 19147
(215) 218-0110   gazela@usa.net   www.gazela.org
Activity Location: Penns Landing area

For the cost of insurance plus dues (around $85/year) and a pair of kakai pants to go with your Gazela shirt, you can be crew on the oldest, largest, (sweetest) wooden, square-sailed ship still sailing in the world. This is an old Portuguese cod fishing boat that is retired from fishing off the coast of Greenland and lives near Penn's Landing in our fair city. The volunteer crew does maintenance (paint-ing, tarring, etc.) in the winter and sailing in the summer to places like Nova Scotia, Boston, NYC, and Norfolk. You'll feel like you're part of an old sea adventure as you hoist sails from the yardarms, but you'll sleep very well after evenings of socializing and singing sea shanties. I did this—it was super. (Each volunteer contributes 50 hours of maintenance to apply for a sail berth.)

Liberty Sailing Club

Pier 12, 235 North Columbus Boulevard, Philadelphia, PA 19106
(215) 627-SAIL (7245)   www.libertysailing.com

If you would love to go sailing, cruising, or racing nearby after work or on weekends, the Liberty Sailing Club is for you. Try out a free sail on Tuesday evenings before you decide to join—great for beginners. If you're experienced crew, you can take a series for new skippers both in the classroom and on the water, including racing skills. LSC's sailing year is long, with boats on the Delaware from late March until the Saturday after Thanksgiving. The club holds many events such as lectures, slideshows, trips, classes, and social activities including barbeques, a Chinese Banquet, Mid-Summer Night's party, Crab Fest, and more. LSC cooperates with the Liberty Sailing School where you can take lessons from certified instructors.

Philadelphia Sailing Club

(610) 668-1234 (hot line) www.webcom.com/psc
Activity Location: The Cynwyd Club, 332 Trevor Lane, Bala Cynwyd, PA 19004

This excellent 22-year-old sailing club charters boats for 14 weekend local sails, usually on the gorgeous Chesapeake Bay. On the 32'-51' boats are sailors with a range of experience, from novices to seasoned experts, so beginners learn first-hand on the water. The club organizes and conducts instructional courses in various aspects of sailing. Members are men and women of all ages who meet monthly for business and socializing. There are US and international sailing trips to the Caribbean, Tahiti, Greece, and many more, appropriate to the season. If you've been thinking about sailing, this is a terrific way to get started.

☼ 3rd Wed./mo except December   ☎ 8-9:30pm

Windsurfing Club

(610) 648-4446 (John Janssen)
Activity Location: Marsh Creek, Yardley, PA

This windsurfing club meets on a pretty casual basis because they always need the third party (the wind) to come and he shows up when he feels like it! Communications between members often take place via voice mail because they spend so much time on the water, away from their phones! Windsurfing takes place at Marsh Creek, as well as Nockamixon Lake or Peace Valley, so take a lesson at Ebbtide Windsurfing, grab your board, and join up with fellow splash-sailors!

Skating: In-line, Roller & Ice

Drive Sports

2601 Pennsylvania Avenue, Philadelphia, PA (across from Art Museum),
& One Boathouse Row, Philadelphia, PA (near Lloyd Hall)
(215) 232-RENT & (215) 235-RENT   jen@bladinaction.com
www.drivesports.net

If skating tickles your fancy, be sure to call for an indoor skate lesson and then test your mettle on the sidewalks along the Schuylkill River and Kelly Drive. Look for the Drive Sports van where you can find out about classes; they will provide the rollerblades and gear. So, whether you ride, roll, run, or walk, the Drive is for you to glide along with all the other outdoor enthusiasts. Also, on the weekends from April to October, you can enjoy the whole road on West River Drive, closed to cars and open for fun and fitness.

Games & Sports

Landskaters Inline Skate Club: *City Skates*

P.O. Box 128, Collingswood, NJ 08108
(856) 988-9898   info@landskaters.org   www.landskaters.org
Activity Location: Phila. Museum of Art, 26th & Benjamin Franklin Parkway,
Phila., PA

If you are a good in-line skater, this is the group for you. You are ready to skate around the city if you can negotiate curbs, stop on hills, and stop for traffic, at the least. All ages of skaters, men and women, don protective gear (required) and skate the city, checking notable Philadelphia spots on Saturdays, Sundays, and Tuesdays. You don't have to be a member to join Landskater's City Skate events. Club members take trips to cities around the country, where they meet up with local groups to skate. The biggest skate weekend of the year in Philadelphia is June 25-27, Freedom Skate Weekend, when clubs from around the country gather for a variety of exciting skating events. Call for information about which days fit your skating ability.

☼ Int: Suns. (10am-12noon); Exp.: Tues. (7-10pm); Adv.: Sats. (7-10pm)

💰 $32/membership, for newsletter, t-shirt, and trips

Penn In-Line Skating Club

http://dolphin.upenn.edu/~pracpenn/pp13a_orgs.html#hobbies

On the above web site, the University of Pennsylvania lists its myriad student activities. They include all kinds of hobby groups, such as amateur radio, paintball, flyfishing, an in-line skating group, and much more. I was told that some groups are open to non-Penn students and others are not; you have to ask each group. They look so terrific that I thought you might want the listing so you could check the great things happening on Penn's campus and call for info.

River Rink at Penn's Landing

(215) 925-RINK www.riverrink.com

Not only can you skate every day of the week from the end of November until February 28 on Penn's Landing, but you can take lessons to learn how to skate as well! Group lessons are held on Saturdays and Sundays with 4-5 different levels of classes offered. The class runs for four consecutive weeks, with two sessions of classes per season. The cost was $60, including skate rental, but if you signed up for both sessions, the rate was reduced.

☼		🕐	
Mondays-Thursdays		6-9pm	
Fridays-Saturdays		12:30-10:30pm	
Sundays		12:30-9pm	

Skiing

Blazers Ski Club

P.O. Box 13052, Philadelphia, PA 19101

(215) 829-8100 (hot line)   www.blazersskiclub.org

Activity Location: Harrambee Institute, 66th & Media, Phila. PA (West Phila.)

Blazers is the Philadelphia chapter of the National Brotherhood of Skiers, a predominately African American ski club with a strong commitment to training minority youth. However, the ski club has an active adult program (over 200 members) where you can learn to ski, meet friendly and interesting people, take various trips, and do exciting things. There are ski trips in the Poconos, Vermont and Europe, and a semi-annual Summit for a week, held in the Rocky Mountains, with 82 clubs participating. Other social events include local networking brunches, golf outings, sailing, and lots of local and regional biking events, including some with other bike groups. This is an all around social club.

☼ Meetings every 2nd Tues./mo from September to June

Fall Line Ski Club

P.O. Box 1535, Cherry Hill, NJ 08034

(856) 931-4462   www.fallline.org

Activity Location: Day's Inn, Rte. 73 & Fellowship Rd., Mt. Laurel, NJ

"A Delaware Valley ski club that never stops." Well-established with over 625 members 74% of which are single and equally divided between male and female. Experience levels range from beginners to advanced. Ski trip destinations include New England, western US, Canada, and Europe. For beginners, the season begins with a week of lessons, lodging, and meals at Mt. Tremblant, Canada. For non-skiers, there are many non-skiing events, enjoyed by all in the club, such as golfing, hiking, parties, white-water rafting, biking, and more. At the meetings, people get information about the group and upcoming events, and indulge in great socializing. There are also three special events each year: Spring Fling, Snoball, and the Christmas party.

☼ 1st & 3rd Tues./mo   ⏰ 8pm

Killington Resort

4763 Killington Road, Killington, VT, 05751

(800) 621-MTNS   info@killington.com   www.killlington.com

I know it's not in the area, but if you really are serious about learning to ski, you should check out the slopes in Vermont. Killington offers a 5-day/night Learn-to-Ski week starting at $347 (in 2001). That includes lodging, lift pass, lessons, and equipment. Not bad. And I'll bet you meet lots of nice people in the lodge. There is also a lovely summer package, including golf, tennis, and the like.

Games & Sports

King of Prussia Ski Club

P.O. Box 60146, King of Prussia, PA 19406
(610) 26-KOPSC (hot line)   www.kopsc.com
Activity Location: Holiday Inn, 260 Mall Blvd., King of Prussia, PA 19406

This year-round sports and social club provides a variety of activities. Meetings, which are open to nonmembers as well as members, have themes such as a ski equipment and fashion show, dancing, games, and talent shows. There are social activities all through the year. The group sponsors include happy hours, biking, in-line skating, tennis, softball, sailing, car rallies, ice-skating, dinner dances, and banquets. KPSC joins with other clubs to do community projects, and offer learn-to-ski clinics, ski racing clinics and club ski nights held at local ski areas, has a ski racing team. These are only a few of the exciting activities sponsored by this group. This is a *very active* group!

☼ 3rd Tues./mo from September to April

North Penn Ski Club

819 Chestnut Street, Lansdale, PA 19446   call Scott 215-234-0358
(215) 997-USKI   http://hometown.aol.com/DSchoneker/NPSC.html
Activity Location: Meetings at Elks Lodge on Trewigtown Road, Colmar, PA

Scheduled speaker/activity followed by business meeting.Try the ski trips every month, local, national, and international, as well as events like sailing trips on the Chesapeake, bike rides, hikes, fun tours, picnics, and outings to games (speed racing). A general all-around outdoor group.

☼ 2nd Thurs./mo from Sept. thru April   ⏰ 7:30pm

New Hope Nordics: *A Cross-Country Ski Club*

P.O. Box 52688, Philadelphia, PA 19115
(215) 283-2840 (president Rico Paolino)   www.newhopenordics.com
Activity Location: Jesse Soby American Legion Post, Richardson & Bellevue Aves.,
Langhorne, PA (1/2 mi. south of the business district, behind the bank)

The only ski group in the area devoted to cross-country skiing, this group takes trips to NY state and Vermont often during the ski season. Plus they include a terrific list of places to ski on their web site. There is socializing after the skiing and occasional events, such as summer picnics, holiday parties, and trips to the TK Club in Conshohocken for Cajun dancing, and the like. You don't have to be a member to attend the meetings, but do be sure to tip the friendly bartender.

☼ One Tues./mo   ⏰ 8pm

Swimming & Scuba

Aqua Hut divers taking a break

Aqua Hut Dive & Travel

51 Rittenhouse Street, Ardmore, PA 19003
(610) 642-3483   Christine@aquahut.net   www.aquahut.net

Learn to scuba dive and you too can hunt for underwater treasure with these divers! Aqua Hut offers classes year round, and the location, format, and class schedule varies depending on the needs of the clients. From the pool, divers graduate to local diving spots or exotic Caribbean waters. People get to know each other through classes, trips, and special events and do lots of socializing around the water! If diving is not for you, snorkelers are always welcome.

Blue Horizons Dive Center

1100 S. Columbus Boulevard, Philadelphia, PA 19147
(215) 462-7587   mail@bluehorizons.net   www.bluehorizons.net

Everything you can imagine having to do with scuba and snorkeling is done at Blue Horizon. There are lessons (beginning through instructor), trips, both local (NJ coast) and international (Caribbean, Pacific Rim-Mayalasia), and others. I was told there is a very strong community of divers here, with a coffeehouse atmosphere on weekends and evenings when divers are chewing the diving fat. For the non-scuba people, BH offers a full component for snorkelers who join the divers on trips. This is a full-service diving center with certification programs as well.

Games & Sports

Tennis & Racquetball

Northeast Racquet Club & Fitness Club

Krewstown Road & Grant Avenue, Philadelphia, PA 19115
(215) 671-9220

If you are looking for a place to play racquetball or tennis, consider this club where you can take lessons, rent courts for you and your playing partners, and join a playing league. It is for players of all skill levels. This is also a full-service fitness club, with weights, treadmills, a pool, hot tub, steam room, physical therapy/chiropractic services, and more.

💰 Racquetball: $75/yr membership with pay as you play at $12-16hr/court
Tennis: $75/yr membership with pay as you play at $25-35/hr/court

Philadelphia Tennis Club

422 East Locust Street, Philadelphia, PA 19144
(215) 844-9941

This is a membership tennis organization with an open tennis contract. You pay by the season, which goes from March to October, to play on outdoor softcourt and clay/hardcourt surfaces. For those who wish it, instruction is offered, as well as team competition and round robins for singles and doubles.

💰 Around $200/season

"Dr." Art Carey's main prescription (for getting fit):
Go out and play.
Go out and have fun.

Princeton Tennis Parties

(609) 799-8214   swansonint1@home.com

Activity Location: Princeton Indoor Tennis Center, 92 Washington Rd. (Rte. 571), Princeton, NJ

Tennis parties take place on a regular basis for single and married players of all levels. The format of the events is that married players go on the court at 7pm, eat and socialize at 7:45pm, and go back on the court at 8:30pm. Single players go on the court at 7:45pm, and break from 8:30pm to 9:15pm. People are grouped with others at their level as much as possible. Members enjoy other activities, including socializing at holiday parties.

☼   1st, 2nd & 3rd Sat./mo from October to April

💰   For individuals: 1 party $30, 2 parties $56, 3 parties $78

Swarthmore Adult Tennis Camp

444 East 82nd Street, New York, NY 10028

(800) ACE-2442   greatennis@aol.com   www.tennisresortsonline.com

Activity Location: Swarthmore College, Swarthmore, PA

"Designed for all level club players from beginner to advanced. The emphasis is on teaching tennis skills and strategies. It's ideal for players who want to play lots of tennis, improve their game, meet other tennis enthusiasts and have fun." (from the web site) There are programs designed for the weekend, 3-days, and 5-days, so you can choose your course. Also, there are special weeks for singles and for advanced players. From June to mid-August. Resident and non-resident.

💰   Runs from $335 (weekend non-resident) to $850 (5-day resident, including accomodations + tennis program)

Tennis Farm

235 North Aberdeen Avenue, Wayne, PA 19087

(610) 687-2557 or (800) 7-TENNIS   http://tennisfarm.com

You don't have to belong to a fancy country club to find friends with whom you can play tennis. The Tennis Farm offers playing opportunities and lessons for all levels of players in Center City, Chestnut Hill, Pottstown, Wayne, Moorestown, and Wilmington. At scheduled times, men and women at your skill level will be ready to play fun matches, team matches, and ladder matches against other branches of the TF. After the matches are over, enjoy the social comaraderie. It's all set up for you.

Games & Sports

 **Here are some extra resources to check out**

Books

• *Short Bike Rides in Eastern Pennsylvania* (Bill Simpson)
  Hoops Nation: A Guide to America's Best Pickup Basketball (Chris Ballard)

Activities

• *MS 150 City to Shore Bike Tour,* (215) 271-1500

Web Sites

• *www.skitops.com,* Ski Tour Operators Association
• *www.gorp.com,* Guide to Outdoor Recreation and Active Travel
• *www.uschess.org,* Chess Federation
• *www.sportsmatchonline.com,* SportsMatch Online helps find partners or teams for all kinds of physical activities while traveling. This is a service that costs an annual fee. Since you are meeting people on-line, use care and common sense when providing information about yourself.
• *www.ACEonline.org,* American Coaster Enthusiasts site. Group has regular events at amusement parks and a national convention
• *www.acanet.org/acanet.htm,* American Canoe Association, a recreation and conservation association
• *www.rivercountry.net,* Bucks County River Country for canoeing and white water rafting, tubing, etc. in Point Pleasant, NJ (215) 297-TUBE
• *www.kittatinny.com,* Kittatinny Canoes in Dingmans Ferry. Go tubing, white water rafting, kayaking, etc. (800) 356-2852
• *www.dcnr.state.pa.us/stateparks/parks,* Pennsylvania State Parks site, with recreation opportunities as well as directions, rules, etc. Great for planning your summer vacation. (For Lake Nockamixon: add "/nock.htm" to the web address.)
• *http://users.erols.com/runadvte,* Runners' Advocate, with information for runners in the Delaware Valley, including a schedule of races, running clubs, and links to other sites for running and training.

Health for Mind & Body

Exercise • Healthy Eating • Personal Growth
Walks for Charity • Yoga & Meditation

Health for Mind & Body

Students doing sitting meditation at Shambhala

Getting a good stretch in a fitness class at Jefferson Hospital

Health for Mind & Body

Although many of us have taken steps toward a healthier life style—meaning that we have given up smoking, hard liquor, and red meat, started eating more fruits and vegetables, and begun taking brisk walks on weekends—there are those who take healthy living much more seriously. (You see them out there, if you're not one of them yourself.) These folks are riding bikes or walking vigorously at 7am. They wouldn't miss their spinning class right after work, and get up half an hour earlier than they need to so they can meditate. They may visit an acupuncturist, a herbologist, or a homeopath; they usually don't drink alcohol and definitely don't smoke. You can tell who they are because they don't just talk the talk, they walk the walk.

Why do they go to all this effort? After all, life is complicated enough. No-foolin' health enthusiasts tell me that they not only want to live longer, they want to enjoy the benefits of an improved quality of life that a 'clean' body and a more serene state of mind allow. They also tell me that keeping in touch with a community whose members put real energy into taking care of themselves supports their efforts not to slide back into unhealthy habits. Health-conscious communities may practice meditation together, prepare and eat delicious healthy foods together, or discuss spiritual awareness and psychological topics. Participants of these groups find teachers and attend classes to learn the latest information about organic/vegetarian diets, movement and exercise, and meditation and healing. Most important, they enjoy each other in a big way, bonding around their mutual efforts toward feeling really good.

You *know* how much better *you* feel when you have an exercise program, no matter what it is. Whether it's walking in Fairmount Park, weekend birdwatching trips, meditating in the mornings, or sculling on the Schuylkill River, finding a regular activity that you love will keep you moving. (Remember Meryl Streep in *Ride The Wild River* rowing alone every morning on the Charles River—didn't that look like a romantic way to exercise?!) We're also more likely to continue with an exercise program when we do it with others who expect us to show up for mutual workout sessions, like a class, several times a week. The point is to find a community to encourage your huffing and puffing and *stretchhh* noises, with an *aahhhhh* at the end. A community with whom you sweat, groan and share the joyful "It's over and wasn't it great!" feeling (easy to say *after* it's over). There's something so satisfying about being part of a

Health for Mind & Body

living, moving group whole, going in the same direction (usually) across the gym, in sync, in communication.

If you're looking for places to do this—places to exercise, stretch and move—you can find them in neighborhoods and studios throughout the city. Most noticeable are the good old reliable "Y's," which have been face-lifted and offer high-quality professional classes for very reasonable prices. It's hard to go wrong at the "**Y**," and some insurance plans will help defray the cost with partial reimbursement if you go regularly. I absolutely love the **Roxborough "Y."** There's always something I want to do there, like swim, take a step-class, do cardio kick-boxing, lift weights (while watching overhead TV), ride the Internet-bike, or take a spinning class. Afterwards I treat myself to a stint in the sauna and come out feeling like a million. It's where I meet and chat with people from my neighborhood while we work out together. We commiserate (*and* keep each other moving) on the gym floor, on the treadmill, and in the locker room.

But there are plenty of other places to take classes that sound interesting, like Pilates, jazz dancing, yoga to music, and exercise using the Alexander Technique. These places, including the **Moving Arts Studio** in Mt. Airy and the **Learning Studio** in Langhorne, also have basic exercise classes as well, enjoyed by many who live in the neighborhood or in the surrounding areas. You can call and ask about their programs, and then visit to see if it's your cup of tea. You probably know that many hospitals offer complete wellness programs, including fine exercise programs, where you may want to work out as a follow-up to a nutrition class in the same place.

If you're a health enthusiast, you are likely quite interested in connecting with others around food subjects, including where and what to purchase, and how to prepare it. Groups that discuss ways to create a diet that improves your quality of life, prevents disease, and makes a caring environment for those you love have come into their own in Philadelphia. Our own now-famous **Christine Pirello** (she's on PBS-TV and writes books) gives the most marvelous classes for only $25, where you discover that macro food is truly delicious. (It's *not* all alfalfa sprouts and tofu! Try the brussels sprouts recipe on page 231 of *Cooking the Whole Foods Way*. It's a mainstay in my dinner party repertoire.) Standing in front of you, she cooks foods you will eat, all the while explaining how food and true good health are intimately related.

Health for Mind & Body

There are more and more stores in the area where organic food can be purchased with advice on how to prepare it. If you haven't yet shopped at **Whole Foods Market** (used to be Fresh Fields), get yourself in there to discover interesting organic products, unusual and exciting grains, and macrobiotic staples, such as umeboshi vinegar and three different kinds of miso. If you want to learn things like how to cook burdock or make an exciting sugarless dessert, keep tabs on the events and hands-on demonstrations at Whole Foods, including special events just for singles. At the other end of town is **Essene**, a fine, high-quality, healthy foods store and café where you can find out about the health community events around town. Check the bulletin board and pick up the publications stacked near the front door. I bought my first mochi in Essene. I loved both the mochi *and* Essene, and make it a point to stop in when I need to get started on my healthy path again.

Breaking bread with other healthy food enthusiasts is a great way to socialize with that community. **Arnold's** in Manayunk offers all kinds of support for raw food gourmets with lectures, breakfasts and potlucks. The **Organic Planet Dinner Club** is a delightful place to enjoy mostly macrobiotic vegetarian food, deliciously prepared. You'll have great conversations if you sit with the regulars at the community table for these feasts once a month. Lindsey, who cooks, also offers classes so you can learn to make what you've been eating. The **Vegetarian Society** gets together for dinners and other events, and I've just discovered **Club Veg**, a national group with a local branch that sponsors many activities for vegetarian folks to find and support each other. All these activities are important because they help counteract the temptations to eat fast food high-fat and high-sugar foods which are always around us. It makes a big difference to have information and support from others who, like you, care about eating well. Since these are issues that people are passionate about, it's understandable that a community has formed around them.

The organizations included in the Personal Growth section of this chapter feature some form of spiritual and/or psychological awareness workshops, as well as movement classes. For example, there are all-around health and wellness centers, such as the **Becoming Center** or the **Oreland Health Center**, that offer a potpourri of sessions on everything from a Course in Miracles to reflexology and stress reduction. Women can attend sessions explaining the *Tanya,* or take an exercise class to relieve menopause symptoms at the **Heart of the Goddess**. They can try

Health for Mind & Body

gardening or cooking as a method of alternative healing, as well as yoga and meditation, at the **Wise Woman's Center**. There are lectures/discussions on the teachings of Jung to learn the wisdom in fairy tales (**Jung Society**), in addition to talks about spirituality at the **Garland of Letters** on South Street. All of these offer a community of people who reflect on and talk about their changing lives (journey) as they seek understanding and wisdom. If you're looking for a weekend retreat, consider **Omega** (see *A Closer Look*, page 283), **Kripalu**, or **Rowe**. Each offers a serene environment away from normal life stresses, with classes and workshops to promote personal growth, as well as meditation and yoga practice. Sometimes getting away from your routines helps you to move forward.

If you're looking for an on-the-spot, one-shot exercise opportunity with a lot of people and a delightful atmosphere, try one of the Walks/Runs for Charity listed in the *Weekend Section* of the *Philadelphia Inquirer* on Fridays. In the fall and spring, you can count on an outdoor charity event almost every weekend. My favorites are the ones for AIDS and breast cancer, which draw lots of people with a common interest in raising money and having a good time with like-minded strangers. It's really fun if you can get some friends or co-workers to make the trek with you, but don't close yourself off from meeting new people walking or running all around you. You'll make friends while you do some good, lose some weight, and end up with roses in your cheeks!

The meditation and yoga class you choose is a very personal thing. You need to find the one that suits your style and your needs. Don't stop after your first try—meditation can make a real difference for reducing stress and improving quality of life. If you don't believe me, try it!

Fortunately, the groups listed here are open to the public (not just the converts), so we may all discover the pleasure of healthy activity. Even though many of the organizations in other chapters are about healthy pleasures, these groups are specifically devoted to encouraging spiritual (not religious), psychological and physical health. Taking part in the classes can change your understanding of yourself. You'll also notice other changes: the length of time you can walk in the woods, whether your stomach hurts after a meal, and how bright your eyes sparkle. It's not *all* hard work—but a lot of fun as well, with a community that enjoys feeling fully alive.

Health for Mind & Body

Exercise

Learning Studio

412 East King Street, Malvern, PA 19355
(610) 578-0600   classes@learningstudio.net   www.learningstudio.net

The Learning Studio offers "fun and informative classes year-round in a wide variety of topics including cooking, art, computers, careers, dance, performing arts and much more. They also sponsor activities for singles, activities that support the mind-body connections, classes in relationships and life enrichment and performing arts. If you like to learn, you've come to a good place! Check the web site for info, or call for a brochure, and see what appeals to you.

Moving Arts Studio of Mt. Airy

550 Carpenter Lane (corner of Greene Street), Philadelphia, PA 19119
(215) 842-1040

Over 40 classes are offered weekly in this sun-filled studio in Mt. Airy, including Pilates, t'ai chi (push hands), self defense, fencing, and creative dance classes. Call and ask about the yoga class where the teacher plays a violin!

💰 $75-$85 for 10-week classes

Mt. Airy Learning Tree

6601 Greene Street, Philadelphia, PA 19119
(215) 843-6333   www.mtairylearningtree.org
Activity Location: various in West Mt. Airy/Germantown

Cardio-boxing is among the many exciting fitness classes offered by the Learning Tree . Also Healthy Weight Management, Water Aerobics, and scads of dancing classes and sessions in mind and body, such as Alexander Technique. Lots of nice people taking these courses will share your interest in movement. Terrific catalog.

Students practice their kicks in Mt. Airy Learning Tree's class *Self-Defense for Women and Girls* by instructors from Women's Anti-Violence Education

Photo by Jonna Naylor

Health for Mind & Body

Thomas Jefferson University Hospital

Gibbon Building, 111 South 11th Street, Philadelphia, PA 19107
(215) 955-6319   www.jeffersonhealth.org
Activity Location: Fitness Center, 1015 Chestnut St., Ste. 100, Phila., PA

Many hospitals have excellent health and fitness programs available to the public. Jefferson's Healthy Neighbors Calendar details a wide range of such activities, including free lectures, classes in kick boxing, aquacize, aerobics, step, and overall muscle toning. Many are conveniently offered during lunch hours or right after work. Special classes for seniors and for weight management.

💰   Unlimited classes $95 for 12 weeks

YMCAs & YMHAs

Activity Location: Around the city and the suburbs

The "Ys" are outstanding organizations for group physical activities, and they're located in many neighborhoods around the city. Local branches offer classes in aerobics, weight training, tennis and sports, martial arts, and swimming. Also look for some real jazzy activities like modern and ballroom dance, volleyball for fun, walking and running races, and more. Some have special groups for singles. Look for programs that interest you at one of the "Ys" around town.

💰   Reasonable

Healthy Eating

Arnold's Way

4438 Main Street, Philadelphia, PA 19127
(215) 483-2266   arnoldsway@compuserve.com

You can network with health enthusiasts at the lunch counter of this friendly health food store. If you want to learn more about mindful eating, attend the lectures on the benefits of eating your food raw, such as how raw foods can prevent and reverse many diseases, held every Saturday morning (8-10am). Learn to be a raw food gourmet on the last Saturday of the month (8-10am). Or check out the potluck meal of raw food on the last Wednesday/month from 6-8pm for only $7. It's free if you bring a raw food to share. There is a free raw food newsletter.

💰   Breakfast lectures and raw food gourmet sessions are free (wow)

Christina Cooks

243 Dickinson Street, Philadelphia, PA 19147
(215) 551-1430   www.christinacooks.com
Activity Location: Essene, 719 S. 4th St., Phila., PA (215) 922-1146

It's good for your body and your soul watching Christina cook, listening to her ongoing rap about how foods can nourish and heal. She fills the space with energy and thoughtful ideas while she brews wonderful smells and colors using the same foods that your mother overcooked. (I loved Christina's dishes!) Try her classes at Essene about two Saturdays/month when she cooks a macrobiotic meal that you'll love and will want to try yourself. A variety of people show up and they are friendly. Call for schedule.

☼ 2 Saturdays/mo   ☎ 10am

☎ Christina Pirello

💰 Still $30/class (it was the same 5 years ago)

Club Veg, Philadelphia Chapter

(484) 530-2660   philly@clubveg.org   www.clubveg.org/phillyevents.htm

This vegetarian educational group aims to teach us all about the benefits of a vegetarian lifestyle, and you'll have a great time learning! Events include potluck suppers, restaurant outings, all-you-can-eat buffet dinners cooked by nationally known chefs and speakers, and more. Recently the Philly Club Veg group joined the Central Jersey Vegetarian Group for dinner at Essene after a tour of historic sites in Philadelphia. Other activities have included suppers in local outdoor parks and trips to NYC for get togethers with other vegetarian groups that focus on food and entertainment. These are great networking opportunities. Look at the web site to find vegetarian activities in the area.

Essene Natural Foods Market and Café

719 South 4th Street, Philadelphia, PA 19147
(215) 922-1146   www.essenemarket.com

Essene is a hub for Philadelphians interested in healthy foods and healing. Learn about macrobiotic cooking and nutrition at 'Christina Cooks' Saturday classes. Check out the free Wednesday evening lectures (7pm) on a smorgasbord of interesting topics, such as acupuncture, Chinese medicine, and mind-body psychotherapy. Stop by and pick up an events schedule, and while you're there take a look at the terrific organic foods department. Open 9am to 8pm (9pm Weds. and Fris.).

☼ Everyday

💰 $30 registration for Christina's classes; others are free

Health for Mind & Body

Whole Foods Market (formerly Fresh Fields)

2001 Pennsylvania Avenue (near 20th & Callowhill Sts.), Philadelphia, PA 19130
(215) 557-0015   www.wholefoodsmarket.com

Also in CC (South St. at 10th), Jenkintown, North Wales, Wynnewood, & Devon
PA and Marlton, NJ

Meet other health-conscious people in cooking classes where you learn to create delicious vegetarian dishes. Also, there are regular health- and fitness-related workshops. For single health enthusiasts: Check out the singles events held about four times a year, where money is raised for a local charity. A newsletter and in-store bulletin board list frequent lectures/demos, or you can sign up for an email events listing.

Organic Planet Dinner Club

(215) 753-7171   organicplanetexp@aol.com   www.organicplanet.com
Activity Location: Cafette, 8136 Ardleigh St., Phila., PA

Not *really* a club—it just *feels* like one to the regulars who come every month to taste and discuss great healthy food. Newcomers are warmly included and people coming alone are invited to join the Community Table where they meet interesting people to dine with. Be sure to call for a reservation. Get on the mailing list for up-to-date info.

☼ 3rd Sunday/mo   ⏰ 2 sittings 5:30, 7:45pm

☎ Lindsay Gilmour

💰 $30/4-course meal

Vegetarians of Philadelphia

P.O. Box 24353, Philadelphia, PA 19120
(215) 276-3198

Part of a vegetarian network, this group shares a dinner about six times a year. Anywhere from 20 to 100 people show up to pool potluck vegan goodies or meet at a fine vegetarian restaurant. The evening sometimes includes a speaker and always includes great socializing. Check out the annual potluck dinner on the Sunday before Thanksgiving.

Vegetarian Society of South Jersey

P.O. Box 272, Marlton, NJ 08053
(877) www-vssj   www.vssj.com

This group supports all activities that encourage a vegetarian lifestyle and "caring, consciousness, conservation and compassion." This includes classes, literature and social activities where people meet to share meals and fun.

Health for Mind & Body
Personal Growth

Becoming Center
250 North Bethlehem Pike, Ambler, PA 19002
(215) 283-9999   www.becomingcenter.com

This health and wellness center offers a full menu of classes to keep you on a strong, healthy course. Their services/classes are based on a holistic approach to healing integrated with traditional medicine, including land and water exercise classes, yoga and t'ai chi, health education, and programs for arthritis, weight management, people in transition, and a Course in Miracles class. Massage and bodywork therapies include massage, acupuncture, and hypnotherapy.

C.G. Jung Society of West Jersey
(215) 985-4525   http://region.philly.com/community/wjjung
Activity Location: Moorestown Community House, 16 E. Main St., Moorestown, NJ

The C.G. Jung Society of West Jersey is a public lecture series which is offered in an open and friendly atmosphere. The lectures and discussions are focused on the applications of Carl Jung's thought to understanding our culture and ourselves. Jung utilized mythology, fairy tales, and folk tales as they relate to the struggles we all face in our lives (for example, "Through the Dark Forest: Drawing Inner Wisdom from the Adventures of Little Red Riding Hood"). There are the Philadelphia Jung Seminars eight weekends a year in Center City.

Garland of Letters
527 South Street, Philadelphia, PA 19147
(215) 923-5946   garlandom@aol.com   www.garlandofletters.com

Browse in this inviting store specializing in information about psychological, metaphysical, new age, yoga, and religious issues (and more). Join its weekly yoga, qigong (internal martial art), or feng shui classes. The classical yoga classes are presented by the SKY Foundation for both beginner and advanced students. Occasional book signings and author talks. $10--15/class

☼ Classes: Mondays-Thursdays. Store is open everyday

Heart of the Goddess Holistic Learning and Healing Center
10 Leopard Road, Berwyn, PA 19312
(610) 695-9494   artemis@voicenet.com   www.voicenet.com/~artemis

For over ten years this women's center has offered high-quality programs for personal growth and spirituality. Topics have included: Woman Wisdom Training and Health Mastery Training, Myth of the Goddess Study Group, Shamanic Journeying, Reiki, and Foot Reflexology. Sessions are scheduled on weekends and evenings. There is a splendid woman's community here.

Health for Mind & Body

Labyrinth at St. Stephen's Episcopal Church

19 South 10th Street, Philadelphia, PA 19107
(215) 922-3807

Take time out to wind your way in peaceful reflection or prayer as you walk the labyrinth laid out on a canvas floor at St. Stephen's. The labyrinth revives an ancient Christian custom and provides a spiritual tool for reflection and meditation. It could take 20 minutes to an hour, depending on how long you want to take. You may also sit in front of the meditation pool filled with rocks and running water. Be sure to call beforehand.

☼ Tuesdays thru Fridays   ⏱ 11am-4pm

💰 Free

Omega Institute for Holistic Studies

150 Lake Drive, Rhinebeck, NY 12572
(800) 944-1001   www.eomega.org

Omega's goal is to offer "effective strategies and inspiring traditions that might help people bring increased meaning and vitality into their lives." Ask anyone who has attended and they will affirm they have loved the place. Omega is a learning community with more than 250 high-quality workshops in holistic health, psychological development, spiritual practice, the arts, relationships, and sports. Examples from the catalog include: Healing Through Sound & Music, The Art of Ritual, The Artist's Way, and (one of my favorites) Play for Dummies. It's a chance to find friends and a community that values self-awareness and renewal as much as you do. Call for a great catalog or check their web site. (See *A Closer Look*, page 283.)

☼ Year-round

💰 Extremely reasonable

Pendle Hill

338 Plush Mill Road, Wallingford, PA 19086
(610) 566-4507   www.pendlehill.org

Pendle Hill is a place that invites seekers: People who choose to explore their spiritual path, sometimes alone, sometimes in the company of fellow travelers. Pendle Hill offers a wide selection of weekend workshops and retreats with topics ranging from artistic workshops for learning art (Painting on Cloth), poetry, and street theater to spiritual programs that cross all spiritual lines (Weekend on Spiritual Autobiography) to personal growth programs (Massage and Energy Work). Founded by the Quakers in 1930, this pastoral retreat center is a haven for serenity, contemplation and community.

Health for Mind & Body

Wise Women's Center

735 South 50th Street, Philadelphia, PA 19143
(215) 727-9473   wisewestphilly@hotmail.com

The center offers alternative healing to all women, using a sliding scale for fees. It promotes spiritual awareness and mental and physical health through a number of programs, including classes in cooking, yoga and meditation, aerobics, gardening, and personal growth (such as stress reduction and "Growing your Business"). Many practitioners offer services here in healing arts such as homeopathy, reflexology, and massage. It's a great place to meet and make friends with a diversity of wonderful women, either in a casual way or a support group. Call for information about current events.

Walks for Charity

AIDS Fund "AIDS Walk"

1227 Locust Street, Philadelphia, PA 19107
(215) 731-9255   AIDSfund@aidsfundphilly.org   www.aidswalkphilly.org
Activity Location: Eakins Oval in front of the Philadelphia Art Museum, Benjamin Franklin Pkwy., Phila., PA

Walk and talk with many Philadelphians in this large charity walk in the city and help raise much needed funds for 58 AIDS service and education organizations. Follow the route along Kelly and West River Drives and then enjoy the live music and entertainment back at the Oval. You may even hear the mayor who is often a featured speaker !

☼   3rd Sunday in October   ⏰ 9am

💰   Free; Preregister to get sponsor packet

National Multiple Sclerosis Society "MS Walk"

1 Reed Street, Su. 200, Philadelphia, PA 19147
(800) 883-WALK   www.pae.nmss.org
Activity Location: 20 different walk sites in the Delaware Valley, including Philadelphia Art Museum, Benjamin Franklin Pkwy., Phila., PA

Your physical health improves when you walk for yourself, and your mental health improves when you walk for someone else! Very festive and fun event enjoyed by many walkers. Watch the papers or web site for the exact day of this annual springtime event. By the way, the web site lists many social activities (e.g., ghost tours, cycling to the Jersey shore, etc.) with proceeds for the MS society.

💰   Raise $75 and get a T-shirt

Health for Mind & Body

Yoga and Meditation

Maharishi Vedic School: *Transcendental Meditation*

(215) 844-1232   Hot Line: (888) LEARNTM   www.tm.org

Since 1974 this nonprofit educational organization has taught TM in Philadelphia. The organization maintains that this very popular form of meditation brings about a deep level of stress reduction and is very easy to practice. Everyone is invited to come by for the free introductory Sunday lectures where you'll learn the mechanics (how to do it) and the intellectual foundation of TM. There are also courses on diet, yoga postures, and advanced TM techniques.

☼   1st Sun./mo

☎   Philadelphia area: Yvonne Jackson

Rainbow Meditation Group

Activity Location: William Way Community Center, 1315 Spruce Street, Phila., PA
(215) 732-2220   www.waygay.org/programs_services.html

Come to meditate and learn about Buddhist meditation practices held at this gay and lesbian center. Meets Mondays at 6pm and Thursdays at 6pm features guest speakers.

Shambhala Meditation Center of Philadelphia

2030 Sansom Street, 3rd Floor, Philadelphia, PA 19103
(215) 568-6070   info@philashambhala.org   www.philashambhala.org

You'll feel very welcome at the center's free initial secular meditation instruction every Thursday at 7pm (please email ahead). Public sitting takes place in this peaceful place from 7pm-8pm Mondays to Thursdays, and Sundays from 9am-noon. Also, there are classes in Tibetan Buddhism, secular Shambhala meditation training, and contemplative arts, such as calligraphy and flower arranging.

💰   Meditation is free; class fees are about $40 for 5 weeks

Sky Foundation

339 Fitzwater Street, Philadelphia, PA 19147
(215) 574-9180   yogasearch@aol.com   www.skyfoundation.org
Activity Location: 15 locations in Phila. area

Sky has programs for people new to classical yoga as well as for people who have practice experience. They offer a variety of nondenominational formats, including weekly classes, workshops, and summer retreats with visiting teachers and experts in related fields. Its sister organization, the Yoga Research Society (215-592-YOGA; www.yogaresearchsociety.com), sponsors an annual conference and lectures for professionals. It's $15 for a single class and $40/series.

Health for Mind & Body

Greater Philadelphia Yan Xin Qigong Cultural Center

www.pyxqc.org

Activity Location: Various including UPenn., Drexel, Temple, Upper Darby & more

For over 7,000 years, qigong has helped people let go of the negative and receive the positive. Following this traditional Chinese method of meditation, these groups utilize the guided visualizations of Dr. Yan, a very well-known teacher who lives in China. This web site provides you with a list of many qigong classes and practice locations in the area. Most are free.

Yoga Garden

31 North Narberth Avenue, Narberth, PA 19072

(610) 664-2705   yogagarden@msn.com   www.yogagardennarberth.com

Practice a variety of yoga styles here, where members are encouraged to listen to and enjoy their bodies. Classes for adults, with one prenatal class, and free meditation evenings once a month, on the second Friday at 7:30pm. Personal growth workshops are also offered, in areas like Expressing Spirituality in Everyday Life. This center is a liaison to the Kripalu Yoga network.

✆   Georgette DuBois, MS, RYT

💰   Classes $10-$15/hour

Photo by Shelly Miller

Serious students practice yoga at the Yoga Garden in Narberth

Health for Mind & Body

Yoga-On-Main

4363 Main Street, Philadelphia, PA 19127
(215) 482-7877   yogaonmain@aol.com   www.yogaonmain.com

You can find a full schedule of yoga for all levels and ages right in the heart of Manayunk. There is a yoga course for beginners and then a slew of regular drop-in yoga and meditation evenings for those who have experience. There are many special events, like candlelight concerts, retreats, and teacher training programs. These are user-friendly classes for people of all ages (like me! I did it and felt great.).

☎ David Newman
💰 Drop in $10-$14 per class

QiGong Research Society: *QiGong for Health & Well Being*

3201 Route 38, Su 201, Mt. Laurel, NJ 08054
(856) 234-3056   faxiang@aol.com   www.qigongresearchsociety.com

Master FaXiang Hou, a fifth generation Master of qigong, teaches exercises along with mindful concentration and breathing techniques for health and calming. He gives many classes, including at Garland of Letters Bookstore (527 South Street), workshops, therapy, and special events. They are well-attended and require preregistration.

An outdoor class at Omega

A closer look at...

Omega

150 Lake Drive, Rhinebeck, New York, 12572
(800) 944-1001   www.eomega.org

Experience a peaceful oasis from a hurried world at Omega. "We have made our campus a healing center, a place where you can relax, rejuvenate, and feel at home in the midst of nature's bounty and a community of warm, caring people." Omega has many excellent and innovative workshops which offer you everything from playful fun (Play and Community Building, Second City Theater, The Joy of Play), improvement of your sport (The Dance of Tennis, Golf & Yoga), dance and music experiences (Drums of Passion, Gospel Music, Dancing from the Inside Out), or an in-depth spiritual experience (Meditation for Beginners, Spiritual Partnership, The Soul of Sufism). Outstanding faculty include Stephan Rechtschaffen, M.D., Caroline Myss, David Darling, Alan Arkin, and Harville Hendrix. If you're not sure where to start, you could try the Introductory Weekend, given about six times a year ($165 tuition only). The beauty of the natural environment, the friendly staff, and wonderful food all support the learning that takes place in the workshops. Take a weekend (or week) for your self and meet others who value their personal growth as well.

☼ Year-round

🪙 Extremely reasonable

Health for Mind & Body

 Here are some extra resources to check out

Web Sites

- *www.earthsave.org*
- *www.veganoutreach .org* (Vegan information)
- *www.peta.com* (People for the Ethical Treatment of Animals)
  All kinds of animal rights topics
- *http://fitness.philly.com/fitnessfinder.asp* Find all kinds of
  fitness organizations, including gyms, boxing gyms, martial
  arts, yoga and alternative fitness programs
- *www.alternativefitness.com*
- *http://dmoz.org/Health/Alternative/*
  Massage_Therapy_and_Bodywork/Schools
  Listing of massage therapy and body work schools

Publications

- *Delaware Valley Directory of Alternative Health Resources*
  Box 35047, Philadelphia PA 19128, (215) 483-7051
- *Creating Community,* P.O. Box 1116, Doylestown, PA 18901,
  (215) 345-6525, www.creatingcommunity.net
  A publication of holilstic and creative arts events, activities, and
  resources covering a wide range of areas including arts,
  entertainment, holistic health, spirituality, movement arts
  (fitness, yoga, and dance), theater, mind/body practices, and
  community service. Bi-Monthly. Subscription $18/year. Free.

Organizations

- *Vegetarian Awareness Network* (800) USA-VEGE
- *Women's Anti-Violence Education*, 1501 Cherry St., Phila., PA
  (215) 241-5720, www.selfdefense.org, Self-defense classes.

Events

- *Annual Pennsylvania Natural Living Conference*
  Bloomsberg University in 1994, (610) 678-4702
- *Peace Weaver Center: Mother Earth Music & Arts Festival*
  Bath, N.Y., (607) 776-2026, www.peaceweavers.com A nonprofit, intercultural, educational community supporting greater
  peace and healing for individuals, families, and groups. Puts on
  a gathering of world music, dance, art, healing arts, yoga,
  meditation and much more.

Hobbies & Clubs

Animals • Arts & Crafts • Astronomy
Cars, Planes & Trains • Collecting • Computers
Cooking & Food • Gardening
History & Genealogy • Language & Culture
Miscellany • Wine & Beer

Hobbies & Clubs

Agility training at Camp Gone To The Dogs

Photo by Dave Guttman

Members of the Road Angels of Doylestown
preparing a street rod for a road show

Hobbies & Clubs

There is a terrific book called *Organized Obsessions* that lists 1001 clubs for people who share a passion to collect matchbooks or pictures of Millard Fillmore and the like. Unfortunately Philadelphia does not seem to have a local chapter of those clubs, but there *is* a local chapter of **Sons of the Desert**, a Laurel and Hardy appreciation fan club, where members really get into the comedy style of that duo and old style vaudeville, and have a lot of laughs at their get-togethers.

Participants who belong to the organizations listed in Hobbies & Clubs are often quite devoted to the subject of their clubs, including those with a serious purpose. If you attend the meetings of the **League of Independent Ferret Enthusiasts**, you will learn everything you need to know about the care and nurturance of your superferret, including how to prepare it for a show. The people you meet at the **Suburban Dog Training Club** sessions (I'm one of them) are extremely invested in the care, welfare and obedience of their dogs, for all the right reasons. There is even a camp in Vermont (**Camp Gone to the Dogs**) where you and your dog can join other dogs/owners for games, long walks, and agility training. To this dog lover, that sounds like a great time! I'm sure I'd feel quite simpatico with the other people there, and so would my dog Rusty.

Each area of hobby interest opens a world of activity and connection for its members. For example, this chapter only scratches the surface of area car clubs, but it should get you started. (When you attend their events, you'll get more info about what else is happening.) You can join a Corvette car club (**Corvette Club of Delaware Valley**) even if you don't own a Corvette yourself, and find out what you need to know if you decide to purchase one. There are clubs for devotees of historic, vintage and classic cars (there *is* a difference), all makes and models, street rods, and so on. There are car festivals with activities for the whole family (games, food, petting zoo, music), so the hobby becomes a nucleus around which everyone finds fun and community. You can find motor-cycle groups for men or women (**Motor Maids**) and even a group that maintains and admires vintage fire engines (**Society for...Preservation of Antique Motor Fire Apparatus**). Model trains (**Chelten Hills Model Railroad Club**) and historic planes (**Delaware Valley Historical Aircraft**) also have their followers. We do love things we can drive!

Hobbies & Clubs

For celestial observers, astronomy clubs (**Chesmont Astronomy Society, Delaware Valley Amateur Astronomers**, etc.) can be found any place where there is enough sky to see the stars. People come together to learn about constellations and planetary bodies and then go out on stargazing parties to see them. This is sophisticated business: You have to go at the right time of year with proper weather conditions, and you have to know how to use a telescope to find the precise stars you are looking for. (We're not just talking Big Dipper here.) Join them and you'll be building a network with those who enjoy learning and star-watching together. And what you're learning about will be there for you to appreciate the rest of your life.

If you're one who gets excited by scratching around in the earth, you may be a true-blue gardener. If you are, trust me: Whatever you want to know about how to improve your garden can be provided at a garden group nearby. Everything. This includes: How to test and enrich your soil; which shade plants survive best in the region; the best way to build a compost heap; identifying the flowers that keep bugs off your tomato plants; and what time of year you should trim your shrubs. The arboretums (**Morris Arboretum, Scott Arboretum**, etc.) and the **Penn Urban Gardening Project** are all-around organizations where you'll find this type of general information in classes, tours and workshops. They also provide on-going help when you get into trouble. Beyond that, there are clubs for people interested in roses, azaleas, daylilies, hardy perennials, ferns, African violets, and any other flower you've ever heard of. Also, your local nature center is an excellent source of information about the flora and fauna in your backyard. I used to be nuts about ferns. The **Schuylkill Center for Environmental Education** (in the Nature Chapter) taught me all I know about them, from Christmas fern "feet" to New York fern spores to the graceful plumage of the ostrich fern. My favorite image is when I almost tripped over JD Wherry, the premier fern expert, lying across a path with his magnifying glass, examining a newly emerging baby fern in the woods. He was 92. He never lost his love of wildlife. Those are the kinds of people you find in gardening groups—people who lose themselves in the everyday miracles of the outdoors.

Computers have become a passion for creative types who can now put together products they never could have dreamed of before hi tech. Find a user group of computer folks and luxuriate in the techy words and instructions for sexy things you can do with your laptop. There is no way to explain it to someone who doesn't have the bug (so to speak). These are like-minded users who speak their own language. Members of **MacBus**, a local Macintosh user group, have saved my life and my book's life on so many occasions I can't count them. Some people in the group are expert enough to take my computer apart and put it back together with no parts left out. Others are just getting the hang of it but getting smarter with each meeting. But we're all there together, month after month, bonded by our common interest in cool ways to do the neatest things. We love the kick of the Mac and welcome new members. (If you go to MacBus, say hi to Todd or George; they'll make sure you feel at home.) PC users can find user groups too; they are listed in the *Delaware Valley Computer User* magazine found in free newspaper boxes.

As you can imagine, food and wine groups are exceedingly popular all across the country, and Philadelphia has plenty of them. **Homebrew** hosts regular Wednesday tastings in an informal setting where you can get the information you need to get started making your own beer. Homebrew also takes part in competitions with other brew clubs, so you can network with the beer community all over the Delaware Valley. If wine is more to your liking, try the **International Wine Tasting** group where you'll taste a variety of related wines, like Cabernets of different years from Chateau Talbot, or sweet Rieslings, or wines that go with game meat. You'll sit at a table with other wine aficionados, sipping and describing the flavors in each glass. It's terrific fun, and, as my old wine teacher used to say, "Wait 'til you see the homework!" Likewise, when you attend a food club, you get to taste the most wonderful concoctions that you will learn to make yourself. Now think about the kinds of people you'll meet in these places. They'll be people who enjoy good food and drink, but who also want to share methods and recipes, talk about the benefits of daikon, and where to buy the best hops. There's lots of info and lots of lively schmoozing going on in these activities. Your kind of people? Check it out!

It was so much fun to research and talk to people about their hobbies and clubs that I had trouble ending the chapter (and this foreword). But I must. So let's just summarize the rest. Remember that there are collectors such as **Walt Disney, Inc.**, and the **Dumpster Divers**, who collect other people's "refuse" for their artwork. There are the art hobbyists, who do embroidery, boat building, quilting and glasswork, to name a few. There are organizations devoted to the language and culture of many nationality groups (**America-Italy Society**, etc.) with high-quality events (from Swedish language lessons to the Festival du Chocolat) for all who wish to learn more about them. And there are meetings for history and genealogy groups, where people study the Civil War (**Civil War Round Tables**), maintain historical houses (**Ebenezer Maxwell Mansion**), and explore their black heritage and genealogy (**African-American Genealogy Group**). Do not skip reading about the groups in this chapter. Then take time to attend a club meeting that tweaks your fancy and ask yourself if that's a community you'd like to belong to. You may surprise yourself!

If you do your research, you will probably find yourself exploring an amazing new interest, alongside people who are as excited (and exciting) about it as you are. All right here in Philadelphia.

Members and guests of the French-American Chamber of Commerce of Philadelphia

Animals

Cat Fanciers' Association, Inc.

P.O. Box 1005, Manasquan, NJ 08736
(732) 265-2521   www.cfainc.org

This cat registry organization is also a liaison to cat clubs in the area. If you call them or email them (from web site), they will give you a list of clubs related to all breeds or specific breeds of cats. Some of the local clubs include: Liberty Trail, Moorestown Cat Fanciers, Conestoga Cat Club, and Cats Incredible. But the best way to meet members of these and other cat clubs, I'm told, is to go to one of the many cat shows around the area and introduce yourself to the club members attending. They can give you the pertinent facts about their clubs and you can go from there. Cat shows are listed on the CFA web site.

American Kennel Club

(800) 252-7894   info@akc.org   www.akc.org

Of all dog clubs in the nation, including the Delaware Valley, one has a great web site. It tells you where to find obedience and show handling classes, clubs for specific breeds, and information on the care and needs of all dogs. If you're looking for people with a common interest in raising, training, breeding, and competing with purebred dogs, clubs are a popular place to socialize and exchange information with seasoned dog show folks. For example, there is a Great Dane Club in Abington, and a Doberman Pinscher Club in Norristown.

Camp Gone to the Dogs

P.O. Box 600, Putney, VT 05346
(802) 387-5673   www.campgonetothedogs.com

If you hate to take a vacation without your dog, this camp might be the vacation that exceeds your wildest dreams. You and your pup can join fellow dog lovers in agility and obedience classes with top national instructors, enjoy dozens of other structured activities together, and/or just relax and enjoy a walk or swim in the Vermont countryside. Only positive training (motto is "Tails Up!") during three one-week sessions in June, July and September. I'm going!

☎   Honey Loring
🏺   About $800-$1,300

Hobbies & Clubs

Greater Philadelphia Dog Fanciers Association

(215) 338-4351 (hot line) GPDFA@aol.com
http://members.aol.com/gpdfa/GPDFA.html
Activity Location: St. Luke's Episcopal Church, Welsh Rd., Phila., PA
(Northeast Phila.)

Try this hot line to find an obedience class for your dog, or for a class where you can learn the skills you need to show your dog in competitions. GPDFA was founded in 1968 to encourage dog fanciers to learn responsible dog ownership and breeding practices. They conduct regular obedience classes; dog shows, matches, and obedience trials; and fun events like the Dog Lovers Bazaar and a Puppy Match. For breeder groups you can also call the PA Federation of Dog Clubs at (215) 842-2407.

☼ 2nd Wed./mo   🕐 7:30pm

Lower Camden County Dog Training Club

(856) 429-9239
Activity Location: 114 Old Berlin Rd., Stratford, NJ

You and your dog will get expert training at low cost in the obedience classes offered by this club, around since 1947. This kind of beginner to advanced training can help you build a strong and caring relationship with your dog. For those interested in showing their dogs, the club offers monthly Show and Go practice training matches for only $7 from September to June. Once a year, they sponsor an AKC obedience trial. (For other New Jersey dog clubs, look at www.barkbytes.com/sclubs/njclub.htm.)

💰 $60/basic training series (6 weeks); $110/year

Philadelphia Dog Training Club

(610) 853-9601   www.members.aol.com/jdicanio/phildog.html
Activity Location: Agnes Irwin School, Rosemont, PA

This is the oldest dog club in the area. It hosts official AKC obedience trials and gives beginner, intermediate, and advanced obedience classes for all breeds and mixed breeds of dogs. You'll learn skills to help you extinguish unwanted behaviors and how to use praise, food, and correction properly. You'll also meet many wonderful dogs and maybe find new friends to walk your dogs with!

Hobbies & Clubs

Suburban Dog Club

4019 Crescent Avenue, Lafayette Hill, PA 19444
(610) 941-6394

*Activity Location: Chestnut Hill Academy, Willow Grove Ave., Phila., PA
(Chestnut Hill)*

This fine club offers classes in dog obedience and show training on a regular
basis for experienced and novice owners (and dogs). They also offer Show and
Gos and rehearsals for obedience trials. My dog Rusty is the proud "parent" of
a graduate (me) who has finally, finally learned how to properly correct him.
Dog shows are great places for fun and socializing. Some members volunteer for
the demo team that visits nursing homes with certified therapy dogs.

☼   Mondays and Wednesdays

Animals: Miscellany

Legion of Superferrets Ferret Show

(215) 946-2747 (voice mail #1)   rose@losnational.com
www.losferretworldnfriends.org

Join with others for information about the care and nurturance of your ferret
when you attend a show put on by this group. This state division of a national
organization gives one show yearly, and members attend others nearby. You can
also look into the American Ferret Association and the League of Independent
Ferret Enthusiasts.

🐾 $30/year

Delaware County Aquarium Society (DCAS)

(610) 447-0786
http://members.tripod.com/~dcas

*Activity Location: Springfield Municipal Building, 50 Powell Rd., Springfield, PA
(Delaware County)*

You can enjoy fish as pets and find peaceful serenity as you watch them in your
aquarium. Check in with this group for monthly meetings with guest speakers,
special presentations (Sunfishes for the Aquarium, Water Testing & Filtration),
bowl shows, auction/raffles of many items each month, and occasional field
trips. Free admission. Newsletter for members.

☼   1st Fri./mo from September to June   🕐 7:30pm
🐾   Membership $10-16/year for individuals and families

Hobbies & Clubs

Arts & Crafts

American Woodworker Show (Greater Philadelphia Show)

(800) 914-9395

Activity Location: South Jersey Expo Center, Pennsauken, NJ

For anyone who works alone in his/her own basement building furniture, crafts or objets d'art, this annual three-day show in November offers seminars (about $10) and a look at all manner of woodworking tools. Plus you'll have the opportunity to network with others who appreciate and understand this craft.

Beads

225 South Street, Philadelphia, PA 19147

(215) 413-2323   www.beadworks.com

You really *can* make your own jewelry and meet others who are talented in this craft. If you're new at this, try the basic bead-stringing class or the earring and linking class. Specialty workshops are scheduled from time to time, such as bead weaving and using macrame and hemp. You can also just walk in, empty handed, put your beads together, sit at the back table, and produce your new pieces! If you really enjoy bead work, check out the South Jersey Bead Society.

💰 $25 for a two-hour class

Byrne Sewing Connection at Byrne Fabrics

422 East Butler Avenue, New Britian, PA 18901 (near Doylestown)

(215) 230-9411   byrne@byrnesewing.com   http://byrnesewing.com

Stitchers listen up! Bryne Fabrics offers sewing and quilting classes, including embroidery, computer designing, needlework, beadwork, and applique. The Chestnut Hill branch (215-247-3485) also offers a few classes. But do stop in and chat and find out about current classes. These are friendly and knowledge-able people.

Delaware County Camera Club

(610)-566-3469   http://members.aol.com/camrclub/dccc.htm

Activity Location: Trinity Lutheran Church, 1141 W. Chester Pike, Havertown, PA

This is a very active club with members of varying experience, including non-photographers who love good photos. They meet every Monday except the first Monday of the month with programs (like Underwater Photography, Tropical Bird and Animal Photography, and In-depth Look at Digital Photography), workshops and field outings. There is a competition on the last Monday for members. About 40 members attend these lively sessions, and total membership is over 100 strong.

Embroiderer's Guild of America: *Philadelphia Chapter*

www.philaega.org/index.shtml

Activity Location: Usually the Radnor Township Library, Rte. 30 toward Devon, left on So. Wayne Ave., in Wayne, PA

If you enjoy needlework—any kind of stitchery for which you use a needle with an eye—or think you *might* enjoy it, you should check out this group that does embroidery and needlepoint. They meet once a month for hands-on stitching, or to listen to a national teacher or a lecture (e.g., how to photograph your needlework for juried exhibition). This friendly group loves sharing and passing on the secrets to these age-old crafts. There is a newsletter and web site for all local branches. (Other branches in Devon, Wynnewood, and Strafford-Wayne. Also, the local chapter of the American Needlepoint Guild meets at the Radnor Library.)

☼ Usually the 4th Wed./mo

💰 $34/year

English Ceramics Study Group of Philadelphia

(215) 635-4948   vicpol@aol.com

Activity Location: Various locations in the area

A small group of collectors that meets more than six times a year to discuss ceramics and hear distinguished speakers who are experts in their fields. They take occasional field trips to local exhibitions and museums and have a national newsletter.

☎ Muriel

Heart Strings

(610) 668-6491

Activity Location: Presbyterian Church of the Covenant, Bryn Mawr Ave. & Montgomery Ave., Bala Cynwyd, PA

Heart Strings meets monthly offering in-house programs with local speakers, including its own members, some of whom are professional quilters. They have an activity every month, such as marking quilts. Everyone brings their own project to work on while they talk, learn, and share quilting skills/tips. About twice a year they bring in two outside national speakers, and twice a year (June and December) they have member parties. All levels are welcome in this casual friendly group of about 25 people (40 members). For a daytime group, try the Main Line Quilters (610-645-0516) which meets at 9:30 am on the 3rd Friday of the month in Berwyn with speaker meetings, trunk shows, and spin-off Bees.

☼ 2nd Thurs./mo   🕐 7:30pm

☎ Tracey

Hobbies & Clubs

Main Line Knitting Guild

(610) 696-3655   www.close-knit.org
Activity Location: Radnor Township Memorial Library, Wayne, PA

The Guild's web page says they are looking for the "community of closet knitters" and it welcomes knitters of all levels, ages, and backgrounds who are passionate about knitting! This very friendly group includes some very talented artists who are willing to share their knowledge and skills. You'll learn a lot from the members, as well as the knitting designers brought in for occasional classes. 50+ members. Also find them (wo)manning a table at the Stitchers Convention in Fort Washington.

☼ Usually 3rd Tues./mo   🕐 7:30pm

💰 $20 covers holiday party, mailings, etc.

Montgomery County Guild of Craftsmen

P.O. Box 1116, North Wales, PA 19454
(215) 412-9209
Activity Location: Meetings at a church in North Wales, PA

You do not need to be an expert craftsman to become a member of this guild. Bring your interest to a meeting and meet other crafters who make jewelry, baskets, wood arts, pottery, and more. At the meetings, members share information about their craft, and hear speakers on topics such as how to prepare for a show and how to market the craftwork. At this local county branch of the PA Guild of Craftsmen, artists are juried and show at the local level. MCGC's yearly show is in October at Montgomery County Community College. Admission is $2—come see these fine works for yourself!

☼ Quarterly

💰 $25/year

Philadelphia Guild of Hand Weavers

3705 Main Street, Philadelphia (Manayunk), PA 19127
(215) 487-9690   www.libertynet.org/~phweaver

This active organization, about 200 strong, does fiber arts, including spinning, felting, weaving, dyeing, and tatting. They provide outreach demonstrations showing how cloth is made, along with workshops, a monthly newsletter, meetings, and an excellent library for guild members.

💰 Reasonable workshop fees & $25 year membership optional

Piece to You, Comfort Quilts: *Peace by Piece*

(215) 885-3686

Activity Location: Jenkintown, PA

This dedicated group of teenagers and adults makes and donates comfort quilts for charitable causes. In the process, they learn about quiltmaking in a comfortable and informal atmosphere, and pass on to the next generation the art of sewing the fabrics of your life. Donations of cotton fabric gratefully accepted! Call to check on the occasional workshops they offer.

☎ Jude

Sophie's Yarns

2017 Locust Street, Philadelphia, PA 19103
(215) 977-YARN www.sophiesyarns.com

If you love yarn, you'll be in heaven wandering around this store. There are classes, too, including basic knitting (Introduction to Sweaters) and advanced knitting (Color Theory for Knitters, Lace & Openwork), on weekends and weekday evenings. For no charge, you can be part of Knitting Circle on Wednesday evenings from 6-8pm.

💰 Typically $75 for five classes.

Stained Glass Classes

225 Race Street, Philadelphia, PA 19106
(215) 923-8122   www.johnbeirs.com

John Beirs has been doing stained glass art for over 30 years. He gives hands-on courses for six-to-eight weeks to truly interested students. Projects include window hangings, glass panels, and boxes. John says you can let your imagination go here. This opportunity is special.

☎ John Beirs
💰 Reasonable

Tangled Web

7900 Germantown Avenue, Philadelphia, PA 19118
(215) 242-1271   www.tangledwebb.com

All manner of knitting and weaving classes are offered at the Web. You can learn to make socks, sweaters, hats, kids' stuff—whatever you can knit. The sweater workshop lasts eight weeks, but you can sign up for each weekly topic separately. Once a month there is a Knit-in free of charge where you hang out and talk yarn stuff. Newsletter.

💰 $15 for one-night class

Hobbies & Clubs

Workshop on the Water

(215) 413-8638   http://seaport.philly.com

Activity Location: Independence Seaport Museum, 211 S. Columbus Blvd., Phila.

Join the crew at the workshop and learn how to build a wooden boat. There are hands-on classes and opportunities for volunteers to get involved—even if you've never picked up a hammer.

Astronomy

Bucks-Mont Astronomical Association

(215) 579-9973   www.freeyellow.com/members2/bmaa/index.html

Activity Location: Peace Valley Nature Center, 170 Chapman Rd., Doylestown, PA

This group of amateur astronomers meets monthly with speakers and presentations and plans extensive activities during the year. The message line gives updates about star watches happening all around the area.

☼ 1st Weds./mo   ⏰ 8pm

Chesmont Astronomy Society

(610) 495-0867

Activity Location: Great Valley Nature Center, Rte. 29 just south of Phoenixville, PA

Join Chesmont for many observations in the area, such as in the French Creek State Park and sometimes farther. In August, they hold a *Star Fest* in Warwick, PA, followed by a full-fledged star party. Over 400 attended last year. But they hold many other smaller star parties locally all year. Meetings feature speakers and updates on what's happening in astronomy.

☼ 3rd Sun./mo   ⏰ 7pm

Delaware Valley Amateur Astronomers

(610) 933-0497   www.dvaa.org

Activity Location: Schuylkill Center for Environmental Education, Hagys Mill Rd., Phila., PA

A group of enthusiastic star-gazing hobbyists dedicated to sharing their knowledge and enjoyment of astronomy with each other and with the general public. Meetings feature talks by professional astronomers and other experts, with time for socializing and refreshments. The club holds free public star parties every four weeks from April to October at Valley Forge Park, and holds classes and clinics for one-on-one interaction between new and experienced astronomers.

☼ 2nd Fri./mo   ⏰ 7:30pm

💰 Free events; about $27 for membership

Villanova Astronomical Society

Villanova University, Villanova, PA
(610) 519-4820 www.villanova.edu to academics (menu A&S)

Although this group is composed primarily of astronomy students from this highly rated undergraduate department, the public is welcome to enjoy the activities. These include several trips a year to major observatories and planetariums, as well as picnics and parties where star studies are a major topic of conversation. The public is invited to attend the excellent and frequent speaker presentations sponsored by the astronomy department.

☼ During school year   ⏰ 7-9pm

Cars, Planes and Trains: Cars

Antique Automobile Club of America (AACA), Keystone Region

350 South Old Middletown Road, Media, PA 19063
(610) 566-6992
Activity Location: Broomall, PA

Meet with this group and discuss past and future activities about historic cars. Plan regular car meets and shows where as many as 200 vintage cars are on display with vintage music, food, and flea markets in the background. You don't have to own a vintage car to belong, just have an interest. Call Robert to find out more, and order the newsletter. Also check out the Historical Car Club of PA (email bud@spokenwheel.com).

☼ 3rd Mon./mo   ⏰ 7:30pm
☎ Robert Burke

Antique, Classic & Special Interest Car Show

(215) 443-6087
Activity Location: Willow Grove Naval Air Station, Rte. 611 & County Line Rd., Horsham, PA

If you own a car that fits in these categories, call to see if you can enter it in this exciting show for vintage vehicles and their owners. Every year different cars are on display, including street rods, originals, and modified. There are plenty of activities for the family too, including a slow drag race (the slowest entry wins) and a petting zoo.

☼ Usually the last Saturday in April

Hobbies & Clubs

Corvette Club of Delaware Valley (CCDV)

(215) 938-7722   www.ccdv.com

One of the oldest and largest corvette clubs in the country with an Annual Cavalcade of Corvettes. At monthly meetings, they swap stories and tips, enjoy speakers, and have dinners and events together. Members (about 400 strong) all own a corvette, but you can have a one-year conditional (non-voting) membership *before you buy* if you're thinking of purchasing a Vette yourself!

East Penn Traction Club, Inc.

greighn@voicenet.com
Activity Location: All around the Delaware Valley

This group of some 230+ members share a common interest in the history and modeling of electric powered rail transit vehicles, known more affectionately as trolley cars. The models actually take their operating current off of the miniature overhead wire, just like the real ones do. In the spring of odd numbered years, the club sponsors the largest trolley-only model meet in the country for a weekend of viewing models, films, model contests and "how-to" clinics. At meetings members present their models and watch movies and slide programs.

Road Angels of Doylestown, PA

P.O. Box 12, Plumsteadville, PA 18949
(215) 257-7618

A monthly meeting for members to plan shows and help each other with information about their souped up, highly painted pre '48 street rods. There is an annual Rod Run in mid July with about 300 cars, trucks, customs, and more, with games, vendors, and music for the family.

Photo by Dave Guttman

Gibson Road Antique Fire Association (local chapter of Society for the Preservation and Appreciation of Antique Motor Fire Apparatus in America)

(215) 638-0531   alf@grafa.org   www.grafa.org
Activity Location: Meets in members homes, Bensalem, PA (Northeast Phila.)

Do you know what a fire muster is? It is the primary activity of this local group of about 130 members who love and appreciate historical fire apparatus (read fire engines!). Besides the monthly meetings, they have Christmas parties and picnics where they display pieces owned by individual members. You don't have to own one yourself. You just have to love it and enjoy socializing. All welcome.

Cars, Planes and Trains: Planes

Delaware Valley Historical Aircraft Association

(215) 443-6039   halpro58@cs.com   www.dvhaa.org

Activity Location: Willow Grove Naval Air Station, Rte. 611 & County Line Rd., Horsham, PA

You only need an interest in historical flight to be part of a group that acquires, restores, and preserves vintage naval aircraft. They meet monthly for speakers, aircraft display events, dinner meetings, and camaraderie between generations of aviation enthusiasts, including pilots. Check out the fine mini-museum as well as the extensive research and reference library. On Saturday mornings, tour the aircraft on the Naval Base.

☼ 3rd Thurs./mo

💰 $25/yr for membership

Pottstown Aircraft Owners and Pilots: Fly-in at Pottstown Limerick Airport

Rte. 23, Pottstown, PA

(610) 272-2598   www.paop.org

Fly in for Sunday breakfast on Labor Day Sunday! Or, if you love aircraft but don't own one of your own, for $5 you can have breakfast and walk around the antique planes, military warbirds, helicopters, and gyrocopters and chat with the owners. For the adventurous, there are helicopter and biplane rides.

Cars, Planes and Trains: Trains

Chelten Hills Model Railroad Club

8000 Old York Road, Elkins Park, PA

(215) 357-3990

You can join these model railroad enthusiasts who meet every week to work on an HO Scale operating layout. They're busy building scenery, adjusting electrical wiring, and cleaning rails and buildings. Two or three times a year in the winter, they put on a show open to the public; the first show is around Thanksgiving.

☼ Every Thursday   🕐 7-10:30pm

💰 About $50 to join; $100/yr dues

Hobbies & Clubs

Delco Area Railroaders in N (DARN)

PO Box 2580, Upper Darby, PA 19082
paul@darn-ntrak.com   www.darn-ntrak.com
Activity Location: Broomall, PA

A model railroaders group that works in very small gauge. Each member
constructs a small piece of a layout to certain specs; then local clubs get together
and plug them in to make a huge layout (as much as 2,000 feet). Monthly
meetings involve planning and designing modules and swapping info. They
prepare for open houses and shows for the public, and may take portions of the
layout to different places for public viewing. Very casual, friendly, and informal
and, by the way, open to all. There are women in this group. (Women are
involved in many cars, trains, and planes organizations.)

🏦 $1/week

Philadelphia Trolley Coalition

(215) 755-7717   www.libertynet.org/trolley

The Philadelphia Trolley Coalition is a grassroots group that supports the
improvement, expansion and preservation of light rail (trolley) lines around the
area. In December they sponsor a party to celebrate the anniversary of the first
electric street car. This is a lighthearted event where you'll find others who
support public transportation and who like a bit of Philadelphia history besides.
Newsletter.

☎ Joel Spivak

Collecting

Double Eagle Coin Club

(215) 222-7760   www.money.org   (American Numismatic Association)
Activity Location: Tabernacle Church, Loretto & Ripley Sts., Phila., PA

This club sponsors a coin auction every week with various dealers who display
and buy coins. Meetings include discussions about what's new in the coin
market along with general information about coins and tokens. Other coin
clubs meet here on other Tuesdays: Benjamin Franklin (1st Tuesday/month) and
Liberty Bell (2nd Tuesday/month). Also check out the Roxborough group at the
American Legion on Ridge Avenue (Philadelphia) on the 1st Wednesday/month
(7pm).

☼ 3rd Tues./mo   🕐 7pm
☎ Dr. Jack Gold

Hobbies & Clubs

Greater Northeast Stamp Club

www.stamps.org

Activity Location: Rhawnhurst Recreation Ctr., Bustleton & Solly Ave., Phila., PA

This information about local stamp clubs was taken from the above web site in Fall of 2001. Philadelphia Chapter No. 18 meets in the Community Room of Elkins Park Square (8080 Old York Rd., Elkins Park) on 3rd Tues., at 7:30pm; Germantown-Chestnut Hill Stamp Club: 1st Tues. and 3rd Wed./mo at the Springfield Retirement Home at 8pm, Greater Northeast Stamp Club: 3rd Thurs./mo at the Rhawnhurst Recreation Center, Bustleton & Solly Aves., Phila. at 8pm, and the Phoenixville /King of Prussia Stamp Club: 1st Wed./mo (except July and August) at Phoenixville Area YMCA, Pothouse Rd., Phoenixville. There are others in the area. Check the web site.

Philadelphia Coin Club

www.money.org (American Numismatic Association)

Activity Location: Ardmore Methodist Church, 200 Argyle Rd., Ardmore, PA 19003

The Philadelphia Club reports that it is has been around since 1935. Meetings usually feature educational programs, often with speakers on interesting topics such as coins from a Central American shipwreck or how a coin is engraved. Every month the club sponsors Show and Tell, led by members with interesting coins, which is followed by conversation and refreshments. Many members attend the national convention, as well as occasional banquets and out-of-town trips with other local clubs. You'll find this is a friendly, welcoming group.

☼ 3rd Tues./mo   ⏰ 8pm

Tuscarora Lapidary Society

(610) 565-8505   info@lapidary.org   www.lapidary.org

Activity Location: Meetings at Springfield Township Building on Powell Rd., Classes at 105 W. Jasper, Media, PA

Explore your interest in all kinds of gem cutting and silver/brass/copper work by coming to a general meeting of this group, ongoing since 1957. Members will explain lapidary activities and speakers will describe shows and provide information on interesting topics such as faceted and cabachon style of cutting, cutting and polishing, bead making and stringing, and pewter and silver work. Check the web site for info regarding the annual show (first weekend in November) when dealers come from around the US, and there are exhibits and demos by members who show you what they do and how they do it.

☼ Meetings on 2nd Wed./mo   ⏰ 8pm
   (except July & August)

Hobbies & Clubs

Walt Disney

PO Box 1116, Lansdowne, PA 19050
(610) 622-5477   www.castlekeepersclub.com
Activity Location: Meets in members' homes all around the Delaware Valley

This club is for anyone who enjoys and is interested in anything Disney. Share information and discuss different collectibles of interest to everyone, as well as the latest happenings at Disney Parks around the world. There are group outings to conventions and to Disney productions in New York, a holiday party, and a summer picnic.

☼ One Sun./mo   ⏰ 1pm

☎ Barbara Kammer

Computers

Macintosh Business Users Society of Greater Delaware Valley (MacBUS)

(215) 402-0700   www@macbus.org   www.macbus.org
Activity Location: Future Media Concepts, 4th & Chestnut Sts., Phila., PA 19104

This terrific group is the Center City Mac user group. We meet to hear about the latest cutting-edge software/hardware products on the market, see them demo-ed, and get inside industry information not yet available to the public. Our membership (about 120 strong) is a diverse group of professionals, entrepreneurs, and any others who love the Mac. Some of us learned how to self-publish books in this group, do our accounting, put sophisticated graphics on a web site, find domain names, and explore the Internet. It's a great group, with a sense of humor to boot. Try us.

☼ Last Tues./mo   ⏰ 6:30-9:30pm

💰 $40/year

Philadelphia Area Computer Society

(215) 842-9600   pacsboard@pacs.phalpa.us   www.pacsnet.org
Activity Location: Upper Moreland Middle School, 4000 Orangeman's Rd.
Hatboro, PA 19040

PACS was formed to help computer users in the area communicate with one another. Over the past 18 years, it has evolved into a collection of over 60 separate small interest groups, which are also open to the public. If you want to learn computer skills and enjoy fellow techies, this is your chance.

☼ 3rd Sat./mo   ⏰ 9am-noon

Cooking & Food

Book and the Cook Festival and Fair

Fair (215) 592-6632; Festival (215) 545-4543   www.thebookandthecook.com
Fair: Philadelphia Convention Center; Festival at restaurants all around the region

For anyone who loves to eat and/or cook, Philadelphia in March is the place to be! The B&C *Fair* offers a weekend abundance of cooking demonstrations, exhibitions, and book signing-author presentations. The festival hosts ten days of cooking classes and fantastic eating/drinking at a diverse array of the finest restaurants in the Philadelphia region. Learn cooking secrets through your own experience, and have a really wonderful time.

- ☼ Annually in March for 10 days
- 💰 Fair: $15 per day; Festival dinners, prix fixe: $25-$85

Chef's Tour of the Italian Market

(215) 772-0739   in www.phila.com under Tours

A behind-the-scenes peek at one of the country's oldest outdoor ethnic markets. You'll visit a Salumeria (Italian deli), learn why southern Italians cook red and northern Italians cook white, visit a kitchen equipment store and a Sicilian pasticceria, and learn what a ghittara is. Lots of history and anecdotes. Very well done—and you'll love your guide!

- ☼ Tuesday-Saturday & Sunday mornings
- ☎ Louise Cianfero Simpson
- 💰 About $30 for individuals; group rates available

Whole Foods Market (formerly Fresh Fields)

2001 Pennsylvania Avenue (near 20th & Callowhill Sts.), Philadelphia, PA 19130
(215) 557-0015   www.wholefoodsmarket.com
Also in Center City Phila. on South St., Jenkintown, Wynnewood, Devon, North Wales, and Marlton, NJ

Meet other health-conscious people in cooking classes where you learn to create delicious vegetarian dishes. Also, there are regular health- and fitness-related workshops. Singles health enthusiasts can check out the events for singles held about four times a year where money is raised for a local charity. A newsletter and in-store bulletin board lists frequent lectures/demos, or you can sign up for an email events listing.

Hobbies & Clubs

Organic Planet Dinner Club

(215) 753-7171   www.organicplanet.com

Explore the world of whole foods for better health for us and the planet. Lindsay Gilmour offers classes such as Italian Vegetarian Cookery, the Joy of Soy, and Warming Winter Soups & Stews. Once a month she has a four-course vegetarian feast at the Organic Planet Dinner Club. It's *really* good! Be sure to call for a reservation.

☼ 3rd Sun./mo, Cafette
   (8136 Ardleigh St., Phila., PA)

☻ 5:30pm & 7:45pm seatings

Reading Terminal: *Saturday Morning Breakfast Club*

Pennsylvania General Store, 12th and Arch Streets, Philadelphia, PA 19107
(215) 592-0455

Activity Location: Meets at Demonstration Kitchen area near Arch Street entrance

Grab some coffee and pastry and head over to the Reading Terminal's kitchen for a lively discussion on the science, history, and culture of cuisine. Reservations are not needed to join the group, where you'll learn about how to prepare Jewish specialities, creative breads, fancy truffles, or winter soups. Founded by Pennsylvania General Store's Michael Holahan, the talks are presented in collaboration with the Philadelphia chapter of the American Institute of Wine and Food. This is a really fun way to start your Saturday (9am), plus you can shop for the ingredients at the market. Free concerts by some of the best Philadelphia jazz artists, and cooking classes are happening at the terminal too!

☼ Saturdays   ☻ 9am

Wok N' Walk Chinatown Tour

(215) 928-9333   www.josephpoon.com

Chef Joe Poon (owner of Asian Fusion Restaurant) has put together a walking tour of his community that is both fun and educational. It includes a light meal, a t'ai chi demonstration, a tour of his restaurant's kitchen with a Chinese vegetable carving lesson, as well as 14 different stops in the community. It's a great way to explore the history and culture of this area of the city.

💰 About $35/individual; group rates available

Gardening

American Rhododendron Society, Grtr. Philadelphia Chapter

(610) 642-4437

Activity Location: Morris Arboretum, Hillside Ave., Phila., PA (Chestnut Hill)

You don't have to be a member to attend a meeting (2nd Thurs./month) and hear a presentation about how to keep your rhodies healthy. This lively group also sponsors workshops, plant sales, a flower show, banquets, and picnics. Members probably have good advice about *all* kinds of planting, all yours for only $28/year. If you are a gardener, a network is invaluable (and fun!).

Delaware Valley Fern and Wildflower Society

(610) 647-9337

Activity Location: Horticultural Center, Phila., PA

Wonderful garden groups like this have been networking for years. DVFWS is 25 years old! Members don't meet indoors often, about twice a year for business and speakers, usually at the Horticultural Center. Several very nice day trips are planned every year, such as to Dingman's Ferry (Environmental Center) and at least one longer trip to visit great wildflower spots around the nation. You can talk to them at their exhibit at the Flower Show. Newsletter.

💰 $8/yr for individuals; $11 for two at same address

Hardy Plant Society, Mid-Atlantic Group

325 West Ashbridge Street, West Chester, PA 19380
(610) 696-5503

A group of over 1,000 members from the Mid-Atlantic region meets all over the Delaware Valley once a month for lectures about well- and little-knownherbaceous plants to help you develop a sturdy garden. Plant sales, a very popular seed exchange, garden tours, visits to members' gardens, and an annual all-day symposium, are some of the popular events here. $25/year for membership.

Penn State Cooperative Extension: *Urban Gardening Program*

4601 Market Street, Philadelphia, PA 19139
(215) 471-2224 (garden hot line)   www.psu.edu

There are over 500 community gardens in the area, producing vegetables galore. With six full-time garden advisors, PSCE responds to calls from garden groups to provide educational help. About once a month, advisors hold workshops in demonstration gardens. That's where you should go if you wish to be part of this garden activity. By the way, gardens are wonderful social places where you meet, and hoe with, your own neighbors. Free newsletter.

Hobbies & Clubs

Pennsylvania Horticultural Society

100 North 20th Street, 5th Floor, Philadelphia, PA 19103
(215) 988-8800   www.libertynet.org/phs

With a mission to advance the art and science of horticulture in our area, the Horticultural Society has much to do with the plantings you see around the city. All gardening enthusiasts are invited to pursue their own particular horticultural interests with the society. What kinds of activities? Be a volunteer at the Flower Show, provide help and expertise at one of many Community Green neighborhood (garden) projects, plant flowers around City Hall, or work with children at PHS Arbor Day or the Junior Flower Show. And that's not all. Call to see how you can be involved. It's a wonderful organization.

Philadelphia Rose Society

(215) 345-6575   http://helpmefind.com/sites/prs/prs.html
Activity Location: Morris Arboretum, 100 Northwestern Ave., Phila., PA

Meetings feature speakers, consulting rosarians, panels, and lots of discussion about how to help your roses flourish. In June, PRS sponsors a big rose show at the Arboretum with a picnic for the awards ceremony. A rose show in the fall, a photo contest in November, and holiday party in December rounds out a great year for this congenial group of all ages. Newsletter with $12/year membership.

☼ 1st Thurs./mo in Mar, Apr., May, Oct., Nov., Dec.   ☑ 7:30pm

Rock Garden Society, Delaware Valley Chapter

(610) 525-8683   www.nargs.org
Activity Location: Main Line area

The Rock Garden Society meets about 10 times a year with terrific information from speakers and members helping members. They go on garden tours and sponsor several plant sales a year.

Village of Arts and Humanities: *Community Market*

2544 Germantown Avenue, Philadelphia, PA 19133
(215) 225-7830   www.villagearts.org

As part of a broad outreach program, the Village has a vegetable farm that runs on a community work-share basis. Volunteers are welcome to help keep it strong, especially those with gardening experience. If you like working with children, you are needed to teach elementary gardening skills so kids can participate in growing their own food.

History & Genealogy

African American Genealogy Group

(215) 572-6063   www.aagg.org
Activity Location: Community College of Phila., 4725 Chestnut St., Phila., PA

A nonprofit, Philadelphia-based, African American genealogy group that encourages and supports genealogy research for those who express a desire to research their family roots. They provide seminars for beginners, go on field trips to archives and libraries, and hold regular conferences. The active sub-groups are where the research gets done. One is a computer user group using genealogy computer programs to do research through the Internet. The others are five states groups where people share info to track down their family origins. It's just $25/year ($20/seniors) to attend subgroups, with no fee for meetings.

☼ 2nd Tues./mo, General Meeting   ☎ 7pm

Atwater Kent

15 S. 7th Street, Philadelphia, PA 19106
(215) 922-3031   www.philadelphiahistory.org

Look at the series of active programs that have been offered at the museum of Philadelphia history. Just a few annual events include: Riding the Rails, a trip on most of the rails in and around the city as a study of Philadelphia's transportation system; a tour of local breweries every October; a summer music series in the AK garden; a street food festival in May specializing in Philly foods; and in February a Books & Authors series with discussions. There are also special presentations about current exhibits. Truly a place for Philadelphiaphiles!

💰 $3

Chester County Historical Society

225 N. High Street, West Chester, PA 19380
(610) 692-4800   www.chestercohistorical.org

If you love the rich local history of the area, CCHS has terrific interactive events where you learn in the company of other history lovers. Programs include Civil and Revolutionary War reenactments, a hands-on history lab, reproductions and artifacts that you can reconstruct, and costumes of historical eras that you can try on! You'll find an extensive decorative art collection (such as tall case clocks, teapots, and furnishings from different periods), with regular lectures, discussions, and local artist (Pippin!) presentations. Recent special exhibits have included War Comes to Chester County, and an extensive show about baseball (Connie Mack and the Philadelphia Athletics). On top of all this, members take day tours, such as genealogical trips to Washington, DC, and NYC, visiting colonial homes in New Castle, DE, and trips abroad.

Hobbies & Clubs

Civil War Round Table Association

(215) 338-4446   hb1865@aol.com

Activity Location: Radisson Hotel in Northeast Phila. on Rte. 1, south of PA Tnpk.

This group, with a membership of more than 150 people (20s to retirees), meets monthly to hear speakers (on topics like Battles & Leaders), followed by lively discussion and dinner. The group also hosts other events, such as trips to places like the Shenandoah Valley and Antietam, where they tour battle sites, go antique-ing, and enjoy great dinners (including one in a haunted barn!). In February and July you're invited to hear whole evenings of member discussions about challenging issues. There are about 10 Civil War Round Tables throughout the area, including Old Baldy Civil War Round Table at the Friends of Civil War Library & Museums in Philadelphia at (215) 289-6484 and (215) 735-8196. Check to see the events of each branch.

☼ 3rd Tues./mo

☎ Hugh Boyle, President

Fort Mifflin

Fort Mifflin on the Delaware, Ft. Mifflin Rd., Phila., PA 19153 (just off I-95)
(215) 492-1881   fortmifflin@earthlink.net   www.fortmifflin.org

True history buffs can call to find out how they can take their interest to a hands-on level by becoming a reenactor—studying Revolutionary and Civil War history and then acting out the battles in a very realistic way. Volunteers are needed to be involved at the Fort as well.

💰 $6/adults; $5/seniors

Friends of Laurel Hill Cemetery

(610) 293-0693

Activity Location: Cemetery Gate House, 3822 Ridge Ave., Phila., PA 19132

The Friends of Laurel Hill Cemetery is a group active in the preservation and restoration of both the grounds and monuments of Laurel Hill Cemetery, one of the first rural cemeteries in the US. They also conduct public and private tours (such as Captains of Industry and Civil War Laurel Hill) to raise funds for historic preservation (such as for the medallion gardens) while explaining the cultural significance of the cemetery to a wide public. Call to get involved in this lovely historic spot along the Schuylkill River.

Hobbies & Clubs

Genealogical Society of Pennsylvania

215 South Broad Street, 7th Floor, Philadelphia, PA 19107
(215) 545-0391   gspa@aol.com   www.libertynet.org/gspa

Founded in 1892, GSPA helps people collect and preserve the vital and personal records of their ancestors. They offer tours (like Philadelphia Cemeteries), conferences, and programs—alone or in conjunction with other historical societies—with lectures for researchers at all skill levels. One program featured Irish genealogists (*from* Ireland) to assist people exploring their Irish heritage. Upcoming in 2001 will be a program on Genealogy and Genetics, exploring the ramifications of the new DNA research findings. Also, GSPA sponsors a week-long camp for family historians, including trips to archives and concluding with dinner, all for about $250 for the whole week. It's a great opportunity to learn how to do your own research and meet others with more experience.

🐱 $25-$35 for membership

Victorian Society, Philadelphia Branch

202 E. Gowen Avenue, Philadelphia, PA 19119
(215) 248-1839

Activity Location: Various locations around metropolitan Philadelphia

Join this local group of people who are interested in the preservation and appreciation of things from 19th Century (1840-1901) and you'll have the chance to tour privately owned Victorian houses as well as fine examples of Victorian public buildings. There are workshops and presentations by preservationists about how to fix up your 19th Century house by architects who have done restoration on Victorian buildings, by historians and writers who specialize in the culture of the period, as well as by experts on antique furniture, china, glassware, clothing, and jewelry. Light refreshments and socializing are part of the these events. Membership includes two newsletters.

Hobbies & Clubs

Language & Culture

Alliance Francaise

1420 Walnut Street, Ste. 700, Philadelphia, PA 19102
(215) 735-5283   www.alliancefrancaisephiladelphia.com
Activity Location: Center City Philadelphia and the Main Line

Take part in this international organization and learn about France through any number of French classes and/or a number of exciting cultural activities. Lunches in Center City, Chestnut Hill and the Main Line, book clubs, films, happy hours and dinner dances, wine tastings, concerts, and excellent lecture-discussions are some of the events where you will have an opportunity to expand your French lingo. If you really want to kick up your heels French style, celebrate Bastille Day with Alliance in July!

💰 Yearly membership $45

America-Italy Society

1420 Walnut Street, Ste. 1206, Philadelphia, PA 19102
(215) 735-3250   americaitalysociety@rcn.com

Regular Italian lunches are the tip of the iceberg offered by the America-Italy Society, where you can practice your conversational Italian. But there are a host of other activities here: Lecture-discussions about Italian painters, about Italian music and about Italy; films; trips to NYC art museums; concerts with members of the Philadelphia Orchestra; and a large language school with classes on literature and conversation. Ciao!

American Swedish Historical Museum

1900 Pattison Avenue, Philadelphia, PA
(215) 389-1776   www.americanswedish.org

Learn Swedish here, either as a beginner, advanced beginner, or in intermediate conversation classes. You might rather absorb Scandinavian culture and beauty in the evenings in a film group (see *Ellis Island*, *The Immigrants*, or *The Settlers*), or a literature group (e.g., *The Immigrants*), both followed by Q & A. Only $3.

Amici

(215) 898-6040 (Nicola Gentili)   ngentili@ccat.sas.upenn.edu

An organization of Italians and Italian-Americans affiliated with the Center for Italian Studies at the University of Pennsylvania which promotes Italian culture. As a member, you may take part in specified activities at the center, such as conferences, colloquia, and film festivals. Conference topics have included Italian Women Writers of the Renaissance and Modern Italian Literature.

Asian Arts Initiative

1315 Cherry Street, 2nd Floor, Philadelphia, PA 19107
(215) 557-0455   info@asianartsinitiative.com   www.asianartsinitiative.com

AAI is a community arts center where artists and everyday people explore and express their diverse experience as Asian Americans. Besides theater and writing groups for Asian Americans, they sponsor a popular monthly Rap Series—presentations of poetry, videos, and performances—for the general public. AAI also hosts classes and workshops for people of all ages and experience. Check out this exciting new addition to the Philadelphia arts community.

Balch Institute for Ethnic Studies

18 South 7th Street, Philadelphia, PA 19106
(215) 925-8090   info@balchinstitute.org   www.balchinstitute.org

Learn about the immigrant experiences and cultural traditions that represent your background and those of your neighbors in programs and workshops for people of all ages. Balch activities encourage lively discussions around public programs, such as the work of Asian women filmmakers as they explore family roots and relationships. These are extremely thoughtful and exciting sessions, with discussion and learning for everyone present. Check the web site for current events that would interest you.

💰 Most programs are $10/person

French-American Chamber of Commerce of Philadelphia

2000 Market Street, 7th floor, Philadelphia, PA 19103
(215) 419-5559   faccphl@aol.com   www.faccphila.org

One of 13 international chambers in Philadelphia, the FACC offers exciting events for the general public once a month with a diversity of topics to accommodate a diversity of interests. These events include a regular networking program for 100-150 people hosted by local restaurants, business seminars (such as Establishing your Business in  France, featuring an expert on the French business economy, Meet the CEOs Business Luncheon), The Chocolate Festival, an annual wine and cheese tasting, and, of course, a tasting of the beaujolais nouveau ("Savor The Reds") in November. All events are held in English but include many French-speaking people as well. Call for information about these activities and other events.

💰 $30 for networking events, including hors d'oeuvres
For members, annual membership dues.

Hobbies & Clubs

German Society of Pennsylvania

611 Spring Garden Street, Philadelphia, PA 19123
(215) 627-2332   www.germansociety.org

This oldest German Society in the country (established 264 years ago) sponsors many programs that convey a youthful vitality, starting with both German and English classes. For newly arrived German people, the English language classes are part of the Epatriarch Program and include Business English and Practical English applications. For the public, the lecture/speaker series looks at the architecture, economy, cultural events, and politics of contemporary Germany. The society sponsors a concert series with performers ranging from the Wistar Quartet to high school choirs singing German songs. One important program features readings about life in Germany for Jewish citizens. There are special group meetings (young people's meetings, a women's auxiliary) and strictly social events such as student parties and a Rathskeller. Newsletter.

Japanese House & Garden

(215) 878-5097   www.shofuso.org
Activity Location: Horticulture Center in West Fairmount Park, Phila., PA

Get a true feel for Japanese culture by experiencing it in this lovely setting in Fairmount Park. Come for the public tea ceremony, offered four times a year, and learn what it signifies as you are served tea by people in traditional Japanese kimonos. Or attend the summer festival with traditional Japanese music, dancing, crafts, and workshops on Japanese cooking, calligraphy, and papermaking.

☼ Open May to October   ☺ 10am-4pm
💰 $2.50/adults; $2/seniors & students

Miscellany

Dumpster Divers

(215) 755-7717

Divers meet monthly at members' houses to throw around ideas (and stuff) with each other, including tips on good dumpsters to dive in and requests for others to look for certain materials for them. About 40 people are regulars in the group, and the membership is all inclusive. That means you are welcome!

☼ lst Thurs./mo

Philadelphia Association for Critical Thinking

P.O. Box 1131, North Wales, PA 19454
(215) 885-2089 www.phact.org

About 120 members meet eight times a year for lectures about paranormal activities and the scientific explanations behind them. If you like tough questions and don't always accept the first answer you get, if you like to challenge unsupported information, you may enjoy this group. PhACT encourages responsible scientific investigation of paranormal and fringe-science claims. Their activities include a newsletter and educational meetings and lectures, such as Keeping Fiction Out of Science, How Do You Know That's Impossible?, and Fanaticism in Cyberspace. This is a well-educated and thoughtful group that asks, "What's the evidence?" Check the web site for topics of meetings over the last few years.

Sons of the Desert: *A Laurel and Hardy Appreciation Society*

(215) 637-5744 http://users.aol.com/twotars/2tars.html
Activity Location: Cannstatter Club, 9130 Academy Road, Phila., PA

Sons of the Desert is a 30-year-old organization dedicated to the appreciation of the films and work of Laurel and Hardy as well as old vaudeville talent. Programs put on by this group feature a few films of that comedic couple, followed by live local vaudeville performers. The group also honors famous Hollywood celebs like Eddie Bracken and Gale Storm (*My Little Margie!*) as well as local TV stars. The banquets are attended by about 95 people and are a lot of fun with lots of laughs!

☼ 2 times a year

Having a great time at a Sons of the Desert banquet

Hobbies & Clubs

Wine & Beer

Dock Street Brewing Company: *Celtic Flavors*
18th & Cherry Streets, Philadelphia, PA
(215) 496-0413   www.dockstreet.com

Look in on a summer Saturday afternoon for a brewery tour that includes tasting several of their beers. Dock Street also has live music on Wednesdays and Fridays, with occasional entertainment.

💰 $5

General Lafayette Inn & Brewery: *Homebrewers Dinner & Competition*
646 Germantown Pike, Lafayette Hill, PA 19444
(610) 941-0600   www.generallafayetteinn.com

Get together 10 to 20 homebrewers with their friends and guests, including restaurant patrons, for food and a brew-rating competition and you have a terrific party! Other interactive events happen here often, like Lafayette's Escape with continental reenactors and Cigar and Ale Tastings. Regularly scheduled live music and a good all-around crowd make this a fun stop. Check the web site for events.

Homebrewers of Philadelphia and Suburbs (HOPS)
(215) 569-9469   www.beerphiladelphia.com/homesweet

Local club run by and for homebrewers in the greater Delaware Valley. At the meetings, the group does business, socializes, tries different beers, and organizes an annual competition, party meetings, and other events. Once a month they meet at a BYO restaurant. Don't forget to check in at Home Sweet Homebrew *every* Wednesday from 6-8pm for a weekly beer tasting, when local or commercial homebrewers contribute their fine products.

☼ 4th Wed./mo

Savona
100 Old Gulph Road, Gulph Mills, PA 19428
(610) 520-1200   www.savonan.com

Enjoy wine tastings every Friday on Savona's outdoor patio (summer) or at the bar (winter) conducted by sommelier, Brice Delclos. He selects four white and four red wines that are connected in some way (French/California, old wine/new wine, same grapes, same country, etc.) for comparison and discussion.

☼ Fridays   🕐 5:30-7:30pm
💰 $17/20/per person includes wine and hors d'oeuvres

Independent Wine Club

P.O. Box 1478, Havertown, PA 19083
(610) 649-9936

Activity Location: Jack's Firehouse, 2130 Fairmount Ave., Phila., PA

Whether you want to know which wine goes with what meat, or you just enjoy learning about types and styles of wine, you'll want to try IWC's wine tastings with lectures and discussions. They are offered almost every Thursday evening, with lots of time for sampling and socializing. IWC also offers other events, such as excellent one-night courses on Monday and Tuesday evenings. Call for their newsletter to whet your palate.

☼ Mondays, Tuesdays, Thursdays   ⏰ 7-9pm

☎ Neal Ewing

💰 $40-60 for each event for non-members

Mt. Airy Learning Tree

6601 Greene Street, Philadelphia, PA 19119
(215) 843-6333   www.mtairylearningtree.org

You'll love the homework for this class in wine tasting at this commuity-based adult education school. Each term there are over 180 classes, from computers to cooking to walking tours.

Photo by Jonna Naylor

Mt. Airy Learning Tree's wine tasting students enjoying themselves during class at Cresheim Cottage Café

Hobbies & Clubs

 **Here are some extra resources to check out**

- *Organized Obsessions: 1,001 Offbeat Associations, Fan Clubs, and Microsocieties You Can Join.* Deborah M. Burek, Martin Connors. Visible Ink Press, Washington, D.C., 1992

- *Longwood Gardens* (www.longwoodgardens.org) has classes and exhibits by horticultural organizations as well as volunteer opportunities. The classes are numerous, from floral design to outdoor perennials to the " Viewing Stones" exhibit by the North American Viewing Stones Society. Call or see the web site for amazing activities. (610) 388-1000, Rte. 1, near Kennett Square.

- *The American Community Gardening Association (ACGA)* is a national nonprofit organization of professionals, volunteers, and supporters of community greening in urban and rural areas.

- *www.communitygarden.org.* Holds a national conference and many events and programs throughout the US.

- *Renningers Antiques & Collectors* (610) 683-6848

- *Downingtown Flea Market* (610) 518-5100

- *Zern's Farmers Market* (610) 367-2461

- *Hot Rod Magazine's Power Festival,* an annual two-day party for race and street-machine enthusiasts with swap meet for nostalgic car buffs and drag racing in a variety of classes. A weekend-long fest that's fun for the family. Maple Grove Raceway in Mohnton, Berks county. Check the web site: www.hotrodpowerfestival.com.

- *Sommelier Society of America* has a Philadelphia chapter with monthly meetings and tastings open to anyone interested in wine. (212) 679-4190.

- *Schuylkill River Dog Run,* 25th Street, Philadelphia PA 19103 More dog walks listed on web site: *http://home.digital city.com.*

- *www.gardenweb.com* is a great web site listing all kinds of gardening info, such as Northern gardening, cacti and succulents, a plant encyclopedia, gardening forums, and much more.

- *www.beerphiladelphia.com* Includes Beer Philadelphia's (Jim Anderson) small venue beer events that "feature selections from our area's fine brewing community, as well as hard-to-find beers, vintage beers, cask-conditioned beers and barleywines for which we scour the globe in order to bring unique pleasures our guests. We also strive to provide an entertaining and environment in which our guests may enjoy themselves." (From the web site.)

Music

Bluegrass/Country • Blues/Jazz • Classes
Classical/Opera • Drumming • Folk
Gospel • Instrumental • Irish • Latin
Multifaceted Places • Singing
Songwriting • Festivals

Music

Musicians gather at monthly Philadelphia Area Songwriters Alliance sessions to offer support, critiques, and resources.

Bring your fiddle or tin whistle and join in at the weekly Wednesday night Irish session at the Mermaid Inn.

Music

*"There's nothing like music, is there Jim? It's social, it's beautiful,
and it does you a world of good!"* – *Tom Gala*
(overheard at a Mark Cosgrove concert, at the Mermaid Inn)

A sk people what their favorite leisure activity is and they will
likely include music right off the bat. But we all have our own
ways to enjoy it. Some hum when they feel good. Others sing in church
or in the shower. Many of us slip in a CD the minute we hit the car. And
some lucky folks play an instrument for others to hear or for their own
satisfaction. My friend Talia can't hear music without moving into a
dance or some kind of movement. Every one of us is nuts about some
performer and style or era of music. Tom was right; music takes us
someplace else. It speaks to our hearts.

And it *is* social! Music events are some of the all-time great places to
find a community you'll like. Just choose your style, plunk yourself down
and look around. You'll be sitting in the middle of a crowd enjoying the
same sounds you groove to. Some people will be dancing, some bobbing
and weaving in their seats, and some will be mouthing or singing the
words. Some, like my husband Jim, just sit, with rapt attention.

You can find all kinds of music activities in every newspaper and on
many web pages. Most of these are musician-audience events, where the
musicians perform and the audience listens and goes home. What
distinguishes the music events in this book is that they include some
kind of activity that encourages interaction among the participants—
performers and audience alike. So the **Philadelphia Orchestra** is listed
because it offers *Concerts and Conversations*, a folk spot (**Cherry Tree**) is
mentioned because it has folk music with food at intermission, or an
ongoing *Open Circle* (**Bucks County Folk Song Society**) is included
because people sing songs together. Clubs that have live music might be
mentioned because they feature dancing lessons (like **Brasils**). These
establishments go out of their way to foster community, making it easier
for someone like you or me to go alone or for the first time and find a
way to be part of what's happening. A list of *Open Mics* and *Festivals*
appears at the end of the chapter, as well as extra *Resources* to help you
find new places of your own with updated info.

Philly has become a city where you can be involved in all kinds of
music—lots of it. If you want to sing, you have your choice of gospel,
folk, sacred and secular choirs, barbershop quartets, and more. I just
discovered **Sacred Harp** singing, where people sing sacred music from

Music

the late 1700s using scores written in square notes. (Remember those funny notes they put on posters about the Renaissance?) The point is to raise your voice with joy and exuberance and not to worry about singing the *right or wrong* notes! It is the experience, not the product, that matters—but it turns out beautifully anyway. Can you believe it?

For more traditional sacred choral singing, you can look into the choir at a church in your neighborhood. If you are a really good singer, go for an audition with the **Mendelssohn Club** or **Singing City**. If you make it, the experience will be glorious. If you don't, show up for the annual Sing-In with Singing City and pretend you made it! (I'll be the froggy-throated alto/tenor singing my heart out.) Also, there are several excellent organizations that will teach you gospel singing—not just the notes, but the breathing and the awareness you need to sing gospel well. These are multicultural, non-denominational groups that use music to bring people together in good fellowship, and they welcome newcomers.

If jazz is more your thing, rejoice in the exciting resurgence of blues and jazz in the city. Both small neighborhood spots (**South Street Blues**) and fancy places (**Zanzibar Blue**) have a full roster of fine per-formers. At South Street, I felt like I was *in* the band, I was so close to them, and talking with people I'd never met before was easy. **Ortliebs** is another very friendly **Jazzhaus** that's been around for years. There's an active jazz audience there. To *learn* more about jazz, take Harrison Ridley's courses at **Temple University Center City**. He is a great teacher and you'll hear jazz in a whole new way (theme-response and all that).

Opera is having a revival in Philadelphia too, largely because of the fine productions by the **Opera Company of Philadelphia**. Take another Temple CC class on your lunch hour about the current opera OCP is performing. You'll be treated to excellent teachers with a sense of humor who sing and play musical themes on a piano so you can't miss them when you hear them performed. Or take trips to the amazing Met in New York with various groups like the **Opera Club** and **Settlement Music School**. Another form of classical music currently attracting interest is Renaissance music, excitingly performed by several local professional groups such as **Piffaro**. You can volunteer for them (and others) and meet the community of music lovers who make it their business to be out and about hearing fine music. They form a social and information network where you'll learn about events you won't want to miss. They could become your compadres in musical excursions.

Maybe because folk music reflects stories about human life, the community around folk music is especially warm and welcoming. Try **Mom and Pops** or the **Mermaid Inn** on folk music nights and experience the camaraderie among the people in the room. You can tell that this is an important social network for the people there and one that newcomers can become a part of by just showing up. Another very rich folk music community is the **Philadelphia Folk Song Society**. PFSS sponsors events (e.g., *Spring Fling*) and also has regular monthly sing-ins for members in their homes. The *PFSS Folk Festival* in August is absolutely not to be missed. Camping is the most fun (if you don't mind port-a-potties for the weekend) where music is played all night long at different campsites. People wander from site to site listening to Irish ballads here, a jug band there, and a duel of fiddles down the road. You'll think you're in music heaven.

If it is the time in your life to learn to play a musical instrument, go for it. Excellent instruction is available at **Settlement** and **Temple University Center City** music schools where classes are reasonably priced and with discounts for seniors. Do you know what this means? *You* can make the music you have heretofore only listened to. It comes from *your* instrument (or voice) sweetly or not yet sweetly, but *you* are making that musical sound. Then you can put that sound together with the sounds made by your new musical friends and you have a song, a tune, a symphony. If the hard work of practice doesn't put you off, you will be hooked. Making music now becomes part of your self-definition. ("I am a musician.") And you now have a network that is part of the social life you really want.

Whether you want to make music or listen to it, look through this chapter and find the music that is your kind of music. It is a long chapter because there are so many places holding interactive music events. Call to explore what's happening when, and ask the questions that will guarantee your comfort level. Now get the courage and go. Go again. Go a third time. Now decide if this feels like a network you want to include as one of *your* communities, a place you can go on Friday nights (or Wednesdays, etc.) when you want to be around music and people you can talk to.

Gone are the days when you have to be "good" to be allowed to sing and dance and have a compatible community to sing with. Music is for us all and it's a fine way for us to get to know each other.

A closer look at ...

Philadelphia Folk Festival
Old Pool Farm near Schwenksville, PA
(215) 242-0150   www.folkfest.org

The Philadelphia Folk Festival is an amazing three days and nights of traditional and contemporary folk music, blues, and a bit of everything else that's fun. A typical day could include contra dancing at 11am, listening to Tom Paxton close up in shady Dulcimer Grove, checking out the crafts after lunch, relaxing in front of one of three small stage events, and then enjoying outstanding performances from big name or lesser known singer-songwriter/musicians (in 2001, Arlo Guthrie, Solas, Richie Havens) in the late afternoon and evening. The dancing lasts all day, if you want to do that. (Many do.) Another part of the Festival is a sea of tents comprise the campground community where some of the finest music of the weekend takes place all night long. Don't expect to get a lot of sleep if you camp, but do look forward to an extraordinary weekend that will keep you coming back to see old and new friends. (This year was my 20th.) Try volunteering. You'll meet people and get in free. Check out the Spring and Fall Flings as well, smaller folk events, also sponsored by the Philadelphia Folk Song Society.

☼ Weekend before Labor Day

💰 About $18/day; camping & all-Fest
   ticket: $110 in 2001. Kids under 12 free

Bluegrass/Country

Bluegrass Jam

(215) 659-8623
Activity Location: Washington House, 136 N. Main St., Sellersville, PA
(215) 257-3000

Jim Simpson plays mandolin as he hosts this jam, a favorite of bluegrass lovers around the Philadelphia area. Bring your instrument and play tune after tune with the regular players on upright bass, banjo, and guitar. Washington House is about an hour out of the city, but many think it's well worth the trip. Try to catch Jim's group, Choppin' Wood, playing in local clubs like the Mermaid Inn.

☼ 1st Tues./mo   ⏰ 8-11pm

Holmesberg Country Jam

(215) 624-6614   fmoore@icdc.com   www.holmesbergjam.com
Activity Location: Linden Avenue Boat Ramp or the Nite Owl's Tavern,
7900 Frankford Avenue, Philadelphia, PA (1 mi. south of Academy Rd. exit, I-95)

You can take in traditional bluegrass at the Holmesberg Country Jam, which has been bringing musicians together for 30 years. If you're lucky, you'll hear an original from songwriter and regular Fred Moore. This group used to meet in a kitchen/backyard, but now makes fine sounds in the Linden Avenue Boat Park along the Delaware River from May to October. During the rest of the year or inclement weather, look for them at the Nite Owl. Free.

☼ Thursdays   ⏰ 8pm-12am

Mermaid Inn: *Old Time Music Jam*

7673 Germantown Avenue, Philadelphia, PA 19118
(215) 247-9797

Some say this is the only old time music jam in the area. On the fourth Tuesday of the month at 8:30pm, bring your instrument and enter in.

Pinelands Cultural Society: *Sounds of the Jersey Pines*

Albert Music Hall, 125 Wells Mill Road (Route 532), Waretown, NJ 08758
(609) 971-1593

If you like country, folk and bluegrass music, you'll want to be in tune with this longtime music group that sponsors two types of terrific musical events. Every Saturday night, musicians play to their heart's content for 25 minutes each. And four times a year the group sponsors special programs with a theme, like *Pine Barrons Festival* and *Bluegrass in the Pines*. Only $4 to attend.

☼ Saturdays   ⏰ 7:30-11pm

Music

Blues/Jazz

Jazz Vespers

Old Pine Street Presbyterian Church, 4th & Pine Streets, Philadelphia, PA
(215) 925-8051   oldpine@libertynet.org   www.libertynet.org/~oldpine

Jazz musicians integrate their music with a spiritual celebration at area churches once a month. Find this uniquely beautiful experience also at the First Presbyterian Church of Haddonfield (856-429-1960) on the first Sunday.

☼ 3rd Sun./mo.   ⏰ 5pm
💰 Free with offering

23rd Street Café Jazz Jam Session

233 North 23rd Street, Philadelphia, PA
(215) 561-2488   www.23cafe.com

Held in a café that seems more like a club, this eight-year-old jam session features classical jazz, Dixieland, and '40s and '50s style jazz. Sign up on the list and play with the many regulars who show up every week. Very welcoming and fun.

☼ Tuesdays   ⏰ 7:30-11:30pm
💰 Free

Bucks County Blues Society

P.O. Box 482, Levittown, PA 19058
(215) 946-4794   tjc3@voicenet.com   www.bucksnet.com/bcbs
Activity Location: A.J. Sports Bar, 5316 New Falls Rd., Levittown, PA

Since 1977, BCBS has held over 200 concerts, usually featuring nationally known blues acts. Every year it holds a Halloween concert, a Rhythm & Blues Picnic in July, a Mardi Gras Show, and the Spring Fever Foot Stomper Festival. Join the group on Thursdays at A.J. Sports Bar for a hoppin' blues jam (Blue Thursdays).

H.I.G.H.W.I.R.E. Gallery

137 North 2nd Street, Philadelphia, PA
(215) 829-1255   tosmos@voicenet.com   www.highwirestudios.com

All kinds of cross disciplinary performance art emerges at Highwire: Poets meet musicians, percussionists and filmmakers; selfmade instrumentalists meet writers and dancers. Performers from New York, Europe, and the West Coast join local artists for amazing multidisciplinary theater. Call them for mailings or stop in on First Friday.

Mill Creek Jazz and Cultural Society

4624 Lancaster Avenue, Philadelphia, PA 19131
(215) 473-4273

Mill Creek helps to sponsor a wide range of community activities, from gospel music to roller skating in a large facility. It is involved in presenting first-rate musical concerts with world beats like jazz, gospel and reggae. There are also music classes ("all instruments") and workshops and dance classes. The society publishes *Jazz Philadelphia* and *Gospel Philadelphia* for those who want to keep up with these wonderful traditions in the area. Call to be put on the mailing list.

Ortlieb's Jazzhaus

847 N. 3rd Street, Philadelphia, PA 19123
(215) 922-1035   www.ortliebsjazzhaus.com

Don't mind the water buffalo staring at you in Philadelphia's oldest and very popular jazz house. World-class musicians play bebop as fine as you'd want to hear, right in front of you. A great bar for socializing, this place maintains a solid core of regulars, including students, neighborhood and center city people, and musicians after hours. Attended parking lot is available right outside. This place is a treasure and there's no cover.

:Ö: Tuesday-Sunday

Music

Philadelphia Clef Club

736-38 South Broad Street, Philadelphia, PA 19146
(215) 893-9912   clefclub-jazz@mindspring   www.clefclubofjazz.8m.com

The PCC is a mecca for jazz in Philadelphia offering music instruction and performances that highlight the rich jazz history of Philadelphia. Some of the programs have included: Jazz in the Sanctuary, Clef Club Student Ensemble, Jazz Camp, and Private Instrument Instruction. This is the place to hear the finest musicians in the world for reasonable fees. Some programs are MC'd by jazz expert Harrison Ridley.

Warmdaddy's: *Blues Jam*

4 South Front Street, Philadelphia, PA 19106
(215) 627-8400   www.warmdaddys.com

A good size crowd shows up each week for this open jam session. A variety of blues styles are played and it's all pretty wonderful. By the way, for blues performances, Warmdaddy's is outstanding; for jazz *and* blues, try Zanzibar Blue.

☼ Tuesdays   ⏰ 8pm

Classes

Settlement Music School

416 Queen Street, Philadelphia, PA 19147
(215) 336-0400   info@smsmusic.org   www.smsmusic.org

This first-rate longstanding musical organization has six branch locations that provide excellent and reasonable classes in all sorts of orchestra and band instruments and voice. If you learn your instrument, you can be part of the adult chamber ensemble that meets every Wednesday morning (Tuesdays at the Jenkintown Branch).

💰 Reasonable. Offers financial assistance based on documented need.

Temple University Music Prep

1616 Walnut Street, Philadelphia, PA 19103
(215) 204-1512   www.temple.edu/music/musicprep

Both experienced musicians and rank beginners can take private or group instrumental lessons and performance classes in jazz improvisation and singing at Temple. Plus there are exciting music appreciation courses, Friday afternoon classes with the Philadelphia Orchestra, a three-week evening course that includes concert and dinner, and a course with the Philadelphia Opera Company. Wow. Fall and spring terms.

Classical/Opera

Delaware Valley Opera Company

(215) 725-4171   www.libertynet.org/dvoc

*Activity Location: Hermitage Mansion, 700 E. Hermit Ln., Phila., PA
(off Henry Ave. in Roxborough)*

Enjoy fully staged operas inside and outside of this lovely mansion in the Park. No reservations are required and you can bring your own lawn chair and flashlight and meet a community of opera lovers. On some evenings, a buffet dinner is offered; on others, you are encouraged to bring your own "picnic on the grass." These are very special evenings for opera/nature buffs. About $15.

🦽 Some Thursdays and Saturdays   📷 6:30-8pm

Music Group of Philadelphia

*P.O. Box 41107, Philadelphia, PA 19127
(610) 527-9122   www.musicgroupofphila.org*

Fifty volunteer singers specialize in a cappella singing of the works of new composers and works seldom performed. The group has about six concerts a year, including some holiday concerts where the audience is encouraged to sing along. There are receptions for mingling on concert evenings.

Opera Club

*1346 Joan Drive, Southampton, PA 18966
(215) 322-1364   operaclub@hotmail.com*

Activity Location: Academy of Vocal Arts, 1920 Spruce St., Phila., PA

This exciting forum focuses on opera and vocal arts. About 10 times a year, members preview local opera productions and explore literary, historical and musicological topics. Meetings feature singers, conductors, and stage directors, and regularly include live and recorded music, all in a friendly, informal atmosphere. In the past, programs have included attending the performance of Schoenberg's *Gurrelieder*, and a concert, lecture and dinner commemorating the 50th anniversary of the death of Richard Strauss. Annual dues about $35/year.

Opera Company of Philadelphia

(215) 928-2100   www.operaphilly.com

Activity Location: Academy of Music, Broad & Locust Sts., Phila., PA

Great opera is now firmly established in Philadelphia! If you haven't seen the productions in the last few years, treat yourself to a glorious Sunday afternoon (or weeknight evening) of excellent singing. Ticket holders can take advantage of the fine introductory talks one hour prior to curtain at the Doubletree Hotel.

Music

Philadelphia Orchestra: *Pre-Concert Conversations*

260 S. Broad Street, Philadelphia, PA 19102
(215) 893-1900   www.philorch.org

The orchestra provides many opportunities to join the classical music community. Subscribers can attend special Pre-Concert Conversations where they meet soloists, orchestra musicians, and composers to discover insights into the evening's programming. They also can dine in the Academy before the concert (Bravo!) or kick up their heels in the party atmosphere of the holiday concerts (For Halloween, come in costume!). The Friday Afternoon Lecture Luncheons offer fascinating lecturers, celebrity guests, and a buffet lunch (8 people for $200) hosted by the Rittenhouse Square Committee for the Orchestra (215-893-1956). Singles: check the Singles Chapter for the SOLO group of the Orchestra.

PIFFARO: *Philadelphia Renaissance Wind Band*

739 North 25th Street, Philadelphia, PA 19130
(215) 235-8469   piffaro1@aol.com

PIFFARO inspires a group of devoted followers (I'm one of them) to show up eagerly at every concert to hear these unusual instruments played by this creative troop with a theatrical flair. Many take on volunteer responsibilities at the concert, such as greeting the audience-guests, passing out programs, and manning the box office. Other volunteers help by preparing mailings, designing brochures, or assisting with sets and costumes. It's worth it. Finding community with members of this group is a pleasure.

Settlement Music School: *Opera Trips*

Jenkintown Music School Branch, 515 Meetinghouse Road, Jenkintown PA 19046
(215) 885-3345   www.smsmusic.org
Activity Location: Bus pickup in 4 locations—Bala Cynwyd, Willow Grove, Jenkintown, & Center City Phila., PA

Join enthusiastic opera lovers for trips to the Kennedy Center in Washington, D.C., the Lincoln Center in New York (Metropolitan Opera, or New York City Opera), and, in the spring, the New York City Ballet. Opera club members subscribe to a minimum of four operas, but if you call a few weeks before the event you may find tickets available. Selections include traditional favorites as well as premier events of modern works. We opera fans believe that the finest opera productions in the world are now accessible and affordable with this group.

🏛 Approximately $170, includes ticket and bus transportation

Women for Greater Philadelphia:
Concerts by Candlelight at Laurel Hill

530 Walnut Street, Independence Square, Philadelphia, PA 19106
(215) 627-1770

Activity Location: Laurel Hill Mansion, Edgely Dr. in East Fairmount Park, Phila., PA, (215) 235-1776

For over 24 years, this summer concert series has offered classical music in the lovely historic Laurel Hill Mansion. The Jubal Trio, the Wister Quartet, the American Society of Ancient Instruments, and Allen Krantz and Edward Schultz have played over the last few years. Each concert is followed by a reception where a regular following discusses the music and has a chance to talk to the musicians.

☼ Sundays   ⏰ 7:30pm

💰 $15/each concert ($12/seniors), series tickets for 4 concerts are available

Drumming

Pro Drum Center

363 North Easton Road, Glenside, PA 19038
(215) 887-1462 www.prodrum.com

Visit this amazing store filled with every conceivable type of percussion instrument and decide if you want to sign up for lessons. The center also teaches piano, guitar or bass with 4-week group Bodhran workshops from time to time.

💰 $50 for four 30-minute lessons

RhythmSong (formerly Gourd-Love Drum Club)

(610) 524-6280 dkern@libertynet.org   www.rhythmsong.com
Activity Location: West Chester, PA area

Come and prove that all people are born to make music. Be the music! Approximately once a month, this six-year old group brings experienced, talented and positive teachers to make all kinds of percussion music with all who attend. Sometimes there are all-weekend or all-day Saturday funshops with nationally known world musicians, such as Sankofa Dance Theater, Paulo Mattioli, and Tony Vacca. Traditional and original rhythms, songs, and group playing. Joyous.

☎ Debbie Kern

💰 $20-25

Music

Folk

Bucks County Folk Song Society

(215) 579-4540   www.bucksfolk.org

Activity Location: Wrightstown Friends Meeting House, Rte. 413,
2 miles north of Newtown, PA

This 30+-year-old folk society helps us all to learn about and appreciate folk music by providing a regular venue for mostly local folk music artists. Each month members host a song circle, a break for sharing food brought by volunteers, and a jam session. Sometimes there is a featured performer. About 40-70 people attend each month and newcomers are welcome. A monthly newsletter is included with membership which costs $20.

:☼: 1st Sun./mo   🕰 6:30-10pm

Cherry Tree Music Co-op

(215) 386-1640 (hotline)   www.cherrytree.org

Activity Location: St. Mary's Parish Hall, 3916 Locust Walk (between Spruce and Walnut Sts.) on the University of Pennsylvania Campus in West Phila., PA

Outstanding folk concerts are held on Sunday nights in Philadelphia's eclectic coffeehouse. It's been an all-volunteer, cooperative (no leader) outfit for 25+ years of performances, mini-folk festivals, and other events. To be more involved, you can join the volunteer staff. Best to call first, then show up at 5pm and help with chairs, equipment and other basic tasks to produce a great show. Mingle with other folk lovers for coffee and brownies at intermission.

:☼: Every Sunday evening   🕰 7:30pm

💰 Between $10-13

Folk Factory Coffeehouse

(215) 848-6246   polson@igc.apc.org   www.folkfactory.org

Activity Location: Unitarian Universalist Church of the Restoration,
6900 Stenton Ave. and Gorgas Ln., Phila., PA 19150

Good music and progress for social change are the mottos at the popular concerts at the Folk Factory. Each month the Folk Factory holds an acoustic concert featuring nationally known performers (2nd Friday, 8pm) and an open stage/open circle (4th Thursday, 7:30pm) with a regular audience of about 25-30 people. A very comfortable and interesting crowd to talk to while you munch light snacks at the reception after the concert. Sign language. (See page 82.)

:☼: During academic year: 🕰 evenings
    Concerts 2nd Friday, Open Stage 4th Thursday

💰 Sliding scale: concerts $8-$25, Open stage $2-$5

Godfrey Daniels Coffeehouse
7 East 4th Street, Bethlehem, PA 18015
(610) 867-2390   www.godfreydaniels.org

This weekly open mic is worth the hour drive from Philly. Or you can go for the monthly blues, swing, or sing-jams. Concerts by well- known performers on the weekends. Membership gets you a calendar of events and ticket discounts.

☼ Open mic on Sundays   ⏰ 7pm start

💰 Open mic $2.50; concerts $9.50-$17.50; $30 and up for membership

Green Willow Folk Club
(302) 798-4811   www.greenwillow.org
Activity Location: O'Friel's Irish Pub, 600 Delaware Ave., Wilmington DE, just off Rte. 95 (1st Delaware Ave. exit in Wilmington)

This club sponsors friendly events in an Irish pub, where the tables are close together and people talk to each other easily while eating and listening. Mostly Celtic and British Isles concerts, and often musicians from same, taking place about once a month, usually Mondays. No smoking inside.

☼ Usually Mondays   ⏰ 7:30pm

☎ Reservations suggested because limited seating

💰 About $15

Lansdowne Folk Club
304 Congress Avenue, Lansdowne, PA 19050
(610) 622-7250   info@folkclub.org   www.folkclub.org
Activity Location: Twentieth Century Club, 84 S. Lansdowne Ave., Lansdowne, PA

For over five years, this club has presented concerts with local and well-known folk performers. It's easy to meet others who love folk music by volunteering, performing at the open stage, or just hanging out in this beautiful space during the show.

☼ Thursdays   ⏰ 7:30pm start

💰 $15 advance, $18 at door

Music

Mom & Pop's Coffeehouse

(215) 547-1124 (for info)   SDeckhart@aol.com   www.fortissimo.org
Activity Location: United Christian Church, 8525 New Falls Rd., Levittown, PA
(215) 946-6800

The concerts at Mom & Pop's are held in a church sanctuary with the alter as the stage, lofty ceilings, and very comfortable seating. An atmosphere both congenial and homey is created for both performers and audience, with homemade baked goods and tea and coffee for milling around during intermission. Between 50 to 100 people show up for performances—new faces and regulars—and volunteers are welcomed. Usually the first and third Fridays of the month, but call first. Mailing list. Just $7.

☼ 1st & 3rd Fris./mo (Sept.-May)   ⏰ 8pm

Philadelphia Folksong Society

7113 Emlen Street, Philadelphia, PA 19119
(215) 242-0150   pfs@pfs.org   www.pfs.org or www.folkfest.org
Activity Location: Germantown Academy Arts Center, Morris Rd., Fort Washington, PA

If you want to be involved with folk music, this is the group to try first. On a regular schedule, you can sing and sup with local artists at a monthly sing-event in PFSS members' homes, attend concerts by prominent musicians in the intimate setting of a member's home, learn in workshops hosted by a society member for all skill levels, or enjoy nine monthly concerts of top music artists at the Germantown Academy. PFSS also sponsors the *Philadelphia Folkfest*, the most wonderful three days for singing and instruments you can imagine on the weekend before Labor Day. Plus there are two annual weekend retreats, the *Fall Fling* and *Spring Thing*, which are full of music, dance and jam sessions. Are there more superlatives that I could use? Call for a full newsletter of events and see for yourself.

💰 $25 individual, $20 sr/$40 family

West Chester Folk

325 Dean Street, West Chester, PA 19382
(610) 436-0497   tmb@myxa.com www.westchesterfolk.org
Activity Location: West Chester University, West Chester, PA & Grand Opera House, Wilmington, DE

This is a friendly folk group that sponsors about six traditionally oriented folk music concerts a year and occasional jam sessions with the audience afterwards. Last year the performers included Sara Grey, Bruce Molsky, and Andy Cohen and Larkin Bryant. Check the web site for location addresses.

💰 $10

Gospel

Evelyn Graves School of Performing Arts

5447 Chester Avenue, Philadelphia, PA 19143
(215) 727-7796   egdrampro@aol.com

The Evelyn Graves School and Theater Group offers rich cultural activities for both adults and children. Classes are designed to train and develop artists and strengthen self esteem through sacred dance with modern ballet and jazz movements, drama, art (including drawing, painting, and jewelry-making), piano, and creative movement. Gospel singing is taught with appropriate breathing, articulation, and vocalization techniques. There is a strong motivation to preserving the African-American heritage through these fine multicultural activities.

Philadelphia Gospel Seminars (Edwin Newberry Choir)

P.O. Box 21425, Philadelphia, PA 19141
(215) 549-3777
Activity Location: St. Paul's Lutheran Church, 5900 N. 5th St., Phila., PA (Olney)

This is an interdenominational, interracial group whose aim is to promote cultural unity through the power of gospel singing by offering an affordable gospel music seminar to all people in the local community. Since 1983, over 2,000 participants have learned new gospel music, vocal techniques, and choir decorum, and enjoyed fellowship with people from all walks of life. This group perform in the U.S. and Europe. (They sang for the Pope!) An annual seminar ($45) offers a week of learning gospel singing and choir techniques, with many songs taught by the composers of the pieces. Plus there is a Saturday night performance. You can try this and see how you love it!

💰 $3/mo dues; $45 for the week-long seminar

Music

Instrumental

Philadelphia Classical Guitar Society

(215) 567-2972   www.phillyguitar.org

Activity Location: Classical Guitar Store, 2038 Sansom St., Phila., PA

This musical group presents guitar concerts, supports education in guitar, and provides a social setting for people who love the instrument. You do not have to play to belong or attend the functions, such as the Sunday afternoon informal guitar salons where members of the society play, or the master classes by virtuoso guitarists. However, you'll *want* to be a member to attend social events like picnics with guitar playing, food and fun. The society also presents formal concerts for the general public, featuring some of the finest guitar players in the world, and a large student recital at guitar festival days. Food and demonstrations are included.

Philadelphia Recorder Society

philrecorder@hotmail.com   http://users.erols.com/vfitz

Activity Location: Settlement Music School, 6123 Germantown Ave., Phila., PA

This group plays music by composers of the Late Middle Ages, Renaissance and Baroque eras, but also ragtime, folk tunes, and modern compositions. They start their meetings playing easy pieces and then tackle more challenging music. Other activities include performing for local charities and holding workshops.

☼ One Mon./mo (usually the 3rd)   ☉ 6:45-9pm

💰 $35 annual membership dues

Irish

Glenside Pub: *Irish Session*

122 South Easton Road, Glenside, PA 19038
(215) 576-9354

John Brennen and his friends keep this Irish Session going every Thursday. It's a fun, friendly night out. Bring your instrument and join in or just listen to the jigs and reels. Enjoy an Irish ale and the good food reasonably priced at the Glenside.

☼ Thursdays   ⏰ 9pm

Irish Bards: *Irish Session*

2013 Walnut Street, Philadelphia, PA 19103
(215) 569-9585   www.the-bards.com

Bob Michel plays banjo, concertina and the flute and runs the Irish Session in this nifty pub that looks like it's in an Irish village and has a very nice Irish owner (Patrick Whelan—say hi when you go). Kevin plays the button box accordion, and you can bring an instrument or a song to sing and join the group. Musicians get a complimentary beverage. It's common for families to attend.

☼ Sundays   ⏰ 5-9pm
💰 Free

Philadelphia Ceili Group: *Irish Festival*

(215) 849-8899   PhilaCeiliGroup@aol.com   www.philadelphiaceiligroup.org
Activity Location: PCG: Commodore Barry Club, 6815 Emlen St., Phila., PA
Festival: Memorial Hall, Fairmount Park, Phila. PA on the 2nd Sat. in Sept.

In 2001, PCG sponsored the 27th annual Irish Festival in September with workshops and concerts at Memorial Hall in Fairmount Park. Reported as the oldest traditional Irish music and dance festival in the country, it's a wonderful event where internationally known musicians (such as Mick Moloney) play real traditional Irish music on several stages happening at once. You can learn ceili, step dancing, and traditional Irish music the day before and play/dance your heart out at the Festival. On Friday nights, the PCG holds an Irish session at the Commodore Barry Club in Mt. Airy. Dancers are welcome; you can learn Ceili there. Call for newsletter.

Music

Latin

Asociacion de Musicos Latino Americanos (AMLA)

P.O. Box 50296, 2726 North 6th Street, Philadelphia, PA 19132
(215) 223-3060   amla@libertynet.org   www.amla.org

AMLA offers the spectrum of authentic Latino music, including all the Caribbean sounds, with affordable classes in a wide range of music and dance, including Latin percussion and salsa dancing, and much more. Consult the *Pulso Latino* page on the AMLA web site for the latest AMLA eventsLatin music being performed in the area. AMLA's fabulous Street Fair on 5th Street (from Lehigh to Indiana Avenues) is held each September. You won't want to miss it! Ask about the Cultural Treasures program, a workshop/lecture series on the historical and cultural underpinnings of Latin music (such as Salsa on film).

💰 $40 individual membership

Multifaceted Places

International House: *International Music Series*

3701 Chestnut Street, Philadelphia, PA 19104
(215) 895-6537   ihouse@libertynet.org   www.libertynet.org/ihouse

Explore the music of gifted international performers, from Bulgarian wedding to Pakistani gypsy to Afro pop to Cape Briton fiddle music. Concerts are held monthly at IH, where international students live and study and where all Philadelphians can enjoy interactive cultural events of high quality. Call for a calendar, which also lists film, dance and discussion programs.

☼ Fridays and Saturdays   🕐 8pm

Mermaid Inn

7673 Germantown Avenue, Philadelphia, PA 19118
(215) 247-9797 www.themermaidinn.net

Considered one of the best folk music bars in the city, there's music every night at the Mermaid. Attend the Irish Session (Weds.), Bothy Club open mic with concert (1st & 3rd Mons.), Open Circle with sing-alongs and originals (1st & 3rd Thurs.), Bluegrass Jam (3rd Tues.), Acoustic Blues Jam (4th Tues.), and great weekend concerts. Comfortable, welcoming, and unpretentious. (See page 78, **Cafés,** for additional info.)

☼ Mondays - Saturdays   🕐 9pm

Music

Sedgwick Cultural Center

7137 Germantown Avenue, Philadelphia, PA 19119
(215) 248-9229 info@sedgwick.center.org www.sedgwickcenter.org

The Sedgwick, dedicated to building community through the arts, provides a common meeting ground for artists and audiences of many ethnic backgrounds, religious traditions, age groups and socio-economic levels from Philadelphia's historic Northwest. Come to hear outstanding concerts by all types of musicians, including jazz (such as, Philadelphia Heritage Art Ensemble, and Orrin Evans Trio), meditation music, a feminist vocal ensemble (SheWho), and a popular singer/songwriter like Garnet Rogers. (I heard Garnet; he is terrific!) When you go, you'll enjoy talking to the folks you find sitting next to you, or joining you to admire the local artists' works on the center's walls. No matter what neighborhood you're from, you'll be part of the community here.

  Very reasonable

Singing

Anna Crusis Women's Choir

P.O. Box 42277, Philadelphia, PA 19101
(215) 864-5991 annacrusis@snip.net www.annacrusis.org

Anna Crusis Women's Choir holds open auditions annually, typically in June. The choir seeks women of every conceivable cultural, musical, and personal background. They sing secular music, especially songs with political and feminist themes and songs from all nationalities and cultures—all beautiful music. They perform for many organizations.

  Rehearsals are every week from 7-9:45pm.

Bucks County Choral Society

(215) 598-6142 (for info) bccs@comcat.com www.buckschoral.org
Activity Location: Doylestown area

This well-known independent choral group of about 70 volunteers sings sacred and secular classics, including major choral works with local orchestras. To join, you'll need previous choral experience, good sight-reading skills, and a voice that will blend with the choir. The society gives one three-concert series a year and at least three or four other concerts for local organizations.
Directed by Dr. Thomas Lloyd.

  Tuesday evenings from September to May   7:30-10pm

  Small membership plus costs of choir materials

Music

Choral Society of Montgomery County

Montgomery County Community College, Box 400, 340 DeKalb Pike, Blue Bell, PA 19422

(215) 641-6518   www.mc3.edu/evact/cultural/choral_society.html

This select adult ensemble sings the entire spectrum of choral literature, including such notable works as the *African Santus, Carmina Burana* and *The Messiah*. The Choral Society has presented workshops for the public featuring internationally known musicians/music groups. It sponsors *Living Program Notes* before performances of major works to inform audience members about the music they are about to hear. You can take part in the music experience in many ways with this singing group. Call for upcoming events.

Mendelssohn Club of Philadelphia

1218 Locust Street, Philadelphia, PA 19107

(215) 735-9922   www.libertynet.org/mcchorus

For those of you who can really sing, here's your chance. This fine all-volunteer group that sings sacred and secular pieces holds open auditions for semi-professional singers. Sight-reading is essential to sing the finest choral music of many cultures, traditions, periods and styles, including works by new composers. If you qualify, you may be singing with the Philadelphia Orchestra at the Mann Music Center, as well as presenting concerts in many churches and the Academy of Music, sometimes with other choruses.

☼ Rehearsals on Wednesdays   🕑 7:30-10pm

Northeast Oratorio Society

(215) 745-9596

Activity Location: St. James Lutheran Church, Castor and Pratt Sts., Phila., PA

If you love to sing and like being around others who also love to sing, try this choral group. It requires an audition and the ability to sight-read, but you don't have to have a perfect voice. This is music you stand still to sing—concert versions of sacred and secular pieces—anything from Bach's B Minor Mass to Handel's *Elijah*. Recently affiliated with a community orchestra, the group performs at least twice a year at its own concerts and for other organizations. There are about 40-50 members, many of whom are soloists for the group.

☼ Mondays   🕑 7:30-9:15pm

Music

Philomusica Chorale

(215) 646-1975   chvmard@aol.com

Activity Location: Presbyterian Church of Chestnut Hill, 8855 Germantown Ave., Phila., PA

Philomusica welcomes people of various ethnic and national backgrounds. This group of between 40 to 60 volunteers sings a diversity of musical selections and performs all over the area, often in northwest Philadelphia or eastern Montgomery County. The repertoire includes major works, plus international folk songs, Broadway hits, madrigals, and more. An audition is necessary, but don't be intimidated—a sight-singing class is held to help you develop skill. If you love to sing, go for it! Directed by Mardia Melroy.

☼ Mondays   ☎ 7:30pm

Sacred Harp Singing

(610) 896-1565   mmckenzi@haverford.edu.
http://members.aol.com/_ht_a/sacredharp/home
Activity Location: St. James United Church of Christ, Myrtle & Warwick Road, Havertown, PA (next to the Grange)

There is no harp other than the harp of the human voice in this non-denominational, social, singing group. It is a cappella hymn music in three- and four-part harmonies from books of "shape note" music, such as *The Sacred Harp* (1991), and other old and new compositions in shape notes. The singers sit in facing sections around a "hollow square" and take turns leading tunes at their chosen pace and pitch. This method relates to late 1700's sacred music before instruments were used in church ceremonies. The music is exciting and was meant to excite singing congregations. It still does. The whole experience is exuberant as people sing at full volume in a joyful yet serious celebration of life. Absolutely everyone is welcome and the only prerequisites is the love of music. Just show up and sing.

☼ 2nd Fri./mo   ☎ 7:30-9:30pm

Singing City Choir: *Sing In!*

123 South 17th Street, Philadelphia, PA 19103
(215) 569-9067   singcity@libertynet.org   www.libertynet.org/singcity

This group has been uniting people through music since 1948. If you wish to audition, check the web site for things to consider, one of which is a weekly rehearsal on Tuesdays at the First Baptist Church on 17th and Sansom Street. If you can't be a member of a great chorus (like me), you can join this fabulous choir for an afternoon of singing choral masterpieces (such as *The Messiah*) for the annual winter Sing-In. It is an absolutely thrilling afternoon. I rarely miss it.

Music

Singing in the Moment

(215) 233-0777

Activity Location: Close Philadelphia suburb

Explore the songs within you in workshops that focus on discovering and exploring one's inner world of rhythm and sound in a safe, playful environment. Using hundreds of instruments from around the world as well as your voice, you'll engage in drumming and singing, listening for both rhythm and melody, in solos or ensembles—all facilitated with caring appreciation and a great sense of humor.

☼ Most Saturdays   ☻ 9:30am-12:30pm

Sounds of Liberty Barbershop Chorus

(215) 636-9012 soundsofliberty@hotmail.com

Activity Location: Philadelphia Protestant Home, 6500 Tabor Rd., Phila., PA

If you can carry a tune and love to sing, this men's group that sings barbershop in four-part harmony would love to have you join them. It's a great group of about 35 who sing their hearts out every Tuesday night.

☼ Tuesdays   ☻ 7:30-10pm

Valley Forge Chorus of Sweet Adelines

(610) 525-8879 www.sweetadelineintl.org

Activity Location: Freedoms Foundation, Martha Washington Bldg., Rte. 23, Valley Forge, PA

This woman's barbershop singing group welcomes new members without barbershop experience. Barbershop style gives you a chance to really enjoy four-part harmonies. About 50 strong, the Adelines rehearse weekly, perform in places like Longwood Gardens and Rose Tree Park Summer Festival, and compete once a year with other SA choruses. Besides blending their voices, they occasionally have parties and other social events with other choruses. This kind of singing is so much fun it can be addictive.

☼ Tuesdays   ☻ 7:30pm

Workmen's Circle Chorus

(215) 742-0346 schwartzpb@juno.com

Activity Location: Northeast Regional Library, Bustleton & Cottman Aves., Phila.

You don't have to be Jewish to love Yiddish choral music. About 25 women and men rehearse on Mondays to sing this lively and moving music. The group has been singing and performing in the area for 70 years. If you can sing in Yiddish, call for an audition; otherwise, call about performances. It's $15/year to join.

☼ Mondays   ☻ 1pm

Songwriting

Philadelphia Area Songwriters Alliance

(215) 233-0384
http://members.aol.com/philasong/philsong.htm
Activity Location: In members' homes

For over 12 years, this group of acoustic musicians has been meeting in each other's homes to critique the songs they are writing and offer support. They also discuss venue and songwriting resources, collaborate with other groups, and present member showcases at area coffeehouses. In 1999 they produced a CD called *Declaration*. If you are a songwriter and want to join them, give a call About $10 a year to belong.

☼ Once or twice a month   ⏰ 7-10pm

Philadelphia Songwriters Association

songwritersphila@aol.com
Activity Location: Recording studios and cafés in the area

PSA offers very practical, nuts and bolts help to songwriters who want to better their writing craft and to develop a business plan to help them successfully market their songs. Meetings have an exchange of useful songwriting business information from members, a guest speaker from the industry, and songwriting critiques with fellow writers. All styles of music are welcome.

☼ Mostly on Mondays, once or twice a month   ⏰ 7:30-10pm

Festivals

Augusta Heritage Center Arts Workshops

Davis & Elkins College, Elkins, West Virginia
(800) 624-3157   www.augustaheritage.com

Augusta offers 200 week-long intensive classes in music and dancing. You'll find Cajun/Creole, French Canadian, guitar week, Irish week, old-time music week, Swing week, and more. Every one I talked to who has attended these workshops has just loved them.

☼ Summers

Music

Bethlehem Musikfest

25 West 3rd Street, Bethlehem, PA 18015
(610) 861-0678   www.musikfest.org
Activity Location: Concerts throughout the city

If you love music, you'll love this eight-day celebration. There are ten stages within a four-block area so you can walk around to your heart's content and listen to everything from Cajun to country to classical to folk to dance bands. Over 650 artists perform and there are 1000 performances. Plus there are street performers and lots of children's activities.

☼ Beginning of August   ☖ Noon-11pm
🏃 Mostly free

Brandywine Friends of Old Time Music:
Delaware Valley Bluegrass Festival

P.O. Box 3672, Greenville, DE 19807
(302) 475-3454   www.brandywinefriends.org
Activity Location: Salem County Fairgrounds, Woodstown, NJ

"The Brandywine Friends of Old Time Music is a non-profit organization that is dedicated to the preservation and presentation of the traditional music of the United States known as "old time" music: fiddle, banjo and string band music, particularly that of the Southern Appalachian mountains; classic early country music; and also including bluegrass." (From BFOTM web site.) Formed in 1972, BFOTM presents the Delaware Valley Bluegrass Festival and other events during the year. Call or check the web site for upcoming events.

☼ Friday to Sunday of Labor Day Weekend
🏃 $60 weekend ticket with camping
   $10/yr membership BFOTM

More Festivals ...

Appel Farm Arts & Music Center, 457 Shirley Road, Elmer, NJ
(800) 394-1211, Folk Festival hosting both big names & area artists on 1st
Sat in June, 11:30am-8pm, $24 advance, $28 at gate.

Bach Festival of Philadelphia, (215) 247-2224.

Bridgeton Folk Festival, 181 East Commerce Street, Bridgeton, NJ 08302
Activity Location: Ampitheater at Sunset Lake, Bridgeton,
3rd Sat in June, 11am-8pm.

Jam on the River, Great Plaza at Penn's Landing, Memorial Day Weekend,
(800) 611-5958.

Cultural Festivals, Cannstatter Volksfest Club, 9130 Academy Rd.,
(215) 332-0121. Call for dates of ethnic festivals like their German Festival.

Peco Energy Jazz Festival, (800) 611-5958.

Philadelphia Lesbian & Gay Music Festival

*Shady Brook Farm Annual Amaizeing Corn Maze Festival
& Concert Series*, 931 Stony Hill Rd., Yardley, PA, (215) 968-1670,
Super G Labor Day Family Weekend, and five-week Concert Series-Folk
and Blue concerts.

Web sites

- *www.fortissimo.org* major web site for Philly folk music
- *www.chorusamerica.org/northeast.html* for choral singing

Music

Open Mics, Jam Sessions, Karaoke

Fergie's, 1214 Sansom Street, Philadelphia, PA, (215) 928-8118
Variety, Mondays, 9pm

Finnegan's Wake, 547 North 3rd Street, Philadelphia, PA, (215) 574-9240
Irish Session, Wednesdays, 8pm, Lm Dennis Brennan 3/8

Grape Street Pub, 105 Grape Street, Manayunk, PA, (215) 483-7084
Mondays, 8:30pm

John & Peter's, 96 South Main Street, New Hope, PA, (215) 862-5981
Variety, Monday, 8:30 sign-up, 9pm start

McGillin's Old Ale House, 1310 Drury St. (between Sansom & Chestnut
sts.), Philadelphia, PA, (215) 735-5562, Wednesdays, 10pm-1am, Karaoke

Rusty Nail, 2580 Haverford Avenue, Ardmore, PA, (610) 649-nail
Live audition nights, Variety, Wednesdays, 9:30pm, call manager,
Chris Braccili a day to a week ahead of time to get an audition.

The Point, 880 West Lancaster Ave., Bryn Mawr, PA, (610) 527-0988
Wednesdays, Open Music Circle, 8pm, Tuesdays, Open Mic, 7:30pm, Folk,
Acoustic

South Street Rhythm and Blues, 21st and South Streets, Philadelphia, PA
(215) 546-9009, Thurs., Karaoke, 9:30pm, $4 cover

Open Circle at the Mermaid Inn

Nature

Bird Watching • Fishing

Hiking, Walking & Orienteering

Miscellany • Nature Centers, Parks & Friends

Nature

Wissahickon Trail Club clearing a bike trail
in Valley Green in Fairmount Park

Photo by Rob Burbank

Elderhostelers learn about mountain ecology during a day hike at the
Appalachian Mountain Club at the Pinkham Notch Visitor Center, NH

B eing outdoors restores my soul. Being outdoors, when I pay attention to being outdoors, lifts the blues, takes me out of the humdrum place I'm in, and gives me perspective. Conversely, when I stay inside too long, I start to get "funny." Getting outside is not a luxury in my life; it's a necessity. How about you?

Sometimes it's nice to be alone outdoors. But it's also nice to do outdoor things with friends or with a community of outdoor enthusiasts. Since the love of nature is so universal, you'll find a rich blend of people of all ages, personality types, and multicultural backgrounds in that community. They'll all be out there–listening to birds, admiring the colors of spring wildflowers, and watching (breathlessly watching) the sun go down over Hawk Mountain.

Have you been thinking that it's time to slow up a bit and appreciate the sounds and smells of your life a little more deeply? When you stop and listen, you actually *will* hear the birds. (Every so often, I do that. It's quite remarkable.) If you really want to hear them, hook up with the **Audubon** folks for first-rate guided bird walks in prime bird watching areas, where you can identify birds, count them (for official bird counts), photograph them, study their habitats, improve/conserve their habitats, and more. Birding has become a hot activity for outdoors people, so you'll find lots of good company who want to meet regularly for early Saturday (or Sunday) morning walks.

Women in ever larger numbers are taking to the streams and woods for outdoor adventures. We are learning to fish, camp, and hunt (if we wish) for a whole weekend in a program called **Becoming an Outdoors Woman** sponsored by the State of New Jersey. Then we could join the **Delaware Women's Fly Fishing Association** for regular fishing activities with a great collection of fishing cronies. You fellas can join us in groups like the **Main Line Fly Tyers** club, which meets all year, to hear speakers talk about no-fail fly fishing techniques. Club members go on some great fishing expeditions. There are also loads of fishing tournaments on the fresh-water lakes of Pennsylvania and on the Atlantic Ocean. Tournaments are hosted by sporting and conservation groups, which sponsor all kinds of fishing and other outdoor events for the general public.

If you're new to the area and are looking to find an interesting social network, try spending time with a local hiking club. They do lots of

Nature

different activities every weekend that don't require much skill or knowledge and include lots of socializing along the way. Besides long walks, short walks, "real" hikes, and backpacking, club activities might include snow shoeing, climbing, "volksmarches," biking, skiing, conservation projects, parties, and trips. The schedule of activities for many hiking clubs will blow you away. They are so varied and exciting, you'll have trouble waiting for the weekend. One year the **Sierra Club** had Thanksgiving dinner on top of a mountain. One member drove the dinner up the mountain (that would be me), the rest of the group hiked up the mountain, and everyone enjoyed the reward at the top!

There are all kinds of hiking groups. Some are small, some are geared toward a specific population, and some focus on city walks while others explore hills and valleys all over the Delaware Valley. Smaller groups may hike most often in a specific geographical area, such as the **Chester County Trail Club**. The large groups include the **Sierra Club,** which has a strong conservation agenda, the **Outdoor Club of South Jersey,** where volunteer members lead the activities, and the **Appalachian Mountain Club**, which networks with many other outdoor groups, like one of my favorites, the **Philadelphia Canoe Club**. If you are single and want to spend time with other unattached buds, check out the large clubs with special groups for singles. The hiking community is very large across the country. You can network in this larger community when the local branch of a national organization like the Sierra Club or the Appalachian Mountain Club connects with their counterparts in another city, like the DC branch of AMC. For *lots* of reasons, hiking is a great way to socialize. At the same time, you'll get your exercise (painlessly), lose weight, reduce stress, and put roses in your cheeks! (As soon as this book goes to the printer, I'm going!)

For education about the natural world, look to your local nature center. There are so many in the area that I could not put them all in this book, but there is bound to be one near you. Their programs are *very* reasonable and are led by experts on a huge number of amazing and practical topics. Look at these: Growing medicinal herbs; photographing subjects in nature; learning about wildlife and wild flowers; testing your garden soil; learning to find shade plants for your backyard or setting up a bird-feeder. Nature centers provide hands-on projects, like trail building in the Wissahickon, and ongoing gardening classes. They also sponsor dinners, tours of gardens and special botanical collections, canoe trips, camping trips, tours along historical canals and farmlands, barge rides, and star gazing on critical observation nights. You name it and you can probably find it. By the way, volunteers are much needed at nature centers, where indoor and outdoor work needs to be done. Volunteering will give you a firm place in the nature community and link you to hundreds of others who share your interest in and commitment to the natural environment.

For such a large metropolitan area, Philadelphia has extraordinary outdoor natural resources. Outside the city but within an hour's drive are the Atlantic Ocean, the Pocono Mountains, the Chesapeake Bay, and the gentle hillside trails in Amish country. Running through the city limits are the fabulous natural areas of Fairmount Park. You can run in the Wissahickon Gorge, play in or walk along the creek in Pennypack Park, ride your bike from Center City to Valley Forge, and see not another living soul for some parts of your trip. People are always coming together to hike, bike, glide, row, watch, listen and learn in the outdoors here. If these are your passions, be prepared to find plenty of new friends while you're enjoying the beauty and having fun. So get off the couch and com'on out!

Tree planting at Schuylkill Center for Environmental Education

Nature

Valley Forge Audubon Society enjoying birding excursions

Bird Watching

Bucks County Audubon Society

6324 Upper York Road, New Hope, PA 18938
(215) 297-5880   mail@bcas.org   www.bcas.org

Go on bird counts throughout the region with this group, or just enjoy bird watching within BCAS's 120 acres of trails, woods and streams. The Honey Hollow Environmental Education Center runs several hundred workshops (e.g., *Natural Landscaping*) a year, plus it has seasonal festivals. A great place to volunteer—lots of neat things to do.

:☀: Year-round

Mill Grove Audubon Wildlife Sanctuary

P.O. Box 7125, Audubon, PA 19407
(610) 666-5593   www.montcopa.org
Activity Location: Intersection of Audubon & Pawlings Rds.; 4 mi. from PA Turnpike; 2 mi. from Rte. 202

View the amazing artwork of John Audubon in his first American home, now a National Historic Landmark. Join others on the Saturday morning bird and wildflower walks or Sunday afternoon family walks through the sanctuary's five miles of trails. Try the special events like the Apple and Maple Sugar Festivals. This is a museum and a wildlife sanctuary.

💰 Free

Valley Forge Audubon Society

P.O. Box 866, Paoli, PA 19301
(610) 544-4217   www.audubon.org/chapter/pa/vfas
Activity Location: Meetings at Delaware County Community College

A very active group that goes on bird walks and birding trips two to four times a month, spring plant walks, and Thursday morning hikes on trails all over the area, from Cape May to Princeton Park. The society sponsors guest speakers on the first Friday of the month. You can go along with members for hikes and walks before joining this very welcoming group.

:☀: September-June

💰 Free walks, memberships $20 individual (introduction), $38 family

Nature

Wyncote Audubon Society

1212 Edgehill Road, Abington, PA 19001
(215) 233-9090   http://members.aol.com/sialia1/index.htm
Activity Location: Schuylkill Center for Environmental Education, Hagy's Mill Rd.,
Phila., PA (Roxborough)

WAS is one of the nation's oldest nature clubs with about 2,000 members. Not
all attend the monthly meetings, however, which are open to the public with
speakers and discussions on birding and wildlife topics. It sponsors field trips
that explore areas such as *Wildlife rehabilitation, Bird migration, How to spot
butterflies,* and *Gems of the Wissahickon.* Members may join a photography
group, assist in conservation activities, and enjoy fellow nature enthusiasts.

☼ 3rd Fri./mo. from September-May   ⏰ 7:30pm

💰 Membership $20, includes newsletter

Fishing

Dame Juliana League of Fly Fishers

P.O. Box 178, Kimberton, PA 19442
frenchcreek@djlflyfishers.org   www.djlflyfishers.org
Activity Location: Kimberton Fire Company Fair Grounds, Route 113
(1.8 miles South of Rte. 23), Phoenixville, PA

From September to April this group of 120 members has monthly speakers on
fly fishing or conservation. Members go on fly fishing trips together and in
summer do stream improvement work. Lots of fathers-sons and families in this
group too.

☼ Last Mon./mo.   ⏰ 7:30pm

💰 $20 to sign up, then $15 annually

Delaware Women's Fly Fishing Association

1612 Pine Street, Philadelphia, PA 19103
(302) 764-5075   oreflyfish@aol.com   www.halcyon.com/wffn/clubs.htm#PA

DWFFA believes that "A woman's place is on the stream." Women fly fishers
meet and network as they fish together in a friendly and supportive environment. Novices can enjoy learning with the help of experienced fisher women.
They'll be fishing two or three times a month in the spring, summer and fall.
They go to local streams or have fully guided overnights. In the winter, they go
bowling, and have fly tying lessons and other social activities. But mostly they're
about fishing and the camaraderie it affords!

💰 $25/yr membership, newsletter

Main Line Fly Tyers

(215) 885-0917

Activity Location: Schuylkill Center for Environmental Education,
8480 Hagy's Mill Rd., Phila., PA, (215) 482-7300

A group of men and women that meet to discuss the best fishing spots and the tried and true techniques of fly tie fishing. Experts are invited to discuss their expeditions and fishing wisdom with the group. Beginner and advanced classes are offered so everyone can be included on the group fishing trips.

☼ 3rd Thurs./mo from Sept.–May   ☎ 7pm

☎ Dave Baker

New Jersey Division of Fish and Wildlife: *Governor's Annual Surf Fishing Tournament*

Pequest Trout Hatchery and Natural Resource Education Center,
601 Pequest Road, Rural Rte. 1, Box 389, Oxford, NJ 07863
(908) 637-4125   www.njfishandwildlife.com

Activity Location: on Rte. 46, 9 miles west of Hackettstown (Warren County), NJ

On the first weekend in October over 1,000 people compete in surf fishing at New Jersey's Island Beach State Park. Call to pre-register. At the Trout Hatchery, you can take free monthly fishing classes or explore its 4,000 acres. The center also has an annual open house. It's free.

New Jersey Division of Fish and Wildlife: *Becoming an Outdoors Woman*

220 Blue Anchor Road, Sicklersville, NJ 08081
(856) 629-7214   www.njfishandwildlife.com
Activity Location: Programs run throughout New Jersey

Part of a nationwide program to teach beginners a range of skills like fly fishing, canoeing, kayaking, cooking over a fire, hiking, camping, and scuba diving. It also includes outdoor survival skills, hunting, and the proper use of firearms. About nine one-day or weekend workshops with lots of hands-on practice.

💰 $35 for 1-day, $180-$300 for full weekend

Nature

Ocean City Marlin and Tuna Club

P.O. Box 1120, Ocean City, NJ 08226
(609) 398-2332

The club sponsors 12 fishing tournaments a season for area boaters, often with Friday night barbecues where participants get together with other marlin and tuna fisher people. Catch a big fish and win a prize at the annual awards banquet. And the club takes physically challenged kids out fishing for a day each season. Call Mike Engelman. About $40 per person.

☼ Saturdays from June to November ☎ 8:30am-3pm

Trout Unlimited of Perkiomen Valley

P.O. Box 730, Green Lane, PA 18054
(610) 718-0304   fhenry@vrintr.net   www.perkiomenvalleytu.org
Activity Location: Upper Perkiomen Library, 2 miles north of Green Lane on Rte. 29

A volunteer conservation group for the Perkiomen Valley Watershed. Members restore stream beds with plants and fencing on three to six Saturdays a year, go on day trips together, and enjoy slide shows on fishing techniques. There's also time to socialize at meetings.

☼ 3rd Mons./mo ☎ 7pm

☎ Scott Repa

🏵 $30 national dues

Trout Unlimited, Southeastern Montgomery Chapter

P.O. Box 154, Abington, PA 19001
(215) 379-0185   www.physics.upenn.edu/~wk/stream-restoration-project.html
Activity Location: Pennypack Ecological Restoration Trust, 2955 Edge Hill Rd., Huntingdon Valley, PA

A national organization for the conservation of streams for salmon and trout. Come help out with stream improvement projects, go on fishing trips, or educate kids during *Fish-o-ramas* in June. This group has an annual picnic and monthly meetings. There are also chapters in Doylestown, Valley Forge, Media, and Perkiomen Valley. $30 national dues, $20 chapter dues

☼ 2nd Tues./mo ☎ 7:30-9pm

☎ Joe Veasey

West Chester Fish, Game & Wildlife Association

P.O. Box 511, West Chester, PA 19381
(610) 873-9062

This wildlife association stocks trout in West Valley Creek, maintains a section of the stream, and supports environmental advocacy for all Chester County. The group puts on community events that are fun and interesting, such as a trout rodeo and a bass rodeo, and holds public meetings with speakers on environmental topics. It also sponsors a hunter safety class. About 500 members in this first-rate group. Go to the web site and find a number of watershed organizations that you can work for and enjoy.

Hiking, Walking & Orienteering

Appalachian Mountain Club, Delaware Valley Chapter

(215) 979-1174   info@amcdv.org   www.amcdv.org

This first-rate, enthusiastic, well-attended outdoor organization sponsors a variety of outdoor activities for all ages and experience levels: day-hiking, biking (regular road biking and mountain biking), canoeing, backpacking, climbing, and snowshoe trips. Beginners who are non-members are welcome on many trips, but membership makes keeping updated much easier since there is an extensive newsletter. Members have to supply their own equipment. If you are at all interested in being outdoors, look into their activities. Membership is $40 a year.

Appalachian Mountain Club of Delaware Valley

Nature

Batona Hiking Club

6651 Eastwood Street, Philadelphia, PA 19149
BobLeo@aol.com   http://members.aol.com/Batona
Activity Location: Hikes within 2 hours of Phila., PA

Founded in 1928, Batona is the oldest hiking club in the city. Hike with the club (5 to 12 miles) and a Batona leader in the Wissahickon Valley, in the Pine Barrens, on the Appalachian Trail, or some other beautiful spot. There are no meetings, just hikes "every Sunday rain or shine" and sometimes more often, frequently including a stop at a country diner after the hike. They meet at the end of a transit line, then carpool to the start of the hike, so you do not need your own car. They also maintain three trails, go cross-country skiing and backpacking, have moonlight hikes, and go on trips to places like Scotland and Costa Rica. There's an annual banquet for stories and memories. Check the *Inquirer's Weekend* section for hikes every weekend.

💰   50¢ each hike, send $2 for schedule

Chester County Trail Club

P.O. Box 2056, West Chester, PA 19380
(610) 594-1540   cctrailclub@hotmail.com   www.cctrailclub.org

CCTC has daytime hikes all over the Delaware Valley almost every weekend for enthusiastic outdoor lovers of all ages. Most weekends you can choose between a short hike (under 5 miles) or a longer activity (about 8-15 miles), with an occasional backpack and/or overnight trip of varying degrees of exertion. Members also vacation together; there have been international hiking trips to England, Ireland, Switzerland, and New Zealand. Closer to home, traverse the White Mountains, Appalachian Trail, and Horseshoe Trail with this group. Send $7 for a three-month schedule. (For the Keystone Trails Club list of local hiking clubs go to: www.pennaweb.com/kta/clubs.htm.)

Delaware Valley Orienteering Association

14 Lake Drive, Spring City, PA 19475
(610) 792-0502   frankdvoa@aol.com.   www.dvoa.us.orienteering.org
Activity Location: Events throughout Delaware Valley

DVOA says orienteering "is like a treasure hunt and road rally on foot." When you register, you get a detailed field map that helps you find your way through the course. There are 45-50 events year round. All are open to the public and have instruction for beginners. There's an annual summer picnic and winter meeting, and opportunities to network with other outdoor clubs. All welcome.

💰 $7 per map non-members, membership $16/individuals, $26/family

Horse-Shoe Trail Club

P.O. Box 182, Birchrunville, PA 19421
(610) 208-5620   http://n99.com/hst/

A small but friendly group that has monthly hikes along this 130-mile trail which runs from Valley Forge National Historic Park to the Appalachian Trail. You don't need to be a member to join the hikes, but you do have to be a member to receive *Blaze*, the club newsletter with hike listings and other important information about the Horse-Shoe Trail.

☼ 4th Sun./mo from September-May   ☎ 9am-3:30pm
💰 Free hikes, membership $15 and up (goes to trail preservation)

Liberty Bell Wanderers: *Volksmarch Club*

(215) 699-9246   http://hometown.aol.com/lbwvolks1/lbw.html
Activity Location: Verenigung Erzegebirge, 130 Davisville Road, Warminster, PA

"A whole different type of walk" for "fun, fitness and fellowship" are the themes of the American Volkssport Association nonprofit groups, like this one, which emphasizes noncompetitive physical fitness for people of all ages. They host a dozen walks (*volksmarches*) a year in scenic or historic areas. You get an easy map to follow when you register for a 10-kilometer walk, as well as walk information about the sights you will see along the way. If you want it to be an official volksmarch for which you get an award, you must complete the trail before the stated finish time. But don't worry, you get plenty of time. Attend the monthly meetings, find out more about the volksmarchers, and help plan events. There are more than 600 AVA clubs nationally. Call (210) 659-2112 for info.

☼ 3rd Wed./mo   ☎ 7:30pm
💰 Free hikes, $10 membership with newsletter for individuals or families

Mosaic Outdoor Club of Pennsylvania

P.O. Box 2813, Cherry Hill, NJ 08034
(215) 922-3345   www.mosaics.org/philly

"The Mosaic Outdoor (Mountain) Clubs are a network of nonprofit organizations dedicated to organizing outdoor, active, and/or environmental activities for Jewish adults. Great activities here: hiking, biking, camping, canoeing, rock climbing, backpacking, skiing, sailing, kayaking, scuba diving, snorkeling, skating, volleyball, horseback riding, and more! Benefits of belonging include enjoying outdoor experiences with other Jewish people, participating in activities that you either couldn't or wouldn't do on your own, and finding out how rewarding volunteering can be." (from Mosaic web site) Try activities with the national Mosaic Club, also.

Nature

Outdoor Club of South Jersey

(856) 427-7777 (hot line)   www.voicenet.com/~ubert4/ocsj

OCSJ provides low-cost opportunities for people of all ages to appreciate and gain knowledge of the outdoors. The activities are led by volunteer members and take place 52 weeks a year. Backpacking, bicycling, camping, canoeing, cross-country skiing, hiking, and a practical experience course in basic backpacking and wilderness survival are among these popular activities. Although most take place in South Jersey state parks and forests, local rural roads, and small rivers of the Pine Barrens, the club also takes trips to exciting locations all over the country. When you visit the web site you won't believe all the outdoor events you can do with them—it's fantastic!

💲 Membership for an individual is $8

Philadelphia Trail Club

(215) 233-2944   http://m.zanger.tripod.com
www.aldha.org (Appalachian Trail Club)

You don't have to be a member to join this friendly group for a hike on Saturdays and Sundays. They hit the trails for short hikes and long hikes (from 8-12 miles) in the Wissahickon Valley and Valley Forge. Twice a year the club takes part in trail maintenance on the Appalachian Trail. They also go on quarterly excursions to places like Nova Scotia or Austria for some super hiking.

☼ September-June

💲 Free hikes, membership is $10 year

Sierra Club, Southeastern Pennsylvania Group

P.O. Box 34659, Philadelphia, PA 19101
(215) 592-4063 (592-4073 outings hot line)
www.sierraclub.org/chapters/pa/southeastern

The Sierra Club is one of the most influential organizations in the nation, supporting public programs about the environment. This branch has a rich agenda of activities that informs people about local and national conservation issues, with opportunities for advocacy. Local conservation projects involve trail maintenance, stream cleaning, etc. The club also has many terrific outings to enjoy the outdoors, including hiking, biking and ski trips. Locations for hiking have included: the North Broad Street Mansion Historic District, the Lehigh Gorge, and trail work along the Wissahickon Creek. Members of this club sometimes get together with members of other hiking groups, like Appalachian Mountain Club, for outdoor events. If you're single, check out Sierra Singles.

💲 Hikes vary from free-$15 for non-members; membership $35/individual

Springfield Trail Club

(610) 485-4331   SpringfieldTrailClub@Prodigy.net
http://pages.prodigy.net/javelin   www.pennaweb.com/kta/clubs.htm
Activity Location: Hikes usually leave at 8am from the municipal parking lot (you can take SEPTA) behind the WAWA, at Powell and Saxer Aves. in Springfield, PA

Hikes with swimming/wading and overnight camping trips on the local Springfield Trail or on the Wissahickon Gorge Trail, Horseshoe Trail, or Peace Valley Park are all part of the schedule for this club in 2001. Some hikes are noted as difficult or easy, so you can choose for yourself. There is one business meeting in the fall and one Christmas party, so it seems that hiking is what this group loves to do most. The club is a member of the Keystone Trails Association, whose web site for local chapters is printed above.

☎   Bill Grunwell

Wanderlust Walking Club

(215) 725-2011

Walk, talk and see a different part of the city each week while getting some exercise with this informal, friendly group. These non-strenuous walks always start near a bus line. Check the *Philadelphia Inquirer's Weekend* section for times and places.

☼   Saturdays   ⏰ 1:30-3:30pm

💰   Free

Nature

Miscellany

Academy of Natural Sciences

1900 Benjamin Franklin Parkway, Philadelphia, PA 19103
(215) 299-1000   www.acnatsci.org

This international museum of science provides research and public education about the environment and its diverse species. Its stated mission is "to expand knowledge of nature through discovery and inspire stewardship of the environment." (from the web site) Familiarize yourself with the numerous excellent activities here. Exhibits, tours, and many interactive events take place regularly. You can be involved as an exhibit guide volunteer or assist with the live animals. You can also attend the films and lectures presented by Earthwatch and the Geographic Society of Philadelphia.

☼ Year-round

💰 $30/yr individual membership, entrance fee about $9, seniors $8.25

Bucks County Community College, Continuing Education: Cape Cod Whale Watch

434 Swamp Road, Newtown, PA 18940
(215) 504-8668   www.bucks.edu/~whales

Each year the college offers four whale watching trips off Cape Cod between May and October. They are three-day weekends filled with whale watch cruises, guided nature walks on National Seashore, and slide and film presentations on whale identification and behavior. They are magnificent. When I went, we saw over 30 whales! It was a very good day.

Friends of Fox Chase Farm

8500 Pine Road at Shady Lane, Philadelphia, PA 19111
(215) 728-7900   www.foxchasefarm.org
Activity Location: Pennypack Environmental Center, 8600 Veree Rd., Phila., PA

This is an all-volunteer group (about 400 strong) formed to maintain and preserve this pastoral treasure. Volunteers actively support the farm by assisting with the physical maintenance (sheep shearing, etc.), fund raising, guided tours, and other public events. New people can attend a bimonthly meeting with other supporters of the working farm to hear guest speakers and socialize, or help with the farm's four seasonal festivals (hayrides, crafts, garden produce), Sunday tours, or holiday and "spring green" plant sales.

☼ Year-round

Nature

Natural Lands Trust

Hildacy Farm, 1031 Palmers Mill Road, Media, PA 19063
(610) 353-5587   members@natlands.org   www.natlands.org

This nonprofit regional land trust works with communities to proactively protect significant open lands in the Philadelphia region. Members can help plant trees, remove invasive vines, monitor blue bird boxes, and do fundraising. They also go on canoe trips, star and bird watch walks, and tours of lesser known preserves. Social activities include cookouts and a campfire concert series.

💰   Membership is $35+

Nature Conservancy, Pennsylvania Chapter

1100 East Hector Street, Suite 470, Conshohocken, PA 19428
(610) 834-1323   pa_chapter@tnc.org   http://nature.org/pennsylvania
Activity Location: Work projects throughout the state, such as the Poconos, South Chester County (Oxford), Harrisburg, etc.

Protect rare and endangered species with this nonprofit international environmental organization. Locally you can attend work parties, where people work to benefit these rare species and their habitats by cutting down trees, mowing, removing invasive plant species, etc. People of all ages enjoy working together on about six projects each month for this cause during all seasons. You can also go on work projects all over the world with this group.

Nature Centers, Parks & Friends

Wissahickon Environmental Center at Andorra Natural Area

Tree House, Northwestern Avenue, Philadelphia, PA 19118
(215) 685-9285

Something's always going on at Fairmount Park's Environmental Education Center in the Wissahickon Valley. A bimonthly calendar lists events to keep you busy with adult night walks, full moon walks, gardening and trail building projects, early morning birdwalks, nature trips, and special workshops on topics like "Fishing in the Wissahickon" and "Native American Craft and Game Days."

☼   Year-round

💰   Programs are free, donation welcome

Nature

Bowman's Hill Wildflower Preserve

P.O. Box 685, New Hope, PA 18938
(215) 862-2924   bhwp@bhwp.org   www.bhwp.org
Activity Location: 1635 River Road (Rte. 32), 2 1/2 miles south of New Hope, PA

The preserve is a botanical collection of Pennsylvania native plants in a naturalistic setting. Wander through the two dozen trails and discover beautiful native wildflowers, trees, shrubs, vines, and ferns. You can also attend thought-provoking lectures on topics like "Nature Photography," "Knowing Native Plants," or "Managing Ecosystems." You can go on a guided tour everyday, or one of many field trips to other plant communities. If you volunteer at the Preserve, you'll meet fellow native plant enthusiasts.

- ☼ Open everyday   ⏰ 9am-5pm
  Guided walks from March-November at 2pm
- 💰 Free admission to Preserve, $3/individuls ($5/family) for guided walks

Campus Arboretum Association at Haverford College

370 Lancaster Avenue, Haverford, PA 19041
(610) 896-1101   www.Haverford.edu

This beautiful 216-acre arboretum/college campus has one of the largest pine tree collections (300 varieties) on the East Coast. Take the guided tours, or attend lectures by experts in the field. Members go on two trips a year, have an annual lecture with dinner, and attend special garden tours.

- ☼ Year-round
- 💰 Free, membership $25/yr

Churchville Nature Center,
Bucks County Department of Parks & Recreation

501 Churchville Lane, Churchville, PA 18966
(215) 357-4005   http://communities.phillyburbs.com/home/CNC

Get their activities guide full of great things to do. Every Sunday you can go on family naturalists walks. Attend the Star Party campfire or Lenape stories campfire. Take workshops on birding, join the Saturday morning birdwalks (7-9am) or help with the butterfly count in July and August. The center also runs natural history trips (like "Frog Safari" in the Pine Barrens), canoe trips, day hikes, backpacking, and family camping trips. It's very pretty at the Churchville location.

- 💰 Low cost

Friends of Philadelphia Parks

Boelsen Cottage, West River Drive, P.O. Box 12677, Philadelphia, PA 19129-0077
(215) 879-8159   friends@philaparks.org   www.philaparks.org

This coalition of groups and individuals works to save and maintain Philadelphia Parks. Among the quite sociable activities sponsored by the Friends are several park clean-up days each year. Once a month architect and historian Bob Thomas leads all-day or half-day tours/hikes in places like Manayunk at sunset, farms in Lancaster County, and along local canals. FPP carpools hikers to hard-to-reach locations and can help you find an FPP group near you to join.

💰 $35 individual membership; tours are $10 members, $15 non-members

Friends of the Delaware Canal

At the Lockhouse, 145 South Main Street, New Hope, PA 18938
(215) 862-2021   fodc@erols.com   www.fodc.org

Take a barge ride with this group while listening to a concert or having dinner. Friends of the Canal support the preservation and historical interpretation of the 60-mile canal that runs from Bristol to Easton. They also offer walking tours, bike rides, hikes, canal clean-ups, and special social events. Terrific pictures of the canal on the web site—check it out!

☀ Weekends

☎ Susan Taylor

💰 Memberships $25/individual, $35/family

Friends of the Wissahickon

8708 Germantown Avenue, Philadelphia, PA 19118
(215) 247-0417   friendswis@aol.com   www.fow.org

This very active group offers you a chance to do conservation field work with others every Saturday morning (10am-noon) as well as regular trail repair every month, sometimes with mountain bike enthusiasts. There are also information meetings with high-quality lectures and guest speakers on many wildlife topics. Plus these folks do lots of hiking, nature walking, and mountain biking—all good fun, sometimes with dinner afterwards. An excellent newsletter lists many activities you can join with ongoing opportunities for care and conservation of this fabulous park. (My Dad calls it the Wissahickon Gorge, as indeed it is. I think it feels like deep woods Oregon right in the Philadelphia city limits!) If you haven't been to Valley Green, that's a good place to start a walk in the Wissahickon. Enter from Henry Avenue and Wise's Mill Road.

☀ Year-round

💰 $35 individual membership

Nature

Gloucester County Parks & Recreation:
Scotland Run Park Nature Center
(856) 881-0845

Activity Location: Academy St. (County Rte. 610), Clayton, NJ

Scotland Run presents a series of free workshops on how to enhance your yard to provide for the needs of wildlife. Workshops are given on topics like "Backyard Habitats for Wildlife," "Butterflies and Hummingbirds," "A Wildflower Meadow and Pond for Wildlife," and "Basic Gardening Skills." Many other programs are offered as well, including bird walks, outdoor activities, and a star party. Great stuff!

💰 Many activities are free

Green Lane Park and Nature Center
P.O. Box 249, Green Lane, PA 18054   *www.montcopa.org/parks*

Activity Location: On Rte. 29, 3/4 mile north of Green Lane (intersection of Rte. 63 & Rt. 29), Nature Center (215) 234-8497, equestrian info (215) 234-2877, boat rental (215) 234-4863

Take year-round classes on medicinal plants, butterfly gardening, or bird watching on the weekends. Also find hiking, mountain biking, and equestrian trails, as well as tennis, volleyball, camping, ice skating, and fishing. Rent a battery-powered rowboat and relax on its vast and beautiful reservoir (3 hours for $10, additional charge for non-county residents).

☼ Boating in April-October

✳ John Heinz National Wildlife Refuge at Tinicum
8601 Lindbergh Boulevard, Philadelphia, PA 19153
(215) 365-3118   http://heinz.fws.gov

The largest natural wetlands in the USA, only one mile from Philadelphia International Airport, are a haven for migratory birds. Over 280 bird species have been recorded here. The center sponsors walks every weekend to see the birds, as well as wildflowers and small animals, with talks and nature programs in indoor classrooms. Volunteers are very important here. If you would like to help, you can be involved in many ongoing programs. Join the Photo Group to help document the refuge's natural resources, help produce educational materials, or participate in a trail maintenance group.

💰 Programs are free, Friends group membership $10/individual

Nature

Peace Valley Nature Center

170 Chapman Road, Doylestown, PA 18901
(215) 345-7860

14 miles of beautiful nature trails in the woods and meadows near Lake Galena are the setting for a Saturday morning bird walk (7-9am) along the trail, a Sunday afternoon (2pm) family nature walk, or a singles nature walk on Saturdays (10am-noon) every other weekend. There are also a paved bike trail and boat rentals (sailboats, canoes etc.). Join the Friends of Peace Valley Nature Center to raise funds for the center, or volunteer to help maintain the trails.

☼ Year-round

🌢 Free

Pennypack Ecological Restoration Trust

2955 Edge Hill Road, Huntingdon Valley, PA 19006
(215) 657-0830   pert@libertynet.org   www.libertynet.org/pert

Explore the 650 acres of woodlands, meadows and wetlands, join the Saturday morning bird watchers, attend monthly naturalist programs, or take day trips led by an expert naturalist. Or become involved and help the volunteer group that cleans up the Pennypack Creek.

☼ Year-round   🕝 9am-5pm

🌢 Programs: free or $3 for non-members, Membership: $35 individual, $50 family

Pennypack Environmental Center

8600 Veree Road, Philadelphia, PA 19115
(215) 685-0470   http://users.erols.com/hgabr/pec.htm

This center offers a full calendar of educational events that are a lot of fun, like guided bird and wildflower walks, Friday evening campfires, orienteering programs, stargazing lectures, and day trips to Hawk Mountain or Bowman's Hill Wildflower Preserve. Check the web site for information or call for free program calendar.

☼ Year-round

🌢 Free or low cost

Nature

Scott Arboretum of Swarthmore College

500 College Avenue, Swarthmore, PA 19081
(610) 328-8025   www.scottarboretum.org

The web site says this arboretum emphasizes "living trees, shrubs and herbaceous plants which are hardy in the climate of eastern Pennsylvania and which are suitable for planting by the average gardener." Stroll the grounds, maybe bring a picnic, and then hear an outdoor evening concert. Attend lectures, free guided tours (for example, "Berries, bark and buds"), horticulture workshops ("Green wreaths"), and trips relevant to the season. Or get in shape with a group that power walks through the arboretum from March to May (noon-1pm). Really, you have to check the web site or call to hear the many events that take place here.

☼ Year-round

💰 Membership $30 individual, $40 family, many free events, workshops additional $20-30

Schuylkill Center for Environmental Education

8480 Hagy's Mill Road, Philadelphia, PA 19128 (Roxborough)
(215) 482-7300   www.schuylkillcenter.org

The Schuylkill Center offers a wide variety of outdoor and indoor natural history and environmental science programs for all ages, including seasonal festivals, guided walks (I loved the fern walks), bird walks, star gazing, and special events ("Bat Prowl!"). They also sponsor trips, such as a Cape Cod whale watching excursion or a nature walk in the New Jersey Pine Barrens. Since SCEE is right here in the city, you might want to consider being a volunteer. Ask about the NAButterfly Association that meets and takes field trips in their enjoyment/study of butterflies.

💰 $3 admission for adults

✳ Tyler Arboretum

515 Painter Road, Media, PA 19063
(610) 566-9134   TylerArb@aol.com   www.tylerarboretum.org

There are many ongoing activities at this 650-acre arboretum. Every Wednesday you'll find a bird walk and a "Stop and smell the wildflower walk." Other days, look for "Name that tree," "Explore the secrets of the pinetum," evening owl prowls, and trips to places like the Forsythe National Wildlife Refuge (NJ). For fun and socializing, come by for the annual pancake breakfast with maple sugar demonstrations or the Pumpkin Day Festival.

☼ Year-round

💰 $3 admission, membership $30

A closer look at ...

Photo by Steven Goldblatt

Morris Arboretum

100 Northwestern Avenue, Philadelphia, PA 19118

(215) 247-5777 www.upenn.edu/morris

"The Morris Arboretum of the University of Pennsylvania is a place of beauty, an historic landscape, a teaching garden, and a collection of scientifically documented trees and shrubs." (from Morris brochure)

Although the primary mission of the Morris Arboretum is teaching and research, what you experience when you go is the amazing natural beauty of this 92-acre Victorian garden and landscape. You'll walk by ponds and streams, a rustic log cabin, rose, rock and fern gardens, meadows, and quiet woodland walks. It's a lovely place to find peace and serenity whenever you need it. But when you're refreshed and ready for activity, you'll find plenty of that at Morris too. "People and plants need each other" is a theme filtering through all the workshops here, such as the healing plants seminar, identifying fall trees, butterfly gardening, and lawn care. There are concerts, like a cappella songs of the Renaissance, held in the garden, and silent auctions of plant treasures while you enjoy cocktails and hors d'oeuvres. For those who want to be active and involved with Morris, volunteer guides for walking tours are warmly welcomed and given continuing education classes (field trips, workshops and lectures). You can also get your exercise by helping plant and maintain the gardens. Make your way to Chestnut Hill and take a walk around Morris Arboretum and you'll be hooked.

Weekdays: 10am-4pm; Evenings: Call for hours

Weekends: 10am-5pm (April-October); 10am-4pm (November-March)

Admission: $6 adults, $5 seniors, $4 students. Kids under six & members: free

Nature

Hikers from the DV-Appalachian Mountain Club on the trail

Here are some extra resources to check out

Awbury Arboretum, (215) 849-5561, www.awbury.org

*Briar Bush Nature Center, 1212 Edgehill Road, Abington, PA
(215) 887-6603*

Chanticleer, 786 Church Rd., Wayne, PA, (610) 687-4163

Great Valley Nature Center, (610) 935-9777

Lower Merion Conservancy, (610) 645-9030, www.dragonfly.org

Ridley Creek State Park

*Silver Lake Nature Center, 1306 Bath Rd., Bristol, PA, (215) 785-1177,
on www.phillyburbs.com web site*

*The Riverbend Environmental Education Center, (610) 527-5234,
www.gladwyne.com/riverbend, 1950 Spring Mill Rd., Gladwyne, PA*

*Wissahickon Valley Watershed Association,
12 Morris Rd., Ambler, PA 19002, (215) 646-8866, www.wvwa.org*

Seniors

Community Service • Dancing

Games, Sports, & Fitness

Lifelong Learning • Senior Centers • Travel

Seniors

Photo by Jim Harrison

Elderhostellers learning about the desert soil

Intergenerational planting project by members of
the Lutheran Settlement House

Now that *I'm* a "senior" I wonder what it means. When I was young, I used to think that being "old" meant that you had wrinkles, walked very slowly, and talked about the good old days.

Now that I'm a senior, I have revised this notion. First of all, I know that "old" people are as smart and as interesting as anyone else (and maybe more so). They may or may not walk slowly, but even if they do, they can often dance, go on bird walks, and mentor small children as well as anyone. I know now that age is really a function of how you live and what your attitude is about yourself, your community, and life in general—just the way it was when you were younger.

One very good thing about being a senior is that usually you have more discretionary time and thus, more choices: You can choose to do more things that you *want* to do instead of the things you are *supposed* to do. Your kids, if you have them, are usually grown, so you don't have to spend 24/7 caring for them and ferrying them around. Your finances usually are in some kind of sync with your living standard, which means you know what you need and have adapted your income to cover those items. You have probably stopped running after the brass ring in your career and know now that you aren't going to be president of the United States or your company, or write the *Connecting* bestseller and go on all the national talk shows. So now you get ready to relax and read the paper at a more leisurely pace.

Read the paper? Wait a minute! *Now* is the time you can choose that community service activity you've always wanted to do but haven't had the time or energy for because your day job and home responsibilities took all you had. (I am ready to be an advocate for something in Harrisburg. I just haven't figured out which crucial issue I want to fight for...) *Now* you can pursue your passions, like learning to do a sexy Tango or study the unique features of Philadelphia architecture. *Now* you can plant every kind of fern in your so-satisfying garden or walk the Delaware Canal at 7am, with terrific conversation afterwards with your walking friends over a bowl of steaming steel-cut oatmeal. Maybe you're ready to do interesting research for the **League of Women's Voters**, who let you know how much they appreciate your time. At any time of year, you can drive across the country without a specific destination, taking three months instead of the two to four weeks that you've always had for vacations. And how about that class in art history that answers the questions you've had about why paintings with geometric people are considered great art. If you wish, you could revisit great authors like Darwin or Dickens that you haven't read for forty years, and discuss them in your local **Great Books** club. You now have time to take special care of your self by taking classes in yoga and meditation to clear your mind and move forward on your path. And, really importantly, you can spend quality time with friends and family, forging deeper connections with people who mean a lot to you. You can choose just what you want to do at this time in your life.

People of *all* ages can do any of the activities in this book. But if you are over a certain age, there are special opportunities ("benies") for you in a number of groups. My all-time personal favorite best stuff for people 55 and over are the get-away programs offered by **Elderhostel** (See page 390.). Don't take my word for it, just get the catalog or read it online and drool over almost every workshop in some of the most beautiful and exciting locations in the U.S. (and abroad) for incredibly cheap prices. Try courses like "Late Tchaikovsky Symphonies" or "Ghost Towns of the Old West" for about $600 a week, including room, board and classes. There are thousands of great-sounding courses in resorts and universities all over the country. (It may be cheaper than staying home—I love it!) Plus you meet other lively people who, like you, can't wait to learn, talk, build, and jump around in the world.

Many older people wish to "give back" to their communities. Seniors are especially suited for community service activities because they have more flexible time and more life experience and wisdom to bring than their younger counterparts. (As a senior I know these things.) There are many types of service projects especially suited for seniors. How about a working vacation where you teach English or build a community center in Central America? If you'd rather get involved in your area, there are opportunities to mentor teenagers, nurture sick kids, or support families with disabled children in their homes; assist seniors or people who are ill with their meals or transportation; take part in political activities; and be involved in the arts, historical organizations, and museums. There is a need for just about any kind of work you want to contribute. The main guideline is that you should be sure you choose something you *really care about* so you keep coming back. And the more you give what you love to give, the more you get back. You know how that works.

Seniors are welcome to dance in lots of places around the area, but if you're looking for other seniors to sashay with who remember the same steps you learned in the '40s and '50s (like the Hokey Pokey), you'll find those places too. Places like **Mr. D's Social Dance** offer genuine partner dances, like the waltz, jitterbug, polka and cha-cha, with mostly seniors in attendance. And somewhere in the area you can find Arnie Zacharius teaching folk dance in a senior center. He's a good teacher and lots of fun. Make no mistake, you will smile wider, jounce (you know what I mean!) higher, and live longer if you dance, no matter what your age. Trust me.

Look in the Games chapter and the Nature chapter for most of the outdoor activities in the area. But there are several neat events set up just for seniors, like the **Walking Club** at the **Bryn Mawr Presbyterian Church**. Indoor games like bridge are held at the **Jewish Community Centers**. Hang out there and play, whether you're a cutthroat player or a total novice taking your first class in bridge. The centers have other games and activities as well, including dynamite trips to plays and musical events. If you're *really* a player (even if you're not that good), look into the **Keystone Games** in Lewisburg, PA, where seniors get together every summer to play games of all kinds. Lots of dancing, social activities, and informational sessions as well.

Scientists tell us that we maintain all our brain cells and stay smart if we use our heads. Keep learning, thinking and following your curiosity if you want to keep up with (and maybe surpass) the kids. Where to do this? Take one of the outstanding programs for seniors offered at the **University of Pennsylvania** or **Temple University** that are designed for daytime schedules at low cost. Or audit one of the regular university courses and avoid writing papers or taking tests. If you'd rather stay closer to your house, look into the lifelong learning programs offered at colleges in your neighborhood (like LaSalle, Chestnut Hill, Penn State-Ogontz or Montgomery County Community College, etc.). Ask about all types of classes at your local Art Center (**Fleisher, Cheltenham, Abington** or **Allen's Lane**) as well as organizations like **The Learning Studio** and the **Mt. Airy Learning Tree,** which have ever-changing fun courses for very reasonable fees. Classes are an exciting way to expand your horizons, exercise your brain like a high school student, and meet those who are just as interested in moving forward as you are. Oh—and don't forget TARP (**Temple Association for Retired People**) classes and the other Temple discussion groups for people who have Friday lunchtimes free. They bring in classy speakers to talk about extremely interesting topics and stimulating discussions that will knock your socks off. Finally we have the time and place for this!

Since we seniors can take the time to travel in a more spontaneous way, there are many discounts to take advantage of, like "this weekend" air fares. My physical therapist Alice (who helped me recover completely from a serious broken leg) loaned me a terrific book called **Unbelievably Good Deals and Great Adventures That You Absolutely Can't Get Unless You're Over 50** (Joan Heilman,1998, Contemporary Books). It outlines great deals for airfare, car rental, lodgings, sports trips, and the like, and reminds you of the upside to being a senior. If you are traveling alone, there are planned theme trips in groups that take advantage of the keen interests of older people and are protective of the single person. Take the time to travel. It breaks up your usual routines and introduces a broader perspective into the fixed notions we have about life and society. When we explore how others live, their beliefs and customs, we understand them and ourselves a bit better. Don't you feel changed when you return from a trip?

Back in Philadelphia, check out all the fine senior centers located all over the city which have a multitude of programs covering all levels of ability and age. As a young 60-year-old, you'll find computer classes, ballroom dancing, and strenuous exercise classes. As an older 70-year-old, there are board games, exciting trips to NYC for a play, and less strenuous dancing and exercise classes. The activities are designed for everyone and cost very little or are free. What you'll find is a delightful community that shares bright ideas, jokes and laughter with people who are moving forward to learn new skills and more about the world. These are places filled with life. Go see for yourself.

I don't think "retirement" means you don't work anymore. I think it means you restructure your activities to fit your style and do the things you choose to do, without income as a major factor. You can be as busy as you want to be. My father says he doesn't know when he had time to work. He is 89. Dear God, let us all be so lucky.

Community Service

AARP Volunteer Talent Bank

733 Walnut Street, Philadelphia, PA 19106
(215) 629-7445   vtb@aarp.org   www.aarp.org

If you're over 50 and want to volunteer your time, AARP will match your skills
and interests to community service projects and nonprofit organizations in your
area. It also uses volunteers for its *Tax Aid, 55 Alive Driving, Connections for
Independent Living*, and *Grief and Loss* programs. Call—there's a lot to do.

Center for Intergenerational Learning at Temple University

1601 North Broad Street, USB206, Philadelphia, PA 19122
(215) 204-6970   www.temple.edu/cil

This center sponsors 16 excellent programs involving youth and older adults.
They include *Family Friends*, where older
adults (55+) provide in-home support to
families who have children with special
needs; *Time Out*, where college students
provide respite for caregivers of older
adults; and *Across Ages*, a drug prevention
program matching high-risk youth with
adult mentors who spend time together

Photo by Madeline Polss

after school and on weekends. Check the newsletter for other activities, such as
the Intergenerational Learning Retreat.

💰   Some programs offer stipends

Executive Service Corps of the Delaware Valley

119 Coulter Avenue, Suite 200, Ardmore, PA 19003
(610) 649-2284   escdv@philly.infi.net   www.libertynet.org/escdv

The goal of ESCDV is to mobilize the management and technical talents of
both active and retired executives and professionals to provide (volunteer)
management consulting assistance to nonprofit clients. Strategic planning,
human resources, marketing, information systems, and fund-raising are among
the activities the volunteers do. ESCDV provides training and holds periodic
networking meetings of volunteers to discuss experiences and share insights.

Seniors

Foster Grandparents

990 Spring Garden Street, 7th floor, Philadelphia, PA 19123
(215) 685-3627

If you are 60 or older, you can be a volunteer to give one-on-one support to neglected children. You can also mentor teenagers and young mothers or care for premature infants and children with disabilities. Locally, there are thirty-two volunteer stations around the city, including St. Christopher's Hospital. Receive a tax-free stipend, meals, and reimbursement for transportation. This program is through the Mayor's Office of Community Services.

Graduate Hospital: *Volunteers*

1800 Lombard Street, Pepper Pavilion, Philadelphia, PA 19146
(215) 893-2279   www.graduatehospital.com

Although open to adults of any age, many hospital volunteers are seniors because they have the time and willingness to serve. Become a liaison between families and doctors in the surgical lounge, visit patients on the floors, help with cooking, art and music classes (didn't know they had these, did ya?), do office tasks, or assist in the day-care center. There's also a need for cancer survivors to encourage cancer patients. Holiday parties for volunteers. Graduate is but one of many hospitals that need volunteer services. You'll get free lunch and parking.

Hometown Senior Center: *Meals-On-Wheels*

302 South Jackson Street, Media, PA 19063
(610) 566-0505   hometownseniorcenter@juno.com

Many senior centers not only offer programs and classes but also have volunteer opportunities. (You can give and you can get, or both!) Hometown needs volunteer drivers for about an hour a week for its home delivery meal program. Each volunteer goes through orientation and training and receives mileage reimbursement. They have other volunteer activities as well. Call for info.

Retired Senior Volunteer Program, West

227 North 18th Street, Philadelphia, PA 19103
(215) 854-7077   www.volunteersinvt.org

Those 55 or older who want to contribute time and experience to their communities may consider volunteer assignments through RSVP in settings like hospitals, nursing homes, schools, day-care centers, museums, historical sites, and arts organizations. Many help with literacy and the America Reads Program. There is an RSVP in every county so you can work close to home. For example, the Montgomery County RSVP has 1,500 volunteers and trains them to become Medicare counselors, friendly visitors to homebound elderly, literacy tutors, or volunteer executive consultants. Some programs offer reimbursement.

Dancing

Associated Polish Home of Philadelphia

9150 Academy Road, Philadelphia, PA 19114
(215) 624-9954   www.magyarclub.com

Get out your string tie and cowboy boots for Monday night country and western dancing, open to all ages. Wednesday is ballroom dancing night to a live band for people 40 years and up. There are weekend dances for members but you must have a sponsor to join.

☼ Mondays ($6)   ⏰ 6:30-10:30pm
   Wednesdays ($7)   8:30-11:30pm

Cannstatter-Volksfest-Verein Club

9130 Academy Road, Philadelphia, PA 19114
(215) 332-0121   www.cvvphilly.com

It's mostly an older crowd that jumps up to fox trot, jitterbug, waltz, and move around to the music of a live accordion player in the bar/lounge of Cannstatter. This is one of many social activities enjoyed by a nice group of members at this, the oldest, German-American club in Philadelphia. $30/year membership.

☼ Sundays   ⏰ 7pm

Charles Weinstein Retiree Center: *Line & Folk Dancing*

2115 Sansom Street, Philadelphia, PA 19103
(215) 568-4080, x170

Arnie Zacharius, a joyful dance teacher, teaches line and folk dancing weekly here. This center for retirees, originally established for retired members of the men's garment union, is now open for all retirees with a quest for learning. In addition to dancing, there is an extensive program of activities, such as choral singing, drama, sewing, and art classes. Opera and classic films are shown every week on a 42-inch screen. Find friends and neighbors while you play. Free.

☼ Mondays-Fridays   ⏰ 10am-2pm

Juniata Park Older Adult Center: *Ballroom Dancing Class*

1251 East Sedgley Avenue, Philadelphia, PA 19134
(215) 685-1492

For those 55 or older, a ballroom dancing class is open for fun, learning new dance steps, and meeting new dancers. Don't stay home when you could be dancing! Just $1. (Also check out the other programs, like t'ai chi, here.)

☼ Fridays   ⏰ 12:30pm

Seniors

Mr. D's Social Dance

(215) 997-2316

Activity Location: VFW on Jenkintown Rd., (near Ardsley RR station) Glenside, PA

Mr. D kids that this is the best dance on Monday nights because it's the *only* dance on Monday nights! But I doubt it. I think his sparkling personality gives it a special welcoming charm. What kind of dancing? "Everything!" That means Ballroom, Jitterbug, Line, Cha-cha, and more. Mr. D plays one Billy Ray Cyrus piece every Monday ("Where'm I going to live when I go home?") or they won't let him leave. Live music by the Ritchie Moore Trio. It is a great evening for some 160 people 40 years and older and they welcome newcomers.

☼ Mondays   ⏰ 8:30-11:30pm

💰 $7, refreshments included

Watkins Senior Center

326 Watkins Avenue, Upper Darby, PA 19082
(610) 734-7652   www.watsencen.com

Show up for line dancing and/or ballroom dancing for a $1 donation. If you're not a dancer, try the discussion groups, arts and crafts, t'ai chi, muscle toning with weights, or bingo and a hot lunch ($1.25) daily. Join the Watkins folks for fun trips to places like Atlantic City, or for monthly Sunday dances for $4.

☼ Mondays-Fridays   ⏰ 9am-4pm

Muscle toning class at Watkins   Watkins Center pool players

Wayne Senior Center: *Line Dancing*

108 Station Road, Wayne, PA 19087
(610) 688-6246

Another venue for line dancing and *many* other senior activities (trips, arts and crafts, exercise, etc.). If you live nearby, check out this friendly community where people are enjoying their interests and loving their dancing.

☼ Fridays   ⏰ 10:30am

Games, Sports & Fitness

Bryn Mawr Presbyterian Church:
Walking Club for Older Adults
625 Montgomery Avenue, Bryn Mawr, PA 19010
(610) 525-2821 x839   www.bmpc.org

This lively group keeps fit and enjoys a walk of approximately two miles (45 minutes) in the Bryn Mawr area three times a week, weather permitting. Newcomers are greeted warmly and joined by an experienced walker. The senior adult office also sponsors lunches, trips, socials, workshops, and more. Call for the newsletter.

☀ Mondays, Wednesdays & Fridays   ⏰ 9am

☎ Beth Ann Force

JCC, Kaiserman Branch
45 Haverford Road, Wynnewood, PA 19096
(610) 896-7770   www.phillyjcc.com/branches/kaiserman.html

This center offers an open bridge game on Tuesday nights from 7:30 to 10pm and on Friday mornings from 9am-12pm. Bridge classes are offered as well. Seniors will find a full cultural program here, with classes ranging from opera and music appreciation to movie talk, world affairs, painting, fitness, and more. Call to find out about all the exciting activities, including trips sponsored by all branches of the Jewish Community Centers (www.phillyjcc.com).

Keystone State Games, Inc.: *Pennsylvania Senior Games*
P.O. Box 3131, Wilkes-Barre, PA 18773
(888) 445-4559 x7   paseniorgames@aol.com   www.keystonegames.com
Activity Location: Shippensburg University, Shippensburg, PA

This *outstanding* games week is a social and recreational yet competitive experience that keeps you fit and offers lots of new lasting friendships. Numerous competitive games include golf, bocce, darts, swimming, racquetball, tennis, and more. Find workshops in swimming, line dancing, and race walking, plus many social activities with informational sessions by AARP. This is a very lively week for people over 55 who love to have a good time.

☀ Annually in summer

💰 $26/entrance fee; campus housing for $42/night, includes three cafeteria meals

Seniors

Lower Merion Senior Center: *Bingo, Pinochle, and Bridge*

36 Ardmore Avenue, Ardmore, PA 19003
(610) 649-5290

This is a full program recreation center with pinochle, bridge, and exercise activities. But that's not all. The center also sponsors a wonderful *Creative Writing* group, usually from September to June on Wednesdays, taught by a local college professor. A very active *Current Events Discussion* group meets every other Friday. Check out the computer labs to start surfing the web and sending email!

☼ Open Mondays to Fridays   ⏰ 9am-1pm

💰 $15/yr

Neshaminy Activities Center for Senior Citizens

1842 Brownsville Road, Trevose, PA 19053
(215) 355-6967

There is a wide range of activities at Neshaminy, including bowling, pool, and cards. You can take classes in computer skills or arts and crafts (such as ceramics and quilting). The center also sponsors speakers who will inform you on all issues relating to seniors. Enjoy their many trips, parties, and picnics, and if you like to jump about, be sure to attend the country line and regular line dancing events.

💰 $10/yr membership

T'ai chi at the Wellness Center at Ralston House

Lifelong Learning

Borders: *Seniors Reading Group*
515 Route 73 South, Marlton, NJ 08053
(856) 985-5080   www.borders.com

Among the many reading groups sponsored by Borders is a fine seniors book group, which is going into its third year. About 20 people come together to discuss a variety of fiction and nonfiction, books with international scenes, political biographies, and some classic authors such as Willa Cather. Check the newsletter for upcoming books and regular events, like author speaker/signings

☼ 1st Fri./mo   ⏰ 11am

Holy Family College: *Professional & Community Development*
Grant & Frankford Avenues, Philadelphia, PA 19114
(215) 637-7700   www.hfc.edu

Many senior classes in arts, hobbies and leisure, Civil War and history, and computer classes are offered here. Too many to mention but you can call for the catalog or check the web site and pick your favorites.

Montgomery County Community College
Central: 340 DeKalb Pike, P.O. Box 400, Blue Bell, PA 19422   (215) 641-6300
also West Campus: 101 College Drive, Pottstown, PA 29464 (601) 718-1800
www.mc3.edu

Seniors (60+) receive discounted rates when they take part in MCCC's Daytime Enrichment Program, open to the general public. There are many wonderful classes given through this program, including computer fundamentals (Introduction to the Internet, or Word Processing), art (hands-on studio classes in drawing, sculpture, etc. and classroom based classes in art history and art appreciation), and general interest courses (the Writings of Lewis & Clark, conversational languages like Spanish and French, Life Story Writing, and Financial Planning). You can have really enjoy learning here!

Rosemont College: *The Forum*
1400 Montgomery Avenue, Rosemont, PA 19010
(610) 526-2980   randrews@rosemont.edu   www.rosemont.edu

Focusing on philosophy, literature and culture, the Forum is a special 6-week program offered each semester to those 55+. Courses about Spanish Civilization, Irish Literature, and Marx and Freud are examples of classes offered. Attend the kickoff party and meet the instructors and other students.

☼ 6 weeks   ⏰ 10am-2:30pm
💰 $65

Seniors

Senior Associates Program

University of Pennsylvania: College of General Studies
3440 Market Street, Philadelphia, PA 19104
(215) 898-7326   www.sas.upenn.edu/CGS/noncredit/senior_assoc.shtml

People 65 years and older may audit two classes per semester at the College of General Studies. No grade/credit is received, but students may be as fully involved in classroom discussion and activities as the instructor permits. Special registration periods are scheduled each semester when members of the CGS staff and senior volunteers are available to help with course selections.

💰 $50/minimum donation per course

Settlement Music School, Jenkintown Music School Branch: 60 Plus or Minus Chamber Music Players

515 Meetinghouse Road, Jenkintown, PA 19046
(215) 885-6166   info@smsmusic.org   www.smsmusic.org

These exciting chamber music groups take place at two of the five branches of Settlement on Tuesdays from 9:30am until noon for new and experienced ensemble players. Settlement has many wonderful musical programs at reduced fees for seniors wanting to learn (all levels) to play instruments and to sing.

Temple Association for Retired Persons (TARP): Friday Forums

1515 Market Street, 5th floor, Philadelphia, PA 19102
(215) 204-1505   www.temple.edu/tucc

You can't say enough about TARP. Excellent instructors teach 165 courses a year on a wide variety of topics for people who have retired. You can become computer literate (even expert!), learn a foreign language, write short stories, or delve into art history. Stop by for the *Friday Forums* at noon, a free lecture, and discussion on current topics that is open to all ages.

☼   Programs from Monday to Friday   ⏲ 10:30am-2:30pm

💰   Unlimited classes at TUCC with $165 yearly TARP membership
     Friday Forums are free

Senior Centers

Chestnut Hill Senior Center

8700 Germantown Avenue, Philadelphia, PA 19118
(215) 248-0180

This active center offers classes in languages, computers, literature, t'ai chi, opera, art, and more. It hosts monthly birthday luncheons as well as exciting day trips. (One year the seniors went to Lake George for vacation.) About 25 seniors attend each day. The average age is 70, but all ages are welcome to enjoy the classes.

☼ Monday-Friday   ☎ 9am-3pm

💰 $20/yr membership plus $1-$4 fee for some classes

Coffee Cup

247 S. 10th Street, Philadelphia, PA 19107
(215) 627-8048

Start your day with coffee (10 cents) and pastries, or check out the lunch for $1. Lots of great socializing going on here, with friendships developing all the time. This is a branch of the Philadelphia Senior Center (215-546-5879) so you could call the center for more info too.

☼ Monday-Friday   ☎ 10am-2pm

Havertown Center for Older Adults

1105 Earlington Road, Havertown, PA 19083
(610) 446-2070

If a trip to the Masonic Temple followed by lunch at the Spaghetti Warehouse appeals to you, call the Havertown Center because these seniors go on these kinds of trips all the time. Other programs include country and western line dancing, an exercise program, t'ai chi, art (oil painting, cartooning, and water colors), Italian classes, computer classes, crafts (a memory quilt is a current project), and many games, including mah jong, bridge, poker, pinochle, bingo, and checkers. This active social group of people 55-90 years has a walking program, puts on nostalgic fashion shows, and organizes picnics. You can't miss here!

☼ Monday-Friday   ☎ 9am-4pm

💰 Lunch is $1.25
    Set fees for trips and computer classes

Seniors

Lutheran Settlement House

1340 Frankford Avenue, Philadelphia, PA 19125
(215) 739-6041

Seniors and high school students get together to discuss history projects and go on trips together as part of an intergenerational program at LSH. Plus it offers lectures, music, exercise, trips, games, a daily hot lunch, and a social worker on staff as a resource on senior's issues. The average age is 75, and they do have a good time!

Intergenerational Christmas party

☼ Monday-Thursday   ⏰ 8am-9pm
   Fridays   8am-6pm
💰 Small donation

Philadelphia Senior Center

Main Branch: 509 South Broad Street, Philadelphia, PA 19147
(215) 546-5879   www.paseniorcenter.com

Just celebrating its 50th anniversary, this multipurpose center for people over 55 provides terrific up-to-date classes in computers, physical fitness and body dynamics, a variety of arts, and dancing of all kinds. Every Friday there is a trip, often to New York City or Baltimore. Plus, there's an annual trip to more distant places such as London. About 300 participants attend each day. The center will also assist with social services. There are many senior centers in the area. Check the web sites above to find the one closest to you and for the event schedules.

☼ Monday-Friday   ⏰ 8:45am-4:30pm
✉ Diane Reed-Small
💰 $1 for lunch, class fee varies

Ralston House: *Wellness Center*

3615 Chestnut Street, Philadelphia, PA 19104
(215) 386-2984

Join the weekly groups practicing t'ai chi, yoga, and Feldenkrais movement or kick up your heels with a line dancing class. Ralston House also sponsors an annual health fair with free medical screenings. Ralston also houses the Institute for Aging (geriatric medical services) of the University of Pennsylvania.

☼ Year-round   ⏰ 9am-12pm
💰 Free or $3, pay per class

Senior Citizens Center of Ardmore

117 Ardmore Avenue, Ardmore, PA 19003
(610) 642-9370

The philosophy of this center is that education is a lifelong process. Anyone 55 and over can enjoy active classes on topics such as creative writing and computer skills (with hands-on lab). There are speaker/discussions about important issues for "Life after 50." The center also emphasizes health and fitness, so many seniors take part in exciting water exercises, yoga, or a regular walking club. Other benefits, including meals, are available.

💰 Most programs are free

Southwest Senior Center

6916 Elmwood Avenue, Philadelphia, PA 19142
(215) 937-1880

All types of classes are offered here, including yoga, ceramics, Spanish, computer classes, discussion groups, painting, dancing plus parties, and casino trips. Stay all day and enjoy a hot lunch too.

☼ Monday-Friday   ⏰ 8:30am-4pm
💰 50 cents daily donation plus minimal cost for classes

Travel

Alaska Wildland Adventures

Box 389, Girdwood, Alaska 99587
(800) 334-8730

"Adventurous tours for the older traveler who desires something out of the ordinary yet requires a higher level of comfort and less physical activity than our other trips." You spend Alaskan nights indoors with private baths but still go on yachting and hiking trips and see wild animals in their natural habitats. It helps if you can walk for two hours.

💰 About $3,095 (as of May 2001) for 7 days

Seniors

Global Volunteers

375 East Little Canada Road, St. Paul, MN 55117
(800) 487-1074   www.globalvolunteers.org

Join a team for one to three weeks and work on much needed human and economic development projects, like teaching kids in the Mississippi delta area, or building community facilities such as schools or community centers abroad. From all backgrounds and of all ages, the volunteers become "servant-learners," working with and learning from people in 19 countries. An extremely rich experience awaits you here. "You're going where?"

💰 US $450, plus transportation; international $1,185-2,395 (in May 2001)

Interhostel

University of New Hampshire, 6 Garrison Avenue, Durham, NH 03824
(800) 733-9753   www.learn.unh.edu

This university-based program offers adults age 50 and older two- and three-week learning and travel programs all over the world. University experts lead mini-classes, presentations and lectures, and sightseeing and field trips to understand the culture, art, and history of the host country. Groups average 30-40 people.

💰 $600-1,300 (1 week US); $2,500-3,500 (2 weeks int'l) w/air, lodging, food

Travelearn®

P.O. Box 315, Lakeville, PA 18438
(570) 226-9114   or   (800) 235-9114   www.travelearn.com

"For over 24 years, Travelearn has provided educational international vacations for adults 30-80 through more than 300 universities and colleges nationwide." (from Travelearn web site) Alaska, Galapagos Islands, Peru, Costa Rica, China, and Kenya are just a few of the places you can go. While traveling, meet the local people, see the sights, and be part of lectures, seminars, and group dis-cussions. Their motto: "For people who take their minds with them on vacation."

Photo by Steven Goldblatt

A collaboration of volunteers, teacher and learners, at the Morris Arboretum.

A closer look at ...

Photo by Rob Burbank

*On an Eldershostel program, Appalachian Mountain Club hikers
visit a maple sugaring operation at Pinkham's Notch, N.H.*

Elderhostel

11 Avenue deLafayette, Boston, MA 02111
(877) 426-8056 www.elderhostel.org

Meet interesting and stimulating people from many backgrounds while you take classes in everything from underwater mammals in Monterey, CA, to golf in Arizona to studying Mozart at the Peabody School of Music in Maryland. Elderhostel believes that turning 55 is just another beginning and is the time to discover new avenues for self-enrichment. Short-term learning adventures designed just for Elder-hostelers are offered in a worldwide network of dynamic programs for adult learners. While challenging and thought-provoking, there are no exams, homework or grades. We'll study at colleges, universities, muse-ums, national parks, and environmental education centers all over the U.S., Canada, and in 100+ other countries. Most domestic Elderhostel programs last five or six nights in pleasant hotels, motels, inns, and other facilities. You'll share experiences with 20-40 curious classmates. Eldershostel also sponsors inviting volunteer vacation trips, such as monitoring activities of humpback and blue whales in the Monterey Bay, sponsored by Oceanic Society Expeditions. Whether traveling by yourself or with a spouse or friend, Elderhostel is a friendly, accessible and secure way to explore new places and challenging ideas. Call for the catalog—as big as one from Sears & Robuck—and be overwhelmed by the terrific places to go. And it's cheaper than staying home! See you there.

☎ For people age 55+ (and spouse or adult travel companion of any age)

👛 Average tuition, including lodging and meals, is about $105/day

 **Here are some extra resources to check out**

Books

- *Unbelievably Good Deals and Great Adventures That You Absolutely Can't Get Unless You're Over 50,* Joan R. Heilman, Contemporary Books, 1988
- *Successful Aging,* Robert Kahn, Reviews results of study of aging in America.

Web Sites

- *www.maturetravelers.com,* A site for vacationing adults 55 and older
- *www.personalhistorians.org,* Association of Personal Historians (800-449-7483)
- *www..storypreservation.com,* Center for Life Stories Preservation
- *http://fantastic50plusonthemove.homestead.com*

Organizations

- *Philadelphia Corporation for the Aging*
  642 North Broad Street, Philadelphia, PA
  (215) 765-9000; Senior helpline (215) 765-9040
  philcorp@voicenet.com
  Publishes a fine local newspaper, *Milestones*
- *Gray Panthers,* (215) 729-6575, www.graypanthers.org
  This national organization of intergenerational activists works for social change around issues of health care, jobs, housing and peace. They work to change laws and attitudes for social justice.

*It takes great passion and great energy to
do anything creative, especially in the theater.
You have to care so much that you can't sleep,
you can't eat, you can't talk to people.
It's just got to be right.
You can't do it without that passion.*
~Agnes De Mille

Singles

Annual Events • Art, Music, & Theater
Community Service • Dancing • Denominational
Outdoor Groups • Professional Singles
Singles Groups • Special Interests

Singles

Members of Dynamic Diversions enjoy a sailing trip on the
Chesapeake Bay

Single Volunteers of Bucks County gather for the Tour de Cure
for the American Diabetes Society

I f you are single, then this chapter is just for you. Actually, the whole book is for you, but this chapter lists places where you *know* there will be single people to meet. I was single for 17 years (between marriages) and I can tell you there are lots of opportunities for fun for singles in Philadelphia. However, you will not find them if you only hang out in front of your VCR or go to the movies/dinner with the same old friends every Friday. Instead, you need to make a commitment to find people and things that are new to you, where you can go "exploring." It's time to revel in your adventurous spirit!

There are some real advantages to being single. One of these is that you can spend your time in whatever activity or group you choose, without conferring with any other person. If you feel like folk dancing on Wednesday night, there is no one to ask or check with about doing that. If you want to join a theater production for six weeks, there is no one whose schedule you will be inconveniencing but your own. Also, you can do those things you've always wanted to try but would just as soon not tell anyone about. Things like taking voice lessons—because you've always wanted to try out for musical comedy. Or joining an on-going horror film group, or trying your hand at golf. It's easier to keep certain activities under wraps, thereby avoiding unnecessary questions ("You're going to do *that!* Whatever for?!" or, worse yet, paroxysms of laughter...) and raised eyebrows from skeptical friends. No one needs to know your whereabouts every Thursday evening when you're practicing your latest tap dancing steps.

You can also use the time when you're not in a relationship to do some serious personal growth. You know, mind-body stuff: Doing morning yoga and breakfasting on fat-free granola in silence; keeping a journal; making conscious and deliberate behavior changes that you've known you need to make; and having TV-free, herbal tea, quiet, good-book-reading evenings. These are things that are harder to do with someone else around. These special periods are golden opportunities to "remember your spirit." (Credit to Oprah for a great phrase.)

The choices you make when you're single reflect what you're truly about—or at least they should. This is a time to consider and mull over what you care about, what you want to spend your time doing, and the kinds of people you are seeking to have in your life. As you look through all the chapters in this book (which I certainly hope you are doing), you

Singles

may be pleasantly surprised to find events and happenings that you would love to do. The only reason you haven't done them already is because you didn't know about them. You may also find activities that you had never considered for yourself, but now that you think about it, they sound like they could be fun. There you go. Starting a new chapter in your life.

Looking through this chapter should introduce you to the many activities singles groups are enjoying. They are dancing, clearing trails, skiing, dining out, attending theater and musical events, and meeting in discussion groups to talk over everything from spirituality to politics. There are activities that welcome just about anyone, and those for specific populations, such as certain age groups, gays and lesbians, vegetarians, religious denominations, or people of a particular size or height. Really, there are more groups out there than you can imagine.

Problem is, where do you start?

To decide, think about what you love to do and then see if there is a group set up that does that. For example, many singles want to spend time "giving back" to their communities. The **Single Volunteers** and **Philadelphia Renaissance** are two groups that concentrate on community service. Members of Single Volunteers join with Habitat for Humanity to help build houses for deserving families, and take part in projects like outdoor plantings and clean-ups with conservation organizations. But while they're clearing vines, they're also having a lot of fun together, and meeting others who share their values about service. Renaissance hosts social hours and get-togethers where many young professionals socialize with others with whom they have wielded a paint brush to benefit the school kids of Philadelphia (and other projects). Renaissance believes that this city is also going through its renaissance and they want to contribute to it and be part of it. Wouldn't you like to spend your time with people who feel that way? (Check in the Community Service chapter, too, for the many "Young Friends" organizations that support Philadelphia's cultural organizations. Many of their members are single.)

If music is your passion, and you are a classical music enthusiast, **SOLOS (Single Orchestra Lovers)** offers terrific evenings at the Philadelphia Orchestra. First you'll have networking time in a fine restaurant, followed by premier seats for one of the finest orchestras in the world. If you don't know a lot about this kind of music, go to an introductory concert where the concertmaster will give you a quick course about what you're hearing, coupled with a happy hour, all hosted by SOLOS.

Single theater lovers who prefer not to go alone will be glad to know about two theater evenings designed for them. After the second Friday night performance, the **McCarter Theater** in Princeton hosts a theater party with discussion, food and dancing, all related to the theme of the play. Even though it is open to all, many single people attend. The **Ritz Theater** (*theater* theater, not the movie house) designates a night for single people on the Thursday before a play opens, with a performance preview and discussion about the play afterwards. It's a chance to meet others who put theater high on their interest lists.

We all like to socialize around food and drink, so many singles groups do just that. One excellent national organization, the **Single Gourmet**, has a terrific local chapter, where people get together to have dinner at the finest (but not always expensive) restaurants in the city. Not only do they enjoy excellent dining experiences to be had in Philly's amazing new restaurants, but also they have lively evenings with other single people who truly enjoy fine dining. I really like food-discussion gatherings because it ensures that you're going to have a good time (eating), and it gives you something else to do besides stare at somebody while you talk. Also, there are lots of people there, so you don't have to carry the ball the whole time. Besides dinners out, Single Gourmet has great parties and takes some very intriguing trips to sample the local food and activities. If you're into healthy food, you'll find good company with the **Single Vegetarians** or at **Singles Nights at Whole Foods**. These groups eat together and share ideas for preparing tasty meals that keep them strong and energetic. Another national organization, the **Wine Brats**, has local events where hundreds of members get together for events with titles like "Sushi, Wine and Sake to Me." They are rollicking good fun with lots of good tasting, but you need to make reservations as early as you can.

Meeting new people is so much easier when you are doing physical activities outdoors. Outdoor groups for everyone, including singles, are in great abundance around the Delaware Valley. To name just a few: **Sierra Singles** is very active with many social activities and hikes. There's camping (**Outdoor Singles**), skiing (**King of Prussia Ski Club, Fall Line Ski Club** and many others), golfing (**American Singles Golf Association**), tennis (**Princeton Tennis Parties**), sailing (**Dynamic Diversions**), and many others. (Check the groups in Games & Sports because many have lots of single members.) Don't worry if you have never done these sports. An enthusiastic attitude and sincere willingness to try will endear you to your fellow playmates. If you'd rather meet someone in broad daylight without mind-altering substances, if you'd rather meet people who are actually doing what they love instead of talking about it, if you'd rather meet people with patience to teach (or learn) how to fall on skis or paddle small rapids properly, these are the best places to get involved. And most outdoor groups have an enthusiastic social component to their gatherings, so look forward to some fun parties!

Some groups for singles offer a full program of different activities. This means you'll do many different things, like discussing topics of interest, playing volleyball, learning dance steps, and so on, with the friends you've made in the group. The **Professional and Business Singles Network** is one of those full program groups. They've been offering dances for over 20 years, often with a discussion or a dance lesson first. Plus they have house parties, discussion groups, outdoor events, and trips. Since PBSN has a large singles membership, you have a chance to expand your network of single friends to pal around with on a Friday night. Call for the newsletter that details numerous activities in different neighborhoods almost every night of the week.

You may want to attend singles groups where you feel you already have membership. This includes those groups that share a religious bond, that are gay or lesbian, or where you are in the same age or cultural/racial/national group. When you are pretty clear that you are looking for a partner for life, these choices are important, and you can find singles groups of these kinds. One example is **Parents Without Partners**, that provides all kinds of opportunities for single parents to get out from under and have a good time. Their social activities are located in country clubs and large halls in many neighborhoods and suburbs around the city, so you should be able to find one that is fairly close to your house (and won't waste babysitter time traveling). These folks are nice and know how to have fun. If you're a single parent, you may want to socialize with others with whom you can share your concerns about raising kids by yourself. And some of their activities include the kids.

Just my opinion.
For several reasons, I think it's important to have a goodly number of single friends (and join a singles group) if you are single. One reason is

that you can share common issues about being single here, now, in this city and these times, with them. No one understands those issues like you all do. The humor and seriousness of the situation is important. It's also important to go out and play with single friends where you don't feel like a third wheel.

A second reason is that, as a single person, you may be very interested in socializing where you have a good chance of finding romance. Actually, you can find romantic partners in all the chapters throughout this book because singles are very active. Some very interesting single people do not go to singles groups because they aren't "looking" but are busy living their lives. Great. But sometimes you want to socialize where you don't have to worry that the person you're attracted to is attached. While attending a singles activity can be fun in its own right, it also should hold the promise of meeting a good person for a relationship. In a singles group, everyone is a potential partner. At a singles activity, you can enjoy flirting when you feel attracted to someone without worrying about a spouse hitting you with an umbrella.

And third, a good reason to join a singles interest group is that you want to be in situations where the friends and potential romantic partners you meet will see what you are really like. They will learn most about you when they see you in action, taking part in something you love and care about. And you will learn more about them, too. A relationship that emerges from an interest shared over time has a better chance of succeeding because it is built on more realistic information about each other. You don't have a lot of time to perfect your image when you've just tipped over in a canoe together!

A final note: Try to get perspective on what you really care about. Some single people are so invested in finding a partner that they are distracted from living the life they have. They spend a great deal of time going around looking for just the "right person" to get connected with. To them I say: Being in a relationship is hard work, too. There is no free lunch either way. Why not look for *your* people in the groups where you share interests and values, so the relationships you find there become a wonderful satisfying people network? What is really important is to find intimacy and love and great pleasure in your network of friends, canoeing partners, and tried and true companions. There's a strong possibility that you'll find among them someone to love with whom you really are well-matched. And you'll have a great time while you're looking.

A closer look at...

Dynamic Diversions

P.O. Box 1775, Southeastern, PA 19399
(215) 849-9944   dynamicdiversion@hotmail.com
www.dynamicdiversions.org

Dynamic Diversions is a non-profit, outdoor, recreational organization that sponsors activities such as biking, canoeing, cross-country/downhill skiing, glider soaring, hiking, hot-air ballooning, horseback riding, rock climbing/rappelling, sailing, white water rafting, adventure travel, and more. They offer day-long, weekend, and week-long diversions. Recent activities have included: a waterfall hike in Jim Thorpe, PA; canoeing on the Schuylkill and Brandywine Rivers; ultralight flight in Havre de Grace MD (with a licensed pilot); biking along the Delaware Canal; hiking in Ricketts Glen State Park; and rock climbing in Bucks County. Upcoming activities will include an African Safari in Kenya for 10 days and sailing in the British Virgin Islands. These excursions are well-planned and well-attended by an interesting and lively group of mostly single people. The variety of activities insures that you'll find something to enjoy, along with very nice people who share your interests. Check the web site for excellent photos of DD's adventures if you're having trouble deciding what to do first.

☼ Year-round   ☎ Joe Feisel

💰 Many 1-day activities about $13/person including full course lunch

Annual Events

Breast Health Institute: *Annual Singles Charity Ball*

834 Chestnut Street, Suite 315, Philadelphia, PA 19107
(215) 830-0587
Activity Location: Varies

Kick up your heels at this annual gala featuring swing, modern, and oldies music and dance lessons for those who need a brush up. Dress is casual to dressy (no sneakers, please), with free food, drink, and door prizes for a crowd mostly 30+. Have a great time!

🏵 About $30, if you preregister.

Leukemia and Lymphoma Society of America: *Bridesmaids' Ball*

2401 Pennsylvania Avenue, Suite 2D1, Philadelphia, PA 19130
(215) 232-1100   www.leukemia-lymphoma.org

Do you really want to win the "Dress from Hell" contest? If you have a sense of humor you'll love this mock wedding, complete with garter and bouquet toss and cutting the wedding cake—easy ice breakers for finding a dance partner to twirl to the Elastic Wasteband. You also might win a nice (*really* nice) prize, like a trip to Jamaica. This distinctive event for young professionals in their mid-twenties to early forties offers guests a chance to mingle with friends, meet new people, and enjoy good food, drink, music, and dancing—and hey, it's for a very good cause. Also ask about the networking party for young professionals ("Port Connection") in October. Held in late Spring from 9pm to 2am.

Philadelphia Magazine: *Singles Party of the Century*

1818 Market Street, Philadelphia, PA 19103
(215) 564-7700 x2045   www.phillymag.com

This is a big party in June where the winners of Philly Magazine's "Most Wanted Singles" contest (selected by public nomination and judged by *PM*-appointed celebrities) are invited to join the rest of us for a really good time. Get next to your favorite 'most wanted' and ask her/him the secret of successful singleness. Or do some high-step dance with another cool partner (Or by yourself!). Cosponsored by STAR 104.5.

🏵 About $50.

Singles

Art, Music & Theater

Art Lovers Exchange

P.O. Box 265, Bensalem, PA 19020
(215) 638-9866   trannel@sprynet.com

If you are looking to meet other single people who are enthusiasts/creators of the cultural arts, such as music, fine art, theater, dance, literature, film, photography, crafts, etc., this is the place. This group helps people make contact with each other through an autobiographical profile in the newsletter published every six weeks.

☎   Ann Keesee

💰 $52/6 months; $68/one year with a $3 fee for each profile received

Classical Music Lovers Exchange

Box 1239, New York, NY 10116
(888) 408-CMLE   info@cmle.com   www.cmle.com

Unattached music lovers with a keen interest in classical music can exchange biographical profiles relating to their common interests.

💰 $65 for 6 months of mini-bios

Film Bill of New Jersey

(856) 795-6836   (Call Fri. to see what they're going to see the following Wed.)
go2movies@yahoo.com   www.go2movies.com
Activity Location: Ritz Theater in Voorhees, NJ

This is an easygoing way to meet people—going to and talking about movies—and this is a nice group with which to do it. They meet every other week on Wednesday nights (reduced price of $5), take in a film, and go out after and have a bite, usually at a diner or Applebys. Some people think you can find out a lot about people by their reactions to characters in the movies. What do you think? No dues.

☼   2nd and 4th Wed./mo

MacCarter Theatre: *After Hours Theatre Party*

91 University Place, Princeton, NJ 08540
(609) 258-ARTS   www.maccarter.org

Attend the second Friday performance of the play series, then talk and dance afterwards with the lively theater crowd that includes many (but not all) singles. There is live music/entertainment, often following the theme of the play, catered food and drinks, and even door prizes. This is a double fun-whammy for singles who are looking for others who love the theater. Phone the box office for info.

Singles

Puttin' on the Ritz Productions: *Mixer for Singles*

Ritz Theater, 915 White Horse Pike, Oaklyn, NJ 08107
(856) 858-5230

Theatrical singles: On the Thursday night before a show opens at the Ritz Theater (playhouse, not movie), there is a singles event, including a preview of the new play and a social after at the reduced rate of $10. It's a great chance to mill around and talk about the play no one else has seen yet. If you're a budding thespian, there are classes and theater seminars here, too.

📞 Lori Jo Jamieson

Single Orchestra Lovers (SOLOS)

260 S. Broad Street, Philadelphia, PA 19102
(215) 893-1956   www.philorch.org

SOLOS is sponsored by the Philadelphia Orchestra Volunteers to provide a comfortable forum for singles over 40 to encounter like-minded, cultured singles for fun, friendship, and romance. Although they offer a number of different events, the basic program is a Tuesday evening orchestra performance with premier seating, preceded by butlered hors d'oeuvres with cash bar cocktail hour and a buffet supper at upscale restaurants like the Ritz Carlton and the Union League. SOLOS has also put together a happy hour at Toto's with tickets to a new program offered by the orchestra. There is also an Informational Concert—a short concert with a musical explanation by the orchestra concertmaster ($15). Call for info and reservations.

💰 $80/single ticket; $139/two events; $270/four events

Young Friends of the Art Museum

P.O. Box 7646, Philadelphia, PA 19101
(215) 684-7750   www.philamuseum.org

There are many "Young Friends" organizations that include many singles who give time- and energy-support to the cultural institutions of the city. (See the Community Service chapter for many of them.) YFAM is a fine example of one of these. It is a very friendly group of young professionals, many single, whose mission is to raise funds for special projects for the museum through a variety of educational and social activities. Besides being given membership in the museum, they are invited to three fund-raising events—the Young Friends Black-Tie Ball (to which the public is also invited), a Rodin garden party, and a holiday party. During the year, there are many events, such as First Friday Happy Hours, gallery tours at local galleries, and day trips. For greater involvement, some members join subcommittees to plan special events.

💰 $100/yr

Singles

Community Service

Friends of Landmarks

321 S. 4th Street, Philadelphia PA 19106
(215) 925-2251   landmarks4@aol.com

The mission of this group is to sponsor events that are cultural in nature but great fun as well, in order to raise money to support four fine historical house museums (Physick, Powel, Grumblethorpe, and Waynesborough). An arm of the Philadelphia Society for the Preservation of Landmarks, Friends is for people 21-45, and includes many outings, parties, trips, and other exciting events. Other benefits include tours of historical places, advance notice of lectures (such as "Childhood in the 18th Century" and "Spotting Fakes & Forgeries in Antiques"), Oktoberfest, Holiday Cheer party, wine tastings at the museum-houses, and a newsletter.

Philadelphia Renaissance

(215) 925-4555   phillyperk@yahoo.com

A premier group for young professionals (25-40) who are interested in exploring Philadelphia, working on interesting short-term community projects in the city, and socializing with others who value community service. Lots of singles attend the regular happy hours that are easy-going, low maintenance, and highly social affairs. Volunteer opportunities have included school and park clean-ups with Philadelphia Cares, the Thanksgiving volunteer event put on by the Little Brothers of the Frail Elderly, the Art Museum's Holiday Candlelight Tour of the Fairmount mansions, and activities with the volunteers from the White Dog Cafe. Find your niche with other young committed civic-minded people.

☎ Bret Perkins

Single Volunteers of Bucks County

(215) 968-1983   svofbc@yahoo.com
www.homestead.com/svbc   singlevolunteers.org
Activity Location: Churchville Nature Center, 510 Churchville Lane, Churchville, PA 18966

Attend a meeting where singles come together in a positive, friendly atmosphere to offer a hand to their communities. At the meeting, you'll find sign-up sheets for many community service projects, such as Habitat for Humanity, groups that feed the homeless, Interfaith Housing, Aid to Friends, the Wild Flower Gardens at Churchville, and EarthDay at Bowman Nature Center. You'll be working with a group of SVBC members, so you'll have lots of conversations and meet new people while you do some good. Terrific.

☀ 2nd & 4th Tues./mo

Urban League Young Professionals

P.O. Box 34775, Philadelphia, PA 19101
(215) 841-5103   www.libertynet.org/ulyp/member.html
Activity Location: Meetings at The Enterprise Center, 4548 Market St., Phila., PA

The ULYP is the volunteer arm of the Urban League of Philadelphia and welcomes all individuals of any age, sex, race, political affiliation, and profession. This group, which includes many single people, is very active in community service programs, such as those that serve food to the homeless, and others that mentor young children. Other committees for members to join include fundraising, professional development, and historical challenge. The Urban League is a prominent service organization in the city, with many opportunities to interact with others who want to make a difference.

☼ 2nd Tues./mo from September to June   ⏰ 6:30-8:30pm
💰 $35 annual dues

Dancing

Singles Scene

(215) 247-2561

Activity Location: Unitarian Universalist Church of the Restoration,
6900 Stenton Ave., Phila., PA 19150

Singles Scene offers a three-phase program for singles over 21. The activities begin at 7:30pm and end at 12:30am. Phase I, 7:30 to 9:30pm: Refreshments, socializing, conversation, and soft music in a cafe setting. Phase II 9-10pm: Discussion groups and/or workshops. Phase III, 10pm to 12:30am: Dancing. This is a lively group where diversity is welcomed and appreciated.

☼ Every Saturday   ⏰ 7:30-12:30pm

Singles USA

(610) 358-4772 (hot line)

This large, happy, dancing group meets at the Ramada Inn in Essington, NJ, on Fridays at 9pm, at Pompeiis in Media, PA, on Saturdays at 9pm, and Sundays at Barnaby's in Havertown, PA. (These places and times change, so be sure to call before you go.) Singles USA dances have become an institution in the area, hosted by Jim Scala, who informs by postcard, newsletter, and an updated hot line. Generally an older crowd. Enjoy!

💰 Only $5

Singles

Denominational

Bryn Mawr Presbyterian Church

625 Montgomery Avenue, Bryn Mawr, PA 19010
(610) 525-2821

One very *active* singles group for all ages sponsors educational programs, like small groups for Bible study and spirituality retreats, mission work (such as cooking and collecting linens for the homeless), and fellowship. Fellowship activities are not explicitly Christian-based and include progressive dinners, trips to the theater and sporting events, outdoor activities such as hiking, biking, and skiing, and various gatherings for specific age groups. Other activities have included: Culture on a Budget (orchestra and theater for $25 or less) and a First Friday dinner and lecture for $10. Call to get the newsletter and updated schedule of events.

Chews United Methodist Church: *Adult Singles Fellowship*

319 Black Horse Pike, Glendora, NJ 08029
(856) 227-4362 (hot line)

This Christian group welcomes singles of all ages and all denominations to its activities, including holiday parties, dinners in members' homes once a month, 3rd Saturday breakfast gatherings (9am) usually at the Freeway Diner in Deptford, a support group (2nd Tuesdays), and occasional events like bowling, movies, etc. There is also a singles Bible study group and adult singles fellowship (2nd Fridays) with a speaker followed by a social hour and refreshments.

Christian Entertainment & Fellowship Network

(215) 858-4957   www.cefn.org

This nondenominational ministry seeks to provide spiritually and socially uplifting entertainment and fellowship opportunities to Christian singles. Although these spiritual, non-alcohol events are geared to singles, all are welcome to come and have lots of fun. Look for information in the papers about their big annual event taking place in May, when 60-80 congregations from all over the Delaware Valley come together to celebrate and inform people about their events. A great multicultural networking party. Check the web site for information about many Christian events in the area.

Church of the Saviour: *20 Something*, & *Focus*

651 N. Wayne Avenue, Wayne, PA
(610) 688-6338 x242   www.20something.org or www.focussingles.org
Activity Location: Sunday mornings at Saturday Club, 117 W. Wayne Ave., Wayne

You'll find a group you can enjoy with one of these four singles groups. *20 Something* and *Focus* (for people between 40 and 60) hold Sunday morning worship and devotional speaker/discussion groups, as well as participate in a wide range of nonreligious social activities, like volleyball, hayrides, movies, dances, and ski trips. Call to find out their schedules. C.O.M.M.O.N. Creed (30s and 40s) has socializing and Bible study, and a Young Adult group (18-25) is slated to begin in Fall 2001.

Free Spirit Singles

(856) 795-2300, x1

Activity Location: Lighthouse Event Center, Landmark One Apts., 1900 Frontage Rd., Suite 113, Cherry Hill, NJ 08034

Singles can enjoy social and educational activities from a Christian perspective here, offered by family therapist Nancy Gearhart, with a group meeting on Thursdays , and a social evening one Saturday a month (7:30pm). Activities include movie nights, dance lessons and parties, singing, speaker/discussions, and special events. Free Spirit is "dedicated to providing a safe environment where singles can meet and have fellowship with new friends." (from FSS brochure).

☼ Thursdays   ⏰ 7:00pm

Jewish Professional & Business Singles

(215) 752-2179

Activity Location: Congregation Beth Chaim, 350 East Street Road, Feasterville, PA

JPBS is a nonprofit singles group that sponsors Shabbat at 8pm at Congregation Beth Chaim on the fourth Friday of the month, followed by coffee, cake, and socializing with the congregation. This group of people (aged 39 and over) hosts house parties, dance parties, and trips such as the Stardust Dance Weekend (with Umbrella Singles) with 50 dance workshops (Latin, Swing, etc.) and parties.

☼ 4th Fri./mo   ⏰ 8pm

Singles

Mosaic Outdoor Club

P.O. Box 2813, Cherry Hill, NJ 08034
(215) 922-3345   www.mosaics.org/philly   philly@mosaics.org

Mosaics is a national nonprofit organization providing a way for "outdoors-oriented Jewish adults of southeast Pennsylvania and New Jersey to meet and enjoy their common interests" (from their web site). Activities have included moonlight strolls, daytime hikes in the Wissahickon, cross-country skiing, historical reenactments at Washington Crossing, silk-screening T-shirts and other crafts, and canoeing on the Schuylkill. Check the web site for past and present events. There is social networking with other branches of this club.

Our Lady of Perpetual Help

Main Street, Maple Shade, NJ
(609) 634-5699   goxraygo@aol.com

This is a dynamic Catholic younger singles group, ages 21-40, who enjoy socializing, having fun, and making and meeting friends. Their activities include sports events, ice skating, hiking, game nights, eating together, happy hours, and holiday parties. In the summer they might visit Penns Landing, the Philadelphia Art Museum, or the Omniverse Theater. Most activities are on Friday nights and weekends, with a monthly planning meeting.

☎ Peter

St. Andrews, The Apostle Spiritual Center

(856) 784-8501

For singles over 40, this group enjoys socializing, hearing motivational speakers, and attending musical events, such as Gilbert and Sullivan operettas.

St. Mary's: *Singles Group*

Main Street, Williamstown, NJ
(856) 546-2343

This informal nondenominational group hosts myriad interesting activities for singles over 30, many in their 40s and 50s: plays, dancing, dinners out, game nights, ice skating, movies, country and western dancing, karaoke, brunches, Super Sunday (and other holiday) parties, and spiritual events for those who wish them. On a regular basis this group has weekly bowling, pinochle every other Thursday, and about two activities every weekend. About 50 people (out of a membership of 200) attend each activity.

☼ 1st Wed./mo meetings

St. Peter's: *Singles Over 21*
P.O. Box 1404, Merchantville, NJ 08109
(856) 663-3759

These activities for Catholic and Christian singles are for all ages over 21, including those never married, widowed, or annulled-divorced. Come and enjoy many types of social activities, including theater or movies nights, dinners out at various restaurants (every month they choose a special spot), dances at different churches, holiday parties, picnics, camping, hiking, a shore excursion in summer, and vacations (such as to Myrtle Beach). It costs $14 a year to join and you get a newsletter to let you know what's happening.

:☼: 1st Fri./mo meetings

Unitarian Singles
(610) 873-3432   (Shawna Tobin, Main Line Church) uusingles@aol.com

The suburban Unitarian churches (Collegeville, West Chester, Main Line, Media, and Wilmington) are sponsoring this lively group of singles of all ages (20-60). They have dessert and coffee following their events, attend movies and the theater, have game nights and book discussions, and take trips to museums and Longwood Gardens. Whatever they're doing, they're having fun and you don't have to be a Unitarian to join them.

:☼: 2 Sats./mo

Young Jewish Leadership Concepts
P.O. Box 313, Langhorne, PA 19047
(215) 750-9552 (YJLC)   lou4YJLC@aol.com   www.israelencounter.org

YJLC is an independent, nonprofit group begun in 1986 offering social events, travel, and community service for Jewish young people in their 20s, 30s and early 40s. They attend the Israel Encounter National Young Professional Tour once a year. Social events include parties, and weekend outdoor trips like skiing and rafting.

Singles

Outdoor Groups

American Singles Golf Association

(215) 579-0591   (800) 599-2815   www.geocities.com/philadelphia_asga

Activity Location: Conshohocken Marriott, Regatta Atrium, Conshohocken, PA

Get your golf game in shape while you meet outdoor singles. ASGA offers fun and fellowship on the fairways with other single golfers, mostly 35+. At monthly meetings, this group gets together to socialize and share info about upcoming events. Besides regular golfing games, there are social activities and networking. This is Philly's local branch of a national group that has more than 45 chapters across the country which sometimes get together for a golf extravaganza.

☼ 2nd Wed./mo   ⏰ 6:30pm

Dynamic Diversions

P.O. Box 1775, Southeastern, PA 19399

(215) 849-9944   dynamicdiversion@hotmail.com   www.dynamicdiversions.org

"Our 24th year of outdoor adventures," states the newsletter of this terrific group that organizes hiking, biking, canoeing, sailing, downhill and cross country skiing, white water rafting, hot air ballooning, rock climbing, and many other outdoor activities. Well-planned activities and a very nice group comprised primarily of single people. I love this group. (For more information, see *A Closer Look*, page 400.)

☎ Joe Feisel

💰 $15/yr plus fee for activity

King of Prussia Ski Club

King of Prussia Ski Club, King of Prussia, PA

(610) 265-6772 (hot line)

This is a year-round sport and social club for people (many singles) 21 and over. They meet at the Camelot Ballroom and other locations for dancing, happy hours, and many outdoor activities such as downhill and cross-country skiing in the winter and biking in the summer. Call the hot line for a list of upcoming events.

Loners-on-Wheels

P.O. Box 1355, Poplar Bluff, MO 63902
(215) 885-8750   www.lonersonwheels.com

A nationwide camping group for singles, mostly 45+. You receive a national
newsletter giving the local contact persons for campouts anywhere in the USA,
and you can attend any that you want. A terrific group of people to meet with
under the stars in every state.

🐱   About $45

Outdoor Club of South Jersey

(856) 427-7777 (hot line)   www.ocsj.org

Not a singles group, but one whose membership includes single people, this
club provides low-cost opportunities for outdoor activities all year, including
backpacking, bicycling, camping, canoeing, cross-country skiing, hiking, and a
practical experience course in wilderness survival. All activities are led and
organized by volunteer members, so you have the chance to create your own
outdoor experience to share. Most activities are in the South Jersey area, but
there are national and international events as well. OCSJ is strongly committed
to respecting the outdoors.

Outdoor Singles

P.O. Box 2121, Horsham, PA 19044
(215) 672-2706

This is a social group and outdoors community where members put together
about 240 events a year for the group. You can join them outdoors on Saturdays
and Sundays, on Mondays for weekly walks, for Wednesday evening suppers, or
at Glenside for Contra dancing on Thursday nights if you love dancing. They've
taken snow-walks, bike hikes, camping trips to places like Assateague Island,
VA, and Rickett's Glen Park, PA, with shore activities in the summer. If you
want to go, call the hot line and show up, or send $12 for a newsletter that lists
all events as well as the phone contact person.

🐱 $12/newsletter with event listings

Peace Valley Nature Center: *Singles Birdwalk*

170 Chapman Road, Doylestown, PA 18901
(215) 345-7860

This walk takes place about every other Saturday from 10am to noon. Call for
the event dates, and enjoy nature with other singles.

Singles

Princeton Tennis Parties

(609) 799-8214   swansonint1@home.com

Activity Location: Princeton Indoor Tennis Center, 92 Washington Rd. (Rte. 571), Princeton, NJ

Tennis parties take place on a regular basis for single and married players of all levels. Events are planned so that married players go on the court at 7pm, break to eat and socialize at 7:45pm, and are back on the court at 8:30pm. Single players go on the court at 7:45pm, and break from 8:30pm to 9:15pm. As much as possible, people are grouped with others at their level. Other activities include holiday parties.

☼ 1st, 2nd & 3rd Sat./mo from October to April

💰 For individuals: Attend 1 party $30, 2 parties $56, 3 parties $78

Sierra Singles

P.O. Box 34659, Philadelphia, PA 19101
(215) 592-4063, Box 6   bowens5953@aol.com
http://pennsylvania.sierraclub.org/southeastern/pages/singles.html

Sierra Singles includes about 600 people who share values and a commitment to explore, enjoy, and protect the natural world. Along with conservation and trail cleanup activities, they sponsor about 50 activities, including an eco-awareness discussion, every month. These include local hiking and hiking trips, road rallies, attending baseball games, camping trips, biking and canoeing, house concerts of folk music and jazz with pot luck suppers, and an orchestra trip once a month. Members also attend Zydeco, Swing, and Waltz dances. Call for a jam-packed newsletter.

☎ Barbara Owens

Tennis Group

(856) 546-9409
Activity Location: Mt. Laurel Racquet Club

All levels of tennis players are invited to join these singles who meet to play mixed doubles once a month. Call Joe for more information.

☼ 1st Sat./mo

☎ Joe Quigley

Professional Singles

Professional & Business Singles Network

P.O. Box 590, Villanova, PA 19085
(610) 359-9733 (hot line) or (800) 537-3859   www.pbsninfo.com

What I like best about PBSN (besides the really nice people there) is that it sponsors such a wide variety of social activities *all over* the Delaware Valley. This means you can probably find activities, such as Swing dance lessons, house parties, brunches, and happy hours in a pub, restaurant, or country club, fairly close to your home. Specific events might include: taking Cha Cha lessons at the Abington Country Club, dancing to hits ranging from the '60s to current songs at the Fort Washington Holiday Inn, or partying on the tall ship Jolly II Rover on Penn's Landing. You could join other singles for dinner at the Tango Restaurant in Bryn Mawr, discuss books in Manayunk, or attend a regular series of performances at the Philadelphia Orchestra or the Pennsylvania Ballet. And these are just the tip of the iceberg. Ralph Israel has really worked to create a comfortable niche for singles to meet new friends. Take a look at the Singles Register or the PBSN web page and see what you think.

South Jersey Single Professionals

(856) 642-1033   sjsp2030@hotmail.com
www.geocities.com/southbeach/palms/2722
Activity Location: Monthly meeting at Voorhees Community Center, the brick building behind police station near the corner of Haddonfield-Berlin Rd. & White Horse Rd. in Voorhees, NJ

SJSP is a social group for single people from 21 to 45 that has been active for ten years. It is informally organized and run by members for members with no dues. They plan two-three events every weekend, such as house parties, happy hours, dinners, brunches, movies, tennis, special trips (NYC, Renaissance Fair), and club hopping. Their regular meetings on Thursdays give people a chance to learn about events, and socialize with old and new friends. Newsletter delivered on email is free.

☼ 2nd Thurs./mo   ⏰ 8pm

Singles

Singles Groups

Connections

(856) 662-0138
Activity Location: Cherry Hill, NJ

Get together with other single people and discuss issues related to singleness, such as "Understanding Body Language and Other Rituals." Then you'll feel okay about asking a new person to kick up their heels with you at the dance that follows. This is a friendly group whose members do many other things together, like attend jazz concerts, have a St. Patrick's Day (and other holiday) dinner, or attend the Holistic Health Expo. The format changes, so be sure to call first.

☼ First Thurs./mo   🕑 7:30pm

Fabulous 50s Plus

1 Langcliffe Court, Mt. Laurel, NJ 08054
iamatraveler2@aol.com   http://fantastic50plusonthemove.homestead.com

A popular group for singles that is affiliated with (and shares some activities with) Singles On the Move. The calendar of events has included happy hours, Greek dinners, buffet and dancing evenings, and a monthly meeting on Mondays at the First Union Bank in Westmont, NJ. Great web site.

Just Singles

Activity Location: Michael's Restaurant, 3340 Street Rd., Bensalem, PA

You just have to show up at Michael's at 8:30am on Saturday mornings to get in touch with this group of energetic singles over 30 (and most over 40). It's worth it: Between 30-50 people meet for breakfast and plan group activities, ranging from dances, bus trips, movies, and bowling. You'll meet new single people who are from all over the area. (This reference was obtained in 1999. There is no way to check if they are still there, so they may not be! But don't you wonder...)

☼ Saturdays   🕑 8:30am

💰 Pay your own way—no member fee

Parents Without Partners, Greater Northeast Chapter #582

(215) 332-0622   pwpphila@hotmail.com   www.expage.com/page/pwp582

There are many chapters in the area of this well-structured, tried and true, international organization for single parents of all ages. Each chapter selects its own, including picnics, discussion groups, dances, weekend trips, bowling, and sporting events. Some activities are with children, many are without. You must attend an orientation to join.

💰 Dues vary by the chapter, usually between $30-$50

Single Parents Society

(609) 392-4430

Activity Location: Paso Doble Ballroom, 4501 New Falls Rd., Levittown, PA

You'll find dancing and free refreshments at these get-togethers for single parents in eight locations. Get really fancy with a dance lesson at the Paso Doble Ballroom, followed by dancing to live music and a DJ on Tuesday nights from 8:30pm to midnight. Locally, you can attend a Friday night dance from 8:30-11:30pm at St. Thomas Aquinas Hall, 17th & Morris Sts., Phila., PA (215-465-2298).

💰 $6 members/$7 non-members

Singles on the Move

Washington Township, NJ
(856) 589-2834   singlesonthemove@yahoo.com
www.homestead.com/singlesonthemove1/singlesonthemove.html

All singles are welcome to meet new friends and have fun doing the variety of activities offered by Singles on the Move. What do they do? Roller skating, bowling, sailing, movie discussions, as well as many happy hours, shared pot-luck and restaurant dinners, and dancing parties. They also have a walking group and a breakfast club. Just about anything you want! Most members are around 40-50 years old, but all are welcome.

Tower Club

(610) 828-0808   www.tall.org/clubs/pa/tcop

The Tower Club of Philadelphia, established in 1942, is a not-for-profit social organization for tall adults. Many singles attend, but married couples are welcome as well. Their web site says it best: "Our goal is to promote friendship and provide entertaining outlets for our members. We also offer community support to tall teens and adults. Activities include dances, parties, movies, museums, concerts, picnics, theatre, restaurants, sports, cultural activities, occasional kid-friendly events, local trips/tours, special events, visiting other tall clubs, and attending TCI's yearly convention." Open and closed events.

Umbrella Singles

(800) 537-2797   stardust@catskill.net   www.stardustdance.com

For large-group dancing to live bands, Umbrella Singles sponsors resort week-ends in the Catskills and Ballroom dance weekends (five times a year) at the Stardust Ballroom in New York. At the Stardust, it's 'round the clock dancing, classes every hour, top Latin bands, and a DJ, with about 800 people in attendance, most of them single and older (40+).

💰 Events start at $200 for accommodations, food, cocktails, and dancing

Singles

Yardley Singles

Yardley, PA
(215) 736-1288 (hot line)   www.yardleysingles.org

You don't have to be from Yardley to enjoy the weekly dinners-out (from pizza to fancy meals) with this group of 40+ singles. About 300 members strong, they welcome everyone to their Friday night dances (9pm-12am), house parties, and trips to the movies, their summer volleyball games and canal walks, special events, cruises, and more. Call for their newsletter.

Special Interests

Concerned Singles Newsletter

Box 555, N. Stockbridge, MA 01262

A nationwide group (since 1984) that links singles of all ages concerned about social justice and the environment.

Whole Foods Market: *Singles Nights*

2001 Pennsylvania Avenue (near 20th & Callowhill Sts.), Philadelphia, PA 19130
(215) 557-0015   www.wholefoodsmarket.com
(Also has stores in Jenkintown, Wynnewood, Devon, North Wales, and South St.)

If you like meeting people in grocery stores, this is the place to do it! About 90 singles attend the parties and fundraisers for worthy causes sponsored by this healthy foods Mecca about four times a year. A sample of typical activities includes massage, food tastings, special cooking classes, speakers about singles activities in the area (theater, natural lifestyles, etc.)—but there are different topics each time. Stop by the store for monthly calendar to find out what you want to attend.

🕝 7-9pm
💰 Suggested donation is $5

Main Line School Night: *How to Be a Great Conversationalist*

260 Gulph Creek Road, Radnor, PA 19087
(610) 687-0460   www.mainlineschoolnight.org

This class teaches you to become a creative and entertaining conversationalist, to pick up on clues from body language, and to figure out other people's intentions. Classes like these at MLSN or Temple Center City are filled with singles who want to branch out, go more places, and meet more people. Sounds like you can't lose with this one. Call for Main Line School Night's catalog of lots of interesting courses where you'll meet the interesting people taking them.

Science Connection

(800) 667-5179   www.sciconnect.com

Single science or nature enthusiasts (includes the social and medical sciences) might be interested in finding like-minded singles who wish to attend science-related outings in their area. This longstanding national group provides a data sheet to members about others in the group. People then contact each other directly for coffee or to attend group outings together.

Single Booklovers

Box 117, Gradyville, PA 19039
(610) 358-5049   SBL@compuserve.com   www.singlebooklovers.com

A popular 30-year-old group that serves the needs of cultured singles who like to read. Connections are made via member profiles which describe favorite books and cultural interests. SBL sponsors dinners twice a year, and some members have started book discussion subgroups and get-togethers.

☎   Bob & Ruth Leach

💰 $72/yr

Single Gourmet

P.O. Box 30119, Philadelphia, PA 19103
(215) 732-0260   www.singlegourmetphilly.com

Members of this upscale and friendly group make fine dinner companions and good friends. They plan dinners at some of Philadelphia's most exciting restaurants (such as Tangerine, Steven Starr's Moroccan dining sensation), as well as tried and true good food places (like an April Fool's dinner dance at Braddock's Tavern in Medford, NJ). About every other month there is a mixer at Monte Carlo's Living Room, with no set seating, which includes dinner and dancing. And once a year, there's a splashy trip to Jamaica that you won't want to miss.

☎   Florence Weltman

Single Gourmets on a
trip to Jamaica!
(1998)

Singles

Single Route at Liadis Travel

3129 West Chester Pike, Newtown Square, PA   19073
(610) 353-8330   www.liadis.com

If you want to travel alone but are interested in more than a "drink 'til you drop vacation," Liadis has done the research for you. It offers high-quality vacations with good values for singles with interesting activities like digs in Sonoma, biking from inn to inn in the Northeastern US, and culinary tours in Italy. Or, if you want a relaxing beach vacation solo, it can steer you to it.

Singles Scene (*Philadelphia Weekly*)

1701 Walnut Street, Philadelphia, PA   19103
(215) 563-7400 x138   www.philadelphiaweekly.com

With its pulse on local happenings, the *Weekly* sponsors singles events that coordinate networking with having a great time. At least three events are held each month (one being a lesbian/gay event), including Happy Hours and music nights (like jazz at local hot spots). There are also concerts in Rittenhouse Square and special activities, like theater evenings with mingling, cocktails, and author Q & A, as well as a ghost tour ending at City Tavern (rumored to be haunted on that evening). This crowd is usually between 25 and 40 years old.

Spirit Singles Book Discussion Club

(215) 489-9008 hot line   http://members.nbci.com/spiritsingle
Activity Locations: Discussions in five locations, in Doylestown, PA, Devon, PA, Montgomeryville, PA, Newark, DE, and S. Jersey

A unique way to meet other spiritually minded singles is to attend a book discussion group about your favorite spiritual books. Groups are well-attended by a diverse membership of men and women mostly between their 30's-50's of all religious denominations. Books chosen for discussion have included *Relax, You're Already Perfect* (Schneider) and *Four Agreements* (Ruiz). Spirit Singles also has social events like a New Year's Eve party, potluck suppers, movies, community service, hikes, concerts and more. The discussions are free and a volunteer runs the group. This information was obtained from their web site. $15 for newsletter of events.

☼ 4th Sun./mo   ⏰ 4pm

Singles

Tri-State Vegetarian Singles of South Jersey
(877) 999-8775 (Vegetarian Society of South Jersey)
www.vssj.com (Vegetarian Society of South Jersey)

Test the produce power of this group that meets about once a month for some lively activity, including house parties, hikes with the Outdoor Club of South Jersey, food talks and meals, bike rides, and picnics.

💰 $20

"Wednesday Night Supper Club" at The Learning Studio
412 East King Street, Malvern, PA 19355
(610) 578-0600   classes@learningstudio.net   www.learningstudio.

This is a fun place to meet new singles and eat tasty, interesting dishes! The web site welcomes you to "Join our guest chef for this "hands-on" interactive cooking class. You'll dine, imbibe, mingle, and learn some new cooking techniques." (from LS web site) Please B.Y.O.B. to share. Sign up for this class early. There is often a waiting list for women. Also, check out the many other classes for singles at the Learning Studio, such as Turbo Dating in which you spend 7-8 minutes with different people to find out whether you want to get them better. This is done in a "confidential, non-confrontational fashion" and is age-segmented.

💰 Members Club $36 Non-members $42
   B.Y.O.B. $5 materials fee paid to instructor

Wine Brats of Philadelphia
(215) 731-2000   peterb@libertynet.org   www.winebrats.org

This local chapter of the national group of Wine Brats sponsors some truly fabulous and fun events where fine wine can be tasted and discussed with aficionados you have only just met. Sex and Wine in the City (Circa), Sushi, Wine and Sake To Me (Fish on Main), and Rioja Festival (Philadelphia Art Alliance) are a few examples of the tantalizing events with this group. Generally about 250 people show up for the evenings that usually start at about 6pm and are reasonably priced around $25-$45. Brats is for everyone, but lots of singles attend. Register early.

☎ Peter Breslow

Singles

Participants of Philadelphia Renaissance help in a Fairmount Park clean-up day with Philadelphia Cares

 Here are some extra resources to check out

Web Sites

- *www.hotclubs.net,* lists clubs in the Delaware Valley that feature music and dancing
- *www.sisterspace.org* a fine, large group that offers a variety of actvities in the region for the multicultural lesbian community
- *www.funn.org* (Friends United in Need Network) Info for young professionals on fun events and volunteer opportunities
- *www.greensingles.com* Fill out a profile sheet to meet single adults who are members of environmental, vegetarian, and animal rights communities
- *www.phillydance.com* is a terrific web site with tons of local dance groups all around the Greater Philadelphia region

Publications

- *Al Klimcke's* regular column in *Courier-Post* is outstanding for singles (and other) activities in the Delaware Valley, especially NJ

Theater

Classes • Community Theater
Drama Discussions • Improv • Performance
Puppetry, Juggling, & Magic • Volunteering

Theater

The Philadelphia Jugglers Club

Photo by Coy Butler

Walnut Street Theatre's Adopt-a-School (Samuel Fels High School) production of "Runaways"

Theater

L ive theater is so much more exciting than a movie, don't you think? Can't you feel the buzz in the house, the connection of the players, and the involvement of the audience in what is happening? There is just something magical about the world of theater!

Experience the magic yourself by attending one of the many quality productions right here in Philadelphia almost every weekend, from mainstream popular shows on Walnut Street to intriguing experimental works on South Street. And as the number of theatrical productions expands, so does the active theater community. You can be a part of this community in lots of ways, whether as an actor, a stage-set builder, an usher, or a fundraiser, or as part of a theater-going discussion group.

The closest I ever came to being part of the theater world was when I was the comic lead in a high school play. It was very exciting. Just the *stage* was exciting. I was terrified and thrilled. It was all I could do not to bungle my big—supposed to be funny—line, to be delivered at just the right moment. (It worked!) But what I really remember was the way our disparate group bonded as the weeks went by. We, and only we, knew the mystery of the story world we were presenting—how it would look, feel and unfold. Together we were tied to the success of the production (and the fear of its failure) and by the history of an intense period of working/playing together to make this thing real. We were creating something where there had been nothing before.

Now, thirty (er, forty, Ruth) years later, I realize I've been longing to be involved in theater again. But I have not tried. Why? Because I've been thinking that theater is only for special people—people with talent, people who are beautiful or can sing or dance. About that I am dead wrong.

To be a part of a theater production, you just have to love it, and be willing to give plenty of time and energy in a relatively short period of time. How do I know? I asked the people who are involved in community theater all around the area. They explained to me that the community theater movement aims to give regular neighborhood people the opportunity for all kinds of theater experiences because theater is *about* and for people. Everyone has a place in their productions. That is good news!

Theater

But the best news is that there are so many fine local theater groups that schedule two to three productions a year, and that welcome your participation. They need enthusiastic volunteers to set the stage, including costume makers and light/sound technicians, as well as folks to create play-worlds out of paper, paint and wood. One group, the **Players Club of Swarthmore,** utilizes a very sophisticated technical stage-set shop with all kinds of tools. You'll learn all the shop skills you need to create the sets for their fine productions.

Want to try your hand at acting? Taking drama classes will help you overcome stage fright, develop solid acting skills, and become an accomplished actor. Listen to just a few of the exciting classes offered in the area: Scene study, Juggling, Stage combat, Playwriting, Improv, and Developing a one-person show. Many outstanding professional, and semi-professional theater groups, like the **Hedgerow Theatre**, **People's Light & Theatre**, **Freedom Theater**, and **Arden Theatre**, have acting classes where students are taught by very fine professional actor-teachers. From there, you can audition for their productions. Or you can try for a part in a community theater (such as **Stagecrafters**, **Dramateurs**, or **Playcrafters of Skippack**) where auditions are open to all. If you're willing to learn and take direction, you might get a great part!

Neighborhood art centers, such as the **Cheltenham Art Center** and the **University City Arts League,** frequently include theater arts in their programs. These are fine introductory classes that could give you an idea about whether adventures in theater are what you are looking for. These classes vary in price, scholarship opportunities, and acting philosophy, but they are all solid theater programs. To find the right theater experience, you can collect catalogs, ask around, or call the centers and ask for details about their programs. One nice thing about doing theater projects is that you can try it for the life of a play, about six-eight weeks. If it turns out not to be your favorite thing, you can gracefully leave after that. (But you'll probably be hooked.)

Another way you can take part in theater that is a little less time-consuming is to volunteer for non-stage activities: Ushering, helping with programs, funding activities, and office work. These responsibilities are the backbone of theater organizations and give the productions a professional environment (and the money to stay alive). Making a play happen is the result of many peoples' work, and the experience of working together on such a cooperative venture is an exciting way to network. It is a bonus that volunteers are a neat group of people to spend time with. They are dedicated to theater and are willing to give time and energy to help provide a cultural experience for the community. As a volunteer, you may also see a lot of free plays, too!

Some of us are fascinated by theater arts without wanting to be *in* a staged play. Improv theater classes provide an opportunity to act out feelings, ideas and situations spontaneously, sometimes without words. Improv looks like a lot of fun, and the players at places like **Comedy Sportz** are very clever and zany. Try going to an interactive Saturday night performance and see if you don't get your laughter for the week there. Your next step may be to sign up for one of their workshops. You can also learn to use your acting skills to do problem solving (**Full Circle Theater**) or handle tricky communication situations.

If you like to think and talk about plays and playwrights, there are many theater-goers' discussion groups that meet to discuss new plays, classic plays, and plays by local playwrights. Some of these groups take place in theaters, where the play on tap is discussed by members of the audience, theater and history experts, community leaders, and the actors and playwright. **InterAct** has regular Monday night playreadings with many discussion groups through the season. The **Philadelphia Dramatists Center** hosts "dynamic impressions" on some Sunday afternoons, as well as other workshops about theater throughout the year. **People's Light and Theatre** has "Playback Thursdays," a full discussion of the current production with the cast of characters and audience involved. Not only do these opportunities enhance our understanding of the plays we see, but they give us a chance to talk with the performers and other audience members. Some innovative theaters invite reaction from the audience even as the performance is taking place (**Painted Bride** and **Second Stage**). The active audience becomes part of the play. In all of these groups, if you go more than once, you'll get to know the theater community—and maybe become a regular member.

Philadelphia has *so* many exceptional interactive theater experiences. If you love theater, you're in the right place to be part of an energetic theater community.

Theater

A closer look at...

© 2000 Photo by Jeanie Chadwick - Mamarazzi Photography

The Philadelphia Fringe Festival

Box Office: National Showroom, 113-131 N. 2nd Street, Philadelphia, PA

(215) 413-1318   www.pafringe.org

Every year in Old City the Philadelphia Fringe Festival presents a jam-packed schedule of risk-taking performances by local, national, and international artists amid an atmosphere of celebration and fun. There's something for everyone during these two weeks, including special outdoor events, shows for families, post-performance talks, a new event to honor the dance community, and lots of surprises. You don't know who—or what—you're likely to run into on the street. Or in the Box Office Lounge. Or at the Late Night Cabaret where everybody ends up for a drink and discussion about the performances. Stay late and have great conversations about the work you've just seen with the people who created it. Artists include dancers, choreographers, directors, actors, musicians, puppeteers, and pranksters. If you want to earn free tickets to festival-produced shows (and other benefits), become a volunteer. It's fun and you can help out as an usher, box office staff venue ticket seller, house manager, or in one of a myriad of other useful jobs. The Fringe is more than a time to see lots of great shows; it's a time for everyone (even you!) to jump and play.

☼ Lasts about two weeks, from the end of August to the beginning of September; Weeknights: 6pm-midnight; Weekends: all day + evenings

💰 Shows are between $3-$35 (most are about $10). Discount $3/show with Fringe membership

Classes

Actors' Support Services

(215) 205-6800   vitorio007@aol.com

You can learn all aspects of acting in various mediums (film, stage, commercial, and industrial) in these classes, which especially encourage developing actors who are Hispanic and bilingual. Look into the Basic Acting class, as well as services in how to get started, how to promote yourself, and how to get organized for an acting career.

☎   Victor Antonio Corsino

Arden Theatre Company

40 North 2nd Street, Philadelphia, PA 19106
(215) 922-8900   info@ardentheatre.org   www.ardentheatre.org

People who are serious about the theater can look into the Arden Professional Apprentice program, where they learn every aspect of working in a professional theater company, from box office to development. This is a full-time position with pay, for those selected. For theater lovers: Arden holds open-play readings of new plays and post-show discussions for each performance on selected nights. Call for the schedules of readings and discussions. Volunteers are also welcome for many important supportive activities here.

Bushfire Theater

52nd & Locust Streets, Philadelphia, PA 19139
(215) 747-9230   thebushfire@earthlink.net

Three to four plays are presented each year in this 400-seat theater, with audience receptions with cast and director at final performances. Classes take place for African-American playwrights and performers. Subscribers may attend free readings and workshops of new plays. The Writers Cafe has workshops, while the Cafe-Theater sponsors jazz, blues, etc. Volunteers are welcome to usher and help in the office. Alfred Simekins is the artistic director.

Centre Theater

Montgomery County Cultural Center, 208 DeKalb Street, Norristown, PA
(610) 279-1013   www.artscc.org

This group is developing a society of artists who collaborate in performance and share space with other companies. They offer fine, highly supportive, acting classes, including movement, improv, and playwriting classes, usually by request. Find open auditions for every show in this professional theater, plus many volunteer opportunities. It's only $10 a week for eight weeks.

Theater

Cheltenham Center for the Arts

439 Ashbourne Road, Cheltenham, PA 19012
(215) 379-4660   www.libertynet.org/cheltenham/cca

Cheltenham Center offers a variety of educational classes for adults and children that are fun and information packed. Let your acting talent shine in a frequently scheduled "Scene Study for Adults" class and see where you go from there. Check out the many classes described in the catalog or on the web site.

Freedom Theater

1346 North Broad Street, Philadelphia, PA 19121
(215) 765-2793   www.freedomtheater.org

Freedom Theater is the largest African-American theater in the country and has a world-class repertory company. It offers terrific classes in acting (Performing Arts Training Program), vocal arts, and dance, building on the artistic voices of students of all levels and ages. Classes for adults are two/three time a week for 10 weeks. The public attends student performances, and post-performance talks with the professional cast. Volunteers are also welcome in many activities here.

Hedgerow Theatre

64 Rose Valley Road, Rose Valley, PA 19063
(610) 565-4211   www.hedgerowtheatre.org

This terrific theatre allows auditions from the community, but you might want to take one of the fine classes here first. Classes in acting, scene study, and performance are available for all levels. Theater auditions are held in March, and playwrights can submit work to the *Stage Reading Series* for presentation. Volunteers are welcomed for every aspect of the theatre—ushers, box office, publicity, set building, costumes, and lighting, to name a few.

💰 $150-195 for a 10-week class; theater tickets $17-19

Mike Lemon Casting (Mike Lemon, CSA)

413 N. 7th Street, Su 602, Philadelphia, PA 19123
(215) 627-1571   www.mikelemoncasting.com

This premier casting company with 18 years experience offers 14 classes, including *Film Acting, Film Audition, the Basics of Acting, Continuing Scene Study*, and a class for acting in commercials. One class, the *Business of the Business*, will help you prepare pictures, a résumé, learn audition skills, etc.—a must for all levels of actors preparing for acting as a vocation. Also look for *Actor Training Fest*, a weekend intensive workshop that includes useful information such as voiceover, improv, acting techniques, and more.

Montgomery County Cultural Center

208 DeKalb Street (Rte. 202 N), Norristown, PA 19401
(610) 279-1013   www.artscc.org

This center sponsors classes, non-equity professional theater, and concerts. You can apply to be involved in all aspects of theater here, acting, stage building, costume design, etc., as well as activities that support the production, such as ushering. There are occasional Sunday afternoon in-house oncerts ("Dessert Concerts") that feature local musicians and where you can enjoy a bit of sweet and good conversation. Their publication, *In The Spotlight*, describes the many opportunities for you to be involved in this suburban cultural meeting place.

Next Studio

340 N. 12th Street, Ste 417, Philadelphia, PA 19107
(215) 413-0975   www.bratproductions.org/next.htm

Next offers quality classes in techniques and methods not found in traditional theater programs, all taught by professional actors and/or directors. Classes include: *Evolutionary Movement Studio, Practical Acting, History of Comedy*, and more. Classes are very reasonable (10 weeks for between $190 and $240) and all ages are welcome. Free on-street parking.

People's Light and Theatre Company

39 Conestoga Road, Route 401, Malvern, PA 19355
(610) 647-1900 or (610) 644-3500 (box office)   www.peopleslight.org

This well-known innovative arts program is open to beginners and advanced acting students. It includes terrific acting classes, such as *Scene Study, Comedy, Movement* and *Improv*, and new classes like *Animal Dreams: Exploring Character Development*, and *Juggling and Unicycle*. This is a fine theater with excellent performances. You will love these classes.

💰 $175-$260/class

Puttin' on the Ritz, Inc. (Ritz Theater)

915 White Horse Pike, Oaklyn, NJ 08107
(856) 858-5230

If you've decided to scratch that thespian itch you've been carrying around from high school days or want to brush up on a specific talent you have, the Ritz probably has just the right class or workshop (e.g., *Stage Combat*) for you. For theater-goers: On specified evenings, the audience can discuss the performance with the cast and crew. Did you ever want to know how a set is built or how an actor prepares before going onstage? This is the place to find out. You can also volunteer in all areas of theatrical production. There are many ways to be active!

Theater

Photo by Coy Butler

Summer at the Walnut Street Theatre

Walnut Street Theatre School

825 Walnut Street, Philadelphia, PA 19107
(215) 574-3550   wstschool@aol.com   www.wstonline.org

This is the largest theater school in the Delaware Valley and the oldest continuously running theater in the country. Courses are taught by professionals in three different levels of study: Discovery, development, and mastery. There are 12-week classes in *Beginning Playwriting, Technique and Scene Study, Voiceovers and Dialects,* or *Intro to Shakespeare*. Students can audition for understudy roles in theatre company productions. The school showcases productions in the theatre studio. Individual coaching is available. Ticket holders can attend post show discussions held twice during the play's run.

💰 $260-$325 for a 12-week class

University City Arts League

4226 Spruce Street, Philadelphia, PA 19104
(215) 382-7811   ucartsleague@aol.com   www.ucartsleague.org

Although it is not the largest department, the League offers fun speciality theater classes like *Developing a One-Person Show, Success as a Spoken Word Artist or Rapper*, and a workshop in *Improv* for people who work too hard, think too much and who want to play more. Call for the League's brochure of classes.

💰 Very reasonable

Wilma Theater

265 South Broad Street, Philadelphia, PA 19107
(215) 893-9456   www.wilmatheater.org

Guided by artistic directors Blanka and Jiri Zizka, the Wilma Theater presents bold, innovative productions in its new 300-seat, state-of-the-art theater. The studio school offers *Playwriting, Acting, Improvisation, Audition Techniques,* and more. Attend post-production discussions on selected Saturday matinees.

☼ 10-week classes

💰 $190-$340 for 10-week classes

Community Theater

Dramateurs, Inc.

P.O. Box 255, Norristown, PA 19404
(610) 539-2276   www.barnplayhouse.org
Activity Location: The Barn Playhouse, Rittenhouse Blvd. & Christopher Lane, Jeffersonville, PA

An exciting community theater (since 1937!) with volunteers who come forward to do all aspects of theater production for the four shows put on each year. Try out in the open auditions for actors, or be involved in making costumes, doing makeup, props, lighting, publicity, and more. Check out the web site or call for the newsletter.

Old Academy Players

3540-44 Indian Queen Lane, Philadelphia, PA 19128
(215) 843-1109

Think you might be the next Grace Kelly? She got her start at this community theater, which was founded in 1923. Housed in a building built in 1819, the theater puts on six shows a year, welcomes production volunteers, and holds open auditions. A friendly group of theater lovers supports this neat theater.

☼ September-June

Playcrafters of Skippack

Store Road off Rte. 73, Skippack, PA
(610) 584-4005   www.playcraft.org

In this community theater, volunteers handle all aspects of the theatrical productions. Come to an open meeting in the big old red barn theater on the first Tuesday evening of the month at 8pm and see how you might be involved: Acting, ushering, props, costumes, box office, etc. By the way, you don't have to be *from* Skippack to do this—just share a love of drama.

Theater

Players Club of Swarthmore

Fairview and Chester Roads, Swarthmore, PA 19081
(610) 328-4271   tickets@pcstheater.org   www.pcstheater.org

You are invited to be involved in this "professional theater at a community level." (from the web site) Audition with others who come from all around the area; schedules are posted on the web page, with phone numbers to call. Are you interested in building things? How about sound and music? Lighting? Costumes or makeup? Props? Stage crew? If any of these areas of technical theater interests you, then you should come by and give the Swarthmore players a hand because PCS has one of the best technical theaters around.

Stagecrafters

8130 Germantown Avenue, Philadelphia, PA 19118
(215) 247-8881   www.thestagecrafters.org

For over 70 years, this Chestnut Hill community theater has been presenting plays. Find open auditions for each of the season's six shows. Volunteers are needed for all aspects of these excellent productions: costumes, lighting, building sets, and props. This is a very committed group of people.

💰 $12 to attend the show

Drama Discussions

InterAct Theatre Company

The Adrienne, 2030 Sansom Street, Philadelphia, PA 19103
(215) 568-8077   interact@interacttheatre.org   www.interacttheatre.org

Join this group on Monday evenings for a series of short fiction works read by professional actors. And if you like to talk theater, this is the place. After the first three Sunday matinees of each play, a discussion with area scholars, community leaders, and artists takes place, and on Tuesdays and Wednesdays, artists and audience talk about the play after the performance. These contemporary productions of new and socially relevant theater do stimulate conversation!

Theater

People's Light & Theatre Company: *Talkback Thursdays*

39 Conestoga Road (Route 401), Malvern, PA 19355
(610) 647-1900   www.peopleslight.com

After each Thursday evening performance (except previews) you can join the post-show discussions called *Talkback Thursdays*, when the cast, artistic team, and panel guests put each play in context. You also can be involved and volunteer as an usher. Be a part of this outstanding theater.

💰 $23, reservations required, series tickets available

Philadelphia Dramatists Center

1516 South Street, Philadelphia, PA 19146
(215) 735-1441   pdc@libertynet.org   www.libertynet.org/pdc/main1.htm

This nonprofit member organization and center for dramatic writers offers screenwriting circles, musical theater, radio play workshops, playreadings, social events, short play festivals, actor resources, and a library of plays. Volunteers are welcome. Many free events are open to the public. Drop by on Sunday afternoons or Monday evenings for dynamic impressions. Exciting events for all.

💰 Membership $25/yr, $5 for newsletters

Philadelphia Theatre Company: *Meet the Artists*

230 South 15th Street, 34th flr., Philadelphia, PA 19102
(215) 985-1400   info@phillytheatreco.com   www.phillytheatreco.com
Activity Location: Plays and Players Theater, 1714 Delancey St., Phila., PA

This excellent professional theater company of contemporary American drama sponsors discussions for the public with the actors and writers of the plays that are performed. These include pre-performance wine or micro-brewery tasting social events as well as post-performance panel discussions and symposia led by community leaders and experts, with significant participation from the audience. PTC also offers volunteer opportunities to usher and work in the office for those who wish to support the theater and see a free play. Call for the newsletter to be up to date on the events happening here.

Theater

Plays & Players Theater

1714 Delancey Street, Philadelphia, PA 19103
(215) 735-0630

This long standing community theater uses the community in all its plays, both in acting and production. Call to find out when you can audition. If you take the First Night Series, you can attend the Opening Night Reception, mingling with actors in the cast, enjoying wine and hors d'oeuvres. On Mondays, playwrights bring new plays to be read by local community actors. Plays & Players also offers classes from time to time. Keep in touch with this place.

Prince Music Theater

1412 Chestnut Street, Philadelphia, PA 19103
(215) 972-1000   www.princemusictheater.org

The Prince is a nationally renowned company with innovative productions of contemporary music theater in all forms, including opera, musical comedy, music drama, cabaret, and film. They often feature *Meet and Greet* sessions after selected performances where audience members can meet the creators and actors for a lively discussion. The Cafe at the Prince is also a lovely gathering place to meet and talk about the show.

Theatre Alliance of Greater Philadelphia

P.O. Box 40028, Philadelphia, PA 19106
(215) 413-7155   info@theatrealliance.org   www.theatrealliance.org

The Alliance works to create a strong, healthy, diverse, arts community in which theater is highly valued. The web site details theater alliance programming, such as StageTix, annual auditions, the Barrymore Awards, and a biannual Philadelphia Theatre Conference with panels, workshops, and networking. Actors can check their Philly Talent database for casting information. These activities are the tip of their iceburg—so stay in touch with the web site for more event info.

Theatre Double: *Underground Voices*

1619 Walnut Street, Philadelphia, PA
(215) 557-9421   thtrdbl@aol.com

This is a series of staged play readings followed by a wine and cheese reception and discussion of the plays, which are often new works by emerging playwrights, many female. Theatre Double puts on many world premier plays by both established and newer writers. Receptions follow the performances on opening nights. Also check Blue Box Productions, a company that shares the play space and frequently holds receptions after performances.

🏺 Free play readings

Comedy Sportz
performing
on Saturday nights

Improv

Comedy Sportz

(877) 98-LAUGH   www.comedysportzphilly.com

Activity Location: The Playground at Adrienne Theater, 2030 Sansom St., Phila. PA

Act out the characters of your fantasies, play in a nurturing environment—all of it is fun and provides much needed stress relief. Comedy Sportz instructors offer nine sessions (two hours once a week) of improv workshops in the spring and fall for everyone, no matter what your experience. You can see the pros in action any Saturday night (either at 7:30pm or 10pm) for only $12. There is extensive audience interaction, and the tables are so close, you'll laugh out loud with others enjoying the show. I can't stay away from these performances!

☎   Bobbi Block

💰   About $160/9 lessons

Theater

Full Circle Theater

Center for Intergenerational Learning, Temple University, 1601 North Broad St., Room 206 USB, Philadelphia, PA 19122
(215) 204-6970   www.temple.edu/CIL/Fullcirclehome.htm

An intergenerational ensemble of actors which uses interactive and improvisational theatre techniques to engage audiences to explore social concerns and develop strategies for problem solving. Sixty actors offer workshops/performances for more than 200 groups a year. Call to find out where to audition.

Playback Philadelphia

133 Rochelle Avenue, Philadelphia, PA 19128
(215) 508-3468   pbphil@erols.com   www.playbacknet.org

Playback is an original form of improv theater where the audience tells true stories from their own lives and sees them spontaneously enacted by the actors. Great classes use sound, movement, spoken word, and music to create human sculptures, vignettes, and full-length story enactments. Sarah Halley is the director. It's about $185 for a 10-week class.

Performance

Allens Lane Theater

Allens Lane Art Center, Allens Lane & McCallum Street, Philadelphia, PA 19119
(215) 248-0546   www.allenslanetheater.com

Come out for this semiprofessional theater's open auditions and classes. Or gain hands-on skills by volunteering to paint sets, collect props, or assist with lighting. Ushers are also needed. Audience can bring picnics to share with friends in the café-style theater before the show. Informal setting with thought-provoking plays.

☼ September-May

💰 $10/show, $35 for season (5 shows)

Brick Playhouse

623 South Street, Philadelphia, PA 19147
(215) 592-1183   www.libertynet.org/thebrick

This is the place where theater artists come to play and experiment. All kinds of activities take place here: Professional actors reading the plays of budding and experienced playwrights, followed by audience feedback and questions; writer circles; and the *1-Minute Festival*. It's a great place to meet alternative theater people—since events are held almost every weekend from September to June. Look for the *Best of IT* performances. The audiences are part of the action here.

Drama Group

288 West Haines Street, Philadelphia, PA 19144
(215) 844-0724

Activity Location: The First United Methodist Church of Germantown
6023 Germantown Ave., Phila., PA

This small, friendly, supportive group makes theater happen. Beginning and experienced performers as well as technical crew are welcome to be involved in all areas of production. They present two shows a year and have a great party in June. Members get ticket discounts, newsletter, and a subscription to *Stage Magazine*.

💰 Tickets $8, members $5

Eastern Cooperative Recreation School

(215) 729-6738   www.ecrs.org
Activity Location: different places in and outside of the city

ECRS typically sponsors about 7-10 events a year: four weekends, two one-days, two week-long camps. These activities are great fun, but you learn about leadership and cooperative play as well. You can try acting and singing in a supportive atmosphere, such as performing in small improv scenes or reading from famous plays, like *On Golden Pond*. ECRS events are usually attended by between 30 to 100 people of all ages and backgrounds.

💰 Very very reasonable

☎ Karen Wisnia

Philadelphia Fringe Festival

211 Vine Street, Philadelphia, PA 19106
(215) 413-9006   www.pafringe.com
Activity Location: Many venues in Olde City in early September every year

A 16-day festival of theater, film, art, spoken word, and music events. There are daytime art classes, lunchtime theater, and many, many evening performances. international, national, and local artists will fill the neighborhood with their works. (See A Closer Look, page 426.)

💰 Average ticket price $10

Theater

Shubin Theater

407 Bainbridge Street, Philadelphia, PA 19147
(215) 592-0119   shubintheater@erols.com

Denise Shubin opened this interesting little theater so performers and play-wrights could perform their works. Shubin collaborates at all levels of play development and encourages new thespians to contact her about support for performances and play reading. Check out these innovative performances.

Puppetry, Juggling & Magic

Spiral Q Puppet Theater

3114 Spring Garden Street, 2nd flr., Philadelphia, PA 19104
(215) 222-6979   spiralq@critpath.org   www.spiralq.org

Create puppets that express the frustrations and victories of urban life. Puppets and banners are created through a collaborative process and are displayed in city-wide and neighborhood parades, pageants and performances. Spiral Q also runs artists-in-residency programs to create neighborhood pageantry with giant puppets, based on each community's story. A very open and welcoming group. The web site tells all. Find out about an open studio where you can participate.

🐷 Free

Philadelphia Jugglers Club

(215) 808-8859

Activity Location: Year-round in Lloyd Hall, Boathouse Row on Kelly Drive

The more the merrier for this group, which for 20 years has been riding unicycles and tossing balls, clubs, and all kinds of props in the air. Very welcoming to newcomers, they'll teach *you* how to juggle. About 20-40 people show up to have fun. The group also holds a free two-day festival in October.

☼ Mondays   🕐 7:30-9:30pm

Society of American Magicians
& International Brotherhood of Magicians

47 Weldon Avenue, Trevose, PA 19053
(215) 364-8132   mmille8430@aol.com

Activity Location: Northeast Phila., Drexel (PA), Collingswood (NJ)

If you show an interest in magic you can be voted into these groups and attend monthly meetings, expand your repertoire, and perform in club shows that raise funds for charities. Or call Mike Miller to find out where to see live magic shows in the area.

🐷 $35-$65 a year includes monthly magazine

Underground at Ron's
(215) 233-0777

An eclectic mix of 15+ minute performances takes place in this 65-seat theater. This is a venue that encourages many emerging artists, as well as some well-established performers, to showcase their talents for a highly interactive, supportive audience. All types of artists perform here, singing, playing, making comedy, and more. It's joyous and lots of fun, and usually happens once a month.

Awakening the Hidden Storyteller
Box 181, Springhouse, PA 19477
(215) 646-2150   robin@comcat.com   www.robin-moore.com

These are workshops by Robin Moore, a master storyteller, who uses special techniques to assist people creating spoken and written stories. He also teaches classes at Cheltenham Art Center and the University of Pennsylvania General Studies Program. Four times a year he performs his one-man show, *Vietnam: A Soldier's Story*, followed by a discussion group for those who were in the war.

☎   Robin Moore

Patchwork
455 West Harvey Street, Philadelphia, PA 19144

This regional storytelling guild is open to all interested performers and audience members. Through its newsletter you can find out about its four local story-swapping groups that have monthly swaps in members' homes, plus many storytelling events throughout the Delaware Valley. Performers from the entire East Coast take part in the guild's annual gathering of storytellers in July. Write for listings of upcoming events that you can attend.

💰 $20/yr

Volunteering

Walnut Street Theatre Volunteer Troupe
825 Walnut Street, Philadelphia, PA 19107
(215) 574-3550, ext. 558

When you become an usher in this beautiful theater, which has been a mainstay in Philadelphia's theatrical arena, you'll get to see the high-quality performances for free. You can commit for the series or for a single performance.

💰   Free

Theater

 **Here are some extra resources to check out**

Organizations

- *Theatre Alliance of Greater Philadelphia*
  P.O. Box 40028, Philadelphia, PA 19106 (215) 413-7150
  www.theatrealliance.org. TAGP supports the local theater
  community in many ways and is an important information
  resource center for theater groups. Every June, the TAGP
  sponsors open auditions limited strictly to local actors.

- *The Philadelphia Chapter of the International Guild of
  Costumers*

Publications

- *In the Spotlight*
  Montgomery County Cultural Center, 208 DeKalb St.,
  Norristown, PA 19401   www.artscc.org
  A monthly theater arts newsletter filled with audition
  notices and a calendar of current and upcoming produc-
  tions in the suburban area.

- *Stage*
  9 E. rose Valley Road, Wallingford, PA 19086
  (610) 565-2094
  A monthly newsletter with information for performers
  (including auditions) in the Philadelphia area.

Online Resources

- YESand, an online news source for the improv theater
  community

Writing & Poetry

Hear An Author • Poetry
Writing & Reading Groups
Workshops & Conferences

Writing & Poetry

An author entertains his audience with his readings
in a Chestnut Hill bookstore

Photo by Jonna Naylor

Alan Elyshevitz teaching a poetry class
at the Mt. Airy Learning Tree

Writing & Poetry

As word-loving creatures, it makes a lot of sense that writing stories and poetry, letters, and journals would appeal to many of us. Writing tells *our* stories—stories about our loves, our mothers and children, our travels and adventures, our dreams and travesties, and the reaches of our souls. When we write, we connect with each other and tell about ourselves.

But writing well isn't easy! As a psychologist turned "author," I found out first-hand just how hard it is to sit down and write. I found out how long I could sit looking at a blank computer screen. And I suffered the embarrassment of an editor changing my verb tenses over and over, or substituting "that" for "who"—things I should have learned in elementary school. There's a lot to know about writing.

Take heart! Help is all around you, in the form of local writers' groups for all stages of your writing development. Whether you keep a journal, compose lyric poetry, write letters to the editor, or are working on the great American novel, having a regular writers' group is a God-send for everything from improving word skills and grammar to the business of getting published. In a group, you'll read a lot, listen a lot, and write a lot—with many critique sessions, bravely endured.

Don't be scared away from writing groups because you are new and have a lot to learn. Putting your ideas on paper is a terrific way to think through what you mean, make sure others understand what you mean, and affirm that your ideas have value. When you participate in a writing group, you build relationships based on mutual respect for all the members' ideas and writing skills. Doesn't that seem worthy of a solid time commitment? And wouldn't you like to build a network with people who really care about their writing projects? Then look for the right group (pun) and go for it!

Philadelphia offers many groups and events to help you get through the writing gate. The listings in this chapter will just get you started. Everyone now knows that the book store giants, **Borders** and **Barnes & Noble**, host a variety of "Hear an Author" evenings with big-deal celeb authors, whom you might otherwise have to pay cash money to hear. Go and find a friendly, interested audience, usually big, comfortable sofas to sit in during the events, and coffee bars for after-the-group conversations. But everyone doesn't know that these same stores have frequent, regular writing *groups* for different writing genres, like mystery, romance

Writing & Poetry

and spirituality, where you can read your writing and poetry aloud to a supportive audience. Also, various writing organizations like **Philadelphia Fantastic** and **Poets and Prophets**, hold their events at these book store giants, which have spread like mad over the entire Delaware Valley. Now you can probably find one near your home, which makes it convenient if you want a local literary hangout where you can hone your writing skills, join a reading group, or just listen to live music on Friday nights. But don't forget to check the other branch stores for special interest groups/events that meet your needs. (Web sites will give you this info.)

Although writing groups in the large book stores may be the most convenient, there are many outstanding groups in other places that might be just what you are looking for. The **Kelly Writers House** at the University of Pennsylvania is one prime example. All kinds of reading and writing events with intriguing titles like the "Laughing Reading Hermit Series" are there every day of the week and are open to the general public. In the 'hoods, you can find smaller, very supportive groups, such as the **Meridian Writers Group** in Mt. Airy and the **Romance Writers Group of Valley Forge**. (Meridian members read their works twice a month on Sundays at the **Sedgwick Theater**, a neighborhood spot well-known for excellent cultural happenings.) As an aspiring writer, you can be a part of these groups, reading your work for thoughtful feedback and learning a lot by listening to others.

When you look around, you'll find that there are first-rate author readings in all the nooks and crannys of the city. Readings provide a safe nonthreatening way to enter the writing scene. Have you found **Big Jar Books** on 2nd Street, yet? It's a cool, funky, book store offering mostly used books, coffee, readings and even a Thursday evening writers group. Or try **Robins Bookstore**, probably the oldest alternative book store in the city and definitely the finest, which regularly schedules readings by well-known authors of color. One of my favorite reading events is the **Bloomsday** reading outside the **Rosenbach Museum** all day every June 16th. People you know read from Joyce's *Ulysses* and other people you know are sitting around outside soaking up the words spoken in Irish brogue. One year John Timoney was a reader and he was terrific.

Keep a close eye on major institutions of learning for regular literature events. The **University of Pennsylvania Bookstore** sponsors scholarly and well-known authors for fascinating presentations in their West

Philadelphia store. **Temple University** offers literature courses, writing groups and poetry events in Center City and on main campus. The **Free Library** also has several author/discussion series (**The Philadelphia Lectures, Café for the Mind**) of very high quality. All of these events draw a mixed crowd of downtown and suburban professionals, as well as artists of considerable sophistication.

Poets are in luck in Philadelphia. The **Mad Poets Society** has everything a poet needs, including a literary journal, an annual festival, trips, regular meetings, and social events. **Poets and Prophets** has for years been hosting readings all around the area, giving new and experienced poets an opportunity to present their works. The **Painted Bride** has two very fine series for poets. Local cafés (such as **Gloria's**) around the area have supportive listeners for poetry readers. People who need writing help can turn to the **Poetry and Literary Forum**. People who want to set their poems to music can do that with the **Underground Poets**. Listeners can attend poetry readings at **Penn's Landing**, and local branches of the **Free Library** (**Lovett Branch**, for example). This is just a small sample of things going on in the poetry community, as you will see when you move out to attend events and network with other poetry fans.

You might want to jump-start your writing activities with a class or workshop, where you'll have an intense learning experience that fuels your fire and gives you a sense of confidence. Try **Temple University Center City** (TUCC), which offers a number of classes geared to different writing styles (mystery, non-fiction, etc.) or **Main Line School Night**. Annual weekend conferences (**Rutgers-Camden Spring Writers' Conference** and the **Mid-Atlantic Mystery Book Fair**) have been successfully networking authors and providing informative presentations for years. (Check the chapters on Discussion Groups, Coffeehouses, and Hobbies and Clubs for other groups and conferences about writing and poetry.)

Writing and poetry activities are a great way for all of us, not just established writers, to listen, think, and talk together about prose and poetry, contemporary issues, and art. And book store/coffee spots can be a great alternative to local pubs just to chill out, browse new books and magazines, and chat with your neighbors. See you there!

A closer look at...

Gay Telese in the Arts Café

Kelly Writers House

3805 Locust Walk, Philadelphia, PA 19104
(215) 573-WRIT   www.english.upenn.edu/~wh

The Kelly Writers House is a place where all types of writers gather to share their work and ideas about writing in a space conducive to conversation and reflection. Many events are held in this 13-room house on Penn's campus, including literary readings, films, art exhibits, workshops, screenings, dinners with visiting writers, and even jazz shows. Try the *Laughing Hermit Reading Series* (readings by published poets on Saturday afternoons), *Manuck! Manuck!* (an opportunity for fiction writers to discuss craft and technique every other Sunday), or *Speakeasy* (an open mic for poetry, prose and anything goes on Wednesdays). Other events include *PhillyTalks* (a dialogue with contemporary poets), *The Play's the Thing*, an open-ended play reading and thinking group designed to get people together to study writing for theater), and *Talking Film* (a screenwriting workshop). KWH also sponsors ongoing interactive webcasts that give participants a chance to talk to famous writers like John Updike and Grace Paley. Or you could also join one of their email writer discussion groups. If you're looking for a place to share your work, learn from accomplished writers, or find an excellent writers group, this is truly an important resource to explore.

☼   KWH programs take place from September to May and are open to the public

💰   Free

Writing & Poetry

Hear An Author

African American Museum

701 Arch Street, Philadelphia, PA
(215) 574-0380   www.aampmuseum.org

Every month you can attend high-quality book signings and presentations by authors whose work focuses on the African-American experience. Also, check out the author series each February called *Amplifying The Word*.

☀ Once a month
💰 Free

Big Jar Books

55 North 2nd Street, Philadelphia, PA 19106
(215) 574-1650   bigjar@telocity.com

This funky little bookstore in the arty section of 2nd Street has a classy selection of primarily used and some new books. You can drink coffee, eat a scone, and watch the activity on First Friday, or attend an occasional performance or author reading. Call or stop in for the events flier—you'll love this place.

Free Library of Philadelphia: *The Philadelphia Lectures*

1901 Vine Street, Philadelphia, PA 19103
(215) 567-4341   www.library.phila.gov

Meet people with ideas at these evenings (formerly called "Rebuilding the Future") where major authors like John Updike, Toni Morrison, Margaret Atwood, and Kurt Vonnegut discuss their recent books. Meet the author, get your book signed, and enjoy talking to the participants about the topic and other books. This is a very social event with refreshments afterwards.

☀ Almost weekly on Thursdays, Sept-May   🕓 8pm
💰 $12 in the auditorium; $6 for video simulcast in the East Gallery

Photo by Nate Clark

Writing & Poetry

Giovanni's Room

345 South 12th Street, Philadelphia, PA 19107
(215) 923-2960   www.giovannisroom.com

Certainly the premier bookstore for gay and lesbian books in the city but you can find other fine contemporary works here too. Giovanni's Room (after James Baldwin's novel) hosts several book clubs, including one for lesbian women, at the current time. The bookstore also sponsors 50 author readings a year. Call for the schedule or send an email. Mailing list.

Joseph Fox Bookstore

1724 Sansom Street, Philadelphia, PA 19103
(215) 563-4184   foxbooks@aol.com
Activity Location: Friends Select School, 17th and the Parkway, Phila., PA

This excellent bookstore can find any book you want, including those out of print. It also organizes a literary series that brings noted writers like Alice Walker and Sebastian Junger to Philadelphia to discuss their work, sign books, and answer questions from the audience. Free.

☼ 12-15 events/yr from Sept.-June   ☒ 7pm

Philadelphia Fantastic: *Readings in Speculative Fiction*

(215) 474-8412   www.voicenet.com/~camille/phillysf.html
Activity Location: Borders Book Shop, 1727 Walnut St., Phila., PA

This terrific monthly event in its third year features programs by published sci-fi novelists and short story writers, some with many books, others with just one. Well known authors and editors also show up. The format, according to Camille is: 7:30pm—chat, readings, chat, more readings and more chat; 9pm—everybody goes out for food/drink, with chat until about 11pm. This sounds like fun.

☼ 4th Fri./mo   ☒ 7:30pm
☎ Camille Bacon-Smith

Robin's Bookstore: *Moonstone Readings*

108 South 13th Street, Philadelphia, PA 19107
(215) 735-9600   www.robinsbookstore.com

This outstanding reading series of poetry, fiction and nonfiction focuses on women and people of color. Open readings follow poetry readings. Free.

☼ Once a month   ☒ 7pm
☎ Larry Robins

Writing & Poetry

Rosenbach Museum and Library: *Bloomsday*
2010 Delancey Place, Philadelphia, PA 19103
(215) 732-1600   www.rosenbach.org

Step into the world of Joyce's *Ulysses* on June 16 of any year. Carefully chosen literary speakers (You'll recognize some of them!), some with Irish brogue, enchant with readings all day at an outdoor seating at the Rosenbach Museum. The reading is incredible as is the fine Joyce exhibition on the first floor. Don't miss it, and look for me. An incredible free event.

☀ June 16   ⏲ 12-7pm

Temple University Graduate Creative Writing Program: *Poets and Writers Series*
(215) 204-1796
Activity Location: currently at Temple Gallery, 45 North 2nd St., Phila., PA

Four to five times a semester, this graduate class sponsors a recognized and emerging author of fiction or poetry who presents her/his work to a public audience of about 50-75 listeners. One evening Robert Coover discussed his recent novel, *Ghost Town*. It's a fine program and a great night out in Olde City!

☀ Thursdays   ⏲ 8pm
💰 Free

University of Pennsylvania Bookstore
3601 Walnut Street, Philadelphia, PA 19104
(215) 898-7595   http://upenn.bkstore.com

This gorgeous new bookstore has one of the finest collections of quality books anywhere in the city, and also offers regular book signings, author presentations/discussions, and music events that are definitely worth watching out for and attending. Check the web site for an up-to-date schedule, open to the public.

Walt Whitman Cultural Arts Center
2nd & Cooper Streets, Camden, NJ 08102
(856) 964-8300   www.waltwhitmancenter.org

Located near Rutgers University in a historic square, this arts center offers a *Notable Poets and Writers Series* with readings and master classes, jazz concerts, and family theater. There are many fine poetry and other special events in April to celebrate Whitman's life.

☀ Year-round
💰 Events are low cost, and free to members $20/yr

Writing & Poetry

Poetry

Free Library of Philadelphia: *Monday Poets Series*
Skyline Room, 1901 Vine Street, Philadelphia, PA 19103
(215) 686-5402

Both experienced and developing poets will love this free workshop series that includes readings with critiques (if you wish) and information sessions that help you find contests, grants and resources. Poets are encouraged to come on a regular basis. Also, there is an open reading series about every other month.

☼ One Mon./mo ⏰ 6:30pm

Gloria's Gourmet Café
2120 Fairmount Avenue, Philadelphia, PA 19130
(215) 235-0566

A literary concert featuring poets, writers, and performance artists. If you want to be part of an open reading, come at 7:30pm.

☼ 3rd Sun./mo ⏰ 8pm

Mad Poets Society
P.O. Box 1248, Media, PA 19063
(610) 586-9318   www.madpoetssociety.com
Activity Location: Reading series in Bryn Mawr (Barnes & Noble Bookstore), Media (at both the Hunt Club Mansion and the Hedgerow Theatre), Haverford (Main Line Arts Center), and West Chester (Chester County Book & Music)

This very active encouraging group runs at least six poetry series in the area; publishes a literary journal called the *Mad Poets Review*; sends out an excellent quarterly newsletter with a comprehensive poetry event listing, has outdoor "Mad Poet Bonfires" in Thornton (near Glen Mills), hosts an annual festival and a young poet's winners competition, holds monthly business and social meetings, and goes on literary excursions. Call Eileen D'Angelo for details.

💰 Free open readings, with membership at $20/yr, including newsletters

Manayunk Art Center: *Poetry Readings*

419 Green Lane (rear), Philadelphia, PA 19128
(215) 482-3363   www.manayunkartcenter.org

All who love poetry can attend these monthly programs on Sundays (2-4pm) in which several featured speakers read their works related to a theme and audience participants are invited to respond. These events have been taking place for 12 years. Also, this art center hosts poetry workshops once a month.

Not Coffeehouse Poetry and Performance Series

(215) 735-7156   www.notcoffeehouse.org
Activity Location: The First Unitarian Church of Philadelphia, 2125 Chestnut St., Phila., PA 19103 (215) 563-3980

Philadelphia has a strong and friendly poetry community. At Not Coffeehouse you'll find a fine example of such with featured poets and musicians performing, followed by an open reading.

☼ Usually 1st Sun./mo   ⏰ 2pm

Painted Bride Art Center:
Living Word Poetry Series & Day of the Poet

230 Vine Street, Philadelphia, PA 19106
(215) 925-9914   www.paintedbride.org

Day of the Poet: A spoken word event often coordinated with a DJ who spins a beat for a diverse group of featured poets. An open reading follows.

☼ 1st Friday at 10pm.
 $7

Living Word Poetry Series: An ongoing series (for 30 years!) that presents mostly published literary artists, including fiction writers and poets. Often one local and one national writer at an event. Call for a schedule.

💰 $6-15

Panoramic Programs, Inc.

(215) 629-3939
Activity Location: October Gallery, 68 North 2nd St., Phila., PA 19106

For five years this warm, friendly group has met to hear 10-12 featured poets in an evening. This is not an open mic, but once you attend you may be asked to read at the next event. They also have CD and book-signing parties, publish a poetry journal, and run GYRO, a program for youth at recreation centers. $5

☼ 2nd & 3rd Fri./mo   ⏰ 7:30-9:30pm
☎ Trapeta Mayson

Writing & Poetry

Philadelphia Cultural Council: *Poetry & Literary Forum*
(215) 685-0592

Activity Location: St. James Lutheran Church, Castor & Pratt, Phila., PA

Poets are invited to listen to guest readers and to share their work with the group during the open reading that follows. Those who read their works may submit material for consideration in the annual anthology. This group has been around since 1986. Bring an original poem or another poet's work you love to read, or just hang out and listen. Ask about the Summer Breeze Poetry series, as well.

☼ Every other Saturday   ⏰ 2pm

💰 $1

Po-Jazz Connection
P.O. Box 4296, Philadelphia, PA 19144
(215) 438-5366

Activity Location: Brave New World, 720 Arch St., Phila., PA

After the featured poet you may have a chance to perform your work (5-minute limit and no profanity) while the Arpeggio Jazz Band creates spontaneous arrangements. Very warm and social gathering.

☼ 3rd Mon./mo

☎ Warren Oree

💰 $5

Poetry in the Park at Penn's Landing
(215) 922-2FUN   www.pennslandingcorp.com

Activity Location: International Sculpture Garden, Columbus Blvd., between Dock & Spruce Sts., Phila., PA

Spend a summer night under the stars listening to the work of two featured poets followed by an open reading.

☼ Wednesdays   ⏰ 5-7pm

💰 Free

Poets' Place at Lovett Memorial Library
6945 Germantown Avenue, Philadelphia, PA 19119
(215) 685-2095   www.library.phila.gov

Come and share in the monthly poetry happenings at Lovett branch of the Free Library. Listen to and/or recite poetry here. Many library branches host events.

☼ 1st Mon./mo   ⏰ 7pm

Poets and Prophets

P.O. Box 449, Swarthmore, PA 19081
(610) 328-POET   bobthepoet@yahoo.com   www.geocities.com/bobthepoet
Activity Location: Borders in Springfield (Delaware Co.), the Ethical Society at 1906 Rittenhouse Square in Center City & many locations in Swarthmore

This informal and supportive meeting of poetry lovers is a *major* poetry group in the Philadelphia area. For over 15 years it has held featured readings all around the area. Look for P&P at the Fringe Festival as well. Free or small donation. Call Bob Small for more information.

Underground Poets Society

(800) 209-2637   poetik1@earthlink.net
Activity Location: The Music Room, 1302 Walnut St., every other Wed., 8:30pm, All That Footwork, 13 North 3rd St., 1st Sun. of month, (spoken word & hip hop).

More a "scene" than a society, Underground Poets present their work as a spoken word performance, often with musical background. Since there are many events to join during the month, check the *Philadelphia Weekly* and *City Paper* for current venues or call for info.

☎ Stephanie Renée

Writing & Reading Groups

Colonial Writers Guild

Activity Location: Jeanes Memorial Library, 4051 Joshua Rd., Lafayette Hill, PA
(610) 828-0441

For over seven years this very warm and encouraging group of 12 to 20 people has gathered to listen to and critique each other's novels, short stories, or poetry. Bring 15 copies of your work for discussion. It's free.

☼ 2nd Mon./mo   ⏰ 7-9pm

Great Books Discussion Series

Free Library of Philadelphia, 1901 Vine Street, Philadelphia, PA 19103
(800) 222-5870   www.greatbooks.org   www.library.phila.gov

Let your imagination soar as you read the greatest words ever written. Then discuss with other enthusiasts what you understand (and don't) and what you think and feel about these universal and classic writings. Great Books groups are held all over the city. Find the one closest to you.

☼ Every other Tues./mo.   ⏰ 7pm

Writing & Poetry

Meridian Writers Collective

P.O. Box 12358, Philadelphia, PA 19119
Activity Location: Sedgwick Theater, 7137 Germantown Ave., Phila., PA
(215) 248-9229

In addition to holding bimonthly readings called *Sunday at the Sedgwick*, Meridian also runs an annual fiction contest with a public reading of the winners. It publishes chapbooks (small books), and has a very fun (and free) Winter Solstice party that has an open mic/reading.

☀ Sundays ⏰ 7pm
💰 Readings $4

Valley Forge Romance Writers

P.O. Box 350, Wayne, PA 19087
(610) 793-2263   http://members.aol.com/jdicanio/vfrw.html
Activity Location: Radnor Memorial Library, South Wayne Ave., Radnor, PA

This local branch of the Romance Writers of America (www.rwanational.com) meets to talk about writing and hear speakers with expertise in writing and publishing romance novels. Speakers include editors from New York, literary agents, and experienced members from the national group. Subgroups form to critique each other's work. VFRW also sponsors fund-raising events for Laubach Literacy. Visitors can attend several free meetings. Newsletter.

☀ Once a month on Saturdays ⏰ 10:30am

Writing & Poetry

Workshops and Conferences

Annual Mid-Atlantic Mystery Book Fair and Convention

507 South 8th Street, Philadelphia, PA 19147
(215) 923-0211
http://midatlanticmystery.port5.com
Activity Location: Wyndham Franklin
Hotel, 17th & Race Sts., Phila., PA

This fall weekend event brings over 500
writers, fans, agents, and editors of
mystery and detective fiction to the city
for workshops, panel discussions, and
book signings. Socialize at the opening
party and/or put a bid in the silent auction.

Annual Rutgers-Camden Spring Writers' Conference

Rutgers University, English Department, Camden, NJ 08102
(856) 225-6490
Activity Location: Fine Arts Building, 4th & Linden Sts., Camden, NJ

For over 12 years, this free one-day event has brought writers together to
critique each other's work in workshops on essays, fiction, poetry, and free-lance
writing. Hear readings by the well-known authors who facilitate the workshops
and hobnob with them at the dinner.

☼ Mid-April   ☏ 9am-9pm

💰 Free, register for lunch ($7) or dinner ($17)

Greater Philadelphia Wordshop Studio

72 West Hillcrest Avenue, Havertown, PA 19083
(610) 853-0296   ahicks@hslc.org
Activity Location: Center City (Trinity Center for Urban Life, 22nd & Spruce Sts.)
and Havertown (St. Faith Episcopal Church, 1208 Allston Rd.)

Using writing exercises, supportive feedback, and manuscript critiques, this
workshop series helps you discover and strengthen your writing voice. Take
inspiration from other writers in the workshop as you work together. Based on
the Amherst Writers and Artists Method.

☼ Mon., Tues., & Weds.   ☏ evenings

☏ Allison Hicks

💰 $315

Writing & Poetry

Main Line School Night: *Creative Writing Classes*
260 Gulph Creek Road, Radnor, PA 19087
(610) 687-0460   www.mainlineschoolnight.org

Over 500 daytime and evening classes are taught by a dedicated and competent faculty in seven easy-to-reach Main Line locations. Among these are several fine writing classes, such as this one. Call for a catalog.

💰   Reasonably priced

Philadelphia Writers' Conference
107 Newington Drive, Hatboro, PA 19040
(215) 674-1639   PWC@pwcgold.com   www.pwcgold.com

Now over 50 years old, the PWC offers workshops with master writers in the areas of fiction, nonfiction, screenwriting, popular short stories, and poetry. Participants can submit a manuscript for professional criticism and contests with an agent/editor appointment as part of the deal. Stay for the "poetry raps" and "fiction raps" after the workshops.

☼   A weekend in June

💰   About $160, some scholarships for seniors, colleges, writing clubs, and others

Rosemont College: *Publishing Conference*
1400 Montgomery Avenue, Rosemont, PA
(610) 527-0200 or (610) 526-2982 Graduate Studies

Rosemont sponsors an annual *Publishing Conference* with experts in the field giving advice on how to find a publisher or self-publish your work. It's a full day of panel discussions and workshops.

☼   Spring   🕐 9am-4pm

💰 $20

Temple University Center City (TUCC)
1616 Walnut Street, Philadelphia, PA 19103
(215) 204-6946   www.temple.edu.tucc

Offering both credit and noncredit courses, Temple's writing courses have included: "Writing Short Stories," and "Mystery and History: A Reading Workshop for Writers." With excellent new selections each semester, you'll have many opportunities to explore the creative writer in you. The catalog will keep you informed about the most recent offerings.

Resources

Gay & Lesbian Activities
Useful Philadelphia Web Sites
Index • About Us • How to Buy This Book

Lesbian & Gay Activities

Gay and lesbian activities are included in all the chapters of this book. These are a variety of additional resources.

Organizations

- *William Way LGBT Community Center*

  1315 Spruce St., Philadelphia, PA 19107 (215) 732-2220 www.waygay.org Premier center for the LGBT community, this place is dedicated to providing a wide spectrum of educational, cultural, social, and health services for Philadelphia's diverse sexual and gender minority community. In addition to providing affordable meeting space and office space for other community groups, we also offer a wide range of programs and services. (from the web site) Women's Fridays, Team Philadelphia (official contingent to the Gay Games, and regular athletic activities), outdoor outings, and Movies on Sundays are just a few of the social activities that happen in this wonderful center.

- *Imago Dei Metropolitan Community Church*

  has a large gay and lesbian membership with a broad spectrum of religious backgrounds.   www.imagodeimcc.org

- *Gay and Lesbian Lawyers of Philadelphia (GALLOP)*

  provides support for the gay and lesbian community, and holds regular social functions (parties, picnics, etc.) to exchange ideas and network.   gallop@libertynet.org

- *League of Gay & Lesbian Voters*

  A non-partisan organization focuses on issues of special concern to the lesbian/gay community in Pennsylvania. Do voter registration and education of voters and legislators. LGLV also sponsors some social events, such as Roller Skating, Gay Day at the Ball Gayme, and cocktail parties.

- *Sisterspace*

  A fine large group that offers a variety of activities in the region for the multicultural lesbian community. Check the web site for many links to lesbian activities in the area. www.sisterspace.org
  (215) 546-4890

Lesbian & Gay Activities

Events

- *Gay & Lesbian Reading Group*
  Held at Borders in Marlton (515 Rte. 73 S.). Phone (856) 985-5080
  Wednesdays, 7:30pm

- *Sisters Nightclub*
  Popular spot where women go to talk and party in Philadelphia
  www.sisternightclub.com

Publications and Media

- *PGN*
  Weekly newspaper for Philly's LGBT community

- *Labyrinth*
  The Philadelphia women's newspaper
  www.labyrinthnews.com

- *Amazon Country*
  Terrific women's music on this station serving the lesbian and feminist
  community for over 20 years. On WXPN on Sunday nights from 9-10pm

Web Sites

- *www.geocities.com/Wellesley/6913*
  The Lesbian Community of Delaware Valley is a non-profit organization
  that wishes to build community among all area lesbians. Activities include
  a monthly Ladies Night Out held at homes and restaurants, bowling,
  hikes, dances, and such. A multicultural group that welcomes volunteers,
  they meet at the Unitarian Church of Delaware County. (610) 534-2119

- *www.communityvisions.org/IAGLBC*
  International Association of Gay and Lesbian Bridge Clubs

- *www.pgmc.org*
  The Philadelphia Gay Men's Chorus holds auditions. (215) 731-9230

Useful Philadelphia Web Sites

- *www.libertynet.org*
- *www.philadelphia.citysearch.com*
- *www.Phila.gov*
- *http://philadelphia.com*
- *www.phillyvisitor.com (Convention Center Visitors Guide)*
- *http://home.phillynews.com/philly 101*
      (Guide for college students, 1998 edition)
- *www.septa.com (Public transport info)*
- *www.gophila.org (Greater Philadelphia Tourism*
      Marketing Corporation)
- *www.philly.com (Philadelphia Inquirer, Daily News)*

Index

About You

If you would like to inform *Connectworks Publications* about your favorite group or organization, we would be happy to hear from you. The next step for us is the creation of a web site that will link to the organizations we think you would like to know about. We will include new, current, interactive activities on this site. We would also enjoy knowing about the groups you have found that work for you. Let us know about your experiences!

You can contact us directly by email: connectworks@earthlink.net or by sending a note to: *Connectworks Publications*, P.M.B. 137, 8500 Henry Avenue, Philadelphia, PA 19128. Or join us at a book signing or a workshop.

Have a great time out there!

About Us

Ruth Harvey, Ph.D.

Psychologist turned author, **Ruth Harvey, Ph.D.** has been writing about connecting through the activities we love since 1981. As a self-publisher, she also wrote and produced the regional best seller *Connecting in Philadelphia, 1st Ed.* (1994), *Philly NiteLife* (1996), and *Connecting in San Francisco* (coauthored with Diane DeCastro, 1998).

A college teacher and counseling psychologist in another life, Ruth is now a full-time writer, speaker, and workshop leader in communication, team building, and social networking. Her ongoing workshops, *Connecting in Philadelphia,* are based on the concept of connecting through your interests and include tips for easygoing sociable interaction. A professional speaker, she also appears as often as she can on local TV and radio programs, encouraging people to take more time off, relax and laugh, meet more people, and grow through the challenges of exciting adventures and meaningful connections.

Janet Gala

Janet Gala is a graphic designer who worked with Ruth Harvey and Diane DeCastro on their book *Connecting in San Francisco.* She graduated from Emerson College, Boston in 1989 with a B.F.A. in Communications. She has worked on many projects, including books and course catalogs, as well as brochures, newsletters, direct mail packages, and music CDs. Clients have included Mt. Airy Learning Tree, Germantown Women's Y, LaSalle College High School, Germantown Mennonite Historic Trust, and Morning Star Studios. Janet loves collaborating with her clients on meaningful, creative projects. She and her husband, singer/songwriter Tom Gala, host a live recording series at the Mermaid Inn.

Did You Borrow This Book? Have one of your own!

If you have your own copy of *Connecting In Philadelphia: 1000 Great Places To Enjoy Yourself And Meet People Who Share Your Interests, 2nd Edition*, you can make notes in it and refer to it whenever you're on the go. You can obtain your personal copy from local bookstores or by completing and returning the form below. For more information contact us at *Connectworks Publications*, call (215) 487-3547, or via email at connectworks@earthlink.net.

_____ YES, I'd like _____ copies of
Connecting in Philadelphia: 1000 Great Places to Enjoy Yourself and Meet People Who Share Your Interests, 2nd Ed.
Please allow 30 days for delivery.

Name _____

Address _____

City/Sate/Zip _____

Phone_____ Email _____

_____ book(s) at $17.95 each $ _____

Add sales tax (7% Philadelphia; 6% outside) $ _____

Shipping and handling @ $3.00/book. $ _____

                              Total Enclosed $ _____

Make your check payable to:

Connectworks Publications
P.M.B. 137
8500 Henry Avenue
Philadelphia, PA 19128

Bulk Orders Invited

For bulk discounts or special handling, please call
(215) 487-3547 or email connectworks@earthlink.net.

Workshops

_____YES, I'd like to receive a free notice of upcoming
events, workshops, or publications
_____YES, I'd like to receive an email of upcoming
events, workshops, or publications

Other Books

_____YES, I want to purchase a copy of

*Connecting in San Francisco: 693 Great Places
to Enjoy Yourself and Meet New People (1998)*
by Ruth B. Harvey, Ph.D. & Diane DeCastro
($12.95 plus $3 shipping & tax)

Contact:

Connectworks Publications
P.M.B. 137
8500 Henry Avenue
Philadelphia, PA 19128